Praise for *The New Rabbi*

"Stephen Fried took what many would consider a mundane topic—
a Jewish congregation searching for a new rabbi—and turned it into
a marvelous journalistic memoir that recorded his own spiritual
development as well as a community's quest for leadership."
—*Publishers Weekly* (a PW Best Book of 2002)

"Engrossing . . . a multilayered account that will resonate with
anyone concerned about the state of organized religion today . . .
The book should keep both Jews and non-Jews turning pages."
—*The Star-Tribune*, Minneapolis

"Writing with clarity, candor and wit, Fried uses the case study of
a rabbi's retirement and replacement to learn what organized religion
means to a suburban congregation and its leaders." —Rabbi Harold
Kushner, author of *When Bad Things Happen to Good People*

"Stephen Fried gets inside the congregational mindset the
way no other writer ever has." —*The Jewish Week*

"The work reads like a good novel. . . . It is the process, and not
just the result, that makes for fascinating reading. . . . Its lessons
can be appreciated by any reader who is interested in organized
religion, congregational politics, and the perils of being a
spiritual leader in any faith." —*The Tampa Tribune*

"No book about Judaism since *The Chosen* has so deeply
affected me. Fried . . . tells a fascinating true story. . . . There is
a lot in *The New Rabbi* that resonates with any reader."
—Father Tom Caswell, *The Inland Register*, Spokane, WA

"A vivid and funny book . . . an intriguing case study that raises
pointed questions in measured tones . . . The rabbi search is clogged
by the factions and intrigue we expect from all church and synagogue
committees . . . but [Fried] never allows us to lose sight of either the
gravity or the comedy." —*Books & Culture, A Christian Review*

THE
NEW
RABBI

A Congregation Searches for Its Leader

STEPHEN FRIED

BANTAM BOOKS
New York Toronto London Sydney Auckland

THE NEW RABBI
A Bantam Book

PUBLISHING HISTORY
Bantam hardcover edition published September 2002
Bantam trade paperback edition / September 2003

Published by
Bantam Dell
A Division of Random House, Inc.
New York, New York

To my father, Jerry Fried, of blessed memory,
and the family he so loved and inspired

CONTENTS

THE
NEW
RABBI

PROLOGUE

When I was a kid, my parents had a Jewish bookshelf. On it were three kinds of books. There were, of course, prayer books and Bibles: some ours, some "accidentally" brought home from the synagogue and someday to be returned. There were handsomely bound scholarly or historic books, most accepted as gifts and never read, except to look up something for Hebrew school. And then there were novels, like *The Chosen* and the "Tuesday the Rabbi" books and even *Exodus*—the pulpit fiction of the day, where the struggle between religious life and real life was explored in language that anyone could understand: the human drama of the intersection of the divine and the secular, the battles between God and man and American culture, the searches for spiritual awakening and the perfect bar mitzvah caterer.

To broach these same subjects in non-fiction, especially the emotional and financial intricacies of American synagogue life, was considered dangerous, "bad for the Jews." And, to this day, that's still basically true. While Jewish bookshelves now teem with a new genre, spiritual self-help and how-to books, there is still very little journalism on the lives of American Jews as Jews. The scarcity is such that a recent book on American rabbis actually resorted to using many examples drawn from fiction—including quotes from fictitious rabbis—to illustrate points that everyone knows to be true, but almost no one dares to write down in narrative non-fiction.

When I first started writing books in my late twenties, I thought about following a congregation while it hired a new spiritual leader as a way of telling a true story about American religion. I was inspired by the fact that a change of clergy in my own hometown synagogue, when I was eleven, had made an indelible impact on my family and my community. You never forget your first rabbi.

But it was just a one-line book idea, and I was at that time only tangentially involved in religious life. I was a six-day-a-year Jew—doing the High Holidays, Hanukkah and two Seders on Passover—which I suppose made me twice as good as the traditional three-day-a-year Jew, but still far from observant or spiritually engaged. So I wrote other books instead.

Then, when I was about to turn forty, my father died. He was only sixty-two. And after years as a wandering Jew, I found myself attending synagogue regularly for the first time since I had set out from my bar mitzvah reception in Sisterhood Hall with my breast pocket stuffed with gift envelopes. I returned for completely selfish reasons: I needed comfort, and the synagogue happened to be a place where I found it.

I took comfort, and I also began taking notes, because I was finding the day-to-day life of the congregation to be endlessly dramatic. Its survival seemed somehow crucial to my own survival. And I started thinking again about a book that would resonate within my generation as the first wave of religious novels had in the 1960s for both Jews and non-Jews. I decided to combine my newfound search for spiritual meaning with my experience as an investigative reporter, and to capture the interior life, the sacred and the profane, of a great American synagogue at the delicate moment of generational handoff.

At any given time, many of the four thousand synagogues and more than 230,000 churches around the country are immersed in the heart-wrenching process of trying to hire new clergy. In doing so, their leaders must anticipate what future generations will expect from their religious institutions. No longer just houses of prayer, they are now big businesses responsible for delivering all kinds of services. Failure to deliver will put spiritual as well as financial solvency at risk.

It just so happened that an extraordinary synagogue, Har Zion Temple in Philadelphia, had recently hung the equivalent of a help-wanted sign—by registering its pulpit opening with the national rabbis' "union," the Rabbinical Assembly of America. Not only was Har Zion an internationally famous congregation, but the rabbi they were replacing was the very one who had been hired away from my synagogue when I was a kid, Gerald I. Wolpe (WOHL-pee).

Har Zion is one of the most powerful and influential congregations in the world. Few American synagogues have produced as many world-class rabbis and scholars, or can match the congregation's ability to put its money where its mouth is. Har Zion is, in every way, rich, with an annual budget of over $4 million, an ambitious Hebrew school that is regularly named the best in the country and a reputation for support-ing intellectual pursuits and social causes. The synagogue's national status has derived from its dominance of the Philadelphia Jewish com-munity, one of the country's largest, as well as the resolve and wealth of its lay leaders. Har Zion is the home of the big *machers*. In Yiddish, a macher is someone who is a big deal or has a lot of big-deal connec-tions, a person with power or proxy who understands how to get things done. All synagogues have their big machers, but Har Zion has a smorgasbord of them. With fourteen hundred member families, the various subgroups within the congregation are larger than many con-gregations.

Har Zion is also well known for the success and career longevity of its clergy: since its creation in 1924, the synagogue has had only three rabbis, each a giant in his own right. Founding rabbi Simon Greenberg left after twenty-five years to become one of the most important voices in the American clergy as vice-chancellor of the Jewish Theologi-cal Seminary (JTS) in New York, which has been considered the Harvard of Judaism. He was later the first leader of the University of Judaism in Los Angeles, which has been every bit Judaism's Stanford.

Greenberg's successor, Rabbi David Goldstein, revolutionized Judaism in a much more regional way, helping to devise and fund many of the institutions—day schools, gyms, summer camps—that became national models for how Jews could create their own American-style communities. It was Goldstein who cemented the synagogue's role in the intellectual life of Judaism by creating the country's first major synagogue scholar-in-residence program. Among his scholars-in-residence was a young Chaim Potok, who ran services at the synagogue's satellite campus in the suburbs in the early sixties and went on to write *The Chosen* and several other best-sellers during his association with Har Zion. Potok and his wife later quit, as did many others, when the congregation elected in the early seventies to leave the ethnically mixed neighborhood of its birth for a suburban setting. While this was happening to houses of worship all over the country, during what came to be called "white flight," it was Har Zion's exodus that *Newsweek* chose to focus on for its cover story on the subject.

By then Har Zion had a new rabbi, Wolpe, who was lured from my hometown synagogue in 1969. A brilliant orator and politician, with a feisty wife and four brainy sons, Wolpe was hired to hold the synagogue together during its uprooting to the suburban Main Line, where its congregants had been relocating after the "there goes the neighborhood" housing restrictions against Jews started to lift after World War II. (It was this intersection of traditional Main Line and Jewish cultures that led a Philadelphia sociologist to coin the term "WASP"—used originally as an abbreviation because White Anglo-Saxon Protestant wouldn't fit on the axis of a graph about social migration trends.)

Wolpe was brought in to save Har Zion from itself. During what would become a thirty-year tenure, he helped the synagogue, and American Judaism, reinvent itself in the new "postwar era"—the one after Vietnam, the Yom Kippur War in Israel, and the civil rights and sexual revolutions in America. But he became best known for his response to a private event that almost ended his career. At the height of his rabbinate, Wolpe's wife, Elaine, suffered a stroke. But instead of leaving the pulpit, he shared the pain and medical dilemmas of her long recovery with the congregation, expressing and evoking emotion in a place where reason and power had traditionally held sway.

In his last act of bravery as a pulpit rabbi, Wolpe agreed to grant me unprecedented access to the private life of his synagogue at this pivotal moment in its history. His wife and family also cooperated fully, including his two sons who are rabbis—especially the celebrated clergyman and author David Wolpe in Los Angeles. Eventually, I was also the beneficiary of extraordinary cooperation from congregational leaders and members of Har Zion, from the grand poo-bahs of rabbinic placement at the Rabbinical Assembly, and from rabbis from across the country who vied for the Har Zion job while their congregations were also seeking new clergy. And I was able to "cover" an enormous number of religious services—and then eat heartily at the postprayer luncheons (especially the little cakes with the bar mitzvah boy's name iced on them). So much of my reporting was done within reach of a buffet table that I could have titled the book *Chafing Dish.*

While this book mixes various aspects of investigative reporting and two kinds of memoir—Rabbi Wolpe's and, to a much lesser degree, my own—it is wholly a work of non-fiction. Even Rabbi Wolpe's memories of his own career were independently fact-checked. Since Hebrew words and Yiddish expressions are part of the shorthand of synagogue life, I've done my best to help the reader talk the talk. Those terms that have not become part of standard English (as bar mitzvah has) are noted in italics when they first appear and then in standard type, because in this multilingual world they are not really foreign words. The trickiest part, however, comes with pluralization, because two different styles tend to be used interchangeably by American Jews. The proper Hebrew plural of bar mitzvah, for example, is *b'nai mitzvah,* but it is more common to hear the Americanized slang "bar mitzvahs." In general, I have deferred to the way people really speak. When there are two terms for the same thing—for example, a skullcap, which is *yarmulkah* in the Yiddish often preferred by older American Jews, and *kippah* in more modern Hebrew—the words are used interchangeably. As for vocalization, most Hebrew words are supposed to be pronounced with the emphasis on the last syllable, but in casual conversation, most Americans instead stress the first syllable.

While I'm not a huge fan of journalistic books with footnotes or end-notes, some readers want or need them. I have therefore made chapter notes available at the website for the book, *www.thenewrabbi.com*. In general, however, all direct quotes come from taped interviews conducted by me or tapes of events, and all observations of events I did not attend were confirmed by at least one other person who was there.

Har Zion, the synagogue I chose to follow for three years—it was only supposed to be one year, but that's part of the story—is Conservative, the denomination that historically has been the most popular and influential among America's roughly six million Jews, and has also been the most influenced *by* American culture. My choice is not meant as a reflection on the other major branches of Judaism: in orientation from right to left, Orthodox (which itself is divided into right-wing ultra-Orthodox and more liberal "Modern Orthodox"), Conservative, Reform (which in recent years has overtaken Conservative in sheer number of adherents) and Reconstructionist. The "Conservative movement," as it is often referred to, just happens to be the one in which I was raised. I have done my best to explain how the denominations differ while still remaining a unified Jewish community, and how the competition between them plays out in attracting families "shopping" for synagogues. But it is not my purpose to debate theology.

Most of the issues and problems confronting this congregation at its time of change are not unique to Conservative Jews, or even to Jews in general. Many Christian friends and colleagues have told me about similar dramas in their churches when there is a change in senior clergy. (And everyone seems to agree that, whatever the religion, once chosen, being the spiritual leader of a large house of worship is probably the hardest job in America.) What all Jewish congregations do have in common, however, is that their senior rabbis are spiritual CEOs, holding the title of *mara d'atra*—"master of the place," the last word on religious decisions and standards within their communities. Yet a rabbinate is not a dictatorship. While its different branches have slightly different theology and observance, Judaism does not dictate belief. Its timeless appeal is as a religion of questions, not answers.

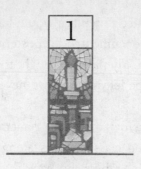

HIS VOICE

WHAT WE MISSED MOST was his voice. Our rabbi could make the most stilted English translation of prayer sound like Shakespeare. His voice was muscular and musical, with an accent that sounded vaguely British at first, but later revealed itself to be all-American, with leftover "aahs" from Boston.

This was not like the voice of God. Rabbis do not aspire to divinity. They have jobs in an industry that has, like many others, shifted from manufacturing to service. Rabbis are employees, religion workers, with unions and contracts and job-related injuries. They have to negotiate dental with the very congregants they must inspire.

Still, while rabbis do not speak for God, some of them have God-given gifts. Rabbi Gerald Wolpe's gift was his voice.

My dad had a story he loved to tell about the day when Wolpe took the makeshift stage of a flatbed truck in the parking lot of the Harrisburg Jewish Community Center. It was the summer of 1967, the height of the Six-Day War. And the rabbi brought home this crisis from halfway across the world with such eloquent urgency that my parents were inspired to pledge to Israel, then and there, every last cent they had saved for brand-new wall-to-wall carpeting. Anyone who ever saw the mud-gray shag they wanted to replace would have to agree this qualified as a miracle. And it was documented for posterity. There was a record album made of the speech. My parents bought that, too.

But then Rabbi Wolpe left us. And we never forgave him for taking the voice away.

I was eleven when he departed, so I remember him only vaguely as an image in confirmation class pictures along the wall—all sideburns and pageantry, dressed, as rabbis did back then, like a human Torah. I vaguely recall him telling us to stop running in the hall between Hebrew school classes at Beth El Temple, and to stop banging on the candy machine.

But I have been following Rabbi Wolpe's lead in my head for decades. When I pray, I still pause where he paused, emote where he emoted. When I hear the *Ashrei,* David's psalm of praise, recited in English, I laugh to myself when I reach the line about giving the hopeful their food "in due season," because I can hear Wolpe giving "due" an extra syllable—"d-yew." The way he articulated "all the wicked . . . he will bring *low*" was enough to keep me from going astray.

One of my strongest memories of growing up Jewish is sitting at Friday night dinner listening to my parents, my Nana and Pop-pop, and my aunts and uncles go on about the politics of the day and Wolpe's sermons. To them, he combined the wisdom of the ages with the morning headlines, name-dropping his way through history, religion and culture.

On the night of *Kol Nidre,* the prayer that ushers in Yom Kippur, the holiest twenty-four hours of the year, they would eat dinner earlier than usual and leave immediately afterward to attend a special service—for adults only. All they would tell us about this mysterious ceremony was, "Oh, you kids wouldn't like it anyway, we have to stand for *hours.*" When the grown-ups returned, they had this strange look on their faces. I assumed they were exhausted from standing. Now I realize it was a kind of awe, the voice still resonating.

✡   ✡   ✡

I would like to hear him again.

On an overcast Tuesday in mid-November, I drive out to the syna-gogue that stole Rabbi Wolpe away. I had seen a story in the *Philadelphia Inquirer,* one that a peppier headline writer would have titled "Tues-day, the Rabbi Gave Notice." Wolpe was calling it quits, announcing a rather elaborate plan of retirement in which he would give the syna-gogue two years to find a suitable replacement and make a smooth tran-sition.

Why now? Judaism is a religion of mystical numbers, starting with "the Lord is One," in its most important prayer, the *Sh'ma.* Wolpe told the newspaper that the numbers just seemed right. Not only would the long good-bye coincide with his seventieth birthday and his thirtieth year on this pulpit, it would be the seventy-fifth anniversary of the found-ing of Har Zion. It would also be the twenty-fifth anniversary of the congregation's controversial relocation from the city neighborhood of Wynnefield to the prosperous suburb of Penn Valley, the heart of what is now called the "Jewish Main Line."

As I'm driving out there, the numbers seem right to me, too. I'm about to turn forty and I just lost my father. I have reached the point in life when all answers turn back into questions. After making the same professional journey that Wolpe did—Harrisburg to Philly, with occa-sional day trips to New York—I have been writing investigative articles and books from here for nearly two decades. Yet our paths have rarely crossed. I did call him once, in the mid-eighties, to get some quotes for a story I was doing. But we've never really *talked.*

For a guy whose voice is in my head, I should know him better.

My first glimpse of Har Zion is through a break in a row of ever-greens in a typical McMansioned Main Line neighborhood. It's a modern sprawl of a building, surrounded by rolling lawns, parking lots, even a fenced-in basketball court and playground. I use the side entrance, where the clergy and staff park their late-model cars while the moms idle in their SUVs, watching their preschoolers, and then me, dash up the steps.

I find Rabbi Wolpe in the largest of a suite of offices, sitting behind a utilitarian desk. He is surrounded by the overstuffed shelves of someone who has actually read the books. On a glass side table are the usual family photos and a bronze of his own head. Half-glasses balanced on his nose, phone to his ear, he waves me in.

Wolpe's face has a certain cartoonish geometry—as if drawn using two perfect circles for cheekbones—and a fleshy ethnicity of uncertain origin. Mostly he looks like a man who works with his hands, dressed in his best suit and tie for a special occasion. Yet when he speaks, his face takes on new character and refinement, the rich charisma of the voice.

He asks—actually, he "aahsks"—how my mother is holding up. Fine, thanks, but that's not why I'm here.

I ask him how *he* is. It's a simple enough question, but I can see it's not one he hears very often. Usually, when people come to visit him, it is to unburden themselves. He pauses, removes his glasses and leans back in his desk chair.

Instead of answering right away, he makes a joke about what it's like to be slipping into his "anecdotage," when new research is mostly dusting memories. He is preparing to give a speech in a few days to the synagogue Men's Club, reflections on the end of his rabbinate. This could be a good opportunity to try out some of his material.

An only child of working-class Eastern European immigrant parents in the Roxbury section of Boston, Wolpe was raised by the Jewish community based at the synagogue Mishkan Tefila. It was a lively congregation, where one of his Hebrew school teachers was moonlighting political historian Theodore H. White, and one of the older kids in shul was young Leonard Bernstein, who played piano at the dinner after Wolpe's bar mitzvah.

Benjamin Wolpe, his father, was a vaudeville singer, part of a "song, dance and fancy patter outfit" on the popular Keith Circuit of theaters. His mother, Sally, worked in the family kosher catering business, which was run by her older sister, Bessie, and Bessie's husband, David. "The family was like a sponge," he tells me. "It absorbed anybody who came into its orbit." There was always a lot of food and, on a moment's notice, forty people could show up for dinner. "It was a happy, supportive, riotous kind of place. From my uncles, I learned you can kiss strong men and not be considered a weakling."

Benny Wolpe died suddenly when his son was only eleven. "I still remember my father laughing," he says. "He was a very funny man, always with a cigar." His mother came home one day and found him dead. Probably a heart attack or a stroke.

"That was the pivotal moment in my life," he says. "In a sense, I've been living in that moment ever since."

I interrupt him. How is it that I don't recall hearing this story when I was a kid? It was not part of the Wolpe canon in Harrisburg or, later, the Wolpe mythology. He says I'm remembering correctly: he did not start speaking so publicly about his father's death until several years after he left Harrisburg. When he reached his mid-forties, and was about to pass the age his father was when *he* died, Wolpe became more open about such things, mostly because he was so fearful that he too would die young. By the time he underwent open-heart surgery at the age of sixty-three, his father's death had become a central metaphor of his sermonizing.

After being widowed, Wolpe's mother began working full-time in the catering business as head waitress. They lived in an apartment above the home of his mother's sister. She and her husband didn't have any children of their own, so they functioned as Jerry's surrogate parents. To some degree, they were parents to his mother as well. Sally Wolpe was never quite the same after the day she took her eleven-year-old son in her arms and told him his father was gone.

He was also taken in by the *shammash,* the sexton, of his synagogue, an elderly immigrant named Mr. Einstein. Even though he was not technically old enough to say the mourner's prayer for his father—those responsibilities don't kick in until age thirteen—Jerry Wolpe still wanted to do it. Mr. Einstein walked him to shul every day before school, and guided him through the traditional mourning process. He taught Wolpe how to recite the mourner's *Kaddish*.

"Ritual can be amazingly effective in allowing you to do something, *anything*, whether it makes sense or not," Wolpe continues. "To be able to say a prayer and be in the company of people sharing the same pain . . . well, that was a saving experience. Mr. Einstein taught me how to *daven*, to pray. He'd sit next to me during the service, and say, 'You know, everybody goes very fast. Don't you go fast. Go as slow as you want.' He was a very short man, with a teaching humor. If I mispronounced something, he'd say, 'What's the matter, did you have a schnapps this morning?' He made me feel incredibly comfortable in a strange surrounding."

But the Kaddish did not relieve the pain. It simply provided him with words to scream at God. His father's death was the genesis of what Wolpe calls his "theology based on anger." His proof of God's existence, he says, is that in order for him to remain *that* angry at something, it *must* exist. It is a view of God that is intellectually provocative and deeply egocentric, just like Wolpe himself. And it is a view of religion driven not primarily by spirituality or joy, but by a time-honored mechanism of coping, a way to process disappointment and loss. As if locked in Jacob's dream, he is forever wrestling with God.

He tells me that the decision to devote his life to wrestling *professionally* was ensured by another incident when he was a teen. One day he returned from school to find his mother banging her head against the kitchen table and wailing. In her hand was a letter from Israel, from a nephew passing on the horrific news that everyone else in her family—forty-two people, including the brother she had begged to leave and come to America with her—had been murdered by the Nazis in Poland. Wolpe had grown accustomed to hearing his widowed mother cry through the night. But never like this.

"Hitler made my mother cry," he recalls. "How else do you fight back? You become a rabbi."

He finished high school when he was sixteen and moved to New York, studying Renaissance history at NYU while living and taking courses at the Jewish Theological Seminary. At sixteen, he was the youngest student ever accepted at the Seminary, in the pretheological department, and one of the first who had been raised in a Conservative synagogue. He had gone to a public school and attended only after-school and Sunday Hebrew school. Before him, all rabbinic students were graduates of full-time Jewish day schools. "It was an experiment," he says, "to see if they could make rabbis out of people like me."

He was also probably the first rabbinic hopeful who boxed and hustled pool. "Who *is* this Irish-looking kid from Boston?" people asked. Especially when the wives of the most distinguished Jewish scholars of the day took him in and invited him to dinner on *Shabbat,* Sabbath. "They were very protective of me, to make sure I ate well and dressed well," he says. "On Friday nights it wasn't unusual to be sitting with Dr. Louis Finkelstein, Professor Louis Ginzberg and Alexander Marx." They were some of the leading religious scholars of the twentieth century.

On Friday nights, he would often make the long walk from the Seminary down to the Park Avenue Synagogue on East Eighty-seventh Street to hear the brilliant sermons of Rabbi Milton Steinberg. Already debilitated from the heart condition that would kill him before the age of fifty, Steinberg delivered his sermons sitting in a chair, but his calm, compelling delivery and intellectual gifts were intact. A passionate Jew and a certified intellectual, Steinberg epitomized everything Wolpe wanted to be. Steinberg had faced the same career choice that was looming for Wolpe, academia or the rabbinate, and had chosen the pulpit while maintaining his ties to classical literature. And when Wolpe listened to Steinberg, who even invited the young rabbinical student to his home on Saturday afternoon after Shabbat services, he was inspired to believe it was possible to become a true Renaissance rabbi.

After nearly a decade of undergraduate and graduate studies at the Seminary and NYU—during some of the most astonishing years in

American and Jewish history, including the end of the Second World
War and the founding of Israel—Wolpe was ordained in 1953 and sent
to Camp Lejeune, the Marine Corps training base in North Carolina. He
was chaplain there during the waning days of the Korean War.

Wolpe suggests we stop here for this session. But before I pack up
my tape recorder and laptop to leave, he tells me a little bit about his
wife and kids. As I know because of a sermon he delivered years ago—
copies of which were circulated widely through the Jewish world (my
parents had a cassette tape of it)—Elaine Wolpe had a life-threatening
stroke in 1986. Ignoring the experts who told him to put her in an institution and get on with his life, Wolpe almost single-handedly nursed his
wife back to health. But while he has given quite a few sermons since
then about her struggle and the lessons learned from it—and frequently
lectures to groups of physicians, bioethicists and spouse/caregivers—he
says he hasn't dared share the real truth of her condition and their life
together. He promises that in one of our next sessions he will finally talk
openly with me about it. And perhaps Elaine will as well.

Wolpe says he knows his marriage faces another test when his rabbinate comes to an end. For the first time ever, it will just be him and
Elaine, most likely living in an apartment far away from the synagogue.
The children are all gone. Proudly, he describes all they have accomplished.

Stephen, the oldest, is a biomedical researcher in Maryland. Paul and
his wife and their two daughters are the only ones who still live in the
Philadelphia area: he is an assistant professor at Penn, and is becoming
known in the field of bioethics. While following in his father's footsteps
in this—Rabbi Wolpe has had a side career lecturing on bioethics for
decades—Paul has also brought his father's insights greater national
attention by getting him involved with his widely known boss, ethicist
Dr. Arthur Caplan, the director of the renowned Center for Bioethics at
the University of Pennsylvania.

David, who is my age, and Daniel, who is much younger than his siblings, are both rabbis. Danny has only recently been ordained, and works as an assistant rabbi at a small congregation in Florida.

David, on the other hand, is arguably the most famous young rabbi in America. While Gerald Wolpe is a legend in the world of pulpit masters, he knows that when most people refer to "Rabbi Wolpe" they are discussing his telegenic son. Based in Los Angeles, David has written four well-received books on Jewish topics. He is widely quoted in the national media. And, after a decade as a traveling lecturer, he has just taken his first pulpit, at tony Sinai Temple in the Westwood section of L.A., where he is one of the highest-paid pulpit rabbis in the world. David is so popular, his father boasts, that if you don't get to shul, to synagogue, by 9:30 on Saturday morning, "you don't get a seat."

Wolpe says he was pleasantly surprised when David came to him and said he wanted a pulpit.

"So," he recalls asking him, "you've decided to go into the retail business?"

The retail business of religion.

I love this concept. Yet, as I pack up my laptop, I realize that capturing this business will mean more than just grilling Wolpe in his office once every week or two. I will have to start attending his services. This synagogue, this retail outlet of religion, is now my beat.

2

BAT MITZVAH GONE BAD

H AR ZION'S MAIN SANCTUARY makes a sensational first impression, especially in the morning when fractured light from the thirty-foot-high stained-glass windows illuminates the outer aisles. Front and center is the *bimah,* the pulpit, a low stage where all the action takes place. Built into its contemporary wood back wall is the Ark, the holy walk-in closet that houses the scrolls of the Torah—the five books of Moses. The Ark is flanked by boxy built-in seats, four on each side. Six are for synagogue officers and those congregants who have been given "pulpit honors" and get to sit on the bimah for part of the service. The two seats closest to the Torahs are reserved for the cantor and, of course, the rabbi.

It is a thrill for me to see Wolpe on the bimah again, the first time in nearly thirty years. Like many modern rabbis, he no longer wears the traditional black ceremonial robes for Shabbat services. In a handsome, tailored suit with an understated blood-red *tallis,* prayer shawl, and a small matching kippah, he looks quietly regal.

He also looks annoyed. With his furrowed brow and all his fidgeting, he looks like he's about to stand up and roar.

There must be close to five hundred people here for the bat mitzvah, already in progress. As Wolpe sits behind her, scowling, the bat mitzvah girl delivers her speech from the lectern. His lectern. She is tall for her age, wearing a plain white dress, looking poised with her long hair tied back under a white kippah. She projects with just the right amount of sentiment.

In a front row is her family. Her sisters, brother and grandmother flank her father, who I recognize as Martin Landis*, one of Philadelphia's most eccentric millionaires, a major property owner and contributor to political campaigns, and one of Har Zion's biggest machers. At the very end of the row, several seats apart from the others, sits the bat mitzvah girl's mother, Michelle*, wearing a smart chocolate-brown suit. Pinned to her short dark hair is a doily of white lace. I don't need a program to figure out that there are marital problems, but that fact is actually listed in the Shabbat program for those who can read between the lines. Even though the father and mother have the same last name, they are listed separately: the bat mitzvah girl, Julie*, is described as "daughter of Martin Landis and Michelle Landis." If their marriage were intact, they would be referred to as "Michelle and Martin Landis."

Up on the bimah, Julie Landis begins a litany of thanks, starting with her grandmother, whose only desire was to live to see this day. She expresses gratitude to the rabbi, assistant rabbi, cantor and Hebrew-school teacher. And then she lapses into a gushy tribute to Daddy.

Looking apprehensive, Rabbi Wolpe rises from his seat and takes a stance directly behind her. As he looms, Julie continues giving thanks for "everything my father has done for me." And then she stops cold. After exchanging a private smile and nod with her dad, she turns to the rabbi to be congratulated. And as she does all eyes turn instead to her mother, who is clenched in her seat, the doily on her head vibrating.

After praising her "brilliant" performance, Wolpe brings the mean-spirited spectacle to an end with a rather perfunctory presentation of a

---

* I have changed all the names in the "Landis" family, as well as a handful of other characters—all marked with an asterisk when first mentioned. There are no composite characters in the book.

certificate of bat mitzvah, along with the traditional gifts from the congregation. Julie takes a seat next to her father, who hugs her triumphantly. But she doesn't even so much as look in her mother's direction. As the hug drags on, the mother stands up and bolts out of the synagogue. A clutch of family members follows.

The sanctuary is abuzz. Usually, the rabbi would shush them. He is, I recall, a big shusher. But today, they *should* be abuzz.

In a moment, he begins the remarks he prepared, a lighthearted riff on the silliness of the Psychic Friends Network. In mid-sermon, however, he stops and calls the rabbinic equivalent of a quarterback's audible. When in doubt, go to the text. He segues into this week's Torah portion, Exodus 13:7–17:16, which includes the parting of the Red Sea—and the Israelites' moments of doubt and faith before the sea is actually parted.

God is irritated, Wolpe explains, because the Israelites are scared and don't know what to do. God sees them on the banks of the Red Sea and says, "Hey, you wanted to be free, this is what freedom is." The point is that "we are products of our choices" in life, the quality of our relationships not so much fated as chosen. His words crackle with intensity, his anger only thinly veiled.

When the sermon ends, he gives the bat mitzvah girl and her father a cold stare. And then he appears pleasantly surprised to see that Michelle Landis has steeled herself to return, walking tentatively down the aisle back to her seat.

After the service, the leaders of the synagogue huddle on the bimah, as I approach them hoping for a word with the rabbi. But Wolpe can't talk to me now. As he makes a beeline for the girl's heartsick mother to comfort and congratulate her, the president of the Men's Club turns to me and says, "That's the worst thing I ever saw in the temple. That man is scum."

When I come to speak with Wolpe several days later, he shakes his head in disbelief over what may have been his worst rite of passage, *ever.*

Over the years, he has officiated at thousands of bar and bat mitzvahs, yet he can't remember one quite like this.

"I'm really sorry you had to see that," he says.

Wolpe looks more tired than usual. He has one of the most coveted pulpits in America, an able assistant rabbi and a full-time program director to help him, luxuries that would answer any rabbi's prayers. Yet the work still takes its toll. The job has eroded him.

He gives me a behind-the-bimah replay. On the morning of the bat mitzvah, Wolpe asked to take one more quick look at the young woman's speech, which had already been preapproved and vetted by the assistant rabbi. The speeches aren't supposed to focus on thanking clergy and family. Wolpe always hated that "revered rabbi, honored parents" stuff. When he came to Har Zion, he tried to get rid of the bar mitzvah speeches entirely, but synagogue leaders balked. So he decreed that the only way thirteen-year-olds would get free airtime on his bimah was if they agreed to donate some of their bar mitzvah money to a charitable organization. He expected them to speak about the cause they supported and how it related to that week's *parasha,* the reading from the Torah.

In this case, when Wolpe skimmed the Landis girl's speech he noticed that a new page had been added, because it was handwritten, not typed.

"The page was this tribute to her father," he explains, elongating the *faah* in father. "And I said, 'You can't recite this, it's an insult to your mother.' So I took the paper away from her."

But, like any good bat mitzvah girl, she had memorized it. "The girl did an excellent job, she's got a lot of presence. How sad it is that, afterward, nobody spoke about how well she did, only what she did to her mother," he says. "It was a gratuitous insult. You don't act out your ire at a child's bat mitzvah."

Wolpe leans back in his desk chair, rubbing his eyes. "I think she's being controlled by the father," he says. "She has rejected her mother—total alienation. Right now the only one she cares about is her father. I

know that the cantor, who spent a lot of time with her while she prepared, very often would try to tell her that her anger was inappropriate."

The synagogue has been dealing with the machinations of Martin
Landis for years. He represents a certain species of big macher, who
gives but wants something back—in his case, control. Several years ago,
he gave fifty thousand dollars so Har Zion could hire its first full-time
program director. Then he tried to micromanage what the program director did, leading to uncomfortable confrontations with the rabbi.

But the daughter is Wolpe's concern. "You know, I worry about her
future emotional health," he says.

So what's a rabbi to do? "I can do one of two things," he replies. "I
can stand up and castigate this man and tell his daughter she sinned
against her mother. Or I can try to turn it into a positive lesson."

He sounds excited about how he was able to adjust his sermon and
find a whole new meaning in a Torah portion he might have otherwise
interpreted on automatic pilot. "This June will be my forty-fifth year as a
rabbi," he points out. "In this period I have preached on this parasha at
least forty-five times. And one thing you struggle with is how to take the
same text, utilizing all the commentaries you can handle, and make a
traditional sermon with new ideas. Every once in a while I have to admit
I get the feeling I've said this before. But what can you do? The verbal
productivity demanded of a rabbi is enormous." Wolpe has spent countless Thursdays racking his brain for material. The occasional fiasco,
however regrettable, is a godsend for sermonizing.

Unfortunately, more inspiration may be on the way. This bat mitzvah
is just the beginning of a contentious spring on the crowded synagogue
calendar. As usual, so many families want their rites of passage celebrated at Har Zion that almost every Saturday will feature not one but
two thirteen-year-olds coming of age. And the Torah honor battles have
already begun.

During each Sabbath service, the week's Torah reading is broken up
into small sections. A brief prayer is recited before each portion is

chanted, and it is an honor to be invited up on the bimah to recite one of these prayers, to receive what is called an *aliyah*. When I was thirteen, the bar mitzvah family got to dole out all the aliyahs. Today, Har Zion is one of many synagogues that reserve some of them for the congregants who attend services every week. The goal is to keep a celebration by one or two families—and their dozens or even hundreds of guests—from swallowing up everyone else's worship. It is a real and present danger, which is why rabbis often refer privately to the typical American bar or bat mitzvah as "the enemy of Shabbat."

While this aliyah gerrymandering succeeds in making sure regular shul-goers get Torah honors, it means fewer aliyahs for the bar mitzvah families—at a time when kids have more parents, stepparents and estranged biological parents than ever. The final aliyah always goes to the actual boy or girl who is coming of age. It is the first of the three events on the bimah that really matter—religiously—about a bar mitzvah: reciting the prayer before the Torah reading, chanting at least one of those small Torah sections in Hebrew, and then chanting the week's *Haftarah,* a longer supplemental reading from Prophets. The ability to perform these three ritual tasks is proof that a young man or woman is ready to participate fully in Jewish services as an adult—and, in fact, could lead the entire service if necessary. Judaism is entirely democratic that way. On Shabbat, the paid clergy usually takes the lead roles. But the whole point of the bar mitzvah is to remind people that any Jew can do it. That's what the event is *supposed* to be celebrating.

But it doesn't always turn out the way the formulators of the bar mitzvah ceremony—a relatively recent addition to Jewish ritual life— had in mind. The social and culinary excesses during the weekend of the event are to be expected. That's old news at Har Zion. It has been more than twenty-five years since *Philadelphia* magazine did a controversial spoof of over-the-top bar mitzvahs—including a cover shot of a young man in a kippah and tallis, suit pockets stuffed with envelopes, and a description of a bust sculpted from chopped liver—leading Rabbi Wolpe to castigate the publication in the temple bulletin.

These nuclear-family wars over bimah time, however, still feel new and shocking, and they are getting worse. Wolpe can think of at least three more bar mitzvahs coming up that he knows will involve family battles over aliyahs. One has already escalated into threats of violence.

"The ones coming up are among the most difficult I've ever had to negotiate," he says. "Who gets the aliyah, will the divorced father put the tallis on the child, will the new husband or wife or paramour have any part in the service? What does the child really want? Or is it what one of the parents *says* the child really wants? These negotiations are more difficult than settling between Israel and the Palestinians."

Wolpe is fascinated by what he calls this "acting out in the synagogue." A house of worship is, of course, supposed to represent a moral center, a place where moral issues are acted out. So, when these fractured families fight, they pull out *all* the moral stops. They are looking for the clergy to take sides. Rabbis have historically been involved in divorces. In traditional Jewish practice, no marriage is dissolved until the rabbis write a *get,* an official decree of divorce, which does not take sides (even though it is technically given to the wife by the husband). Most Conservative Jews don't bother with a get when they divorce. But when celebrating family events in the synagogue, they may seek something even better: a get-even. They attempt to force the rabbi, on behalf of the whole community, to decide which aggrieved ex has been more moral.

Wolpe flashes back to the early seventies and the day he first realized that divorce had become epidemic in his congregation. A young man was caught between his parents, being asked to make choices concerning his bar mitzvah that he really didn't want to make. He didn't want to decide who could come to the separate parties his parents were throwing. He couldn't endure being told again how horrible his mother was. Finally, he walked into Wolpe's office and threw his bar mitzvah book on the desk.

"If this is Judaism," he yelled, "I don't want any part of it!"

Since Wolpe seems to be sharing a lot with me, I'm thinking that now might be the time to ask him to get me into the rabbi search committee.

While I'm compelled by his life, I also want to watch the process of how Har Zion replaces someone like him.

In many religions, new clergy are either directly appointed by the central office, as in Catholicism, or the central office at least handpicks which candidates the house of worship may interview and choose from. Judaism is much more decentralized and democratic than that. Synagogues are relatively free to hire their own rabbis, fire their own rabbis and negotiate salary and benefit contracts with their own rabbis. A small committee of congregants makes all the decisions.

We talk a little bit about rabbi search committees. He is amused to find out that my mom just finished serving on the committee to fill the job at Beth El in Harrisburg—which Wolpe and I can both refer to as our "old shul." It was a very contentious enterprise. While the rabbi who succeeded Wolpe in the late sixties, Jeffrey Wohlberg, was extremely successful in the pulpit for nearly twenty years, the rabbi who followed him, Mark Greenspan, hadn't fared quite as well. A nice enough guy who was better at hand-holding and hospital visits than sermonizing and synagogue politics, he found himself, after ten years and several short-term contracts, unable to get a new longer contract from the leadership and, eventually, unable to get a new contract at all. Many in the congregation were livid about the way he was treated, but many more were livid about the way *they* were treated: there was no major meeting of the membership until after all the important decisions had been made. Many members were talking about quitting.

All this had happened while my dad was dying, so his last religious interactions were with a lame-duck rabbi doing his best not to act embittered. (In fact, Greenspan was spending much of his time undergoing a rigorous, self-imposed course of study and self-examination so he might emerge, for his next congregation, the dynamic leader Beth El always wanted him to be.) Only weeks after my father's funeral, at which Greenspan ably officiated, my mother was invited to join the rabbi search committee. She would call me after the interviews to let me know how they went. I was amazed at how much power this committee actually had.

Not surprisingly, her search committee had a tough time. There weren't as many applicants as they would have liked because word traveled through the rabbi world that the last guy wasn't treated very well. A handful of candidates were interviewed, but they ultimately passed on one rabbi because he seemed too old, and another because he didn't seem to like kids enough.

The rabbi they picked is my age, bright and energetic. The jury is still out on whether he will be able to mend the congregation. And I'm still trying to digest the idea that my *mom* was so instrumental in a process that would affect the spiritual lives of so many people I know. It makes me that much more curious about how the process will go at a synagogue like Har Zion.

I expect Wolpe to be able to deliver me the same ringside seat for the selection process at Har Zion that my mom gave me at Beth El. Instead, he seems sheepish about the subject. He says he made himself a promise before announcing his retirement that he would stay as far away from the search for his replacement as possible. He knows that if he gets involved—even if they beg him to help—he will ultimately be branded as an egocentric meddler who can't let go of the past, more interested in legacy preservation than the future of the synagogue.

So he gives me the name and number of the chairman of the rabbi search committee, and suggests I call. But he can't get involved.

A RABBI YOU CAN CALL JERRY

L OUIS FRYMAN, THE CHAIRMAN of the Har Zion rabbi search committee, is a powerful lawyer whose specialty is making loud problems
disappear quietly. A compact man with oval tortoiseshell glasses and a
poker face, he is impeccably groomed and friendly to a point. Now in
his late fifties, Fryman doesn't attend services the way he once did when
his own kids were small and he and his wife held synagogue offices. But
he remains extremely significant in the corporate life of Har Zion, and
has served in a variety of what he calls "leadership" roles. In addition to
an astonishing array of Jewish causes, he was also the first Jewish chairman of the predominantly WASPy Episcopal Academy. A litigator turned
managing partner of a big Center City law firm—Fox, Rothschild—
Fryman has assumed the role of search committee chairman with a
reputation for clipped efficiency. The last search committee he ran
quickly found an excellent replacement for legendary cantor Isaac Wall,
who had been at Har Zion for forty-six years.

Fryman gives the impression that if a discussion can't be resolved in
one quarter of a billable hour, then it is not worth having. So here I stand,
with about fifteen minutes in which to convince this unblinking man
why, exactly, the rabbi search committee should allow me to sit in on its

meetings for the purpose of writing a book. I quickly assure him that I already have Rabbi Wolpe's blessing on the project.

Fryman seems somewhat intrigued by my request, at least conceptually. He observes that my nascent book project sounds to him like "*A Civil Action* set in a synagogue," which I suppose it could be. There are similarities between a rabbi search and a jury trial, each a convoluted drama ending with people locked in a room casting votes to determine someone's fate.

The last time Har Zion picked a rabbi, in the late 1960s, it was a very uncivil action, and the synagogue nearly destroyed itself. From what little I've heard, Rabbi David Goldstein and the synagogue's leaders battled for years over his "voluntary" resignation. Since Fryman grew up at Har Zion—his father, a garment manufacturer, was an active member—he knows just how bad it was. He also knows how lucky they were to find Wolpe, who had the right combination of skills to help the congregation heal many of its wounds. But the people who discovered a young Rabbi Wolpe in 1969 are now the old *kochers*. While they can still help with the decision, the next generation must make its own imprint or Har Zion will effectively die when the old kochers do.

Competition for Jews is brisk. Younger, hipper Beth Am Israel, a smaller Conservative synagogue down the road with a rabbi who's a former attorney, has been slowly siphoning off younger members. And every year Reform congregations, like Main Line Reform about a mile away, and less traditional Conservative congregations attract a certain number of Har Zion families for just one reason. Hebrew school at Har Zion is still three days a week, mandatory until bar or bat mitzvah age. Every other Main Line synagogue has Hebrew school two days a week at most. For many families, that extra day represents too many missed soccer games. The new rabbi may have to choose between tradition and soccer moms.

Fryman tells me to write a letter to the rabbi search committee, explaining what I plan to do and why they should let me. Then he'll invite me to come in and make a presentation at their next meeting.

☆   ☆   ☆

Several days later, I meet the committee: twenty-one people, seated in chairs arranged in a circle dead-center in Har Zion's all-purpose room—the Fishman-Tobin auditorium, which is bigger than an NBA basketball court and has nicer hardwood floors.

I don't know anyone in the group, but they are recognizable to me as Jews of the suburbs, people like the ones I grew up with. They all have either thick hair or no hair, and share a certain engagement in their dark eyes. While Har Zion is known for its social status, it is doubtful anyone is on this committee just for reasons of prestige, because this is going to be hard work, and a substantial commitment of time and energy. And no matter who is chosen, inevitably many will be unhappy with the selection.

My unusual request to observe the rabbi interviews and deliberations seems to have aroused equal parts of fascination and suspicion. Nobody says so, but it is clear that committee members are concerned about what an unchecked journalist would write about a Jewish institution. All the other volunteer work they do is covered solely by the local Jewish press, which is published by the local chapter of "Federation." The Jewish Federation of Greater Philadelphia is part of a massive nation-wide fund-raising network, a Jewish United Way, which takes great pains to make sure possible donors are never caused great pain by its Jewish media. Har Zion is one of the most charitable congregations in America, and its members are accustomed to being lionized for their good works. In fact, whenever the lay media cover anybody Jewish in anything but a congratulatory way, there is much tongue clicking. For Jews, when it comes to the lay press, no news is good news.

I am grilled by several committee members about confidentiality issues, thanked for my time and then politely sent away. As I leave the auditorium, I'm followed by the man who seemed like the elder statesman of the committee: a tall guy with a bushy white moustache and friendly, crinkled eyes. He also has an unexpected vigor, as I discover when he slaps me on the back, shakes my hand really hard and introduces himself in one gregarious fell swoop.

"I'm Ralph Snyder," he says. "I knew your granddad well, and I knew your dad, too. I was sorry to hear about both of them." He's referring to the fact that my father died only four years after his own father, my Pop-pop, who was also a prominent member of the Jewish community.

I knew of Ralph Snyder. He grew up at Beth El in Harrisburg and became a tax attorney in town, but his wife was a Har Zion girl and eventually they moved to Philadelphia. He was the one who first brought Wolpe to Har Zion's attention, and helped the synagogue poach him—for which his relatives back in Central Pennsylvania have never quite been forgiven.

Snyder confides that there is another "Harrisburg boy" on the rabbi search committee. His younger cousin, Lewis Grafman, a Har Zion vice president, also belonged to Beth El. Now an attorney in his early fifties, Grafman is expected to ascend to the Har Zion presidency in the spring, and will serve his two-year term while Wolpe's successor is being selected. Lew Grafman and committee chair Lou Fryman—"the Two Lews"—are likely to be the driving forces in the rabbi search. Along with Snyder, of course.

We both laugh at what a small town Judaism is, and what a large reach the Harrisburg Jewish community seems to have. While he likes my book idea, he doesn't think there's a chance on God's earth that twenty-one opinionated Har Zionites are going to agree to let me sit in on their confidential meetings. It's amazing that they all agreed to put their chairs in a circle, with so many other geometric shapes available for debate. Still, Snyder wishes me well, says he'll put in a good word for me and recalls once more that my dad was a "hell of a nice guy."

I walk down the long corridor toward the exit to the parking lot. My footsteps are soundless in the carpeted, wallpapered hall. Almost every surface bears some tasteful plaque, in memory or in honor of someone. In my synagogue at home, I would have known most of those on the plaques or their families. Here they are just names, people whose significance I will have to figure out if I am to understand this place.

How does one get to know a community that is both foreign and familiar? It is a problem that I'm sure any new member of Har Zion—any member of any American synagogue, or church, or mosque for that matter—would have. Religious communities are supposed to be welcoming by definition. But they can also be closed and cliquish. We join synagogues and churches to be part of a community of shared experiences, to put our lives into some kind of context. But once inside, the barriers are higher than they appeared from a distance.

This is particularly true in Philadelphia, where all newcomers are viewed with suspicion for the first, oh, ten or fifteen years. In many metropolitan areas, synagogue and church communities have such a large percentage of mobile newcomers that their diversity becomes their strength. But not here. A rabbi once told me that the problem with Philadelphia synagogues is that they have too many Philadelphians. And I knew exactly what he was talking about. It's a city that welcomes you with folded arms.

The next day, I get a call from Lou Fryman. I've been rejected. My proposal to join the rabbi search committee as observer has been turned down, without prejudice.

Even though Ralph Snyder predicted this, I'm still shocked. I have to think fast, and switch into hostage negotiator mode: keep Fryman on the phone, keep him engaged, keep him talking. I ask if the board will reconsider. From the depths of my Jewish knowledge, I yank a precedent I think might be on-point. I recall having heard that rabbis are taught to turn down important requests—such as a request to be converted to Judaism—three times as a test of commitment. Affecting my most rabbinic manner, I let Fryman know I'm determined to follow his rabbi search no matter what, and I intend to ask and keep asking until the committee changes its mind. Then I dash off another letter to them, explaining my interpretation of the Jewish three-strike rule, and await a reply.

In the meantime, I'm off to see "the RA." The Rabbinical Assembly in New York is the "professional organization"—they don't like the word *union*—from whose members Har Zion must choose its next rabbi. Its rules will also govern the rabbi search.

Each major denomination in Judaism has its own seminary for rabbinic training, and its own professional organizations for ordination, peer support and placement. The most powerful of these institutions is Wolpe's alma mater, the Jewish Theological Seminary of America in New York. (The Reform Seminary, Hebrew Union College, is based in Cincinnati and New York and the Reconstructionist Rabbinical College is in Philadelphia; Orthodox rabbis have traditionally been trained and ordained at regional yeshivas, but the "Modern Orthodox" rabbis are trained at Yeshiva University in Manhattan.) Once they have been trained and ordained at the Seminary, Conservative rabbis generally seek pulpits with the more than eight hundred synagogues formally affiliated with The United Synagogue of Conservative Judaism, a professional and support group for the congregations themselves.

The Conservative job-search process is overseen by the ominously named Joint Commission on Rabbinic Placement. But the rabbis are represented and counseled by the Rabbinical Assembly, which also serves as their professional organization and their lifeline to their colleagues. Unless you're an RA member, you can't log onto RAVNET, the rabbis-only Web service, where they privately swap war stories and sermon topics.

The Seminary, the RA, the Joint Commission and RAVNET all have the same New York address: 3080 Broadway, at the northeast corner of 122nd Street. The main entrance is an unobtrusive, vaguely collegiate-looking stone arch, whose door leads to a dingy hallway lined with thick black metal doors. Behind each door is a flurry of academic activity. The halls are bustling with students and teachers who, except for their small, utilitarian pinned-on kippahs, look like the rapt students and faculty of any college.

As I walk in, I suddenly recall that I was here once before—when I was fourteen, and my synagogue sponsored a trip to New York. My strongest memories of the visit are a tour of the Seminary's Rare Book

Room, a trip to the Lower East Side to eat at a kosher Chinese restaurant and then cutting out early with my girlfriend and our mothers to take in a Broadway show. (We thought it best not to tell the rabbi we were ditching the rest of the Seminary visit to go see *Jesus Christ Superstar*.)

I take the elevator to the sixth floor of the Seminary complex, and head down a long hallway looking for the RA, which I expect to be a grand meeting room teeming with rabbis, like Parliament with real beards. Instead, I find a very plain office and an even plainer man from Queens, dressed in a shirt, slacks, a brightly colored tie and Wallabees. He is Rabbi Elliot Schoenberg, the man behind the curtain in rabbinic placements.

Schoenberg led two congregations in New England before leaving the pulpit to become, basically, a rabbi for rabbis—not on theological issues so much as employment matters. If he is having a discussion of Torah or Talmud (the encyclopedic interpretation of the Torah by the early rabbis), it most likely involves how a quote from either source could spruce up a cover letter, or lead to more effective communication in a job interview. Besides his role as matchmaker, he also does some teaching and is a historian of the arcane world of rabbinic placement.

"Congregations all want to hire the same rabbi," he says with a chuckle. "They all want . . ." and he reaches across his desk to grab a page with "The Perfect Rabbi" printed across the top, ". . . someone who attends every meeting and is at his desk working until midnight, someone who is twenty-eight years old but has preached for thirty years, someone who has a burning desire to work with teenagers but spends all his time with senior citizens, basically someone who does *everything* well and will stay with the congregation forever.

"We try to tell them, You're not looking for the best rabbi. You're looking for the best *match*, the best fit. And that's a hard thing for people to adjust to, the idea that the *best* rabbi may not be the best rabbi for them."

I ask him where the Har Zion rabbi search fits into the international placement picture. How would he handicap the upcoming season for Conservative rabbis?

"Har Zion is one of the great plums," he explains. "It's one of the top ten congregations in the country—if there is such a list. It has only had wonderful rabbis, it has only done wonderful things and it has made major contributions to Philadelphia, to the Seminary and to the country. Still, not everybody wants to be rabbi of a congregation of that size and that magnitude.

"We do between sixty-five and eighty placements a year and there are probably twelve to fifteen pulpits every year over six hundred families. During the time of Har Zion's search, you also have Beth-El in Rochester, New York; one in Vancouver; Harrison, New York; Fort Worth, Texas; one in Stockholm, actually; and, oh, Dallas, Texas, Shearith Israel."

The synagogue in Dallas has quite a history. In 1963, it became world-famous, because it was where Jack Ruby belonged when he shot Lee Harvey Oswald. It made the Warren Commission report, as did its rabbi, Hillel Silverman—the son of Rabbi Morris Silverman, who wrote the first widely-used Conservative prayer book. The pulpit is also significant to Har Zion for a completely different reason: in 1969, Congregation Shearith Israel tried to woo a young Jerry Wolpe away from the East Coast. Wolpe interviewed there, but decided to pursue Har Zion instead.

"We also have a very nice congregation in Wilkes-Barre, Pennsylvania," Schoenberg says. He's beginning to sound like a sommelier of synagogues. "But in size, Har Zion is really comparable to Dallas this year, and Vancouver and Harrison, New York, next year."

The first step in the process, he explains, is that the congregation fills out a questionnaire evaluating itself and its needs. Har Zion's pulpit will not be open for another year, and rabbi-hunting season generally runs from January to April, with the new rabbi showing up in the summer and making the first big splash on the High Holidays in the early fall. This means that Har Zion really shouldn't even bother sending in its questionnaire for another year. But the overachievers have already finished their homework, and they want to know from Schoenberg how soon they can post their vacancy on the "Yellow Sheets," the placement list that is the bible of job-searching rabbis.

Congregations are not allowed to advertise vacancies. They aren't even supposed to call rabbis to assess or solicit their interest in changing jobs—although these calls are made all the time. All they can do, officially, is list the opening on the Yellow Sheets, which are updated every month. And then any rabbi who is eligible can apply, through the RA, to be considered by the congregation.

The last time Har Zion hired a rabbi, the process worked differently. The RA and the Joint Commission were more dictatorial back in the sixties: they decided themselves which rabbis should be seen by which congregations, and doled out a handful of résumés. Only if all candidates from the initial panel were interviewed and rejected could the synagogue get more. In 1989, the rules were changed after rabbis complained that the process should be more democratic, the RA's whims less powerful. A rabbi can now apply for any pulpit, as long as certain eligibility standards are met.

"Rabbis don't have free agency," Schoenberg says. "It is a controlled and hierarchical process." They can't break a long-term contract with their current synagogue to pursue a better job. And they have to meet certain requirements of experience depending on the size of the synagogue: the larger the congregation, the more experience necessary. This system is meant to protect older rabbis from being forced out by younger rabbis, and to protect younger rabbis from getting in over their heads.

Since Har Zion is one of the largest synagogues in the country, it's in the highest experience bracket. Congregations, like batteries, are ranked in size from A to D. Only rabbis who have been ordained for at least ten years may apply for a D pulpit like Har Zion.

There's only one exception to the ten-year rule. If a younger rabbi has served as the assistant in a congregation for six years, he or she may apply for that specific senior rabbi position. But, Schoenberg explains, that can't possibly happen at Har Zion. The synagogue's current assistant rabbi, Jacob Herber, is only two years out of rabbinical school. Schoenberg knows this fact off the top of his head. Before graduating to become Rabbi Wolpe's assistant, Herber had worked as *his* assistant at the RA. In that job, Herber explained the placement rules to rabbis countless times. He knows better than anyone that he can't possibly be considered for the post.

"He is not eligible and, also, knowing Jacob, there is wisdom in that . . ." he says, paternally. "How many members does Har Zion have?" More than fourteen hundred families, I remind him. "Well, you need to have been a rabbi for a while to know how to manage and lead such a complex institution . . . Jacob is a wonderful rabbi, an outstanding rabbi and someday will do such a thing. But he needs a little bit more experience, more seasoning. You need some crises in your life."

He says this with authority, backed up, I assume, with insight accumulated the hard way, wisdom that cannot be downloaded. As we talk, I am reminded of the peculiar experience of rabbis—all clergy, really—in the sheer volume of emotionally charged situations, assaults on the human condition, that they must witness and process. These are referred to as "life-cycle events" in the retail business of religion. And after a while, rabbis see and oversee enough of them that they are able to compare and contrast trends and patterns. In any given week, a pulpit rabbi in a large congregation might give two or three eulogies, and might visit three times as many people struggling with life-threatening medical conditions. That's more death and destruction than most war veterans will ever have to process, and for the clergy, there's never a lull in the battle. Then there are the bar and bat mitzvahs, the baby namings, the weddings and the private pastoral counseling sessions, where the weights of various worlds are placed on the rabbi's shoulders. It's enough to create post-traumatic stress disorder by proxy.

I am fascinated by people who have learned things most of us don't imagine can (or should) be known. I remember the hospice nurse who treated my father, and her incomprehensible expertise in the mechanics of death. One night we were sitting up with him when his lungs made a scary, gurgling sound and she matter-of-factly noted, "Oh, that's the death rattle," but explained that, unlike in the movies, it can come and go for days. Two nights later, my brother and I were huddled around Dad, watching for hours on end in case the next breath was his last. At

6 A.M., the nurse got up and turned on the TV to a cable channel with streaming weather and news, muting the audio. When he died fifteen minutes later, we realized why: she knew she would soon be needing to record an exact time of death. She had a specific genius.

Schoenberg is that way with rabbi placements. No matter how unique the circumstances seem, he always knows how it will go. And he knows Har Zion is overanxious. They started too soon and they shouldn't be pushing to have their vacancy listed already.

"I told them they could list it now, but I wouldn't recommend it," he explains. "No one's going to apply because the pulpit isn't open for twenty months. So the congregation won't get résumés for the next ten months. And six months from now people will say 'Why hasn't anybody applied? Doesn't anybody want Har Zion?' Which won't be the case at all, but psychologically it will feel that way to the search committee."

I tell Schoenberg I hope to be able to check in with him periodically. He says he'd be happy to help, the rabbi-placement process is an open one, and maybe what I'm writing will help more people understand its importance and delicacy. We agree to talk again when there is something to talk about. Because regardless of what the search committee at Har Zion thinks, nothing is really going to happen for a while.

Not long after I return from the RA, I get a call from Lou Fryman. It's my second turndown. The rabbi search committee does, however, wish me good luck in writing about whatever I'm going to write about without their help.

Then I call Rabbi Schoenberg again, to make sure I can count on him and input from the RA. He says, actually, well, he's not sure he wants to be involved either. Wonderful.

So I go back to see Wolpe. He seems both unsurprised and unconcerned. Patience, he says. He and I still have plenty to talk about.

Still, I pump him for what he knows about the rabbi search. Very little, he insists. He's doing everything he can to stay out of it.

He has heard one thing, however. In an early meeting, a controversy apparently erupted about whether the next rabbi of Har Zion would be someone they could address by first name. Congregants at Har Zion *never* call Rabbi Gerald Wolpe "Jerry" to his face. It's just not done. Even Ralph Snyder, one of his closest friends, won't do it. He calls him "Rabbi," or "MTR," which is short for *mein teirer rebbi*, Yiddish for "my dear rabbi." Like all Har Zionites, he refers to the Wolpes as "Rabbi and Elaine."

Some on the committee, however, would really prefer a rabbi they can call Jerry. One of the younger members—and, in Jewish institutional life, "younger" generally means close to middle-aged—was particularly adamant. She made a case for a new rabbi who would be more informal, more personal, a leader for a more modern synagogue that is less, as Har Zion is sometimes described, "High Church." Her insistence set off a hailstorm of discussion, a debate reminiscent of the one Woody Allen has with himself when he realizes his girlfriend calls her therapist "Donny," while he reverently refers to his as "Dr. Chomsky."

The debate, of course, is about more than the rabbi's name. It is about the future of Judaism, the future of all American religions, really. Most public prayer in twentieth-century America has been in institutions that are fairly "High Church." We have, in general, preferred a good show to full congregational participation, and charismatic leaders have been valued more highly than patient teachers and scholars because they fill seats. The question is whether baby boomers and the generations after them want their clergy to be as dress-casual as the rest of their lives, or whether the significant return to religion in the 1990s is made up of people who will ultimately desire more formality.

American Judaism in general is leaning toward the right. While fewer Jews affiliate with synagogues than in previous generations, those who do tend to be more closely and actively affiliated. So many young people are becoming observant Conservative Jews, or Modern Orthodox, or something in between (often referred to as "Conservadox") that my alma mater, the University of Pennsylvania, once known as one of the nation's great havens for assimilated Jewish princes and princesses, now has its own kosher dining hall to handle the needs of a burgeoning observant population. And the Reform movement, which was once the most churchlike of the denominations and had the least number of required observances, has been moving toward more tradition and ritual. Reform Judaism still has certain liberal policies. Reform rabbis are allowed to perform interfaith marriages (although more and more of them are choosing not to). Reform congregations are permitted to bar mitzvah children of Jewish fathers and non-Jewish mothers—even though traditionally, biological Jewishness can only be passed along by the mother—based on the modern concept of patrilineal descent. The Reform movement ordains homosexual rabbis and blesses homosexual unions. And Reform conversions have historically been less demanding than those of other denominations. But in many Reform synagogues they have also added more Hebrew to the service, and congregants have even begun to wear kippahs and tallises during prayer, which they never used to do. And they're grappling with the reinstatement of other rules jettisoned long ago.

But recognizing and anticipating trends in Jewish life does not necessarily make it easier to decide which way Har Zion should go. Part of the synagogue's appeal is that it has been ambitious while remaining old-fashioned. Across the nation, some younger congregants voice a desire for more participatory services and smaller congregations. But, still, many Americans prefer to be led in prayer—and everyone likes a good show. The surveys Har Zion did of its search committee and later its congregants both came back with the same result: their number one priority is that the new rabbi be a great sermonizer—or, as they say at the Seminary, a master at homiletics. But most dramatic homileticists don't want to be called by their first names. It undercuts the drama.

While Wolpe finds the debate over his first name amusing, he does not take the subject lightly. A great deal of thought went into how he is to be addressed. Growing up in Boston he had a teacher, an Orthodox rabbi named Mostofsky, who thought he might have a future in the clergy and gave him Talmud lessons. Mostofsky asked him to promise only two things in return. If Wolpe ever became a rabbi, he had to give lessons to any similarly promising student who asked. And he must never let anyone call him anything but "rabbi."

"Once they call you by your first name," he recalls the old teacher saying, "you're not a rabbi anymore."

It is not easy being a man without a first name. It has haunted him his entire career. In fact, he has recently begun seeing a psychiatrist. He wishes he had done it sooner. But he's not accustomed to admitting he needs help. It's not a rabbi thing to do.

"The older rabbis saw themselves as *cley kodesh,* the holy vessel," he explains. "They didn't walk on the same paths as other people. I think some young clergy become too much like their own congregants, too familiar. And when the time comes for them to be used as clergy, the feeling isn't always there. Can you go to somebody you've shared dirty jokes with? Still, I'm not too sure what I'd do if I had it to do over again."

He shrugs and looks out the window. "I've paid a price for not being Jerry," he says.

4

HOW I BECAME A MINYANAIRE

I AM HERE BECAUSE of my father. It is that simple and that complicated. Sometimes I ask myself what I am doing here, mining a rabbi's memory, working in his synagogue. And I always come up with the same answer as Rabbi Wolpe. I am here because of my father.

When I first started showing up for synagogue to say the memorial prayer for my dad, I was surprised to be there. But a rabbi friend of mine was not surprised. It was, he said, as predictable as the seasons: winter, spring, summer, High Holiday and fall.

"We basically get two chances to get you back," he said. "It's either the death of a parent, or kids reaching preschool or Hebrew school age. That's it. You lost a parent before you had kids. Of *course* you're here."

The day after my father was buried, my mother and I went to synagogue. We were there for the weekday morning service, which I could not recall having ever attended before in my life. In my family we did the High Holiday services, an occasional festival, a Shabbat service if we were invited to the bar mitzvah. But never the standard daily services, which have their own names but are generally referred to as *minyan,* the

Hebrew term for quorum, ten adults (or, for the non-egalitarian, ten men). Without ten adults, many of the main prayers may not be recited aloud and the Torah cannot be read. It's the Jewish way of making sure nobody drinks alone.

Walking down the halls I had run through as a child, and entering the small chapel where I sometimes led junior congregation services, I should have felt nostalgic. Instead, the scene was alien to me. The only people in the chapel were a dozen or so creaky adults and they were davening, rocking forward and back, power-praying through page after page of the Hebrew-only service. I flashed back to a moment in this same chapel, years ago, when as youngsters we were asked to participate in "speed-reading" contests. The idea was to read Hebrew aloud as quickly as possible, even though we didn't understand a word of it. It seemed utterly ridiculous to me back then, and didn't make any more sense to me as an adult.

The murmuring confused and embarrassed me. But then, every so often, they would hit a prayer I did recall. Flexing Hebrew school muscle-memory, I jumped right in. It felt pretty good, actually. For a moment I could understand the attraction of getting lost in it, assuming I could ever keep up.

We stood for the mourner's Kaddish, which I knew by heart. The Kaddish is a prayer that makes no mention of death: it is an exaltation of God. To stand and say it in the face of death is a powerful statement of faith. A Kaddish is recited at several other times in every service, but the version slowly monotoned by standing mourners at the end of the service has always held the greatest fascination. As a kid, I would crane my neck to see who rose to recite it. In the middle of a crowd, they were standing so alone. I admired their public solitude.

In a large Sabbath service, only a small percentage of the congregants stand, either those who are in mourning or those who are commemorating a *yahrzeit,* the anniversary of a death. But, at minyan, many people are saying the mourner's Kaddish; it is the reason they have come. The few people seated are often the ones who stand out.

At minyan, the mourner's Kaddish is the only prayer *not* recited at breakneck speed. Saying it felt astonishingly right to me. For perhaps the first time in my life, prayer had meaning. It wasn't just that I was fulfilling my duty as the eldest son to mourn my father. I was moved. It was as if during the prayer some wormhole opened up between where my father was and where I stood. It was gratifying. I wanted to feel that way again. And that evening, I did.

The first seven days of mourning just after a Jewish funeral are called *shiva*, a period when the bereaved stay home and receive visitors all day. In Conservative congregations, mourners generally leave home only to attend shul in the morning, and then the synagogue holds its regular evening minyan at the shiva house. So I said Kaddish in my parents' living room. The next morning, my mother and I went to minyan again. Many of the same people were there and for some reason I was surprised. I knew that Jews were supposed to pray three times a day, but it had never occurred to me that so many people actually did.

On the third morning, there were not enough people at synagogue to pray, so we stood around for a while waiting for a ninth and tenth. (In some synagogues, if you get nine, the Ark is opened and the Torah itself can stand in as the tenth.) And when nobody else showed we just rushed through a skeleton service, skipping many of the good parts, such as Kaddish. I was crestfallen, fearing in some vaguely superstitious way that my father's soul had been dishonored. But then I remembered there would be another service, in our living room that evening. I would catch up with Dad then, mourning him right next to his favorite chair.

When shiva ended and my wife, Diane, and I returned home to Philadelphia, I was surprised I still felt the need to say Kaddish for my father. So I had to find a minyan close to where I lived and worked, and started shopping for synagogues. We had visited a few ten years earlier, when we were first married, but had never actually joined one.

I called up Michael Monson, the rabbi who had married us. I had known him since college, where he ran the Penn chapter of Hillel—the primary campus outreach program of organized Judaism, which is non-denominational, although it caters to the more observant, and is funded by local Federation chapters and private grants. I never actually *went* to his Hillel, except for High Holiday services (the only ones in town that didn't require a ticket), but Michael and I had become friends through a class we were taking. We remained friendly after he left Hillel and worked first for the Conservative movement in Israel—which struggles to get recognition in a country run by the Orthodox—and then as executive director of the non-profit Jewish Publication Society (JPS), the oldest publisher of Jewish books in the English language, which is still located in downtown Philadelphia (or what locals call Center City). Diane and I studied together with him before our wedding, and had urged him to seek a pulpit so we could join his shul. But he had remained in administration, and we remained unaffiliated.

Now I was calling Michael for minyan advice. He belonged to a feisty Center City synagogue, Temple Beth Zion Beth Israel—the merger of two historic Philadelphia congregations that bought a stone church not far from charming Rittenhouse Square and retrofitted it as a stunning urban shul with fiery stained-glass windows. Michael recommended BZBI's morning and evening minyans (while there are three daily services, most Conservative synagogues combine the afternoon and evening prayers into one service around 5:30 P.M.). But he also told me about a rather unusual ultra-Orthodox lunchtime minyan, held in the library of a high-profile personal injury law practice. I checked both of them out.

The BZBI minyan was pretty straightforward—almost exactly the same as the one in Harrisburg, except that the wood in the chapel was blonder. The lawyer minyan, however, was like an alternative universe. The firm's top lawyer, whose face I knew from his local TV ads, had hired his own rabbi to come in every day. Nestled among his law volumes was a small wooden Ark that held a mini-Torah. Only men were allowed to pray in the main library room; in Orthodox services, men and women are not permitted to sit together. If women came to the

minyan—and they sometimes did, because this very Jewish high-rise office building also houses the local fund-raising offices of the Seminary
and other national institutions—they had to sit out in the cramped hallway, separated from us by a folding opaque screen.

The minyan also used a different prayer book than I was accustomed
to: the ArtScroll prayer book, which is popular in both Modern Orthodox
and ultra-Orthodox congregations. The ArtScroll prayer books are much
more detailed and do-it-yourself than Conservative prayer books. In
type so tiny that it could induce the need for reading glasses well before
middle age, every prayer is explained, along with how and why to do
it. Although its theology is a little right wing for my taste, the ArtScroll
is a *prayer's* prayer book. Well-worn copies of the ArtScroll half-size
edition were stacked on the conference table, next to a box of kippahs.
The kippahs were basic black suede on the outside with two printed
panels on the underside. One said "Law Firm of Allen L. Rothenberg,
Mincha Minyan, Mon.–Thurs. 1:30 P.M." The other gave the firm's 800
number.

Unusual as the scene was to me, there were two great things about
this service: there were always chilled sodas on the table and they never,
ever failed to get a minyan. If they came up short, the boss started bark-
ing into the speakerphone, hunting down his associates until he had a
quorum. It was like davening in a David Mamet play.

At BZBI, on the other hand, it was more like *Waiting for Godot*. When
there weren't ten people, the minyan leaders would first hit the phones,
calling any members who lived nearby, and then resort to walking out
on the sidewalk and buttonholing people who *looked* Jewish to see if
they could be guilted into joining the minyan long enough for the
mourners to say Kaddish.

I was becoming a minyanaire. The service only took fifteen or twenty
minutes—they davened so fast, there was barely time to call out the
page numbers—but it resonated through other parts of the day. And as I

kept going to minyan, I found myself getting into a lot of discussions about religion with my friends, Jewish, Christian, whatever. I could break down their responses into four groups, not unlike the Four Sons in the Passover Seder: the wise son who asks why are *we* observing the rituals, the wicked son who asks why are *you* observing the rituals, the simple son who just wants to know what's going on and the son who doesn't even know enough to ask.

Some friends were intrigued because they, too, had recently "relapsed," and were making a return to religion after years of aversion, ambivalence or autopilot. Some had done it for themselves, others because they were embarrassed that their kids, who were in religious day-care or school, already knew more about their religion than they did. My friend Doug, who grew up in a Reform synagogue and had never affiliated as an adult, was suddenly part of a group of young parents who were building a new Conservative synagogue in northern New Jersey. Another friend from that same Reform synagogue, Joanie, was now running a preschool in a Conservative synagogue in Maryland. My friend Kim, who had wandered away from the Catholic Church in her teens, was now very active with her daughter in a Unitarian congregation in Philadelphia. And my friend Ronnie, who had run screaming from Catholicism, was actually being lured back to the faith of her childhood. (She still disagreed with its stands on abortion and homosexuality, but she missed the old hymns.) All of us were suddenly comparing notes with the small percentage of our friends who had always been religious. The "extremists" no longer seemed so extreme. "What is happening to us?" we asked.

A second group was less fascinated than taken aback. "What the hell are you doing?" they asked, either out loud or with their rolled eyes. It was as if our generation had made its own sort of gentleman's agreement about *not* returning to organized religion, or returning grudgingly only for the children. And now I had screwed up everything. My wife and I don't have kids yet. Nor had we succumbed to familial pressure, since my father didn't do this for his own father, and never would have expected me to mourn so traditionally for him. So I had broken the generational pact, and I made those friends feel criticized for their non-practice.

A third group simply wanted to know what religious "relapsing" was like. "What is this?" they asked. "What do you do? Who goes? Do you, like, know how to say the prayers?" As for the fourth group—well, truthfully, the rabbis say that there were originally only three sons in the Seder, and the fourth son was added much later, which is why their questions are so similar. So, to the third and fourth group, I just retold the story of how I became a minyanaire. And I talked about the questions that were starting to occur to me as I sat in synagogue every day, trying to keep up with the praying. Big-picture questions about how religious communities function, and how they keep from falling apart. Liturgical questions, like why we begin the daily prayer of penitence with a request to keep us from falling "into the hand of man." And questions about synagogue life that I picked up from the general shmoozing after minyan.

I would talk about these questions with Rabbi Monson when I bumped into him at shul. He was thinking a lot about the nature of synagogues and rabbis himself, because he was wondering about leaving his executive job and seeking out his first pulpit—at the age of fifty. Apparently he was also discussing this quite a bit with the rabbi at BZBI, Ira Stone, whom I would also see at minyan.

Diminutive in stature, Rabbi Stone has a formidable mind. Bar mitzvah boys often tower over him, and before giving his intellectually challenging sermons, he ascends a booster step behind the lectern so he can see over it. He makes free time that most pulpit rabbis can't to write poetry and meditations on obscure Talmudic texts: he has published several books of each. Not long after we met, we had something in common: his father died only a few weeks after mine. We mourned side by side and later he gave my wife and me a copy of his book of poetry describing the experience of his father's death. It addressed one of the

questions I had for him: how does a rabbi mourn while leading a congregation in prayer?

> *I say Kaddish professionally. I say it for the absent,*
> *for the dead. I say Kaddish for all those the Kaddish-sayers*
> *have abandoned. I say it for the young, too busy, and for the*
> *embarrassed. I mourn professionally, taking into myself*
> *every stray sadness until I am a danger to all innocence.*
> *Until the thought of mourning my own dead weighs on*
> *my chest as if with the weight of my father's new coffin.*

As I hung out more with these two rabbis I became something of a
minyan insider, a mini-macher in the tiny chapel at BZBI. I would sit on
the hard benches and imagine the back stories of all the people who
were there, wondering whom and how they mourned.

Children are supposed to mourn their parents for eleven months.
Parents, spouses and siblings technically have to do it only for the first
thirty days, which is recognized as the official "grieving period"—during
which time friends and acquaintances may only offer comfort and are
not yet supposed to ask mourners how they *feel*. As my own mourning
process unfolded, I felt a constant struggle to balance work, marriage,
exercise and a daily visit to synagogue. And, when I was at minyan, I still
didn't feel as though I was very good at it.

One evening I read a how-to book about various Jewish rituals. It
was edited by sociologist Dr. Rela Mintz Geffen, whose father, in the
small world of Jews, had been the founding rabbi of my old synagogue
in Harrisburg and then took a pulpit in Troy, New York, where he married my eloping Nana and Pop-pop. Rela Geffen was also the ex-wife of
my friend Rabbi Michael Monson: their divorce had been one of my first
inklings about the challenging private life of the clergy. The chapter in
the book on death said that if you couldn't make it to shul every day
during mourning to say Kaddish, there was an alternative. It was
permissible to do a study project in memory of the person you were

mourning. You study something that brings meaning to the person's death, and work on that for a prescribed period each day.

So I asked Michael if he would study with me. Biblical texts that explored the father-son relationship seemed like a logical place to start. I read over the commentary about Abraham almost whacking his son Isaac as a sacrifice, and how Isaac was then hornswoggled by his son Jacob into giving him the paternal blessing that rightfully belonged to his brother Esau. I compared the biblical patriarchs to those of my own family, noting whatever similarities there were between the enterprise of building the ancient pyramids in Egypt and the family furniture business in Central Pennsylvania.

Besides the standard texts, Michael pulled a little treasure trove of yellowed papers from a long-closed file drawer at the Jewish Publication Society. They were writings by Rabbi Chaim Potok on parents and children from the early 1960s—years before he achieved fame with *The Chosen*—that had been done for The Leaders Training Fellowship of the Seminary, an outreach to smart kids. One was a student study guide on the "ethics of child-parent relations," examining various permutations of the Fourth Commandment: honor thy father and thy mother. It is supposedly because of the primacy of this commandment that children formally mourn their parents longer than they do their spouses, siblings, even their own children. In many ways, Potok's study guide not only presaged the "generation gap" of the sixties, but also anticipated the difficulties faced by baby boomers with aging parents at the turn of the millennium. He correctly predicted that the greater question was whether adult children and their parents would ever be able to honor *each other*. As I was struggling to define my role in my mother's life, the writings helped inform some of my ideas about what I had come to think of as "widow management."

So, in the midst of my very personal mourning process, I had fallen in with a gaggle of rabbis, past and present. While I was provoked by their teachings, I also loved listening to them talk shop: congregational politics, national theological politics, fund-raising politics and just plain personal chitchat. It would be untoward of me to suggest that the two rabbis were gossiping, since such talk could be considered *lashon hara,* evil speech, which is a sin. Better to say instead that their observations and asides elevated the common news of temple bulletins to high drama, offering insight into what rabbis and synagogue officers whisper about on the bimah when they lean together and either share a laugh or knowingly shake their heads.

Rabbi Monson was starting to look for a pulpit of his own, and Rabbi Stone had a crucial window coming up in his contractual arrangement with the synagogue: both he and BZBI's cantor would be up for renewal at the same time. But the situation both rabbis were watching with fascination was out at Har Zion. When I heard them gab about Wolpe's retirement and the upcoming pulpit sweepstakes, it sounded as though they were concerned not only for the future of the shul, but for American Judaism in general.

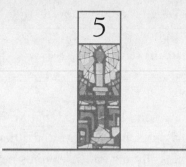

5

STAR OF DAVID

W HEN I ASK, AGAIN, Wolpe claims to have no idea who should succeed him. He has a lot of rabbi acquaintances, whom he sees at Seminary functions and the annual RA conventions, but he doesn't really know many younger rabbis, let alone one he would recommend for his job. He's never seen anyone's *work*. He might be up on the current status of their relationship with their new idiot synagogue president, but it's unlikely that he has heard them deliver a sermon lately. Hard-working pulpit rabbis don't get out much. And when they do, it's unlikely they would bother checking out the competition. They are trying to relax, get in a round of golf, have a nice meal. When he and Elaine are on vacation, Wolpe generally doesn't even tell people that he's a rabbi.

If pressed, Wolpe could probably come up with a few names, the same ones any knowledgeable clergy-watcher would, rabbis of a certain age and experience who might see the synagogue as the challenge of a lifetime. But he knows what Har Zion really wants. They want what every congregation wants: a younger, hipper version of their beloved rabbi, someone who has all of his qualities and none of his imperfections, all of his wisdom plus all of the energy he expended acquiring that wisdom. And, in this case, there just happens to be a rabbi who almost perfectly fits that description.

Unfortunately, they can't have David.

Rabbi Wolpe's third son, David, said he would never become a rabbi—he was, throughout college, an avowed atheist, studying English lit and writing sardonic columns for the campus newspaper. And when he became a rabbi and moved to California, he said he would never take a pulpit. He wanted to be a nationally known writer and lecturer rather than a local hero.

David's fame grew out of the surprise success of his first book, *The Healer of Shattered Hearts: A Jewish View of God* (1990). Published when he was thirty-one, the book invokes his journey from atheist to rabbi. It explores rabbinic views of faith and how God became almost irrelevant to many Jews, and argues nimbly—in reader-friendly bursts of a page or two—that Jews must find their way back to a relationship with God.

His timing was perfect. *Healer* appeared on bookshelves just as a new drive to explore the role of God was sweeping the country—and the popular media, which hadn't been much interested in the deity since declaring him dead in the late sixties. After David was quoted in a *Newsweek* cover story saying, "My father is a rabbi, and a good one, but growing up I never once heard him talk about God," Rabbi Wolpe sent him a printout of the word *God* repeated hundreds of times, with a note reading, "In case *Time* calls you for an interview."

David worked the Jewish lecture circuit hard for nearly ten years, through four books, including *In Speech and in Silence,* which was inspired by his mother's struggle with aphasia after her stroke, and the lighter *Why Be Jewish?* He did countless "special Shabbat weekends" in cities large and small, organized by the B'nai B'rith, the international Jewish service and education organization. He was good on TV, his on-screen skills honed by regular appearances on the A&E series *Mysteries of the Bible.* While he was traveling cross-country, his wife, Eileen, seven years his junior, assumed the role of bookkeeper and ticket master. After four years of marriage, they thought about settling down and raising a family. The positions he had held while earning a living on the lecture circuit were not really career-track jobs. He had been director of the library and then lecturer in Jewish Thought at "the UJ," the University of Judaism in Los Angeles, where he began to study in the early eighties, and where he met his wife. Then they moved back east to be closer to family—his father had had open-heart surgery, his brother's kids barely knew him. During that time he served as an assistant to the chancellor at the Seminary in New York.

The only pulpit he ever considered was at fabled Sinai Temple in Los Angeles, the synagogue that was started in 1906, bolstered by the migration of Jews to the entertainment business and later invigorated by an influx of very traditional Jews from Iran. Sinai is one of the highest-profile pulpits in the country, but it had been a troubled congregation. From 1964 to 1980, it was led by Rabbi Hillel Silverman, whose high profile as "Jack Ruby's rabbi" helped him double the membership. While there, Silverman had a son who grew up to be nice Jewish boy actor Jonathan Silverman. But in rabbinic circles his time at Sinai is often remembered for the way it ended, along with his first marriage. Long separated from his wife, he became involved with a Sinai congregant (although only after resigning from the pulpit, he insisted). He got divorced and married the former congregant the next year, after moving to a prestigious congregation in a Connecticut suburb of New York (where his colleagues sometimes called him "the Hollywooder Rebbi"). After his departure, Sinai went through quite a few rabbis.

David's only real pulpit experience had been his annual gig at Sinai, running the "upstairs" service on the High Holidays, the alternative service for younger congregants who didn't want the pomp and circumstance of the more traditional main sanctuary. He was beloved by the younger big machers in the congregation—especially top movie producer Marc Platt and his wife, Julie, who had been classmates of his brother Paul's at Penn. David and his wife were urged to move back to

California and help rebuild the synagogue. He accepted the job in the late spring of 1997. It may have been only a coincidence that his father announced his retirement at Har Zion just weeks later.

I go to visit David Wolpe in Los Angeles at Sinai Temple. I haven't seen him in years—we were acquaintances in Harrisburg, and later in college. Time has chiseled his face. Shorn of the caterpillar moustache he used to wear, he now looks Hollywood handsome, like a *Jaws*-era Roy Scheider, and his youthful tendency toward self-seriousness has come of age. He is easy to listen to and difficult to penetrate, which makes him almost exactly like his father yet entirely different.

"My father is extraordinarily well defended," he explains. "There is a core to him that is very close to being inaccessible. He is more accessible than he was before my mother's stroke, but he is not of the therapeutic generation. He is a rabbi, and a man who grew up as an only child. He has friends, but they are more or less at an arm's length. One of the reasons he is so successful as a rabbi is that he is warm and intimate without being vulnerable, because vulnerable people in the rabbinate can have a tough time."

Did he pass that on to you? "Yes and no. I have three brothers so I grew up with people close to me. I went into the rabbinate later. He went in at sixteen, so I have friends that predate my rabbinate. Also, I've had two parents my whole life; he didn't. He didn't have a father and his mother, for all her virtues, was about as emotionally distant a mother as you can imagine without being cruel. She wasn't a cruel person, just very self-contained.

"And I'm of a different generation; some call me by my first name. My writings and sermons are, I don't want to say less guarded, but also of a different generation. The spirituality stuff, with all its advantages and disadvantages, can be extremely self-revealing. That's one of the reasons why he's not so comfortable with it."

I ask him about this word he uses to describe his father, *defended*.

"He's not defen*sive*," he explains. "He's defend*ed*. It's somebody whose boundaries are so clear that he can answer intimate questions without them touching him intimately. He'll tell you all this stuff but it's so . . . it comes out so easily that it doesn't feel like you've touched something very deep in him. I'm not saying he can't be touched deeply. But it's hard. He's been in the public eye so much.

"Growing up, I don't think I was consciously aware of it. When we were kids, we just hero-worshipped him. I don't think I saw or took serious note of his flaws until I got older. They don't diminish him. So even if you feel there's some inner thing that you're not getting, he is very warm."

I tell David that sounds a lot like my own father, actually. My dad could also seem warm and easy to talk with. But beneath his affable exterior, he too was "defended," although, when confronted with his inaccessibility, he could be defensive as well. I wonder if this might be true of many fathers of that generation. Either they were distant, omniscient breadwinners like their own fathers, or they approached emotion the way you approach a camp bonfire, moving close enough to get some warmth but not so close that you risk being singed.

"I can just hear my dad saying, 'I don't like all this intimacy,'" David chuckles. "His was a generation who thought that being overintimate was being boundary-less, and not a well-integrated person."

Couldn't it also be a father-son thing?

"I don't know how my father would have related to a daughter," he says. "And since I will probably never have a son, because I will probably never have another child . . ."

David approaches the subject of a recent trauma in his life far more willingly than I would have expected. His thirty-one-year-old wife was diagnosed with endocervical cancer not long after the birth of their first child, a daughter. The condition was discovered by a routine pap smear and, although she escaped chemotherapy, she can't have another child. The personal details of her cancer have been shared in a letter she wrote in the *Sinai Speaks* newsletter. In it, she also explained that she had changed her first name from Eileen to her Hebrew name, Eliana—in keeping with the old Jewish custom of trying to befuddle the angel of death. She now goes by Elli.

While David has not sermonized about his wife's illness, he is writing about it. By a disquieting coincidence, he was working on a new book about "making loss matter," finding meaning in difficult situations, when she was diagnosed. It is his first book with a new publisher, and it will include a foreword from an old friend who has become an unexpected phenomenon in the book world: Mitch Albom, the Detroit sportswriter whose book *Tuesdays with Morrie* was published in September 1997 and still rides high on the hardcover best-seller list. David and Mitch had been best friends on Philadelphia's Jewish Main Line. They attended each other's bar mitzvahs and Albom, who was a musician before becoming a sportswriter, played at Wolpe's wedding, and his wife sang.

I ask David if it's possible that his earlier estrangement from God and the synagogue could have been for a reason other than atheism, a reason less cerebral but more in tune with what he is currently writing about. There is a perception that too much of synagogue life—or the life of any religious community, for that matter—revolves around loss and hurt, and that many of the regular attendees are only there because something about them is incurable.

"That's why many young people don't come back, because religion appeals to the broken," he explains. "But I'm not sure that's what it was for me. My gut instinct about religion was that it wasn't intellectually challenging and thoughtful, like English literature. And I thought that people who believed in God were basically simpleminded, needed a crutch. I was addicted to Bertrand Russell, the most lucid, persuasive atheist you could imagine. His line was, if people were rational they wouldn't need this nonsense, and he ridiculed religion very effectively and I believed it. I was also subject to . . . well, this is my theory about adolescent boys. Why is it that certain adolescent boys love Sherlock Holmes and Mr. Spock and, for me, Bertrand Russell? Because people who seem to be examples of pure reason are very attractive to adolescent boys whose bodies are doing things they don't understand. So they retreat into their heads. This is true for a lot of adolescent boys who find it comfortable to be intellectual and see intellectual models, but don't feel comfortable being spiritual or emotional. I came to religion with a great cynicism and suspicion. I felt it was intellectually weak.

"We were a very head-oriented family, which has advantages and disadvantages. Danny Gordis [a popular West Coast rabbi and UJ teacher who now lives in Israel] and I used to teach classes for 'young professionals'—which is our euphemism for singles. And he told them once that he came from a very intellectual family, and one day he was arguing with his wife about something and she said something that changed his life. She said, 'You know, Danny, you can win the argument and still be wrong.' In his family as in mine, if you won the argument, you *won*."

David began disavowing himself of his early ideas about religion at the UJ, a place that has opened the eyes of many Jews. The UJ began in 1947 as the West Coast feeder campus of the Jewish Theological Seminary. It became financially independent in the seventies, but while its more liberal "California Conservative" culture and Mulholland Drive location brought fresh perspectives, UJ students like David knew that if they wanted to be rabbis, they still had to study at "3080," the Seminary's Broadway address. (The UJ has since opened its own rabbinical school, which, after a several-year skirmish with the Seminary, can ordain Conservative rabbis.)

"It was at the UJ that I saw these were really serious thoughtful people who had read and knew stuff," he says. "It was the first time I thought maybe I had dismissed this too quickly. Maybe it's not all about weak people who need crutches."

Weak people who are rabbis, or weak people who are coming to synagogue?

"Yes, and yes . . . I basically thought, 'My father is a great rabbi, all the others are schleppers.' I don't know where I got that idea, but I had it. I don't think I got it from my dad, he didn't have friends who were rabbis. It's more likely I got it from my mom. That's my guess. You know, 'Your father is a wonderful rabbi, but all the other rabbis—well . . .'"

After a year in Los Angeles teaching Hebrew school and studying at the UJ, David decided to become a rabbi. "When I told my father I was going into rabbinical school, he sat me down and told me everything that was bad about the rabbinate," he recalls. "And I said, 'OK, I'm still going to do it, so tell me something good.' He said, 'Whatever community you go to, you automatically go to the head of the class.' And it's true, everybody wants to connect with the rabbi . . . it is socially liberating. Around the synagogue, if you want to say hello to everyone, you know they *want* you to say hello to them. That's very nice. You don't walk into a room and think, 'Oh geez, I might come up to this person and say hello and they'll think I'm a jerk.' "

I can't help but laugh. This is really the biggest benefit of being the rabbi?

"It's *true*! You say hello to everyone because you're expected to and they love it. It's very big, it really is. I walk into a room and I know that if I talk to someone there it will be appreciated. You're in the hall and there's a bunch of kids there; those kids will *remember* that the rabbi stopped and said hello. Forget what that does for *your* ego, which may not be healthy. But it's a lovely thing to be able to give somebody. It's great. Who wouldn't want that?"

He suspects that the prospect of losing that feeling, that buzz of the welcome hello, is part of the reason his father has agreed to cooperate so openly with me.

"The day that's over, well, that's devastating. So I'm not surprised that he would want something that would carry that on. There are very few retiring rabbis, I think, who would say 'naaah' to someone asking to do a book about their life. And, of course, everybody thinks they can do it right, and not be caught unawares. You know that Janet Malcolm piece in *The New Yorker*?"

Of course I do. All non-fiction writers do. It's the one about the tortured relationship between convicted murderer Jeffrey McDonald and writer Joe McGinniss, which produced *Fatal Vision*—the book, the TV miniseries and the lawsuit. The piece starts, "Every journalist who is not too stupid or too full of himself to notice what is going on knows that what he does is morally indefensible. He is a kind of confidence man, preying on people's vanity, ignorance, or loneliness, gaining their trust and betraying them without remorse . . ."

Actually, I tell David, I've been thinking about that *New Yorker* piece a lot recently. A magazine story I wrote led police to reopen a thirty-year-old investigation of the mysterious deaths of ten babies born to a Philadelphia woman; the day after the article came out, she confessed to murder. While writing it, I spent a good bit of time in minyan praying for moral defensibility, focusing on the line in the *Amidah*—the lengthy standing prayer that is the liturgical centerpiece of the service—when we ask God for "perception, understanding and intellect."

So, yes, I am acutely aware of the issues involved, and how people can be unpleasantly surprised—and surprising—after reading something you write.

David says he too has struggled with some reactions to his writing. Now that he's a widely published author, it's easier to laugh about how his father greeted his first book. "I sent him the manuscript, and he didn't think it was going to go anywhere," he recalls. "I felt he might make some helpful comments, but he said almost nothing about it. His basic attitude was, he was surprised when it was published and he was ten times more surprised when it became popular. The one thing he thought he knew was the Jewish world, and he *knew* that the Jewish world did not respond to this sort of thing—and especially not from his kid. He had rabbis calling him, rabbis he knew, saying what a wonderful book your son has written. I was speaking to the Rabbinical Assembly, to all his colleagues. It crossed boundaries. I think he didn't quite know what to do with that."

The truth is, a lot of people in the Jewish world don't know what to do with the success of David's book—and the rekindled movement toward Jewish spirituality that it represents. While many appreciate what he has done, other rabbis simply roll their eyes. They view

David as a brilliant and handsome communicator but an intellectual middleweight.

He's heard some of the same stuff from his father. After David Wolpe was ordained as a rabbi, he got a teaching fellowship at the UJ. He recalls his father not being thrilled about the position. "My dad didn't want me to go," he says. "And when I asked why not, he said that in his life at the Seminary there were two kinds of people. There were the great scholars and then there were the middle-level bureaucrats. And he said, 'David, you know, you're a nice boy, but you're not a great scholar. And I don't want you to end up as a middle-level bureaucrat.' "

But the retail business of religion has changed dramatically. "I don't think I could have had anything like the success I've had thirty years ago, because I'm not a great scholar, who's going to listen to me?" David says. "But the field of religion isn't like that anymore. You don't have to write a book with a thousand citations for someone to say, 'OK I'll take this guy seriously.' My editor said to me, 'I want you to speak from your own authority as a spiritual teacher.' *Nobody* would have said that at the peak of my father's rabbinate. If he thought it was possible to write a successful book as a pulpit rabbi, as opposed to a scholar, things might have been different for him."

David's first book begins the way his father's might have, with a quote from Samuel Johnson rather than a rabbinic source. In the preface he notes that Johnson once dismissed a book as "both good and original, but that which was good in it was not original, and that which was original was not good." But this kind of self-deprecation does little to hide intellectual friction.

"The Seminary was extremely destructive of people's intellectual self-confidence," David says. "You had to be a great scholar or, basically, it was 'very nice, you can give sermons . . .' "

Today there is "a business of selling spirituality. Jewish groups pay very well for guest speakers. I don't know what other groups pay, but the Jewish groups pay well. I had one or two bad experiences while I was lecturing full-time, but mostly it was a constant flow of joy and of non-entanglement. I would go, speak and leave."

I imagine he must have encountered congregations where he would hear, "If only he were our rabbi."

"Well, remember, you come and skim off the cream. You give your three or four best speeches. The poor rabbi who's there has to speak every single week, you know. He can't only give the speeches he's given a hundred times before and give the answers he's given a hundred times before. He's gotta *work*."

The first of his popular lectures concerned Abraham Joshua Heschel, the twentieth-century mystical scholar, poet and antiwar activist. David knows that some rabbis refer to his work as "Heschel lite."

"I take the kind of thing Heschel did and write it for someone who isn't from another world," he tells me. "Heschel was so much in that world that it was hard for him to understand how much people *don't know*. That's not hard for me . . . the problem with Heschel as I read him is that it's beautiful and wonderful and inspiring but I'm not the same order of human being as Heschel was. I can listen to Heschel but I know I can never *be* a Heschel . . . But people can be a Wolpe, you know."

For many Jews, the first they hear of Abraham Joshua Heschel is from a pulpit rabbi claiming, "I'm not worthy." Heschel died in 1972 but remains the lightning rod in the struggle in American Judaism between intellectualism and spirituality, the head and the heart. He is probably best known to the general public for marching arm-in-arm with Dr. Martin Luther King Jr. from Selma to Montgomery, and for his very public stand against the Vietnam War. But to rabbis, this charismatic Polish immigrant with the wild coif and facial hair of a biblical prophet holds a special place. He is inspiring, challenging, mystical and yearning, like the title of his theological masterpiece, *God in Search of Man,* in which he laid out a philosophy for a return to spirituality that he never lived to see.

"It is customary to blame secular science and anti-religious philosophy for the eclipse of religion in modern society," he wrote. "It would be more honest to blame religion for its own defeats. Religion declined not because it was refuted, but because it became irrelevant, dull, oppressive, insipid. When faith is completely replaced by creed, worship by discipline, love by habit; when the crisis of today is ignored because of the splendor of the past; when faith becomes an heirloom rather than a living fountain; when religion speaks only in the name of authority rather than with the voice of compassion—its message becomes meaningless. *Religion is an answer to man's ultimate questions . . .*"

I was first introduced to Heschel's work at Penn in a course on Jewish mysticism, taught by one of Heschel's most influenced and influential acolytes, Rabbi Arthur Green. Art Green had been a spiritual center for one of the first attempts in the 1960s to take Judaism back from the huge, powerful, establishment congregations—like Har Zion, actually— and begin praying again in a smaller more personal group called a *havurah*. The spirit of the hippie Havurat Shalom in Somerville, Massachusetts, which Art and his wife, Kathy, cofounded, was transmitted to the American public in the pages of *The Jewish Catalog*, which was billed as a *Whole Earth Catalog* for theologically wandering Jews, but was really more like a *Moosewood Cookbook* for a revisionist brand of do-it-yourself Judaism. Originally published in 1973 by the Jewish Publication Society, it became a primer for baby boom Jews, spawning sequels and imitators.

Art Green taught Heschel and mysticism not by lecturing, but by inspiring and manipulating conversations so that, by the end of class, we found ourselves asking the very questions that Heschel had addressed about the place of God and spirituality in a world of American Jews obsessed with building institutions to somehow replace all that had been decimated by the Nazis. Art's course was the first time I was encouraged to unlearn what I'd been taught as a kid about "what Jews believe" and start experiencing Jewish belief as a process of exploration.

When I get home from California, I make an appointment with David's dad, so we can talk about Heschel and spirituality.

Rabbi Wolpe the elder says he remembers Heschel well, since he came to the Seminary not long after Heschel arrived in the mid-1940s. When Heschel left war-torn Europe, he went first to the rabbinical school of the Reform movement, Hebrew Union College in Cincinnati. After five years there as a fish out of water, Heschel came to the Seminary, where he was still a fish out of water, but much deeper water.

There is a story, Wolpe says, about how the Kabbalah—the hard-core writings of Jewish spirituality, mysticism and numerology, which are supposed to be studied only by Torah experts—and the work of mystical popularizers such as Heschel and Gershom Scholem were viewed at the Seminary. Rabbi Saul Lieberman, the great scholar of Talmud, described the mystical texts they were fascinated by as *mishegos,* Yiddish for non-sense.

"But the study of mishegos," Lieberman said, "is still scholarship."

Wolpe continues to view much of the growing spiritual literature as mishegos. But he has an excuse. "I'm a New Englander," he says. "I was brought up and educated in the classical New England form: Emerson, Thoreau, proper English, good enunciation. Classic. That's the way I was educated. Spirituality was not considered to be relevant. You prayed—you did it. Who ever heard of spirituality?"

Most of his memories of Heschel are more secular, collegial. He recalls being on one of the first organized trips to Israel in the early 1960s, and bumping into Heschel on the road to Mount Zion, where people went for a view of the Old City of Jerusalem, still under Jordanian control. Wolpe gave Heschel a ride back to town on his bus. He also recalls running into a frantic Mrs. Heschel at a hotel desk in the Catskills during a Rabbinical Assembly conference: she was short on cash, and he lent her thirty dollars to get back to New York. "Heschel and I had a fine relationship," he says. "But he realized I was not the same as some of the other students who attached themselves to his approach to theology. Whereas my son David is a theologian. That's why David is a spokesman for his generation, while my priorities may have, well, more of an historical context now."

He invokes a metaphor that Heschel liked to use, about fire in the shtetl. "Whenever there was a fire in the shtetl," he explains, "an alarm went off because all the buildings were made of wood. Men ran to their houses to save their wives and children, and then they ran to the synagogue to save the Torahs. 'We've been saving the people,' Heschel would say, 'now it's time to save the Torahs.' "

Heschel used this metaphor to urge people to think more about God and Torah study and spirituality. Wolpe, on the other hand, is using it to explain that he has been, and still is, too busy saving the people.

The fire, the fire of the Holocaust, is still very real to him. He can't get that image out of his head, the one of his mother banging her head against the kitchen table, and wailing over the news of her forty-two relatives killed by the Nazis.

This made him want to fight the fire. He became a Golden Gloves boxer, got involved with the Zionist movement, loaded boats late at night with supplies for Palestine and wondered if he should go there himself. Instead he stayed in rabbinical school. So he was in the auditorium that day in 1945 when the chief rabbi of Paris made his first presentation in America about the true human toll of the Nazi death camps.

"He was talking in French and Yiddish," he recalls, "so it was hard to understand. I was seventeen or eighteen, sitting in the auditorium at the Seminary, and we thought we heard him say that a million Jews had been killed. We looked at one another in shock. 'You mean they burned bodies? You mean they gassed people?' All these horrors have now been assimilated and accepted, so it's hard to understand the shock the first time you realized what happened.

"I think there was a postponement of a religious response to it. Everybody just put off asking 'Where was God?' I think we were caught in the intense emotions of the moment. We didn't have *time* for spirituality. We were building synagogues, building community. The reason people can now talk about spirituality is that they don't have the task of saving the wives and children any longer. We didn't *ignore* Torah. We had a *job to do*."

He doesn't say "dammit," but it's implied.

✿   ✿   ✿

While Wolpe acknowledges that Heschel was "not my cup of wine," he explains that he was deeply influenced by Mordecai Kaplan, the Seminary's other major theological voice. He still treasures the many letters he received from Kaplan during his early years on the pulpit.

Although Kaplan is now best known as the father of Reconstructionism, Judaism's most recent movement, he spent most of his illustrious career, and developed most of his formative ideas, at the Seminary, where he taught every single rabbinical school student for more than fifty years. What he spent most of his life trying to "reconstruct" was Conservative Judaism.

Born in Russia and educated in New York, Kaplan was ordained at the Seminary in 1902, worked for years at a large Modern Orthodox shul in New York and then returned to the Seminary to teach in 1909. There he created a new theology that saw modern Judaism as a *civilization* rather than a religion, its cornerstones of family, community and "peoplehood" perhaps even more important than belief. His ideas on community spawned the move to build a network of Jewish community centers across the country (so Jews from different synagogues would have a central meeting place for social, athletic and educational activities) and the creation of the University of Judaism. Kaplan also championed the notion that God should be viewed less as an independent supernatural being than as a "transnatural" power, a process, a force within the natural world. In his popular history, *Conservative Judaism: A New Century,* Rabbi Neil Gillman paraphrases Kaplan's view as "it is not God who reveals the Torah but, rather, the Torah that reveals the presence of God . . . the authority for what we do and believe as Jews lies not in the explicit will of a supernatural God but, rather, in the community that remains an instrument through which God reveals." Kaplan rejected the idea of Jews as "the chosen people," and sought to eliminate prayers for the resurrection of the dead, the coming of the Messiah, even prayers for rain. His "Program for the Reconstruction of Judaism" was also completely egalitarian, and to prove his point, in 1922, his daughter Judith

became the first Jewish woman to ever have a bat mitzvah, at the synagogue he founded, the Society for the Advancement of Judaism, on
Manhattan's Upper West Side. When Kaplan published, in 1945, a
prayer book that wed his theology to traditional liturgy, he was publicly
excommunicated by a group of Orthodox rabbis, who also burned his
prayer book. While some traditional members of the Seminary faculty
publicly condemned the prayer book, Chancellor Louis Finkelstein did
not allow the ideological battle to affect Kaplan's status there.

Kaplan's impact on rabbinical students was to encourage, even demand, that they develop their own personal belief system before they
could preach to congregants. He also stayed in touch with them during
their first years out of rabbinical school. He was particularly helpful to
Gerald Wolpe during the fifties, when the young rabbi was preaching in
the South and found himself struggling with just how much bullying he
should do from his pulpit when it came to civil rights issues.

Wolpe recalls that his first inclination was to "be a crusader and to
say all the things I felt were proper. But they would abhor people who
came down from the North, dropped a verbal bomb and then took the
train back to New York, leaving the community to deal with the debris
scattered all over the place. I wrote to Dr. Kaplan because he had been
my professor of *Midrash* [the expansive commentary literature about
Torah and Talmud], and we had developed a relationship when I was
being considered for an assistant's position in his synagogue. He would
write to me about the dictatorship of the pulpit. 'You're speaking in the
name of the Torah,' he wrote, 'not in the name of Gerald Wolpe. You can
use the text as a pretext, and if you are cautious, you'll avoid the most
egregious abuses.'

"So, when I was asked what do 'you Jews' think about segregation, I
would say I don't know *all* Jews, but I can tell you what Judaism says
about segregation. Speaking in the name of Judaism, I had a shot at being authentic. And then I could use the text to illustrate. In the Bible
Belt, which that area was, that approach received a sympathetic hearing.
Even though many people were segregationists, they were willing to

discuss text and argue on the basis of being individuals of faith. I never forgot that lesson."

Kaplan fell out of vogue in the fifties—many of his theological innovations long since absorbed into mainstream Conservative or Reform practice—and was supplanted by his charismatic colleague Heschel. But he continued to teach at the Seminary until 1963, when, at age eighty-two, he retired to spend his time turning the ideas of Reconstructionism into a separate movement. "He was persuaded by his son-in-law," Wolpe recalls, "that the only way his philosophy was going to continue was to be a separate movement—even though he had resisted that his entire life."

The Reconstructionist Rabbinical College opened in Philadelphia's northern suburbs in the fall of 1968. Four years later, Heschel died at the age of sixty-five. Kaplan moved to Israel, lived to the age of 102 and died in New York in 1983.

But their disagreement over which is more important, the Jewish person or the Jewish people, is carried on in the endless debate between rabbis and movements, and in the impassioned phone conversations and e-mails of the rabbis Wolpe.

6

THE HIGH HOLIDAY
SEATING CHART

B ARBARA SCHWARTZ LEANS AS FAR BACK as she can in her tiny office cubicle and looks at the massive High Holiday seating chart. She has been studying this life-size crossword puzzle for five months: she must take a rock concert–sized crowd, more than three thousand people, and seat them as delicately and politically as the guests at a small wedding reception in a fractured family. If closeness to God is the prime consideration for successful High Holiday prayer, then Barbara Schwartz is, in many ways, more important than the rabbi. She decides not only who sits closest to God, but who gets the aisle.

There are some decisions she isn't free to make. At Har Zion, congregants still pay higher prices for better seats. Where you want to sit determines the cost of your annual dues. The least expensive package this year runs $1,095 for a family membership, which comes with two reserved High Holiday seats in the back section. New members, or current members who want to buy extra seats, must also agree to an extra "Development Fund Pledge," payable over a number of years. The pledge for the least expensive seats is $800 for a family, payable over three years.

The middle section of seats corresponds to annual dues of $1,220 per family, and a development pledge of $1,500, payable over five years. All two thousand of these back and middle seats are added for the High Holidays only. The front section for the High Holidays is the eight hundred seats of the main sanctuary that are available for free every Shabbat. For these holy days, however, they are reserved for the largest givers, those who pay annual dues of $1,645 for a family, with a development fund pledge of $2,500, payable over five years.

Wolpe has already reserved a pair of tickets for Diane and me. We're in the middle section near the back, Barbara says. I've received a lot of free stuff during my twenty years as a journalist, especially when I was a music critic, but I never dreamed of being comped High Holiday seats.

Why are the seating arrangements at Har Zion tied to the annual dues? Simple. The majority of Jews attend synagogue only on the High Holidays, and apparently the only way to make sure they pay their dues is to print on the bottom of the seat request form, in bold letters, "Tickets can only be sent if all prior and current obligations have been paid in full." This rule raises the stakes on Barbara Schwartz's task, because while some congregants renew their memberships automatically, others ruminate every year over whether they still want to belong to Har Zion, or to any synagogue. Some change their minds about affiliating with the temple, or participating in the Jewish religion, based solely on whether they can get the seats they want.

The High Holiday ticket process is a leading indicator in the annual report of any synagogue's financial health. How many new members are joining? How many current members are resigning? Are those leaving older and relocating to Florida? Or are they active younger members with kids who left in a huff?

In the ebb and flow of these currents, Har Zion usually has no problem filling all its seats. For years there has been a long waiting list of people who ultimately will not get the chance to sit in the main sanctuary at all to hear Rabbi Wolpe's best sermons of the year. Unless there's a last-minute cancellation, people on the waiting list have to pray in the smaller chapel and hear the assistant rabbi's sermon, or find another synagogue.

I watch in fascination as Barbara works the phone, the computer, her pencil-and-paper seating chart: she's like an air traffic controller for the future of the Jewish people. During a brief lull in the action, I ask her how the demand for tickets is this year.

She lowers her voice, so Rabbi Wolpe, who is in the next room rummaging through the morning mail, won't hear her. "We don't have a waiting list the way we used to," she says. "It could be because the rabbis are changing. Don't get me wrong, every seat is filled. But we don't have a waiting list. I think a lot of young people are waiting for the new rabbi. We got thirty-eight new memberships this year, but we've had some resignations. We have 1,430 families. More or less, we always have around 1,450."

While listening to her describe the holiday seating arrangements, I have a hard time imagining where all these seats actually fit. Barbara suggests I go take a look at the main sanctuary. I haven't been in there recently, because the space generally isn't used much in the summer. The smaller Dogole Chapel, which seats just under two hundred, is sufficient for the regulars who continue attending services even after the bar mitzvah high season ends in June and many Philadelphians have begun spending weekends at their summer homes at the Jersey shore.

I wander down the carpeted hall. As I get closer to the sanctuary area, I hear the sounds of construction—hammering, clanging metal, workmen yelling. When I open the door, I'm not exactly sure what I am seeing. The main sanctuary has become the size of a football field. My view from the fifty-yard line is awesome but disorienting. I'm having a hard time figuring out exactly where all this extra space came from. Then I realize: several walls have disappeared. The back wall of the main sanctuary, with the scratchy beige fabric people lean against during services while waiting for congregants to finish a "standing prayer," is gone. The wide walkway between the sanctuary and the Fishman-Tobin auditorium, where all the social events are held, has also vanished, along with the auditorium's front wall. To my left, I can now see all the way to the Ark; to my right, the parquet auditorium floor extends all the way to the kitchen entrance on the far wall.

I talk to Jim Lynn, who seems too young to have been the synagogue's building superintendent for eleven years. He is the construction foreman on this massive project. He explains that the synagogue owns its own set of risers, as well as rows and rows of temporary seats, which are kept in storage all year. Ten days before the High Holidays, workmen begin the arduous task of putting together the risers, a massive steel and plywood erector set, turning the normally intimate sanctuary into a medium-sized arena. It has a larger seating capacity than many of the city's theatrical venues and better sight lines.

It does not, however, have comparable acoustics or ventilation. Every year, the rabbis and cantor hope the synagogue will finally get around to buying a new public-address system, so even their quietest prayers from the bimah can be heard in the cheap seats. And the air-conditioning system, while decent, must be constantly monitored before the holidays begin. Representatives from the company that built the system come out before Rosh Hashanah to double-check everything. The dates of the High Holidays vary according to each year's Jewish calendar. If the holidays come later in the fall—this year they begin on September 21, which is fairly late—or the weather has become unseasonably cool, then the temperature isn't a big problem. But if it's still hot out when the High Holidays arrive, the air-conditioning has to be set at what building personnel call "supercold," or the congregants will quickly become incensed. Younger ones will complain angrily to the synagogue staff, older ones might even pass out. If problems arise, a guard with a walkie-talkie will call to the maintenance staff, which waits in the kitchen during High Holiday services like roadies, ready to run out, take care of any problem and run back.

✿   ✿   ✿

I go back down to the office area to look for the rabbi. He isn't there, so I watch the growing frenzy of holiday preparations. A well-dressed woman walks in with a baby balanced on her hip.

"I need to join," she says. "Can I get two seats on an aisle?" With only four days before Rosh Hashanah, the request goes beyond chutzpah. Barbara Schwartz doesn't even blink. It is the air of absolute entitlement—"after all, we are Har Zion"—that makes the place what it is. And, amazingly, when Barbara checks the computer, a pair of tickets on the aisle is available. Someone with good seats just quit.

Into the office walks Howard Griffel, the synagogue's executive director for the past ten years. The least flamboyant personality in the building, Griffel would make a better cop than a clergyman. But he's the one who actually has to make the place run day-to-day, overseeing the $4 million budget and a staff that, including all the teachers, is the equivalent of more than one hundred employees.

Griffel sees I'm interested in the computers, and, like any detail man, he loves to expound upon his systems. He explains that the computers don't only monitor High Holiday seat assignments. They also generate a list of physicians and their seat assignments, in case of emergencies. The High Holiday aliyahs and the pulpit honors are also computerized, going back five years. This allows the leadership to keep track not only of who has been honored, but who hasn't. Each year, they choose a few members who have never been on the bimah before and invite them up for the High Holidays. Some people decline the honor, because they are afraid of doing something foolish in front of three thousand fellow Jews on one of the most serious days of the year. Others revel in hitting the Jewish lottery. One woman was randomly chosen to hold the Torah on Kol Nidre night. "It was so meaningful to her," he says, "that she bought a plaque in the lobby."

One of the synagogue's biggest operational challenges, Griffel explains, is catering. Har Zion is one of the largest kosher catering halls in Philadelphia. The congregation has contracts with three outside caterers, whose five-year deals to use the kitchen were recently renegotiated. There used to be four caterers, but one decided to drop out after the synagogue raised the rates it charges to use the facility; the synagogue takes between 15 percent and 20 percent of what the caterer charges the client for food. Some of the money is used to maintain the synagogue's massive kitchen, which has just been changed over from electric burners to gas. The synagogue also does some of its own catering and has an in-house cook.

As if on cue, an enormously round guy in his mid-twenties makes a big entrance, draped in a white apron large enough to be used as a table-cloth. Red-faced and a little short of breath, he gulps and says: "I'm scared."

His name is Steve. It says so right on his apron.

"Why are you scared?" Barbara asks, perfectly calm.

"Extended *kiddush* . . ." Steve sputters, "for *520 people*?" He's referring to the news he just received—the order is still in his quaking hand—about a huge in-house catering job scheduled immediately after the High Holidays. The Kiddush is simply a one-line blessing over wine, although there is a longer version recited at home before Shabbat and holiday meals, and in the synagogue at the conclusion of Shabbat and holiday services to sanctify those days. In the parlance of the synagogue, however, "kiddush" usually refers to the food served *after* the prayer in the auditorium: anything from a few cookies, some punch and harshly decaffeinated coffee to an exquisite kosher buffet meal. Har Zion never cuts corners on food. The synagogue's motto, I've heard people joke, is, "If you feed them, they will come."

Occasionally the food at events is paid for by the synagogue itself. But, usually, the food is "sponsored," or even co-sponsored, by families celebrating a bar or bat mitzvah, a wedding, a birth, a big anniversary, a successful operation. At Har Zion this is called an "extended kiddush." If you're hosting a bar mitzvah and you pay to extend the kiddush, you have to cover the cost of your invited guests, plus whoever from the community happens to attend. Prices start at seven hundred dollars for a basic "cold kiddush" for up to 150 guests. The full hot kiddush—with three different noodle or potato kugels and real nova on the bagels, not just lox spread—could run as high as $4,350 for those 520 people. Some synagogues encourage private lunch parties for bar mitzvah guests after the regular kiddush has ended. But at Har Zion, the extended kiddush—with the entire congregation invited—is preferred. Once the Shabbat crowd has been fed, the family is welcome to bring their guests back for an invitation-only kosher dinner party done by any of the synagogue's approved caterers; those prices start in a whole other tax bracket. But some families choose to have their lunch or dinner affairs in more secular, fancier locations, like The Four Seasons Hotel downtown. That's where the more extreme bar mitzvah celebrations take place, the ones with the elaborate party bands that bring their own microphoned dance-instructor/cheerleaders to keep things lively on the dance floor.

Steve, still scared, claims he's never done an extended kiddush *this* big.

"Oh, we do them that big all the time," Howard counters.

Suddenly, Joshua Perlmuter comes running into the office. He's holding the same notice that has Steve so upset, and he doesn't look any happier. An older man with wire-rim glasses and an accent one would assume is Eastern European but in reality comes from Brazil, Joshua is the synagogue's ritual director, the shammash. He teaches kids their bar mitzvahs, tends to all the ritual needs of the synagogue—someone has to roll the Torah scrolls in the main sanctuary to the right place for the upcoming week's readings. He is a quietly fascinating guy, who taught Hebrew school in Rio for thirteen years, moved to Israel with his wife, and then, after working in the automotive industry, won the grand prize in the Israeli lottery—the equivalent of five years' salary—and decided to move to America and be a sexton. His role as a spiritual maintenance man is reinforced by the fact that he and his wife live in an apartment in the synagogue's basement.

"You do know we'll have the sukkah up then," he says.

Barbara brings her hands to her face. "Oh my God!" she exclaims. "The sukkah!"

"I'm scared," Steve says again. And then he walks out.

"Oh, by the way," Barbara says, chuckling, to Howard. "Pam Freydman* resigned. She said she didn't like the letter she got from us." The letter had simply asked her to pay her membership fees: for this year and what she still owes from the previous year. Obviously, the rule about not sending out tickets until the money arrives is sometimes bent. "And she has good seats, too. First row, section three."

"Let's call her up and get those tickets back," he says.

Rabbi Wolpe comes barreling into the office. He wants to talk about his son's latest media escapade. Among David Wolpe's many high-profile congregants at Sinai Temple is a prominent Beverly Hills oncologist named Dr. Bernard Lewinsky. His daughter is, of course, Monica Lewinsky, who has been in the news because of rumors, just recently substantiated, that she had a sexual relationship with President Clinton. Over the past weekend, David gave a sermon damning Clinton for his immorality. This did not surprise his father, because David seems to him extremely conservative. "He's to the right of Caligula," Wolpe jokes.

But then something surprising did happen. An Associated Press reporter in Los Angeles heard about the sermon, and wanted to report that Monica Lewinsky's rabbi—which David is, technically—had castigated the president from the pulpit. When contacted, David repeated the remarks he had made, and the story ran all over the world. David was mentioned on the evening news by Tom Brokaw, who even pronounced the name correctly, although on the late news one anchor called him "Rabbi Wolp."

But then David was asked to do other media: go on CNN, or the *Today* show, as Monica's rabbi. He was thinking about doing it, but Rabbi Wolpe says he talked him out of it. "I told him to shut it down immediately and he did," he tells us. Everyone nods that this was the right thing to do.

His story told, Wolpe announces that he and Elaine will be going to the Catskills next weekend, to stay at the Concord. If he's planning

to leave, I assume he's almost finished writing his Rosh Hashanah sermons. They've been plaguing him for months. He always knows it's time
to start thinking about High Holiday sermons when the Philadelphia
Eagles begin their preseason games. He has been through a lot of painful
August Sundays, keeping one eye on the depressing score and the other
on the notes he's struggling with for the year's two big sermons. One is
delivered the first morning of Rosh Hashanah, the Jewish New Year. The
other is on *erev* Yom Kippur. (All Jewish holidays technically start at sun-
down on the erev, or "eve," of the actual full day.) It is delivered after the
recitation of Kol Nidre, the cantor's mournful prayer, which sets the tone
for the Day of Atonement. Wolpe also gives sermons on the second
morning of Rosh Hashanah, and during the day on Yom Kippur. But
they aren't quite as important. The sermons that matter, the ones that fill
the seats and, this year, will have to cement his legacy, are on the first
day of Rosh Hashanah and erev Yom Kippur.

Usually, he has ample time to work on the second sermon, because
Yom Kippur comes ten days after Rosh Hashanah. But this time the
writing has been especially difficult. And not only because it is to be his
last High Holiday on the pulpit ever. He also had some bad luck. He
wrote what he felt was a pretty well-crafted Rosh Hashanah sermon
summing up his career in the rabbinate. But then David convinced him
he shouldn't deliver it. At least, not on Rosh Hashanah.

David pointed out that his father always has used the first High Holiday for more of a state-of-the-union address about the synagogue,
American Jewry, Israel. The sermon where you bawl everyone out for
not being a good Jew. Traditionally, he has delivered his more personal
sermons on Yom Kippur, to set the tone for the most introspective holy
day.

"Well that's fine," he told his son, "but now what do I do on the first
day of Rosh Hashanah? It's pretty late not to have your sermon." So he
had been up late working on a new Rosh Hashanah address and watching preseason football. He must be satisfied with the sermons—if not the
play of the Eagles—to be making plans to go away and relax.

This will probably be the Wolpes' last trip ever to the Concord, the historic resort that was once so much a part of American Jewish culture. The last of the original Borscht Belt hotels in the Catskills, it will close for good after this year's Jewish holiday season. Only its golf course will survive, although there are hopes that it might one day get a gaming license and reopen as an assimilated New York State tourist site.

"I'm really sick of the place," he admits. "We've been going there for thirty years." He concedes, however, that once the Concord is gone, he'll probably miss it.

While he would never admit it to his office staff, he feels much the same way about being on the pulpit.

7

RABBI AND ELAINE

WALKING INTO THE SYNAGOGUE one morning, I spot her down the hall. Omigod, Elaine. The rabbi's wife. While I haven't seen her since my youth, I've been hearing about her health for years, since the spring of 1986. I remember the time well because Elaine Wolpe had her stroke only weeks before my Nana had hers. My Nana awoke from her coma and completely regained her ability to speak, think and remember, but never stood up again: she spent the next eleven years in bed at the Jewish Home of Greater Harrisburg, which had been one of the many causes she and Elaine Wolpe and others had raised money for in the sixties. Yet even my Nana would say it sometimes, "Omigod, Elaine," because the Wolpes were still so mythologized in Harrisburg, because Elaine was so much younger, only fifty-four when the aneurysm burst in her brain, and because Elaine, the consummate gabber and Jewish mother, could no longer talk.

As I walk closer, I think about all the images Rabbi Wolpe has painted in words for me about her illness. There are certain images he repeats in public: Elaine on the floor of the bathroom after falling in the shower, Elaine lying on what doctors assured them was her deathbed, Elaine coming out of her coma and, for months, being able to speak only

78

two words, the nonsense utterance "kisscove," and the word "prison." These are the images from what has become his stock speech at care-giving conferences, a tearjerker entitled "Mrs. Job." And then there are the images he says he hasn't shared with everyone: Elaine begging him to help her commit suicide, Elaine weeping angrily about the friends who abandoned her, the rabbi going to Elaine's gynecologist to ask how he would take care of her "female needs."

So, Omigod, Elaine, I think, as I approach her and we embrace. She looks pretty damn good for someone people have described to me by shaking their heads and saying "not good." She carries her paralyzed right arm awkwardly, and her stance is a little wobbly. But she presses her hand to my cheek, gives me a kiss and, fumbling for words, bursts out with "Unbelievable!" And I understand in that one word exactly what she is trying to communicate. Unbelievable that she's here, unbe-lievable that I'm here, unbelievable that I grew up, unbelievable that my father is gone and Elaine Wolpe survived.

". . . Mother . . ." she says, her face turning serious, ". . . how? . . ." And I know she is asking about my mom, and how she is holding up in widowhood. I tell her my mother is doing pretty well, all things considered.

". . . Wife . . ." she says, nodding, ". . . dinner . . ." And I know she is asking when my wife and I would like to come to their home for dinner. Soon.

I tell her how wonderful it is to see her, that I want to sit down and interview her sometime.

"Yes, yes . . ." she says, ". . . but *dinner* . . ." She looks at me, commu-nicating in what her son David has described as "the language of plead-ing eyes." And then a herd of Junior Congregation kids come rumbling by, screaming and squealing. Kids, the universal antidote. In a syna-gogue, kids bring relief, hope. They can be anybody's kids; as long as they are in the synagogue, there's hope.

She puts her hand to my face again and shakes her head.

"Unbelievable," she repeats.

✿   ✿   ✿

Rabbi and Elaine sit in the den of the two-story house provided for them by the synagogue. He refers to the house as "the parsonage." It's a term usually associated with the Christian clergy. But, as Wolpe often points out, when the American rabbinate was professionalized "we copied from the Christians"—which explains why rabbis call their jobs "pulpits," a term many Jews associate with Christianity. The Wolpes have lived in the house for nearly twenty-five years, but it does not belong to them. It belongs to Har Zion.

The couple sits in separate easy chairs, leaving the couch for me. I have come to interview Elaine. She hasn't done many interviews since her stroke and I'm not sure she really wants to do this one. Not because she doesn't want to talk to me, but because it is so hard. She suffers from profound aphasia, a neurological disorder that prevents its victims from actually saying what their brains are thinking. To an outsider, her impairment looks like a sort of memory loss, as though she just can't remember what she was going to say. But it is more complex than that. Words, sentences, entire thoughts, literally remain on the tip of her tongue. Forever.

Couples are often described as "finishing each other's sentences." Rabbi and Elaine have taken this form of co-communication to a new level. At some point in any extended conversation, not only does he become her voice but, to some extent, he must read her mind. Sometimes she can utter only one word of a complex thought or memory she is trying to communicate. He must figure out the rest, and quickly, because, like most aphasics, she is prone to giving up in utter frustration. For that reason it is impossible for him to listen to her casually, the way husbands sometimes do with their wives; "uh-huh, uh-huh, you're *kidding,* uh-huh." He must concentrate on her words and make eye contact whenever possible. They have to be astonishingly patient with each other.

Yet her personality remains intact in there. As her son Paul once told me, chuckling, "My mother's entire life is dedicated to the proposition that her opinions are right and anyone who differs with her is at best wrong and at worst trying to undermine the foundations of western civilization. The myth of the family is that because of the stroke she can't control certain things. I think she was pretty much already at the stereotypical extreme end of 'Jewish mother' before this happened."

I ask Elaine a simple question: "Where were you born and raised?" The words come out easily at first, "Cambridge, Massachusetts, all my life, Cambridge." What did your family do? "Gee," she laughs, pausing, "scrap iron metal and, uh, um, uh . . ." She looks to her husband for help, he waits to see if she will find the words. ". . . market, um, uh . . ." She nods to him. "Do you want me to?" he asks. ". . . Yeah." So he explains that her father left the scrap metal business and began selling car radios as a manufacturer's rep. At the sound of "manufacturer's rep," Elaine says, "Ah, yeah" brightly, and then laughs. *That* was the term she was looking for. The laughter is a major part of her communication. When someone is saying what she would have said, she laughs hard and says, "Yeah," like the amen response in a gospel church.

When Elaine speaks words comfortably, her voice is recognizable as her own, one that is well remembered in any congregation where she was *rebbitzin,* the rabbi's wife, because she always speaks her mind. Funny, passionate, judgmental and completely protective of her husband and family, she was a Machiavellian mom—even though, in their male household, she was considered the emotional one, swimming upstream against a current of what they all saw as pure logic.

She grew up active in a Conservative synagogue where her mother— a very modern, educated woman—was the president of everything. Elaine graduated from teachers college and taught third grade, but her heart was in her Jewish commitments, and she always suspected she'd end up married to a rabbi and working as a rebbitzin, which, in those days, was almost a full-time job. These days, rabbis are usually part of a two-career couple, and the spouse does his or her best to keep a friendly distance from the vortex of synagogue life. But in the 1950s, when a synagogue hired a rabbi, they expected to get a couple, a team.

The Wolpes met at an adult Zionist summer camp, where he was a counselor and she a camper. Later, she invited him to speak at her Junior Hadassah group. But they were just friends: in fact, he was engaged to someone else, and Elaine helped him pick out a ring for her. But he later broke off that engagement, and he and Elaine fell in love at a resort outside of Boston, Nantasket Beach, where her family had a summer home and he got a summer job as a rabbi.

They married in 1953, and after Wolpe was ordained they moved to North Carolina, for his first job. At that time, recent Seminary graduates were expected to take a military chaplaincy or a small congregation. Wolpe, who was beyond draft age, chose to serve in the navy, and was assigned to Camp Lejeune, home of the Second Marine Division. They were there during the height of the Korean War and the last hurrah of legendary marine General Chesty Puller. Watching young Americans being trained to kill was a huge culture shock. So was the fraternity of military wives who, in Elaine's view, spent much of the day drinking.

"The wives . . . had *tea* . . . ten o'clock," she says. "Brunch . . . no food . . . oh my *God*!"

Wolpe's "synagogue" shared a red brick building with the commissary. And there was a surprisingly large Jewish population on the base, although many kept their religion to themselves for fear of military anti-Semitism. Wolpe officiated at the first bar mitzvah ever at Camp Lejeune and had an active congregation. There were even four Israeli women who had married non-Jewish marines and always came to borrow the Hebrew magazines he got from the Jewish Welfare Board. At the same time, life on the base afforded the couple their first experience being neighbors to non-Jews. "We were newlyweds in a different society than we ever knew," he says. "Your next door neighbor is a marine who wants to know what it means to be Jewish."

After two years at Camp Lejeune they began to explore the next step in the rabbi's career; by that time, Elaine was also pregnant. One of the other Jewish couples at the base recommended Rabbi Wolpe to their parents' synagogue in Charleston, South Carolina. That led to his first pulpit. Elaine relished the job of rebbitzin. She was active in all the women's groups, especially Sisterhood, the synagogue-based group that tends to involve younger mothers and supports Hebrew school and other local family causes. She was also involved with Hadassah, the women's Zionist organization that raises money for Israeli causes, and tends to skew a little older, so it is often where women go when they outgrow Sisterhood.

Elaine also worked hard as a sounding board for her husband, whose strong voice and liberal politics needed adjustment and modulation to survive in the South. Wolpe had a tendency to speak too loudly when he got excited: it was Elaine sitting in the audience with her finger to her lips that helped train his vocal instrument. And she picked up on words he used in sermons that had unintended double meanings. He used the word *cancer* promiscuously, "the cancer of intermarriage, the cancer of terrorism," until she pointed out how offensive that might be to people who actually have cancer.

They enjoyed the congregation, although it also provided them with a painful learning experience about synagogue politics.

As Wolpe explains it, "There was a teacher there who was very aggressive . . ."

Elaine interrupts, *"Bitch!"* When so few words are available to you, why mince them?

The teacher tried to undercut Wolpe in a way he recalls as "diabolical." The incident led the synagogue to hold a *din Torah,* a rabbinic tribunal. The matter was settled in Wolpe's favor, but the couple recalls it as the worst experience they ever had in synagogue life.

By the time they moved on to Beth El Temple in Harrisburg, they had two sons and another on the way. Elaine quickly established herself as the queen bee of the synagogue, taking leadership roles in all the organizations and acting as the fashion plate for the congregation. She was smart, tough, accomplished and, when it came to clothes, a tastemaker.

". . . I love dressing, I have good taste," she says, ". . . have to dress properly; have to kiss *everybody* and notice*, oh my God*! Unbelievable." They both shake their heads about the way rebbitzin dress today. "The older people in synagogues are not happy about the way the new rabbis' wives dress," he says. "I've seen a lot of rabbis' wives at conventions. They just don't care. If Elaine walked into a supermarket with jeans, somebody would say, 'That's not right.' "

They were in Harrisburg for eleven years; their two younger sons were born there. They loved it for the same reasons I loved growing up there: it was a Jewish community with enough New York transplants to be somewhat progressive in its thinking, but still provincial enough to maintain a fifties lifestyle well into the late sixties. Divorce, drugs—all that came late to the Harrisburg Jewish community, which was determined to squeeze one more generation out of postwar America. Because it was a state capital and the epicenter of the highways that make up many companies' mid-Atlantic sales routes—and, because, frankly, it had a reputation as charmingly insulated—Harrisburg was a nearly perfect mid-size Jewish community. It was a great place to live, and an ideal stepping-stone for a rabbi with ambitions. The community became known for having the largest per-capita giving to Jewish causes in the country. It was buoyed by a booming local economy and several key Jewish family businesses whose success led to major philanthropy: especially the regional supermarket chain Giant Food Stores, owned by the Javitch family, and the national drugstore chain Rite Aid, which was started by a Scranton boy, Alex Grass, who married into one of Jewish Harrisburg's wealthiest families, the Lehrmans, and made them (and everyone else) even wealthier when the company went public.

Within the congregation, Elaine was more political in some ways than her husband. While Rabbi Wolpe was beloved as a public speaker and teacher, and attracted many young members with his fiery sermons and Sunday morning adult education classes, he was not considered a brilliant bedside rabbi. No rabbi can ever do enough hospital and home visits—there is endless demand and only so much supply—but Wolpe tended toward an air of imperiousness that was more useful on the pulpit than in a hospital room. There were times, he can now admit, when he just didn't feel like making yet another hospital visit, hearing another sad story, so he skipped them. It was Elaine's job to humanize him and his pulpit, help make him life-size.

By the late sixties, Wolpe grew restless and was quietly looking at other pulpits. One important consideration was a city where the couple's eldest son, Steve, could get a good science education in high school. Steve was a student at Harrisburg's Jewish day school, which was housed on the second floor of the Jewish Community Center. Like many aspects of the JCC, the school was open to children of all Jewish denominations but its religious bent was determined primarily by the Orthodox (so that the Orthodox families, who were most likely to send their kids to an all-Jewish school, wouldn't be offended by any liberal practices). Steve found his interest in science at odds with the very traditional teachers in the school; it was producing a negative response to religion that disturbed his parents. Wolpe turned down a pulpit in Dallas because the Jewish day schools were no better than Harrisburg's and it was too far from their families in Boston. Then he turned down a pulpit in Boston because it was, well, maybe a little too *close* to family. Philadelphia was perfect geographically. And there was a cardiovascular surgeon there at Hahnemann Hospital—Dr. Victor Satinsky, for whom the "Satinsky clamp" is named—who had developed a reputation as a "Renaissance doctor" by running a very special program for precocious young scientists.

In the winter of 1969, someone from Har Zion called Beth El in Harrisburg asking if it would be all right for a small group to attend Shabbat services and listen to the rabbi. Not long after, they offered Wolpe their pulpit.

Once they were at Har Zion, Elaine again took on a prominent role in the synagogue—especially because they arrived just as the women's movement was forcing Conservative Judaism to rethink its ideas on the role of female congregants. The Conservative movement had officially allowed congregations to become "Torah egalitarian"—meaning women could come to the bimah and read from the Torah—as early as 1955. But, by the early seventies, when the movement was finally going to start counting women as part of the minyan, Har Zion had still not fully allowed women bimah privileges. Just because the movement says a practice is acceptable doesn't mean all synagogues do it: when it comes to liberalization, the rabbi and the synagogue's ritual committee make their own decisions. And Har Zion was Conservative with a capital *C*, especially when it was still located in Wynnefield and serviced a community with many borderline-Orthodox Jews. When Wolpe arrived in 1969, women were not allowed to read the Torah or the Haftarah; they could be bat mitzvahed, but only on Friday night, not Saturday morning.

Elaine lobbied hard for her husband to force Har Zion to become completely egalitarian. Wolpe would have done it immediately, but he knew that would be impolitic, and the synagogue's longtime cantor, Isaac Wall, was dead-set against it. It took nearly three years of public debates and baby steps, beginning with the daughter of one of Har Zion's founders being allowed to open the Ark on the High Holidays. And in early 1972, Elaine Wolpe became the first woman ever given a Torah honor at Har Zion Temple. Cantor Wall, however, could not bring himself to be the one to call her to the Torah: the sexton, Mr. Schwartz, did it, and he retained that special responsibility for some time until the cantor finally acquiesced.

By the late seventies, Elaine had already been president of everything, and three of her four boys were no longer living at home. She began working full-time outside the house—and away from the synagogue. She was the director of continuing education at the University of Pennsylvania Dental School for seven years, then opened a short-lived jewelry store. She ran the administrative side of a congregant's unsuccessful campaign for the U.S. Senate.

The rabbi too was developing more interests outside of the synagogue, and was toying with the idea of going into academia. Over the years, he had developed an expertise in what came to be called bioethics: early in his rabbinate in Harrisburg, he had been asked to lecture to medical students and hospital technicians on how to conceptualize the tough choices that came with modern medicine. When he arrived in Philadelphia, he began giving similar lectures at the Hahnemann

University Medical School. And, in the late seventies, he began pursuing a doctorate in philosophy at the University of Pennsylvania.

He finished the courses and began planning for his thesis. The subject was how medical students feel about death. Through his years of teaching, he had been polling medical students about their attitudes toward death and how medical training affected their feelings. He was especially fascinated by the students who were "frightened silly of death," and wanted to become doctors thinking they could conquer their fear, or maybe even death itself.

Then Elaine got a job with the Bezallel School of the Arts in Israel, as director of its fund-raising efforts in the mid-Atlantic region. When Bezallel started talking to her about a promotion to a more lucrative position as national director, the Wolpes started making plans to dramatically change their lives. Now that most of the kids were finished with graduate school, if Elaine's job worked out Rabbi Wolpe could afford to quit the pulpit at Har Zion at the end of his contract. He could get an academic position, teach and lecture on bioethics full-time.

Instead, they got the bioethics lesson of a lifetime.

The last words she said to him were "good husband." She was responding to the ER doctor who wanted to see if she could still identify the rabbi. Soon after, she lapsed into a coma, and Wolpe was told to call the children. She wasn't likely to live.

After the family gathered for the death watch, the neurosurgeon announced that Elaine would require emergency surgery or she would die. Their eldest, Steve, by then a medical researcher, insisted that they wait until he could read up on the procedure. He proceeded to convince his father to have the doctor delay the surgery. Not operating turned out to be the right choice, and the coma slowly lifted as the brain swelling went down. Elaine lay in bed with a vacant stare for weeks. Then one Friday, Paul's wife, Val, brought Shabbat candles into the hospital room. Val was her only daughter-in-law at the time, so they were the only women in the Wolpe family, the only ones allowed to say the blessing over the candles. Val encouraged Elaine to say the prayer with her.

"*Baruch atah Adonai,*" Val began, praised be God who rules the universe, instilling in us the holiness of *mitzvot,* good deeds, by commanding us to kindle the light of Shabbat, "*l'hadlik ner shel Shabbat.*" Elaine didn't join in. But she did turn to Val and, for the first time, she smiled. And suddenly they realized she was still alive in there.

Elaine doesn't remember any of that. I ask what the first thing is she recalls.

"Wheelchair . . ." she replies, "saw that I was strapped in a wheelchair . . . and outside . . . was a ramp, and *nothing* . . . not in pain, absolutely not . . . the whole right side of body was paralyzed . . . really vague, was a *year.*" For the first time, she doesn't say "omigod." Nothing about the memory is "unbelievable."

She eventually did have neurosurgery to repair some of the damage from the burst aneurysm. And then came the months and years of slow recovery. She was sent first to a rehab facility. Every morning Rabbi Wolpe would call to check in on her, and would hear her screaming in the background. He couldn't take it. After five days, he announced he was going to take her home and care for her himself. Good husband.

They told him it was impossible. He proved them wrong. He brought speech and physical therapists to the house, and their youngest, Danny, volunteered to leave college for a while to stay home and help.

About a month after Danny came back, Wolpe got a call from three past presidents of Har Zion. They asked if he had someone who could stay with Elaine for the day. When he said he did, he was instructed to be in front of his house at 6 A.M. with his golf clubs. A car pulled up and drove them to the airport, and they boarded a private plane to Williamsburg, Virginia, where they played golf all day. They flew back, had dinner at Bookbinders and left their rabbi with a small dose of pleasure amid all the turmoil.

None of the congregants ever really knew how bad it was for Elaine because the rabbi was cagey. "For a year and a half she was not in control of what she said or what she did," he explains. "When she laughed, it was gales of laughter. Every emotion was without restraint. When she cried, she cried incessantly. Remember how angry you would get?"

Elaine nods. He continues.

"As the aphasia became more apparent, there was tremendous frustration. To this day, there is tremendous frustration. There were periods when she was suicidal. 'You should have let me go!' she would tell me. It made me feel terribly sad. You mean I went through all this for *nothing*? When she eventually began to drive a car, I was very worried. I didn't know what she would do. She was in an atmosphere of constant confrontation. Everything was a battle for her, to be understood, to relate to people. And she had to deal with the fact that some of her closest friends abandoned her."

But while some did abandon her, others took their places. In every way, the Har Zion community took care of Rabbi and Elaine. There were times when Wolpe felt he should leave his pulpit, which was being handled day-to-day by his assistant rabbi. There were times when Har Zion's leadership wondered if they should politely suggest that Wolpe leave the pulpit. But, ultimately, Rabbi and Elaine stayed and the congregation stuck with them. When Wolpe spoke about Elaine's illness the next Rosh Hashanah, it was one of the most powerful, painful sermons he ever gave. It set a new tone for his rabbinate—sadder but wiser, more compassionate but less available—and added a new dimension to the legacy of Har Zion.

By then it had been ten years since the synagogue moved to the suburbs, where houses were farther apart and nobody walked to shul, so geographical community was difficult to maintain. The struggle was to create a new kind of *emotional* community, of people who took strength from and gave strength to the synagogue, of people who "lived nearby" in their minds and in their hearts. A veteran rabbi stepping down off his high horse to share his pain—not his anger, his indignation or his disbelief, but his pain—was a powerful thing. Nobody who heard those sermons about Elaine's struggle ever forgot them. And nobody who was part of the synagogue's life when the congregation had to rally for its leader, treat the First Couple as just another family in need, was ever the same.

One longtime Har Zion observer explains it this way. "There are two Rabbi Wolpes," he says, "and he achieved his immortality not through his rabbinate before Elaine's illness, but in his profound work helping her to learn to speak and his way of bringing that to his congregation. He did it through the example of his living a righteous life more than through his preaching.

"Did you know him well before Elaine's illness? He could be a pompous ass. He had become perhaps too full of himself. He probably felt he had become righteous by passing God's test of taking his father from him. But he later found out: there was another test."

8

VERGANGENHEITSBEWÄLTIGUNG, PRONOUNCED FLAWLESSLY

A s I walk into Har Zion on the first day of Rosh Hashanah, services have already begun and Rabbi Wolpe is at his lectern talking about what a small town Judaism is. Today, he says, even Jews in isolated enclaves in Spain know what their fellow Jews are thinking in Russia and America.

Yet there is nothing about the High Holiday scene at Har Zion that brings to mind a *small* town. Some three thousand people are trying to sit quietly, doing whatever passes for whispering at their age, grimacing, albeit politely, when fellow congregants climb over them to their seats, tugging at ties and pantyhose, retrieving yarmulkahs that keep falling off, and riffling through their prayer books looking for the Torah reading, which can be found on page 168.

I can hear Rabbi Wolpe perfectly, but I can barely see him. If not for his elaborate white robes, he would be indistinguishable from the others on the bimah. What I can see clearly is the secular phenomenon Har Zionites refer to as "the fashion show." It's like a Chanel showroom, with the trendier women going either supershort with their skirts or full-on maxi. Under their tallises, the men wear Polo or Armani. Yet nobody seems terribly overdressed or ostentatious. It's more that they've been maximized.

I know almost nobody here. There is something unnerving about being a stranger amid so much familiarity: most of these people have known each other going back three generations. I feel like a guy crashing a family reunion of perfect strangers just because he came to hear the band.

Yet I see people I know *of*. Jerome Shestack, the current president of the American Bar Association, who is also a former president of Har Zion and a friend of the Wolpes. TV personality Nancy Glass. Renowned medical researcher Dr. Michael Zasloff, whose development of a new antibiotic from frog skin has made national news and spawned a hot new publicly traded company. Connie and Joe Smukler, known internationally for their work on behalf of Soviet Jews. And the Mezvinskys: Marjorie Margolis Mezvinsky, the former NBC-TV reporter who, as a U.S. Representative, cast the deciding vote in 1994 on the Clinton tax plan, and her husband, Ed, a former politician (it was his campaign Elaine Wolpe worked on) turned entrepreneur. Marjorie was targeted by Newt Gingrich and lost her seat for supporting Clinton, but gained a friendship with Bill and Hillary; she is currently planning her political comeback.

Amid the sea of people, I am acknowledged by the few I do know. Executive director Howard Griffel, who is posted by the main entrance—arms crossed, walkie-talkie hooked to his waistband—nods hello. I see the Two Lews, search committee chair Lou Fryman and Lew Grafman, who has recently been installed as synagogue president. Both greet me with a curious reserve, as if they're wondering why exactly I'm not at my *own* synagogue. Am I here as a journalist or a worshipper? It's a good question.

Thank God for Ralph Snyder, who always welcomes me with a firm handshake and one of those little "made you look" tricks like anybody's grandfather. He takes a poke at my tie, I look, he laughs. I say I can't believe I fall for it every time. Today, Ralph is also wistful. It is difficult to believe that this is the last time his close friend will also be his rabbi for High Holiday services.

No sooner do I take my seat in far-flung section II than we are asked to rise. The Ark is opened, slowly, dramatically, and two Torahs are taken from it. The cantor gets one and Lew Grafman gets the other because the rabbi will need his hands free for the obstacle course they are about to navigate. The choir is cued: four professional singers, sitting in the front row. And the processional begins, with the cantor leading the rabbi and the synagogue's leaders—officers, board members—down off the bimah.

Why do they take the Torahs out for a walk? Because everyone is equally entitled to honor the handwritten sacred scrolls by touching them. This is never done directly, but by reaching out with a prayer book or tallis, touching the Torah with it, and then kissing the place it made contact. In Judaism, belief in God is optional, something you may wrestle with your entire life. But respect for and fascination with the Torah, the first record of men and women's struggles with belief in God, is not optional. And the Torahs themselves are both holy and wholly accessible. There are endless rules about how to dress, undress, unroll and read them, but they are meant to be read and studied, not worshipped. A Torah is meant to be honored as a living presence, not an icon.

As an author, I'm especially fascinated by the Torah processional for what it represents: people paying homage to a book, which for five thousand years has been copied over by hand, clothed in velvet and jewels, crowned in silver and perpetually read and interpreted. From the most cosmic concept to a single letter, everything in the Torah is open to interpretation and debate. Very early in the morning minyan—often before most people get there, actually—one of the first prayers recited is actually not a prayer at all. It is the thirteen rules for literary interpretation of the Torah, starting with: "An inference may be drawn from a minor to a major premise or a major to a minor premise." There is also a special version of the Kaddish recited after studying Torah.

But the Torah processional has another purpose. It is Judaism's great "meet and greet," an opportunity for the rabbi and synagogue officers to press the flesh with hundreds of congregants as they go up and down the aisles. Wolpe himself kisses hundreds of women, and shakes hands with hundreds of men. He pats cheeks, shares knowing smiles, offers brief condolences. His ability to recall personal information about so many people, pulling out names and particulars effortlessly, one after another, is astounding. How is . . . *your sick spouse's name here*? I was so sorry to hear about *your late relative's name here*. Isn't that wonderful news about *your child or grandchild's name here*. Mazel tov on *your special event here*.

As the Torah processional continues—five minutes, ten minutes— the volume level increases. Many of these people haven't seen each other for months. Some have been down at the shore all summer and just got back. Others have not been here all year, because they live primarily in Florida now and come back only for the High Holidays, some just to hear Wolpe's sermons. People with great tans hug and backslap and swap wallet photos until the choir can no longer be heard above the din. When the rabbi returns to the bimah, he has a major shushing task on his hands. But he finally gets everyone quiet, and the Torah reading proceeds.

The special Torah portion for the first day of Rosh Hashanah is plucked from Genesis 21, in which Sarah bears a son after a lifetime of trying. The aliyahs and the Torah reading go smoothly, and then comes the Haftarah, the supplemental reading from the Prophets. But the reader for today's Haftarah is nowhere to be found. Eventually Wolpe gets up, and, grinning broadly, announces that his son Paul, today's reader, has finally appeared, "sparing you from one of my longest-ever improvisations on the theme of the Haftarah." He gets a big laugh.

Paul is late because he runs the children's service downstairs. He bounds up the steps to the bimah, and gives his dad a hug and kiss. Among the Wolpe kids, David gets much of the attention, but it is Paul who does most of the work. After Elaine's stroke, Paul and his wife, Val, moved back to Philadelphia from New Haven, where he was teaching at Yale, to be closer to his parents. Val, a self-employed career coach, had lost her own mother to an aortic aneurysm, and when Elaine was recovering, she and Paul wanted to be there. They have two daughters who were, until recently, Rabbi and Elaine's only grandchildren. Besides teaching sociology, psychiatry and bioethics at Penn, Paul writes op-ed pieces for various newspapers on bioethical dilemmas. But much of his family's free time is spent with Rabbi and Elaine.

When the sermon finally comes it shows signs of having been written at the last minute. It is, of course, provocatively delivered, gently stirring. But Wolpe can do *that* reading a menu aloud. His best salvos today are aimed at an easy target: country clubs. After announcing that his comments are offered with "the security of knowing it is too late to fire me," he is sardonic about the Bala Golf Club, where "they have given us the privilege of saving them from bankruptcy" by reversing their policy of barring Jews from membership. "We can only pray that soon we can do the same thing for the Merion Cricket Club . . . Who needs the Messiah? We are now really part of the Main Line. All glory be to Heaven!"

During my long drive back home, I can't help feeling a little disappointed. I skipped being with my own wife and family in shul to hear that sermon, and it was not Wolpe's best work. Yet it probably pleased the crowd. As I was leaving, a woman I know came up to me and said she couldn't imagine what the holidays would be like without a Wolpe sermon. She started rhapsodizing about the one he gave after President Kennedy was assassinated.

There was only one problem. Wolpe wasn't at Har Zion when Kennedy was assassinated.

And that, in a nutshell, is the joy and sorrow of being a great sermonizer. Yours is the voice that many people associate with the most important moments in their lives, yet they don't always really remember what you said. And when the sermons are written down, which few of Wolpe's actually are, they often don't read the way they sounded. He

writes for his own voice. His son David has learned the craft of quotabil-
ity: he writes books, and all his sermons are taped and made available by
the synagogue. But Wolpe suffers from the problem of all rabbis who
leave their best stuff on the pulpit: you had to be there.

Someone once told me that when Wolpe walks into a room he can al-
ter people's DNA. But if you aren't there, it is as if it never happened.

If the Rosh Hashanah sermon is only a "B," he will have to make it up
on Yom Kippur. After all, the Kol Nidre sermon is the one that really
matters, the one that is supposed to change lives.

Changing lives is the theme of the entire High Holiday season. Rosh
Hashanah is a celebration of the new year and its possibilities; it signals
the beginning of a period of taking emotional, personal and theological
inventory. The major metaphor of the High Holidays, the "Book of
Life"—which says who will live and who will die in the coming year—is
merely opened on Rosh Hashanah. There are still ten "days of awe" before one's fate is actually inscribed. Yom Kippur, a day of atonement,
solemn fasting, introspection and immersion in past misdeeds, is when
the book is closed for the year. It is the April 15th of Judaism. And, like
a tax day for the soul, it is spent doing last-second calculations of self-
worth, all without the benefit of food or water.

The order of the holidays might seem counterintuitive: why not consider the past year first, and *then* revel in the new one. But the tradition
is more ironic than that. Jews are supposed to make their New Year's
resolutions and then spend ten days pondering how they broke all of last
year's resolutions. That's why the Kol Nidre prayer itself—mournfully
chanted three times by cantors facing their most rapt audiences of the
year—asks for permission to pray and then states, categorically, that all
promises made to God between this High Holiday season and the next
are "hereby publicly retracted in the event they should be forgotten." It
is a pre-apology for the sins you're about to pledge not to commit.

Kol Nidre is supposed to be the most solemn service of the year. But rabbis and cantors often complain that it isn't easy to maintain the high drama when there's so much non-theological *stuff* attached to the evening. For example, since the Torah scrolls have to be out of the Ark during the chanting of Kol Nidre, it has become traditional for all the officers and board members to be invited up to the bimah to hold and carry them. Every Torah the synagogue owns is brought out and marched around the synagogue. But creating solemnity for the chanting of Kol Nidre after such a macher parade is not an easy job.

Also, on Kol Nidre night, it is traditional in many synagogues for the president to address the congregation during the service. The president is usually there for only one reason, to ask for donations during the best-attended service of the year. He doesn't come right out and *say* that if you don't give you might not get sealed in the Book of Life. But it doesn't hurt if his presence on the bimah, and the pledge card on each seat, gives that impression.

Lew Grafman looks like a fiftyish Clark Kent who never gets to loosen up and be Superman. Tonight, he has good reason to be skittish. He must set the tone for his presidency, perhaps the most important two-year period in the synagogue's recent history. During Grafman's term, Har Zion will say its long good-bye to Wolpe and will carry on a yearlong, multievent celebration of the congregation's seventy-fifth anniversary. These could make or break the synagogue's relationship with its wealthy old guard. At the same time, Har Zion must find a new rabbi and raise millions of dollars to erect an addition to its school building to solidify its future with the young parents who will drive the synagogue into the twenty-first century. The congregation hasn't tried to raise sums of this magnitude since the new Har Zion was built in the mid-1970s—which explains why space for the burgeoning Hebrew school is so tight that on Sunday morning one class meets in a converted coat closet.

Grafman is also emotional about Wolpe's last Kol Nidre sermon, although he would never show it. Rabbi Wolpe has been in Grafman's life since he was a child. His grandfather was one of the founders of Beth El

Temple in Harrisburg, and a young Rabbi Wolpe officiated at Grafman's bar mitzvah there. After leaving town for college and law school, Grafman married and began practicing in Philadelphia, specializing in representing movie theater chains. He eventually joined Har Zion and ended up in a law firm with close ties to the synagogue, Cozen and O'Connor, the largest insurance law practice in America. His boss, Steve Cozen, is one of Rabbi Wolpe's close friends.

Grafman does his best to be charming up there, but public addresses are not his forte, and he comes off stiff. Especially when he talks about Wolpe. "The rabbi has agreed to give sermons through the end of the calendar year," he says, making it sound like the result of a protracted labor negotiation rather than a labor of love. He wishes everyone a happy, healthy and generous new year and goes back to his seat. After a few more prayers, Wolpe is on.

From the first, he is mesmerizing. *This* is the sermon he spent all summer writing, and an entire career imagining. He begins by talking about the building we're sitting in, and how he chose the words that would serve as its theme: *shamor* and *zachor,* observe and remember, from the Fourth Commandment. The words, inscribed on the Ark curtains behind him, represent the "maaahr-velous blend" that has defined Har Zion, a congregation that has always seen itself as part of history but still translates that remembrance into religious action.

He threatens to talk about his regrets as a pulpit rabbi, but then retreats, saying it is unfair to burden us—but he'll share just one. He never acted on his greatest rabbinic fantasy, a plan both "diabolical and ingenious" that has lingered in the back of his mind for years.

On Yom Kippur, congregants are supposed to stay in synagogue all day, fasting and praying. Yet at about 12:30 P.M., when the *Yizkor* service is announced, half the congregation gets up and walks out. Yizkor is the memorial prayer for the dead, and many leave because of an old Jewish superstition that it is bad luck to sit through Yizkor if you haven't lost both parents. Others leave because it's a good excuse to cut out after two or three hours of prayer. Then, when Yizkor is over there's often another stampede to the exits, leaving only a few hundred people dotting the three thousand seats.

Wolpe confesses that he has always secretly desired to reschedule Yizkor for six o'clock in the evening so nobody would leave. "I have endured difficult moments in the rabbinate," he says, "by imagining the looks of bewilderment and panic that would spread over the faces of the congregation . . . vainly waiting through the strange machinations of an aging rabbi: 'Did he forget? Should we send an usher? Why doesn't the president *say something* to him?' "

As he speaks, his head moves slowly back and forth, as if driven by an oscillating mechanism beneath his tallis. In this owlish way, he gives the impression of making eye contact with every congregant.

Next he flies off to Barcelona. Rabbi and Elaine recently visited there, and the city, he says, "quickly became one of our favorites." One of the unexpected delights of Barcelona, he recounts, was the Picasso museum—unexpected because he has never been a "devotee of Picasso," and the art history student in him requires him to say so. But this museum included only Picasso's very early work—his portraits of family and friends, planning cartoons and studies for what was to come—as well as a series of copperplate prints he had done near the end of his life. The prints recalled the influences in his career, a tribute to his visual masters. "The Germans, as always, have a word for it," says Wolpe, and the word *vergangenheitsbewältigung* rolls off his tongue as if it comes up in conversation often.

It is "the process of coming to terms with one's own past." It is what Wolpe has been doing to prepare for this sermon and for this year, when there will be a last time for everything he has known as a pulpit rabbi.

He talks about looking at pictures of himself as a child, and notes that there is nobody left alive who knew him then: his last boyhood friend recently died, and he officiated at his funeral. And there is, he says, one Picasso-esque vignette that repeats itself over and over in his mind. He is a youngster, sitting on a large windowsill in the third-floor apartment where he and his mother lived in Roxbury. From there, he can look south over the rooftops all the way to Dorchester Bay. The apartment was once part of a house that had been built by a clipper ship captain, and this very window overlooked the outdoor platform where the captain's wife kept watch for his ship. It was called "the widow's walk." And he recalls sitting on that windowsill and reading and listening, nothing escaping him; novels and poetry, philosophy and plays, and sounds classical and modern, Shakespeare and Browning, Mozart and Cole Porter. He gulped Tennyson's King Arthur and the Dixieland jazz of Pee Wee Russell, along with sages Rashi and Sholom Aleichem. It was exciting and strangely comforting to think that these important voices "were talking to *me,* trying to comfort *me.*" Occasionally he would look up from his book, trying to see the masts of the ships in Dorchester Bay. He knew his father would never return, but he would never stop waiting and searching for him.

Then Wolpe switches gears, giving a meticulous description of a concert of Yiddish music, sung by Mandy Patinkin, that he and Elaine recently attended in a dilapidated former synagogue on New York's Lower East Side. He was enjoying the show until, during a medley, Patinkin began singing "White Christmas"—in Yiddish. At first he felt instinctive resentment, his memories of the music of his rich Jewish youth interrupted by a paean to secular Christianity, the true American culture. But then he realized, it made sense: "White Christmas" and "Easter Parade" had been written by Irving Berlin, a cantor's son who began his career writing "Yidl Mit a Fiddle." Berlin was only one of the songwriters Wolpe adored who grew up listening to Yiddish music but whose ancestry is hard to locate in their most famous work. Jerome Kern and George Gershwin wrote about the struggles of other minorities, but not their own: Kern, after all, penned "Ol' Man River," and Gershwin, *Porgy and Bess,* for which he borrowed a Yiddish tune for the structure of "Summertime." Wolpe laments their professional conversion to American Christian culture, primarily because it was unnecessary. Judaism, he says, "offered me incredible insights about myself and the world around me, but it did not ask for a retreat from a world of Yeats and Auden and Byron and El Greco."

From there he segues into a diatribe against the new spiritualism in Judaism—which he says parallels trends in Christianity as well. He believes some of it is heartening and admirable, but "so much of it has a frightening, simplistic quality about it. It is seductive but avoids the hard questions. It says, 'Don't really pose the soul-wrenching questions. Make it easy and it will sell.' " It is the first time I've truly understood what his problem is with the rebirth of Jewish spirituality: it is, to him, an assimilation to American secular Christianity, "White Christmas" all over again.

And, to him, that isn't what Judaism is supposed to be about. "I have discovered," he says, "that life is volatile and the Torah only makes sense when it is used as a brutal guideline to living in a world that does not always match up to expectations."

He pauses for effect, steps back a bit and rechecks his typed script. It is as if he is taking in air for his last solo. His head starts to sway, and he's ready . . .

I will accept God only if I can confront God. Not benign acceptance, but the eternal wrestling of the soul. Jacob wrestled with You and he came forth limping from the arena. I am damaged as well, and I understand completely the Yiddish lament, "Oh, Lord, You help complete strangers, why won't You help me?"

There's a Midrash where this question is asked with the addition of a poignant cry, "God, it is such a difficult world, why don't You send someone who can change it?" and God answered, "I did send someone. I sent you."

So on this day when so much comes to an end in my life's commitment and there is still so much left to be desired, I have my answer. The world and I clashed many years ago and I felt that God wanted me to help change it. The first time God talks to a Jew, He speaks to Abraham, He tells him to journey to a different place. "*Lech*

Lecha—go from here." God is the Lord of journeys and that should be the destiny of every Jew and it has been mine. It is not going from one place to another; it is the journey of the soul and the journey of the spirit.

God tested me *every step of my journey.* He tested me in ways that I could never imagine. He beat at my soul, my stamina and my faith. He demanded things from me when my own personal needs screamed for my attention, and I was torn between need and duty.

Yet, I kept one personal vow. I never allowed myself to accept the easy answers; I wanted to struggle with each one even when they tore at my heart, mind and soul. I would never compromise with my own spiritual standards. I can only pray that by the honesty of that vow, I made a difference in the lives of other human beings even in the moments when I rebelled and agonized over the inexplicable in His rulings.

And I can only hope that those of you who have listened to me have realized how lonely were the long and brutally demanding hours so necessary to make all the words sound as if they came so easily.

Almighty God, I pray that I have challenged them, Your children, and that I have challenged You with the very justice You proclaimed to the world. Each day I lifted the tears of my soul and have begged that the words of my mouth and the meditation of my heart might be acceptable to them, and to You.

Every night of my life, after I recite the Sh'ma Yisrael, I have closed my eyes to recite a prayer that my father taught me when I was a child. It is a simple and almost childish prayer but it is comforting. It has allowed me the connective serenity of a long silent touch to my father so I could journey with you in your lives to think, to dream, to cry, to hope, to accept and, yes, even to shout to the very gates of Heaven. Each night I have said words left to me by Benjamin Wolpe and have remembered some blessed moments in the task I have chosen.

Lately, however, as I have grown older something remarkable has happened. When at night, as sleep begins to overwhelm me, in the child's eye that still remains I climb once again on that windowsill and I look over the surrounding roofs. And *I can see it*. I can *really* see it. I can see my father's ship enter Dorchester Bay.

For those of you who were part of my journey, thank you, God bless you, Shalom.

His sermon made me cry. I would be embarrassed except that everyone around me is crying, too. But as I wipe my tears, and my wife, who came with me to Har Zion this time, rubs my back, the cantor begins to chant the next prayer. And I am reminded that we are gathered here for something much bigger than this sermon. We are here to pray for ourselves, for our lives. This is the beginning of the most humbling twenty-four hours in the Jewish year. We will pray for another hour or so tonight, return home but neither eat nor drink, and then come back the next morning for an entire day of worship, meditation and contrition.

As Wolpe runs the morning service, he tries hard not to get swept up in the emotion of the day. His sermon on Yom Kippur morning is never a full one: it serves as a curtain raiser to Yizkor, and it always ends with the Yizkor stampede. But this year Wolpe is unusually lighthearted before the memorial service: he recounts a family trip in a Winnebago, shifts to a website he likes that lists the obituaries of uncelebrated but influential people—such as the woman who thought of expanding the SPF on suntan lotion to twenty-five, thirty and beyond, or the man who invented Styrofoam packing peanuts. And then he conjures some vivid images of his late mother's Jean Naté perfume and a shore spot where a congregant still goes to watch the sun set because it is where he and his late brother always did that.

The light sermon may be as much to spare himself as the congregants. Speaking with Elaine that morning, he expressed his fear of "losing it" during the culmination of the *Ne'ilah* service, which tests his emotional and physical mettle every year. Chanted in the late afternoon of Yom Kippur, Ne'ilah is considered the most dramatic prayer in the entire year's liturgy, the moment when, as one cantor has described it to me, "the big guy closes the book and you're either in or out." Kol Nidre is the call to prayer on the Day of Atonement; Ne'ilah is everyone's last chance. It comes at the end of a twenty-four-hour fast when the impassioned pleas are a little more impassioned. And it usually comes with its own light show, because at 5:30 on what is usually an early fall afternoon, the setting sun plays amazing tricks with Har Zion's stained-glass windows, sending beams of colored light careering in all directions.

For the first twenty-three years Wolpe was at Har Zion, Ne'ilah was the passionate performance piece of liturgical legend Isaac Wall, who was the congregation's cantor for nearly fifty years. When Wolpe took over Har Zion in 1969, his predecessor asked him to make only one promise during the transition: never interrupt Cantor Wall during Ne'ilah. Wolpe kept that promise, and was always swept up in Wall's recitation of the prayer. Har Zion's new cantor, Eliot Vogel—he has been there for eight years, but as long as Wall is alive he'll be considered "new"—also has an amazing voice and chants a chilling Ne'ilah.

Wolpe is trying to pace himself and mentally prepare himself for the ending of Ne'ilah, which is chanted with the Ark left open, so nobody can sit down. So he is surprised when the emotion starts washing over him earlier than he expected, fifteen minutes before Ne'ilah ends, during the beginning of *Pesah Lanu Sha-ar,* a three-line prayer sung by the cantor and congregation, asking God to "open for us the gates, even as they are closing." To Wolpe it has always seemed an explosive cry: God, don't shut the book yet, I still have some more to say, let it last a little bit longer. As they sing it, Wolpe's eyes fill with tears, his legs get weak and he staggers off the bimah through a door hidden in the wood paneling next to the Ark, leading to the "robing room." As he stands back there trying to compose himself, he senses the presence of someone approaching behind him; it's Lou Fryman, the head of the rabbi search committee, who takes his shoulder and asks if he is going to be all right. Wolpe says yes, and then peeks back out the door to let Elaine know he is not ill, just caught in the undertow of emotion. And then he looks out. He expects to see the normal crowd: traditionally, about one-third of the congregation returns for the closing prayer. Today, almost every seat is filled.

They have come back for his last Ne'ilah. It is nearing 6 P.M. on Yom Kippur and, for once, his shul is packed. He did not have to resort to postponing Yizkor after all.

As he wobbles tearfully back onto the bimah, someone whispers, "Rabbi, I've never seen it so mobbed."

And Wolpe chuckles, "They came to see if I am really leaving."

9

WHAT, ANOTHER HOLIDAY?

O NLY FIVE DAYS AFTER YOM KIPPUR there is another Jewish holiday, the harvest festival of Sukkot, the Feast of Tabernacles, which lasts seven days. On day one, I attend Sukkot services for probably the first time in twenty-five years. Upon arriving at 9:15, I see that the risers have been taken down and the synagogue is scaled back to its normal size. There are twenty-two people here to worship.

President Lew Grafman is one of them, sitting where he always sits, with his cousin Ralph Snyder, two-thirds of the way up the center aisle on the right side of the sanctuary, the side with the best view of the rabbi's lectern. It occurs to me that I have yet to be at a Har Zion event that Grafman missed, which makes me appreciate how much time the synagogue presidency requires, on top of the demands of his full-time job as a lawyer and his responsibilities as a husband and a father. Not only must he be present at all the major religious services and meetings, but Har Zion has always prided itself on being a synagogue where the leaders usually show up at daily morning minyan. They are also expected to be proficient enough to *lead* the minyan.

As more people shuffle in, I notice a table in the back stacked with the apparatus of Sukkot: javelin-length constructions of woven palm, willow and myrtle branches, wrapped in clear plastic like expensive cut flowers, and small white rectangular boxes, each holding a delicately cushioned citron, which looks like a lemon on steroids. These are *lulavs* and *etrogs,* which are held aloft and shaken during certain Sukkot prayers, in fulfillment of the biblical command to "take the product of goodly trees" and rejoice. It is nearly impossible to share lulavs and etrogs—although I've been at services where they are passed around so everyone gets a shake or two—so the synagogue arranges for congregants to order their own: they run about fifty dollars a set, and since they're living plants, they have to be replaced each year.

Frankly, I'm privately relieved to be without a set because I can't remember what to do with them. Watching the others pray, I am fascinated and humbled by those who actually know what they're doing.

Wolpe speaks from the bimah about the significance of Sukkot, which was once the most important holiday of the year but is now overshadowed by Yom Kippur. He offers a common explanation for its demotion, that it has lost its significance because we are no longer an agrarian society. But I wonder if it is more that we have gone from being a society focused on thanking God for the harvest to a society so introspective that we're no longer impressed with the daily miracles of nature.

Or maybe Sukkot lost its appeal because it is an awful lot of work. Besides taking two mornings away from the office to attend services, you are supposed to build a sukkah, a hut made of raw lumber and adorned with tree branches and fruit, in your yard. And then you're supposed to eat all your meals in the sukkah—some people even sleep in it—for seven days.

After the Torah reading, I watch Wolpe lead the processional— although this time he only has a few dozen hands to shake. When he reaches the back row, he spies Martin Landis and his children, whom he hasn't seen much since the Worst Bat Mitzvah Ever. Julie, the bat mitzvah girl, is a young woman now, wearing a jean jacket over her dress. The rabbi shakes her hand warmly but ignores her father. Even though

Wolpe is still angry, he must concede that Landis is one of the only parents out of Har Zion's fourteen hundred families who bothered to take his kids out of school and bring them to Sukkot services. That counts for something.

After services, we all proceed outside to the sukkah, which is attached to a brick wall near the side entrance. It is large and fragrant from pine needles. The last angry yellowjackets of the season are buzzing around glasses of wine awaiting kiddush. I haven't built a sukkah since I was a teenager. Like most Jewish-American families, we stopped celebrating Sukkot when the kids were old enough to opt out of it and it became clear that my parents and grandparents were only celebrating it for us. As I stand in the Har Zion sukkah, I recall the last one we built in the buggy backyard of our split-level house in Harrisburg in the mid-seventies. There are pictures I treasure of my Nana and Pop-pop sitting in that sukkah, looking youthful, happy, prosperous and utterly suburban. Given my father's negligible abilities with power tools, it is something of a miracle that his sukkah remained standing long enough for the photographs to be taken.

On the second day of Sukkot, attendance is even lower than the first. Even Lew Grafman seems to have taken a day off. Wolpe's young assistant rabbi, Jacob Herber, is given a chance to give the sermon. While he speaks, he oscillates his head the way Wolpe does, making me wonder if he learned this technique from his mentor or whether they teach this in homiletics class at the Seminary. Herber is not a commanding orator. He lacks The Voice and has yet to do all the Renaissance rabbi reading to which this congregation has grown accustomed. Yet he does have a certain quality: a youthful approachability, an easy laugh and a talent for speaking from the heart.

He makes a rather provocative observation about today's parents. In the past, he says, people proudly displayed photographs of their ancestors on the walls and tabletops of their homes. Now, it is mostly pictures of the *children* on the walls. And then we worry that kids have no role models. What is interesting about this sermon is that it's being preached to a synagogue full of grandparents, who spend much of their time grousing about how their grandchildren are being raised—not the way it was in *their* day. But the truth is, one way of understanding today's parents—many of whom are having children later in life, and seem determined to inhabit the world of their kids rather than giving young people an adult standard to strive for—is that they often act more like grandparents than parents. In *my* day, it was the parents who said no and the grandparents who said, "C'mon, why not?"

While Herber is clearly chiding some parents for failing to balance the past and the future, he and his generation of rabbis are deeply invested in making the main sanctuary of the synagogue more kid-friendly. For many years, Rabbi Wolpe was viewed by parents as having a strict "seen and not heard" policy on kids in the sanctuary, until Elaine's health crisis and then grandfatherhood started softening him up. For much of his tenure, he didn't want young children on the bimah at all, or even in the main sanctuary unless they could remain quiet and still. For a long time, he resisted the national trend toward letting younger siblings come onto the bimah at the end of bar and bat mitzvahs to "lead" the closing song, *Ein Keloheinu*. One synagogue officer told me he recalls Wolpe saying, "It's too cute and Har Zion does not *do* cute."

Today, Har Zion does cute. At the end of services, children from Junior Congregation are led into the main sanctuary and up onto the bimah. Herber's wife often comes up to the bimah with their baby daughter, Mychal, and passes her to the young rabbi to cuddle during the closing prayers. The kids make noise and run around, the little girls errantly lift up their dresses; some kids are wearing little "dress clothes," but most wear sneakers, baggy pants, sweaters. For some parents, this is the only reason to come to synagogue. The end of each service becomes a two-minute kiddie pageant.

Six days later, I look at the calendar and see—oh, dear God— another holiday, and I find myself spending yet another morning in synagogue for *Shemini Atzeret*. This is the holiday that seems unable to decide if it is the end of Sukkot—it does include the annual prayer for rain—or the beginning of *Simhat Torah,* the raucous celebration of the ending and restarting of the Torah, which is read Genesis to Deuteronomy each year. With Simhat Torah tomorrow, seven of the last seventeen work days will have been spent in synagogue rather than at the office.

All this extra time in the synagogue, however, does encourage the kind of contemplation rarely allowed in our busy lives. It's an opportunity to consider the prayers, or any other spiritual issues, for several hours with no real interruption but the occasional request to stand up or sit down. During my conversations with Wolpe, we have discussed how clergy members use the time: basically, how do rabbis pray? Any rabbi can recite from memory, incredibly quickly, all the prayers for an entire service. But that's just chanting, repetition, davening. It is useful in creating a sort of meditative or fugue state, which can be gratifying. But I don't know most of those prayers by heart, and reading them in Hebrew doesn't mean much to my untrained mind.

Wolpe says that his way of praying is to pick on one or two phrases from a prayer and focus his attention on them throughout the service. While reciting the rest by rote, he mentally caresses individual lines, teasing out possible meanings. During a Torah reading or the chanting of a Haftarah, a sentence he has read at least fifty times will snag his attention anew, and he will linger there.

On Shemini Atzeret, it is the Yizkor prayer that captures my thoughts. Besides Yom Kippur, Yizkor is said three other times during the year: today, and then twice again in the spring. The whole point of Yizkor, as far as I can tell, is to make people cry on purpose, to give them time and license every once in a while to just admit how painful losses are. The same is true for yahrzeit—the annual acknowledgment of the death of a loved one, marked at home by lighting a twenty-four-hour candle and in synagogue by rising to say Kaddish. Some people find all these rituals morbid, and use them as evidence of Judaism's tendency to be death-obsessed. Personally, I find Yizkor one of the most brilliant aspects of the religion, because it provides an opportunity for contained catharsis, an emotional underground nuclear test. All of us, now and then, burst into tears for what appears to be no good reason, and the reason is often the deaths in our lives, which can never be completely processed. The prayer reminds me of that scene in *Annie Hall* where Alvy Singer suggests that he and his new love interest have their first-date kiss on the way to dinner so they can get it over with and digest their food better. After Yizkor, I digest the rest of my life better.

During the service, I am approached by a woman who asks if I'd like a Torah honor. I'm taken aback, because I feel a bit underdressed for the Har Zion bimah. I'm wearing black jeans, a blazer and a collarless sweater. At my own synagogue in town, where many people pray more casually in shirtsleeves and slacks, my outfit would be unexceptional. At Har Zion, however, men usually wear suits, and everyone but me has a tie.

But being called to the Torah is an honor I never refuse. At my morning minyan, the rabbi or cantor doles out the aliyahs just minutes before the Torah is taken out, near the end of the silent Amidah, and I often find myself looking up from my prayers to make eye contact: "pick me, pick me." It is partly because when you get an aliyah, you are called to the Torah by your Hebrew name, which they ask you for and then chant back at you. The full Hebrew name includes the name of your father— and, in egalitarian synagogues, your mother, too—and I like hearing my lineage announced in the synagogue. I especially like the idea of hearing my father's name spoken from the Har Zion bimah on the day of Yizkor.

I also enjoy what happens after you finish an aliyah. As you walk down the aisle to your seat, people extend their hands to shake yours and wish you a hearty *"yasher koach"*—which I think of as the "Hebrew high-five." Yasher koach is a Yiddishized version of the Hebrew phrase meaning "may your strength be renewed," and it is used specifically to congratulate someone for participating in worship (as opposed to mazel tov, which is used for more general felicitation). Midrash says the first yasher koach was spoken by God to Moses, telling him "way to go" for smashing the first set of tablets after seeing the golden calf.

I get over my sartorial embarrassment and accept the Torah honor, appearing on the bimah in black jeans. My dad, who hated dressing up for any occasion, would have appreciated it. My mother, of course, would be mortified.

The next day, I'm back in synagogue for Simhat Torah, which is as crazed as Shemini Atzeret is somber. The end of a Torah-reading cycle and the beginning of a new one is cause for a huge celebration for the whole family, an evening service where every sacred scroll the congregation owns—whether full-sized or miniature—is paraded around the synagogue in revelry. It's a wild night.

In reality, they aren't really finishing the whole Torah tonight. Some years ago, many synagogues decided that to shorten the length of services, they would return to the ancient practice of reading the Torah through in three years instead of one. The integrity of the parashas—the annual cycle of weekly portions into which the entire Torah was divided during Babylonian times—is maintained by reading aloud one-third of each portion each week throughout the year. Rabbis, however, are free to use the entire parasha to inspire sermons as well as shorter commentaries or teachings called *d'var Torah*. And the congregation still gets the thrill of seeing the last scroll of Deuteronomy read before the Torah is laboriously rerolled back to the beginning of Genesis.

By late in the evening, the kids are so wound up that they are running up and down the aisles screaming, with parents in red-faced pursuit. In the midst of all this cacophony, Rabbi Wolpe and his old pal Ralph Snyder come down off the bimah to relax in the seats abandoned by congregants. They sit, dazed, staring at each other with tired grins, arms around each other's shoulders. They have just survived their last holiday season together as religious leader and congregant, the rabbi and his consigliere. They chat about the end of an era like a couple of Neil Simon characters, laughing, kidding, occasionally bringing their heads close together to share what would have been a whisper, but must be yelled to be heard over the din.

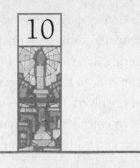

10

JACOB'S LADDER

OVER THE PAST WEEKS, I've had a chance to get to know Wolpe's assistant rabbi, Jacob Herber. Lanky and boyish, with glasses and a reddish goatee, Jacob is both young and old for his age. Young because at thirty-five, most rabbis have been out of school for nearly a decade; he started late and has been ordained for only two years. On the other hand, he had experienced more before the age of twenty than some rabbis do in a lifetime. He has more than earned his slowly retreating hairline.

Rabbi Herber's father is a retired lieutenant in the New York State Department of Corrections: a lapsed Orthodox Jew who became a correctional officer and separated from his wife when the children were young. Jacob grew up living with his mother, a younger brother, and an older half-sister in a small Jewish community in the Hudson Valley. Diagnosed with kidney disease in the late 1960s, his mother had to be dialyzed at home. For several years, his father helped with the painful procedure. Then she started going to a clinic. One of Jacob's last images of his parents together was at his bar mitzvah, where they reunited to make the pretense of being happy and cordial for an entire day.

When Jacob was fifteen, his mother moved the family to Sacramento, where they joined a Conservative congregation. The synagogue community was a relief compared to his dysfunctional family and the stress of his mother's unrelenting illness. During the early 1980s, he stayed close to home by attending college at the University of California's Davis campus, where he got involved in local Democratic politics. Following graduation, he took an entry-level position at the San Francisco law firm of Morrison and Foerster, with the intention of eventually going to law school.

Then his mother died of a heart attack, an all-too-common occurrence for long-term dialysis patients. She was fifty-two. After a long time away from active synagogue life, he decided to say Kaddish for her and joined a Conservative congregation in San Francisco. One Friday night, the synagogue had a special guest speaker, Rabbi David Wolpe, whose talk on Heschel and God and spirituality inspired Jacob to reconsider his future career. He recalled times in his life when he had thought about becoming a rabbi, working with people. Herber revealed his feeling to his own rabbi and before long, Elliot Dorff was calling.

Rabbi Elliot Dorff, an infectiously likable philosophy scholar, is rector of the Graduate School at the University of Judaism in Los Angeles and has a reputation for motivating potential rabbis. (David Wolpe tells a similar story about the call he got from Dorff, helping him finalize his decision to go to rabbinical school.) Convinced, Herber went to Israel for a year and then moved to New York in 1990 to attend the Jewish Theological Seminary. Unable to afford the tuition and high cost of living, he took out student loans—eventually totaling some fifty thousand dollars—and took a part-time job at the Rabbinical Assembly.

"You know, way back when Rabbi Wolpe was a student, they paid *him*," Herber says. "Well, the world has changed, and when I got to the Seminary it was at the height of the recession. Seminary benefactors were hurting, and it was difficult to make ends meet. There was no way they were going to give us a stipend."

We are sitting in Herber's small study, which is part of a suite of rooms dominated by Rabbi Wolpe's office. Herber's lesser space is lined with dark bookcases bearing weighty rabbinic texts. On his desk are pictures of his wife and infant daughter, amid memorabilia from the New York Rangers hockey team—a somewhat risky decoration in a congregation with so many die-hard Philadelphia Flyers season ticket-holders.

Herber's first year at the Seminary was "the greatest challenge of my life," because he sometimes felt culturally ill-prepared. He had grown up attending public school and receiving his Jewish education only during after-school hours—first in Hebrew school, which goes until bar mitzvah age, then confirmation classes, which continue for two more years, and finally taking classes in evening "Hebrew High School." Many of his classmates, on the other hand, were *yeshiva buchers,* having been educated exclusively at eight-year and even twelve-year Jewish day schools. (Most American cities now have at least one Jewish day school for students through the eighth grade; often, when there is only one school, students and teachers will be both Conservative and Orthodox, and, upon graduation, the students will attend public high school. Larger cities may have separate Conservative, Orthodox and sometimes even Reform day schools for grades one through eight, and then a separate Jewish high school. The schools all mix American and Jewish curricula, and tend to use Hebrew as a second language. While *yeshiva* is technically the term for a talmudic academy, it has become a generic term for Jewish schools, whose students are "buchers.")

Besides the day schools, Herber's rabbinic classmates had gone to more observant Jewish summer camps than he had. Consequently, the skills required of the clergy came more naturally to them. This was especially true of his classmate Danny Wolpe, whose brother David had so inspired him, and whose father "Jerry" (as he was called within the Seminary walls) had a reputation as a Pavarotti of sermonizers. Herber had done well on the entrance exams: after nine months of preparation, he was able to place out of everything except Bible. He did well on the liturgy, philosophy and Talmud tests. But he still felt as if he was playing catch-up in his studies.

Working for the Rabbinical Assembly for nearly five years taught

Herber much about being a rabbi that you don't learn in homiletics class. Initially, his job was to place rabbis in High Holiday pulpits because many congregations can't afford full-time clergy, and hire rabbis to freelance for the holidays from a large pool of ordained men and women who, for one reason or another, don't have pulpits. Congregations and rabbis would call Herber, looking for a good match and asking basic questions, such as what was the going rate for the four-day High Holiday gig. (At that time, it was about four thousand dollars.) Then Herber ran a program that helped physicians to become *mohels*—trained in the ritual aspects of performing a Jewish circumcision, a *bris*—in communities around the world that didn't have them. He oversaw programs to train rabbis to serve as kosher supervisors in restaurants, bakeries and other kinds of food preparation businesses. Eventually, Herber was trusted to become involved in the rabbinic placement process itself.

"I got a view of the underbelly of the Jewish world," he says. "Sometimes, the selection committee chairs and synagogue presidents would yell at me because they were angry. The whole process was so frustrating. I'd hear things like, 'Rabbi X was awful and the way he left the synagogue, who is going to take our pulpit?' And then the rabbis would vent about how they were being treated."

But it wasn't all acrimonious. There were plenty of rabbis and congregations just calling for information, and often the selection process went relatively smoothly. And then, right at the peak of placement season, the RA would hold its annual convention, drawing Conservative rabbis from all over the world to compare notes, decry trends and seek the inspiration of their more inspired colleagues. It fell to Herber to help manage the logistics for the convention. So, by the end of rabbinical school, Herber knew an extraordinary number of working rabbis, and had heard many of the horror stories of life in the retail business of religion. He was still regarded as a *pischer,* a little boy, but a pischer who was on a first-name basis with all the big machers of the rabbinate.

This gave Herber a leg up when it came time for him to find a job after rabbinical school. He knew he wanted to be an assistant rabbi, preferably at Har Zion. It was, arguably, the best position open to his graduating class: an important congregation with a major rabbi to learn from. And the synagogue fulfilled his only other requirement: it was in a town with a National Hockey League franchise. If he couldn't be in New York to watch the Rangers at home, he needed to at least be able to see them on the road once in a while.

In his final year of rabbinical school, Herber's life changed dramatically. Not only did he get his dream job but he also fell in love. During vacation, he traveled to Mexico City, the hometown of his best friend in rabbinical school, Felipe Goodman. There, Goodman set him up with a college friend, Cynthia Ickowicz, who was a high-powered lawyer. Trained in Philadelphia at Penn, she was back home representing Mexico's commerce department in side agreements for the NAFTA negotiations with the United States. Herber proposed to Cynthia about a month after they met, and then visited as often as possible during his last year in rabbinical school. They were married just after he was ordained, and within weeks had moved into a cramped apartment in a building down the road from Har Zion. It was the only apartment building in the gently rolling hills of Penn Valley, the Main Line Jewish enclave which was otherwise dotted with homes starting at half a million.

Herber was impressed by the grandeur and ambition of Har Zion, and made peace with its excesses. "The unfair perception of this congregation is that it's where the snobby country club set go," he says. "But there are also those members of the congregation who are really involved and who come Shabbat in and Shabbat out: people who think of Har Zion as a second home. This is a congregation that has the financial wherewithal others do not. But that works both ways. Recently a teacher of mine asked if he could borrow a Torah to take to a Jewish camp in the Ukraine. He came here because he knew we had a lot of Torahs, we could do without one and we'd be willing to lend it."

Herber expected to be at Har Zion for only two years. But then Wolpe announced his retirement, and the leadership—who had grown to like Herber's warm, engaging style, as did many of the synagogue's

younger members—asked him to stay on through the transition. In return, he would be afforded an unprecedented opportunity: he could fill
in as senior rabbi of Har Zion for six months.

Wolpe's last contract with the synagogue includes a half-year sabbatical, which he has decided to take at the end of his term as senior rabbi.
So, until the new rabbi is chosen, Jacob Herber will get to run Har Zion
solo. The plan is that once Har Zion's transition is complete, Herber can
move on to a new smaller congregation, where he can have a pulpit of
his own. He hopes to be able to find a synagogue in a warmer climate, a
southern or western city. But he knows his choices will be limited. There
are only a few such communities that have professional hockey teams.

I ask Herber, as a veteran rabbi placement handicapper, to tell me
how he sees the Har Zion search shaping up. He says he hears that the
synagogue has received at least fifteen résumés from rabbis all over the
country, but they have yet to respond to a single one—largely, he suspects, because they are from rabbis who have yet to develop big national
reputations. He doesn't know everyone who applied, but he fears that
ignoring fifteen candidates could send the wrong message to the rabbinic community: that Har Zion can't be bothered with people it views
as clergy commoners.

"That's a *lot* of résumés for none of them to be up to their standards,"
he says. "A piece of paper doesn't tell you everything about the person.
When they looked thirty years ago, Rabbi Wolpe was not the same Rabbi
Wolpe he is today. I'm wondering how many of these candidates are future Rabbi Wolpes."

He says that Danny Wolpe, his old classmate from the Seminary,
called just before the holidays to ask if anyone had thought about Rabbi
David Ackerman, who leads a small but powerful congregation in Blue
Bell, a town in Philadelphia's northern suburbs. Several other potential
candidates have been mentioned as well. But most disquieting to Herber
are those in the synagogue who are asking why *he* can't be a candidate.

Such comments are extremely flattering, but he doesn't want that. He is not eligible for the pulpit under Rabbinical Assembly rules.

"I believe in doing things the right way," he says. "I don't believe in going against the placement commission rules. And I honestly don't know if this is where I'd want to be a senior rabbi anyway. I was asked to be here to help the successor, not to be an issue for the successor."

The Two Lews came to him to enlist his help in quelling any lobbying effort on his behalf. He says he was relieved to comply. He would not risk being expelled from the RA, "an organization I have respect for and love." He doesn't want to be defrocked.

There have been isolated cases of rabbis and congregations who ignored the rules of the RA, were expelled and then went on to enjoy thirty-year relationships that made the pain worth it. But being at a synagogue for thirty years is now an anomaly. Being a rabbi is much more of a business. And just like every other industry that was once based on lifetime commitments and loyalty and the mutual dependence of company towns, a rabbi is more likely than ever to turn to colleagues and the union for support. Rabbis must stick together.

"I take very seriously my role as Rabbi Wolpe's assistant," Herber says. "There are a lot of things I disagree with him about. But even though we have theological differences, I respect him enormously. I would never challenge him, never distance myself from him with a congregant. There are always people who complain about the rabbi. I'm sure they complain about me, too. When they say something about him, I just won't let myself get pulled into it. I'm here to be his support, to be here when he needs me. I think of myself as working more for him than for the synagogue."

So if he had to guess right now, who will be the next rabbi of Har Zion?

"I have some ideas about who else is likely to apply," he says. "But there's one thing you should know about the process. There is no real rule of thumb. People make changes in their lives for all sorts of reasons. Some are their own doing, and some are not."

11

THE ASK

THE FIRST TIME HE EVER ASKED A congregant for money, it was so easy. The Hillel at nearby Haverford College needed four hundred dollars to buy a new sukkah. Rabbi Herber took it upon himself to call a charitable young congregant and hit him up for the small gift. The check arrived the next day.

But one small gift does not a fund-raiser make. And the pressure to learn how to add zeros—three, four, five of them—weighs on the young rabbi as he recounts to me his first attempt to raise real money, to successfully invoke the biblical command for *tzedakah,* charity. In the fund-raising business, they call this "The Ask." Rabbi Herber's first big Ask didn't go so well.

He stuck closely to what he understood to be the art of the deal for The Ask, carefully considering which of Har Zion's younger congregants would be most likely to care about the cause—the Seminary—and respond to his personal urging to give a donation. Together with the local JTS fund-raising staff, he assembled a field trip to New York, just a limo ride away, to show potential donors what their money would be supporting. And then he followed up with phone calls before arranging for face time with the most likely prospect on his own turf. He came to the meeting with a local Seminary development officer so they could play good cop and really good cop. They discussed the level of the "financial commitment" again. Went over some of the particulars. And suddenly it dawned on the "Askee" that they weren't talking about a one-time gift. They expected him to commit to giving this much *every year*.

"Oh, I can't do that," he said dismissively. A second later, the phone rang and he took the call.

The Ask was over. Weeks of work, erased. Herber and the development officer shared a knowing glance of disappointment. On their way out of the office, the development officer assured Herber it would go better next time.

But it will never be easy for the young rabbi, because it is unclear if his generation will ever have the same sense of duty and philanthropy as their parents and grandparents did. The post-WWII generation of American Jews was good at being guilted. They made money and gave it freely, and those who didn't make much knew they were expected to give anyway. At thirty-six, Herber is somewhere between baby boom and Generation X. His peers barely remember Vietnam, and many are children of divorce and privilege with their own well-developed sense of entitlement. They don't guilt quite so easily. And those who can be guilted are often philanthropically assimilated. They give to medical research, cultural causes, disaster relief and private colleges. Jewish charities are not always first on their list. While American Jews continue to be the country's largest givers per capita, the number of donors to exclusively Jewish charities has declined and the amounts raised annually by campaigns has been flat for over a decade.

Yet some aspects of fund-raising transcend the generations. That's why Herber needs to learn some of Rabbi Wolpe's secrets. Wolpe gives good Ask.

Wolpe doesn't fund-raise by himself. Can't do it. He's not a closer. His predecessor, Rabbi Goldstein—now, *he* was a closer. One of the most amazing fund-raisers in American Judaism. But Wolpe is more like the musician who performs while someone else passes the hat. During the main fund-raising for Har Zion in the early seventies, his partner was Sonny Dogole, whose name is on the Dogole Chapel. Sonny Dogole paid for that, but not just with his own money. No, Sonny was wealthy, but he had something more valuable than money: he could make people wealthier than himself give *their* money. He was the King of the Ask. The new Har Zion exists primarily because Sonny helped put together a deal, a way for the big machers to feel that building a new synagogue was also a great business venture. They didn't buy the land the synagogue was built on. No, Sonny and Joe Gorson (for whom a smaller auditorium is named) made a deal for a handful of Har Zion millionaires to help buy eighty-four acres of choice suburban real estate and then flip most of it at such a profit that the congregation would get its twenty-five acres *for free*. It was sheer genius. And then Dogole and Wolpe tag-teamed to raise the money to build the new synagogue.

It hasn't been the same for Wolpe since Sonny Dogole retired to Florida and "closing" became a profession, a full-time job for paid development officers. But Wolpe is still considered a fund-raising master by the professionals. So when he takes his group to the Seminary, Herber tags along. As do I.

The cost is thirty-six dollars, and as I write out the check, I laugh at the absurd irony of asking people to pay for the privilege of being solicited for contributions.

On the morning of November 19, the sun is rising over Har Zion and two black stretch limos idle in the parking lot. I'm late, so I end up in a car full of people I've seen in shul but never actually met: all the people I know, Rabbi and Elaine, Rabbi Herber, Lew Grafman and his wife, are in the other car. I feel left out. As we get on the turnpike, my limo-mates start asking why I've been hanging around the synagogue so much. They have heard I'm writing a book, but they don't really understand what it's about. Is it a biography, a hagiography, of Rabbi Wolpe?

No, I explain, the synagogue has already commissioned such a book to commemorate Har Zion's seventy-fifth anniversary. I'm writing an investigative book about the inner life of a powerful Jewish community. I want to know what *really* goes on.

So, for the next two hours, they tell me, until my vigorous note-taking causes writer's cramp.

First they complain about who got chosen for the rabbi search committee. "How did they pick *these* people?" one woman wants to know. "They didn't ask me." Instead of the coveted rabbi selection committee, she ended up on the bar and bat mitzvah reform committee. Her daughter, however, got on the search committee because she is the current president of Sisterhood. But nobody is sure how much influence she will exert.

"Some of these older past presidents, they wield too much power," the woman explains. "I'm afraid the older men are going to control everything. The women on the committee are younger and they have less power. Which is funny because in my experience with Har Zion committees, it's the women who actually show up for all the meetings, not the men."

Her friend chimes in, "You know, her daughter on the committee is a good friend of mine, but she'll never have high blood pressure . . . if you know what I mean. She can give up on things."

The first woman begins a monologue on the state of Har Zion. She is small with short-cropped hair, like a brighter, funnier version of George Costanza's mom on *Seinfeld*. Her head bobs whenever the driver swerves between lanes on the New Jersey Turnpike, which he does way too frequently.

"You know, Wolpe is a wonderful speaker," she says, "and he has been wonderful to some people, especially in medical situations. He helps you cut through the emotion and handle it. He can be very incisive. And, yes, Har Zion has a great Hebrew school, the first accredited Hebrew school in the country. It also has an amazing gift shop, and you better believe that gift shop makes big bucks. But there's not enough new programming. The rabbi is weak in that area."

Maybe he views *himself* as the programming, I suggest.

"I don't know. Look, it's hard to get kids to go to Hebrew school. They start to learn that it's 'geeky' to be Jewish, and there's no carry-over from real life into religious school. You get sixteen kids for Saturday morning services. It's so *sad*. My sister goes to a congregation where they have to go to synagogue with the kids at least one service a month before they can be bar or bat mitzvahed. Har Zion has a policy, but it's not adhered to. Beth Am is just down the street, and we have been losing some members to them. Beth Am has a rabbi who is very young, like our assistant rabbi.

"Luckily, Har Zion is still an attractive place to have a bar or bat mitzvah or social event. A *lot* of people join just because of that. But it's not a 'bar mitzvah mill' or anything."

Actually, I've heard people say just the opposite, that Har Zion is a bit of a bar mitzvah mill and some children get through the training without putting forth much effort.

But that's not the problem as this woman sees it. She's more concerned about arrogance than laxity. "Har Zion could be as great as we say it is. But Har Zion holds itself apart from the community. We have the cinderblocks of a synagogue, but we don't have the cement of 'I CARE' holding it together. And Wolpe feels more important than, like, *God* . . ."

She says her husband was one of the officers who approached the rabbi about when he would be leaving. "He was pushed," she says. "But, I'll tell you, my husband was scared to death about how to bring up retirement with Wolpe."

Still, the ladies agree, other major synagogues are going through even more rabbi angst than Har Zion. They mention two other prominent congregations. "My God, at one the rabbi left his wife for his girlfriend. And the other has *the most boring rabbi in America*. But they still attract people, and you know why? Because Har Zion has the only Hebrew school in Philadelphia that's still three days a week!"

The discussion circles back to the upcoming seventy-fifth anniversary book. They're not too happy about that either. It will be a collection of biographies of people in the Har Zion community. The title will be *Connections,* and apparently not everyone had the proper connections to get profiled.

"How does Cantor Wall get to be in there, and not Joshua Perlmuter?" she asks. She cannot believe the synagogue's long-retired cantor is included, but not the current, much-beloved ritual director.

"And Noreen Cook is in there?" she moans. Cook is a vivacious former assistant district attorney who married well—her husband, Robert, runs the family's extremely successful meat-packaging business—and has become very active at Har Zion. At thirty-four, she has three young children in synagogue programs and another on the way. But even though she and her husband are among the synagogue's major new givers, she has only been a member for five years. In Har Zion terms, she's still a rookie.

The woman shakes her head. "This book is very hurtful. And what about Rabbi Herber? He's the heart and soul of this place. When I asked why he wasn't included—oh, yeah, you can be sure I asked—the answer was, 'We don't have enough money.' "

She describes the old days when the synagogue was in Wynnefield. If there was a problem, she says, "they went behind the bimah after services and took care of it. They took money out of their own pockets. The Har Zion way of raising money is not to have an all-out campaign. We're too proud to say 'we can't afford it.' "

The Jewish Theological Seminary, however, is never too proud to say "we can't afford it." Especially to a group from Har Zion. The Seminary runs hundreds of trips like this every year, but this one is special. Har Zion has a long and distinguished history of giving to the Seminary, which is why the institution's first student dormitory in Israel was named the Har Zion Building.

The Seminary tour starts in the Rare Book Room. It is a fascinating collection, part of the Seminary's massive holdings which comprise the largest group of Jewish objects in the world. The Rare Book Room has some of the oldest religious manuscripts ever discovered, including a document that was actually signed by the biblical commentator Maimonides, as well as some of the newest, including *The Anita Hill Megillah,* which transposes the traditional story of Purim with the more recent saga of Supreme Court nominee Clarence Thomas and his sexually harassed associate.

From the Rare Book Room, we are taken to a demonstration of JTS's Internet outreach, the Distance Learning Program that allows people to take on-line courses at the Seminary from anywhere. Next, we tour through the complex, which has many institutional hallways but occasionally a door that opens to something unexpected and charming, such as a grassy enclosed courtyard, serene in contrast to the noisy city streets.

As I stand staring at what appears to be this mirage of a miniature college campus, I'm approached by a couple who came up in the other limo, Jeff and Cindy Blum. They are as friendly a couple as I've met in the Har Zion community. If they regard me with suspicion the way everyone else does, they do an amazing job of compensating for it. Jeff explains that he considered studying at the Seminary when he was just out of college. But he couldn't decide whether he wanted to be a rabbi or a physician. So he became a dentist, specializing in pediatrics, which suits his outgoing manner and quick wit. In addition to mothering their three children, Cindy works for a non-profit educational agency, and makes an immediate impression as a working mom with a lot of heart.

They are funny, gossipy, engaging, and within minutes we are playing "Jewish Geography," the great introductory sport of Jews. Jewish Geography involves quickly identifying wherever you are "from"— hometown, summer camp, college—and then ticking off several rounds of "did-you-knows" until someone both players know is identified. It doesn't matter if either player is especially close to the person they have in common; the point of the game is simply to prove that all Jews, if they try hard enough, know somebody from where you're from.

Our game takes about twenty seconds. Jeff tells me he went to Camp Ramah in the Poconos, so he has to know my high school friend Jeff Rosenschein who was, for many years, the music director at the camp. He does know him, so we both win the game. He asks how Jeff is doing: fine actually, living in Israel, married with five kids, tenured at Hebrew University, working in the software business as a genius-for-hire.

Bonded by our one degree of separation in Jewish Geography, we continue chatting. It turns out that Jeff Blum is a vice president at Har Zion, a job for which he seems a little young. And, more important, Cindy is on the rabbi search committee. Apparently, she's one of the people on the committee who voted to let me sit in on their meetings. I tell her I would love to talk with her sometime about how the selection process is going. Sure, she shrugs, no problem.

Unbelievable. After a year of inquiring, somebody will finally tell me what's going on in the Jewish star chamber that is Lou Fryman's rabbi search committee.

The group from Har Zion is presented with a lovely buffet lunch, after which the chancellor of the Seminary joins us and makes some remarks. Rabbi Ismar Schorsch is only the sixth chancellor the Seminary has had since it was founded in the late 1800s, and since 1986 he has labored to return Conservative Judaism to the kind of primacy it had in the early 1950s, when Chancellor Louis Finkelstein was on the cover of *Time* magazine (which was run by his friend Henry Luce). Schorsch is energetic, thoughtful, clean-shaven and looks a little bit like Buck Henry. Not exactly the bearded, dark visage that Finkelstein presented, but Chancellor Schorsch is still the leader of one of the most powerful forces in American religion. There may technically be more Reform Jews than Conservative in the United States. And there is obviously a rebirth of both Modern and ultra-Orthodoxy going on, with Orthodox rabbis holding enormous power over their American congregants and controlling religious politics in Israel. But real power in America is about national institutions, money, politics, coalitions. In those areas, the centrist Conservative movement has historically been the most formidably organized denomination.

But American Jewry faces huge challenges, he insists, because we can no longer count on anti-Semitism to hold us together against a common enemy. The enemy is now primarily within.

"There is now no external pressure to survive," he says. "We must do it on our own. And in a country that values individualism, it's that much harder to sustain a group where the *group* is valued. That's why Jewish identity is so important: we discover it and then go look for it again. People are shopping around for an identity which might give meaning to our lives. Israel, of course, plays less of a role, so a major component of Jewish identity is declining. The major question is how to negotiate our communal survival in such an open, individualistic society." Schorsch, not surprisingly, believes that Jewish education is the only way. The synagogue needs to be more of a learning community, the Seminary its leading institution of scholarship.

"This is a group with a unique history," he says. "I am *not* going to write the last chapter of it."

Toward the end of the day, our group convenes in the sanctuary. Wolpe gives a nostalgic little talk about what the Seminary has meant to him. He says one of his most enduring memories of his time here was sitting in the Seminary synagogue the day Israel was declared a state. Through the open window, he could hear the bells ringing at the nearby Riverside Church. But they weren't playing their usual tune. On that day, in a rare display of solidarity between the organized religions, the church bells played the *Hatikvah*, Israel's national anthem.

12

ALL THE YOUNG JEWS

JEFF AND CINDY BLUM ARE SITTING in their kitchen discussing who should go first. Both have the day off work. Because the weekends are so crazy with three kids' social lives and synagogue, they arrange their schedules so they can spend one weekday together. But they still have so much left to do on their "day off" that it is best if we tag-team our interviews. The kids are already home from school, so they periodically poke into the kitchen to see what's going on or grab a snack. It is the charming chaos of family life on a tree-lined street in the good-but-not-grand part of Lower Merion.

The Blums are both on the short end of medium height, and have dark hair and eyes. Because of their utter familiarity with each other, they could easily be mistaken for siblings. They met at summer camp when they were thirteen, and, now in their mid-forties, they have been married for nearly twenty-five years.

Jeff decides to go first. He speaks rapidly, a man accustomed to filling in both halves of a conversation because so much of his day is spent around people with their mouths full of dental instruments. At Har Zion, Jeff is considered something of a "rabbi groupie." But, in fact, he is not so much a groupie for the clergy as he is a committed and knowledgeable fan. His best friend is a rabbi in Maryland, his brother is also a rabbi, and he follows the Conservative Jewish clergy as passionately as he follows Flyers hockey and Sixers basketball. If the local sports talk station, WIP, had a clergy call-in show Sunday morning, Jeff Blum would be a perfect host.

He grew up at a smaller Philadelphia synagogue, Beth Hillel, where his working-class parents—his father was a mechanic, his mother a schoolteacher—were involved but not terribly religious. They didn't belong to the old Har Zion in Wynnefield because it was too far away and they considered it too big and fancy-shmancy for their family. But Jeff became friendly with Har Zion kids anyway. He met them at Jewish day school and later at summer camp. He attended bar and bat mitzvahs there. And as he became a teenager, he began to realize that the clergy at Har Zion simply had more talent, more star power, than what he saw on his own synagogue's pulpit. While he remained active at his own shul, learning how to read Torah, he found himself strangely drawn to Har Zion, to its revered cantor Isaac Wall and its dynamic new rabbi Gerald Wolpe.

"I would read Torah at Beth Hillel," he explains, "and after I was finished I would get in the car and race down the street to be there in time for Wolpe's sermon and for Wall's singing of *Musaf*." (The Musaf is the last part of the Sabbath service, which, in more traditional synagogues, includes an operatic repetition of the Amidah prayer—the cantor's version of a sermon.) When Blum was seventeen, Har Zion was looking for Hebrew-school teachers and fill-in cantors for its new second campus in Radnor, at the far end of the Main Line. The synagogue had originally purchased the bucolic site for its summer day camp, but eventually it attracted enough young suburban families to found a small satellite congregation. One of those families was Cindy's.

Blum began teaching bar mitzvah students at Har Zion Radnor and filling in for High Holiday services: it wasn't bad money for something he liked doing anyway. The side income allowed him to pursue his other interests. He was a jazz drummer, he was part of a Jewish choral group and he was a jock: after shul, he would play basketball for hours on end, and when he went to Villanova University, he played on the school base-ball team.

Jeff and Cindy dated during college, and when he started thinking about graduate school, they had a decision to make. Jeff thought he might want to be a rabbi. "But Cindy was not interested in being mar-ried and living in a fishbowl," he recalls. "She said if you want to be a rabbi, look for somebody else." He also knew that he wanted his free-dom, and he didn't think he had it in him to be writing sermons and an-swering to synagogue boards. He didn't have a perfect singing voice, and he doubted his ability to consistently produce "blistering sermons that make the women take out their handkerchiefs." So he went to Penn Dental School. He and Cindy married in 1975. They spent their honeymoon (and the rest of the summer) as counselors at Camp Ramah in the Poconos. They are what are commonly referred to as "Ramahniks."

This has become a familiar campfire tale. For many of the Jews I know who still actively practice some form of Judaism, summer camp had more influence over who they grew up to be than their synagogues or families did. They are Jewish not the way they were raised to be, but the way the alternative reality of summer camp inspired them to be.

In traditional Hebrew school training, kids learn that Judaism can be just as tedious as the rest of school. That's why it is common for young people to disassociate with organized religion the moment their parents will let them: in Judaism, often just after the bar or bat mitzvah. At Camp Ramah, kids have the opposite experience. They often find themselves acclimating to a more observant life than that of their par-ents, because it is packaged in the context of summer fun, not manda-tory education. And since summer camp affords kids the opportunity to reinvent themselves away from their families and their childhood friends, they are assimilated into observant life the same way that most Jews are assimilated *out* of observance.

So, instead of associating Judaism with childhood education, they associate it with being a teenager, coming of age, first loves, even the counterculture. While synagogue life is run by grown-ups, Ramah is run by people brimming with enthusiasm, who return to camp periodically to prove they can still access the teen inside them. The Ramah style of Judaism tends to be very do-it-yourself: there is little centralized religious authority. Most American congregational and Hebrew school life mirrors the hierarchical structure of the traditional Saturday morning service, with the rabbi and cantor preaching to the flock. Ramah Judaism mirrors the minyan; it is more observant, and more communal. Everybody learns how to participate in every aspect of the service, and the only thing separating rabbis and laypeople is the number of years they have studied.

This is, in fact, precisely what the Conservative movement hoped for when it created the Camp Ramah system in the 1950s. The first Camp Ramah was in Wisconsin. Not long after, a wealthy congregant from Har Zion, Abraham Birenbaum, agreed to donate a large tract of land in north-central Pennsylvania for a Camp Ramah in the Poconos. (Birenbaum also had a farm in Bucks County that became a legendary retreat for leading Jewish thinkers, including Heschel and Kaplan.) Har Zion rabbi David Goldstein did most of the aggressive fund-raising necessary to build the camp. Today there are seven Ramah camps: including one in the Berkshires that serves the New York area, one in Massachusetts that serves New England, one in Ontario that serves Canada, one in Georgia that serves the Southeast and one in Ojai, California, that serves the West and Southwest.

There are many Jewish camps that keep kosher and have some observance of Shabbat, but they generally accept any camper who wants a Jewish camp experience. (I spent my summers at one such camp in the Poconos, called Pinemere.) At Ramah, however, campers must be "Jewish" by the traditional Conservative definition: their mothers must have been born Jewish or have gone through Conservative conversion before giving birth. Boys must be circumcised. And, if campers are under thirteen, they must be enrolled in Hebrew school and preparing for a bar or bat mitzvah.

✡   ✡   ✡

Jeff and Cindy Blum are Ramahniks through and through. "Ramah was this incredibly supportive environment," says Cindy, who has arrived to spell her husband and be interviewed. "I always thought our Ramah friends were more important to us than our home friends."

Cindy's paternal grandfather was an Orthodox cantor. Her father became a pharmacist, and her mother worked as a bookkeeper in his pharmacy. She is a classic middle daughter, alternately easygoing or passionate, aloof or annoyed. With a masters in special education, she taught in a suburban Philadelphia public school system before switching to a non-profit agency that helps identify special-needs kids and get them services.

Cindy has powerfully mixed feelings about Har Zion, ranging from great affection to occasional condescension, all stemming from her experiences at the synagogue's suburban campus in the sixties and early seventies. Har Zion Radnor was much more communal and laid-back than the home synagogue in Wynnefield: it always had young rabbis, and its services were intimate, as compared to the pomp and circumstance of the main sanctuary in town. Radnor also had much younger lay leaders. Har Zion traditionally had a one-hundred-member board of directors, all men, to which one was elected for life: it was nearly impossible for a youthful leader to emerge. To remedy that, when the Radnor board was put together in the early sixties, it was decreed that board members had to be under forty. It was one more way in which the Radnor campus felt like the future.

When, in the 1960s, discussions began about moving Har Zion out of the city to follow its members to suburbia, the Radnor members assumed the congregation would be consolidated at their location, and a new synagogue would be built there. But, in the early seventies, Har Zion's leadership decided to abandon *both* locations to erect its current home in Penn Valley, which is in a section of the Main Line much closer to the city. Some Radnor members quit and joined another synagogue in the deep western suburbs. But many of those Radnor members who remained became the new leaders of the new Har Zion.

They stayed, primarily, because even with all the internal turmoil, Har Zion still had the best afternoon Hebrew school in the Delaware Valley, one of the best in the country. Many of these young parents were not going to force their children to go to Jewish day school, as their parents had forced them. Lower Merion, the wealthiest township in the state and one of the finest public school districts in the country, is quite culturally Jewish. The township schools even have an arrangement with the local synagogues, forged by Har Zion's headmaster, Sara Cohen, whereby kids are let out of sports team practices for Hebrew school and bar mitzvah lessons and then are allowed to skip religious lessons on game days. The Blums' kids did not want the extra segregation of attending all-day Jewish school. When Jeff and Cindy revisited the day schools they had attended, they heard a lot of rhetoric about building an "elite" of observant Jews. It didn't sound right to them.

They also found the political attitudes at the day schools somewhat troubling. To Cindy, they were too "right-wing," both in their stances on Israel and their positions on how day-school families should practice their Judaism. Telling people how observant they should be always has its risks: especially since, among Reform, Conservative and even Orthodox Jews, there is often a huge chasm between what people are "supposed to do" and what they actually do. More than the other denominations, Conservative Judaism has always been built on a foundation of pluralism for theology and observance. There is a lot of room for diversity of practice in Conservative synagogues, which is why their membership often ranges to the borderlines of Reform and Modern Orthodoxy. While there is a certain amount of tsk-tsking by the more observant to the less, congregants rarely experience the kind of direct confrontation that kids sometimes get in the day schools. Cindy didn't want her kids preached at.

"There's a great emphasis on observance and the idea that your kid might feel weird if you're not *shomer shabbos*," she says, referring to the strict rules that grow out of the biblical commandment barring "any manner of work" on Saturday, the Jewish Sabbath. Observant

Conservative and Orthodox Jews will not drive a car, or even turn on a light or stove on Shabbat, in fulfillment of that commandment.

"My impression is, if you don't keep kosher," she says, "that doctrine will be sent home and they will keep at you until you *do*." The Blums have always kept a kosher home. They just resent being told they have to.

So much to the shock of their own parents, Jeff and Cindy sent their children to public school as well as Har Zion's Hebrew school. Their son and eldest daughter have already been through the Jewish educational circuit, continuing on through Hebrew high school and a trip to Israel. Their youngest, Samantha, is currently in her next-to-last year of afternoon Hebrew school. "Sammy," as everyone calls her, is a charming star pupil who has developed a funny, buddy-buddy relationship with Rabbi Herber.

So for the Blums, the rabbi search is not just about whether Har Zion will be a great synagogue for their children. It is about the kind of synagogue it will be for them as a middle-aged couple. Will it fill their religious and intellectual needs, challenge them spiritually and cerebrally, and successfully adapt to the needs of twenty-first century American Jews? Will it be the center of the kind of community they want to grow old in?

Cindy tells me that since we first met at the Seminary, she has actually taken on another role in the rabbi search. Chairman Lou Fryman has appointed a small subcommittee that will do the first interviews with all the candidates, and ultimately make most of the decisions. Cindy was pleasantly surprised to be chosen for the subcommittee, which also includes current synagogue president Lew Grafman, former president Dr. Elihu Grossman and eminence grise Ralph Snyder. Alan Greenbaum, the easygoing, fiftyish owner of a family leather business, is in the group: he's currently a vice president, and his inclusion suggests that he might very well be the next president. The other forty-something member is Sisterhood president Lisa Berkowitz.

Carole Karsch, who was the first female president of Har Zion, is also on the subcommittee. A statuesque woman with a shock of gray hair, Carole has been an outspoken power player in Jewish Federation of Greater Philadelphia for decades, and currently serves as the organization's assistant executive vice president. Her presence brings to the committee the perspective of the world of Jewish fund-raising and socializing outside the synagogue—a world that is sometimes seen as competing with the synagogue because it offers a way of participating in secular "cultural Judaism" without necessarily addressing issues of faith or personal Jewish identity.

Carole and her husband, Sam, a lawyer who has also served as president of Har Zion, are close friends of Rabbi and Elaine. And Wolpe has certainly raised his share of money for Federation—money that is used for important local social programs. But Wolpe has also been outspoken about the sometimes divergent goals of the synagogue community and the larger Federation region, because of their differing views of how to "give back" to Judaism. Har Zion has historically been viewed as a big Federation synagogue. And Cindy Blum has some concern that "Federation types" could have too much influence over the process of choosing Wolpe's replacement.

But Cindy is far more worried that her fellow search committee members are grossly exaggerating how desirable this pulpit will be to younger rabbis.

"You know," she says, "some of these people are absolutely *delusional* about who they're going to get for a new rabbi."

As Jeff rejoins us, Cindy is decrying all the résumés that have been summarily rejected. "I feel that some of the names were discarded too hastily," she says. "Once again, it goes to the bigger picture: I think Har Zion is a bit delusional about who they can tempt. There's a newer wave of observant, dynamic rabbis out there. And Har Zion is not what it thinks it is. It's not a huge, shul-going community."

Jeff agrees. "Har Zion is a secular, suburban, country club synagogue," he says, "it's not a havurah, it's not a committed community. I hear this from my good friend who's a rabbi. He says Har Zion just isn't

that huge a draw. I don't know if it's a function of the size or the rich
suburbanites, or just that smaller synagogues around here send more
kids to day school and have more people going to shul."

Jeff and Cindy have sometimes wondered themselves about quitting
Har Zion for a smaller synagogue with a more committed community, as
some of their friends have. Beth Am Israel, just down the road, is almost
a prototype of the type of synagogue many younger Jews say they want:
more informal, more participatory, with a young, intellectually challenging rabbi and bright, politically like-minded congregants. But the Blums
remain deeply attached to Har Zion, in part because of its hugeness and
grandeur and diversity; they remain hopeful that the best of the Beth Am
experience could become one of the many religious services available
at their synaplex. And Cindy still gets goose bumps when she walks
into Har Zion's main sanctuary—a feeling she doesn't get at earthier
Beth Am. There's something temporary to her about the main room
at Beth Am, which has lovely views of the surrounding woods but is so
utilitarian, with congregants seated on folding chairs that can be easily
moved around the concrete floor. Part of going to shul for her is the up-
lifting physical sensation, and when she walks into Har Zion, it feels permanent and self-assured, full of people who know what they are doing.
The old melodies, the traditional rhythm of the service—she connects to
all that. A smaller place has its charms, but it still seems Mickey Mouse
compared to Har Zion.

As we talk, the kids come into the kitchen more frequently, especially
the youngest, Sammy. When she hears us mention Wolpe's assistant, she
bursts out "Yay, Rabbi Herber!" as if rooting for him to win something.

I get the distinct impression that the kids have decided it is time for
me to go. They want their kitchen back, as well as their parents' undi-
vided attention. So Jeff and Cindy and I agree to meet again on their day
off, preferably while the kids are still at school.

As I leave the Blums' home, I feel exhilarated. To paraphrase what a
famous rock critic once wrote after watching Bruce Springsteen perform

for the first time, I have seen the future of Har Zion, and it is the Blums. Their practical enthusiasm makes me realize that for much of a year, I have had access mostly to Rabbi Wolpe's peers, whose primary concern is to preserve the legacy of the synagogue. Both factions, of course, are crucial to any congregation's survival.

The Blums have great affection for Wolpe and are caught up in the emotion of his departure. Jeff, especially, has followed Wolpe so carefully that he can quote lines verbatim from the rabbi's sermons and imitate his every vocal inflection—perfectly elongating the Boston "aahs" until the Jews in Exodus "cutting the calf in half" sounds like "park the car in Harvard Yard." But the Blums have been ready for Wolpe's departure for some time. Even Wolpe would admit that he hasn't had the same energy for the synagogue since Elaine's illness: he has more heart but less passion. And his teaching, once legendary and challenging—I can still remember how my father came home so inspired by his Sunday morning classes, and I've heard similar stories from his congregants at Har Zion—has become a little more routine. The voice is still there, and he still knows how to work a room, but his vigor is depleted and his perspective is now several generations removed. I've still seen him teach brilliantly, but I've also seen him mail it in.

Jeff marks the change from the early nineties, when he sensed that Wolpe was cutting back the number of hours he spent with Hebrew school students, and announced that he was no longer going to attend every Friday night service, leaving some of those duties to his assistant. He blamed the responsibilities of taking care of Elaine and general "agenda fatigue" for his cutbacks. And when Jeff asked around, he found that many senior rabbis skip Friday night services, so they can be with their families and rest up for the big performance Saturday morning. Still, it just didn't seem right. "I don't understand the message," Jeff recalls telling the rabbi at the time. "Can I tell my kids that they don't have to come to Friday night services because Rabbi Wolpe doesn't have to come? Nobody is asking you to preach. You don't have to sit on the bimah. Just come to shul. Hey, we're *all* tired. He said no. He came sporadically but the board excused him because of all the things he did during the week."

Jeff has always been involved in watching and analyzing the incremental drama of the pulpit. But now that he's been made an officer of the synagogue, he has access to all the inside information. So he's like the ESPN of Har Zion clergy, a fan who became powerful enough to actually affect the course of the "sport" he follows. He'll be great fun to watch the rabbi search with. And Cindy, who is actually a player, promises she'll let me know what they're saying in the huddle.

13

THE BURNT-POTATO GUY

RABBI WOLPE HAS STOPPED SEEING HIS SHRINK. He tells me this matter-of-factly during a conversation about something else entirely. He's been going for ten months now, but it has become repetitive. "I felt I was saying the same thing over and over again," he says.

Apparently, he is having similar feelings about his role as a counselor to others. He is afraid he just can't do it anymore. He has been asked if, after retirement, he would be interested in setting up a practice with a therapist. It turns out that for-profit "pastoral counseling," getting paid hourly for what pulpit rabbis have always done for free, is becoming more and more popular among non-practicing clergy members of many faiths. The American Association of Pastoral Counselors, which grew out of the collaboration in the 1930s between minister Norman Vincent Peale and psychiatrist Smiley Blanton, has more than three thousand members offering what is called "pastoral psychotherapy," often at psychologists' prices.

But Wolpe just doesn't want to do counseling anymore. He's not sure he can still give at that level. He is beginning to see too clearly his irritation with what he calls "the nonsense of what happens in the lives of people." It's not that he wasn't always irritated by their pettiness before, he was just more understanding about their feelings—and his own.

"If a woman comes in and says she has breast cancer, then it's a very serious problem," he explains. "But if a guy comes in the next day and says his mother-in-law burned the potatoes at dinner and he's simply not going back there anymore, I may have to hit him over the head. I'm just not as tolerant with the burnt-potato guy anymore. I know it's arrogant on my part: that pettiness is important to the person who has come to me. So, it's probably best that I go off and do other things."

Still, he has heard a lot of amazing stories as a rabbi. A great number of secrets were told in his office; some he is glad to keep, others he wishes he had never heard. He can recall a couple, who are now grandparents, sitting on his couch trying to save their marriage. The woman had a lover, and the husband had found letters that the wife had hidden—not very successfully—in the closet. The rabbi asked her if she wanted her husband to find the letters. "Deep down, if you don't want him to know about the affair, you burn those letters," he said. Eventually, she admitted that she *did* want him to know, and that the affair was a form of revenge.

On the foundation of that admission, they began to rebuild. "From outward appearances, they seem to have patched things up," says Wolpe. "I see them when their grandchildren visit. But human beings are extraordinarily complex, so who can be sure?"

He recalls preventing a murder once when he was at Camp Lejeune. A marine discovered his wife had been unfaithful. He called the rabbi and said he was going to kill her. When Wolpe arrived at the house, the man was sitting on the couch with a gun trained on his wife. At issue was the upcoming bat mitzvah of their daughter. She wanted to invite her new boyfriend to the service, and her husband insisted that if she did, he would kill him right there in the synagogue. He decided, after speaking with the rabbi, not to kill his wife after all—although they did cancel the bat mitzvah and got divorced. The ex-wife later married the boyfriend and moved away. Did they live happily ever after? Wolpe can't say, but at least none of them died on his watch.

There was another congregant he talked down off a window ledge. The man was facing criminal charges, and Wolpe spent hours with him out there, telling him his kids would rally around him and even if he went to prison, he didn't need to end it all. Today the man is a grand-father in his sixties, and he has lunch with the rabbi about once a month. Every lunch begins with the man thanking him for saving his life.

Sometimes the best therapy he has been able to offer is financial as-sistance from the rabbi's special "discretionary fund." Many rabbis have access to such a fund, from which money can quietly be given to avert disasters, with no strings attached and no names on the year-end ac-counting. In the seventies, Wolpe was called to the emergency room sev-eral times because a teenager had been admitted with a drug overdose: he used the discretionary fund to pay the medical bills so the parents, al-ready estranged, didn't find out. He helped prevent several homes from being taken by the bank, and helped settle people who had moved to Israel. In the eighties and nineties, more of the fund went to women who had been left in dire straits by separation and divorce: Main Line moms who suddenly couldn't pay for their children's basic needs.

Last spring Har Zion held an extraordinarily moving rite of passage, which never would have taken place without the rabbi's discretionary fund. It was the computer-assisted bat mitzvah of Leah Zatuchni, a third-generation Har Zionite who has mitochondrial myopathy, a rare genetic condition in which the cells of the body do not produce suffi-cient energy, so the child grows with a normal physical capacity but no strength to use it. What little energy Leah has is expended on the effort simply to hold her head up or to smile from her flatbed wheelchair. She has an ethereal beauty, her heart-shaped face framed by long ringlets of brown hair and the warmth of her eyes emphasized by fluffy bangs. Leah's mind is fine—there's a complete person in there. But nobody had ever heard her voice, because she can produce nothing more than a gut-tural gargle. Then her family found out about a technology that could be used to simulate a voice. Wolpe seeded the project with several thou-sand dollars from his discretionary fund. Federation later kicked in some money; computer equipment was donated. And then Leah's classmates from Hebrew school—Har Zion has one of the few special-needs programs in the country—funneled all their charitable donations for a year to the cause. More than ten thousand dollars was raised for the hardware, software and technical consulting necessary to provide Leah with a computer-generated voice. She typed out her entire bat mitzvah with painstaking patience, letter by letter, in Hebrew and in English. And then the computer was programmed to speak or chant the words in the shimmering vocal inflections of a silicon-chip angel. The keyboard was even equipped with an "Amen" button, so that she could respond to the prayers of the cantor. At the triumphant conclusion of the service, she kept pushing the "Amen" button playfully until the congregation erupted in laughter.

A lot of Wolpe's most intense interpersonal work has been done before and after funerals. He recalls a woman marching into his office right after her father died. She closed the door.

"I'm going to tell you about my father," she said. "He was miserable and he abused me as a child and I've had problems with my own marriage and I'm going to a psychiatrist. I'm going through hell mourning my father, but I'm glad he's dead."

Then she walked out, leaving him to prepare the eulogy.

Nothing a rabbi does is more important than eulogizing. This was one of the first lessons Wolpe learned as a young clergyman, and he learned it from a master. He recalls being lectured on the subject by Dr. Joachim Prinz, the legendary immigrant rabbi who was one of the first to speak out against Hitler from his Berlin pulpit in the early 1930s, and later became well known in the American civil rights movement from his pulpit at the historic North Jersey congregation Temple B'nai Abraham. Prinz was famous for giving the speech that preceded Martin Luther King's "I Have a Dream" sermon at the Lincoln Memorial in the 1963 March on Washington. "Bigotry and hatred are not the most urgent problem," he said that day. "The most urgent, the most disgraceful, the most shameful and the most tragic problem is silence."

Wolpe got to know Prinz in the early fifties when he was a rabbinical student and was asked to help out when B'nai Abraham's assistant rabbi left for a chaplaincy. He recalls Prinz telling him a story about the funeral of his own first wife, who had died during childbirth in Germany only a year after they had married. Prinz explained how devastating her death was: he was wracked with guilt, contemplating suicide. And he said the eulogy preached at her funeral had literally saved his life. While he never revealed to the young rabbi exactly what had been said at the funeral, his message to Wolpe was clear.

"Never fudge on a eulogy," he said. "Sometimes you're tired on a Friday night and you might wing it. But never, *ever,* wing it at a funeral."

I ask Wolpe about a recent funeral at which I know he officiated. The father of Ruth, a friend of mine, died after a long illness. He was not a member of the congregation, and the rabbi had never met him. But Ruth, her husband and their twins had just joined Har Zion. Since she was organizing the funeral arrangements for her bereaved mother, she wanted *her* rabbi to do it.

Afterward, she told me how much Wolpe's eulogy had moved her. He had picked up on things about her father that were mentioned in an article she had shared with him: his love of family, his fascination with Jewish studies and art. Wolpe had taken that information and linked it to the holiday that was approaching, Hanukkah, the Festival of Lights. The central image of Hanukkah is the menorah, a special candelabra with spaces for eight candles, and a ninth with which to light them. The menorah commemorates the miracle of the oil, which was found in the temple in Jerusalem after Jews liberated it from the Greeks; the oil burned for eight days when it should have lasted only one. Wolpe explained that the menorah is also considered the first artistic symbol in Judaism. The adding of a candle each night for eight nights is also associated with the powerful metaphor of extending light in the world. Ruth's dad, he said, had spent his entire life always lighting another candle. He was always "extending the light."

It was as if the rabbi had known him his entire life. That's what Ruth's family said. And that's what so many other mourners have told him over the years after he eulogized their dead with uncanny insight, regardless of whether he knew the person in life. He lets me in on his secret for conveying this sense of utter familiarity. He asks the family questions before the funeral, and then repeats their answers back to them in the eulogy. The less he knows firsthand, the less leeway he will allow himself to improvise and interpret. In fact, in the rare instances when the feedback after a funeral is less than glowing, it is often because he has strayed from what the family told him.

Ironically, when he eulogizes someone he knew well he runs a greater risk of displeasing the family, because then he can share his own memories and interpretations, which may deviate from the family's image. As last words, these better-informed eulogies may very well be more fitting and more "true," capturing the deceased as he or she really was, and really would have wanted to be remembered. But funerals are for the living.

Sometimes, coaxing memories from family members before funerals can be extremely difficult. "It's murder when they have nothing to tell you," he says. "You dissolve into clichés—'he should be remembered, he should be loved,' whatever. Here's someone who had a long life and devoted a great deal of time to you. So, I say, 'Tell me about your mother.' "

"She was a good lady."

". . . and what else?"

"She loved her family."

"OK . . ."

"And she made very good *schnecken*."

"So now I have three pieces of information. And one thing they are saying to me is she really didn't go anywhere or do anything. So I make her 'creating a home where everybody felt comfortable,' try to weave it into something that is positive." It is sometimes easier to write a compassionate eulogy if the family members share negative memories, because at least they are real and allow him to conjure a specific person.

"Sometimes I feel like a eulogy has really gotten through, and other times I'm not sure I made it," he says. "I'm surprised that they come up and say it was so meaningful and touching because I don't personally feel it was meaningful or touching."

His first funeral as rabbi of Har Zion was a test of fire. Just days after Wolpe arrived in Philadelphia, Abner Schreiber, the powerful and controlling Russian-born philanthropist who had recently retired as Har Zion president, lost his wife, Mary. Schreiber was a close friend of Har Zion's original rabbi, Simon Greenberg, and Wolpe assumed the revered clergyman would return to give the eulogy. Instead, when Wolpe visited the family, they started telling him about Mary Schreiber as if *he* would be officiating. He must have looked confused, because Abner Schreiber said, "Rabbi Greenberg is a wonderful man but he always speaks too long. I have heard about you, and I would like you to speak about Mary." The eulogy went well, and afterward the rabbi and his family were treated to their first example of Har Zion luxe. Since the shiva prevented the Schreibers from using their summer homes in the elite Long Beach Island community of Loveladies, the Wolpes were given one of the houses for a family vacation. It was there, together on the breezy barrier island, that they watched the first man walk on the moon.

Schreiber's family was also the cause of Wolpe's first major confrontation with his new congregation on the sticky subject of intermarriage. Jews marrying outside their faith is a huge, complex issue, often identified as the number-one threat to the future of the religion; one-half of America's Jews marry outside the faith, according to estimates, and only one-third of the children of those intermarriages are raised as Jews. Yet it is not a subject that comes up a lot at Har Zion, because everyone knows there isn't much to talk about. Conservative rabbis, like their Orthodox colleagues, are not allowed to officiate at mixed marriages— no exceptions to the rule. They may perform wedding ceremonies only for people who were either born Jewish or have converted under the rigorous training of Conservative or Orthodox rabbis. (Reform rabbis are permitted to decide for themselves whether to officiate at mixed marriages, and at that time it was common for them to do so.) Conservative rabbis are also not permitted to officiate at bar or bat mitzvahs of children whose mothers are not Jewish, and they are strongly discouraged from attending receptions for weddings or bar mitzvahs where the food is not strictly kosher.

Most people have known better than to ask Rabbi Wolpe even to discuss deviating from these hard and fast rules. He tells me about his first run-in over the subject at Har Zion. One of Abner Schreiber's grandsons got engaged to a woman whose father was Jewish and whose mother wasn't. "I wouldn't officiate, and these people went *ballistic*," Wolpe recalls. "They told everybody how I wouldn't officiate, and then said they'd get a Reform rabbi and have it at the Radnor gardens," the lovely outdoor space the family had helped fund at the synagogue's suburban campus. Wolpe then told them they couldn't use the gardens either.

"If they were furious before, you can imagine how they were then," he says. "They were brutal. Then one day I'm in my office and the phone rings. It's Abner, and my heart went down to my toes. I loved this man and I know he loved me. He took a paternal interest in me, and I figured he was going to tell me I should do this—and that would mean the end of a relationship that had been important to me. I picked up the phone. He said, 'Rabbi'—he had this thick accent—'Rabbi, Abner Schreiber here. Rabbi, stick by your guns.' And I burst out crying, literally."

Abner Schreiber had three daughters, one of whom married a Jewish man named Herskovitz, who owned a woodworking company that did much of the gorgeous woodwork at the new Har Zion. Their son is Marshall Herskovitz, who grew up at the synagogue, and went on to become the award-winning creator of *thirtysomething* as well as other successful TV shows and feature films that mine the drama of human love and angst.

I call Marshall Herskovitz, whom I know from writing a couple of cover stories about *thirtysomething* years ago, to see what he remembers about Wolpe refusing to marry his cousin. He says he recalls it vividly—although perhaps not quite as vividly as he recalls Wolpe refusing to officiate at his *own* wedding, because his fiancée wasn't Jewish either. "We had a good, close relationship with him, and I was surprised how adamant his feelings were on the subject," Marshall says. "He sent a letter back to us that was polite but tough. And it turned out to be hard to find a rabbi." But his biggest concern about intermarrying wasn't finding a rabbi, it was confronting his grandfather. "I thought he would react violently against us," he recollects. "But Abner had great respect for anybody who followed their own beliefs and no respect for people who were spineless."

I tell him it never ceases to amaze me how strongly imprinted those early religious experiences are, regardless of how far people have since run from them. Marshall has been in Hollywood for over twenty years, but the details of his life as a young Jew at Har Zion are immediately accessible. It is no coincidence that in his first hit show, the main character was a Jewish man in Philadelphia with a non-Jewish wife, who struggled with the place of Judaism in his life, especially after his father's sudden death. And his most recent TV show, *Once and Again,* focuses on a half-Jewish woman who starts out divorced but later remarries a non-Jewish man who surprises her on their wedding day by learning the Hebrew prayers for the service.

While living in Southern California, where he belongs to a synagogue, Marshall still pays some attention to the greater Har Zion community through his family.

"Did you know Wolpe's son is a rabbi out here?" he asks.

So I've heard.

Wolpe is counting the days until he leaves Har Zion. "Three more sermons to go," he says, without a hint of wistfulness in his voice.

His last Shabbat on the pulpit will be on January 9, and when a new problem comes up in a staff meeting, he says, only half joking, "Why don't you tackle this on January eleventh?" That's when he starts his sabbatical, much of which will be spent on Singer Island in Florida, where many of Har Zion's older, wealthier members migrate for snowbird season. The Wolpes are scheduled to return in the spring for several events commemorating the seventy-fifth anniversary of Har Zion. And then they'll be feted in June, at the annual black-tie dinner dance. It is there that Rabbi Wolpe should be able to formally introduce his replacement.

The only thing he plans to remain involved with at the synagogue is fund-raising. The leadership has asked him to help them raise the money they need to build the new wing of the Hebrew school and expand the endowment fund.

"I have raised a tremendous amount of money for these people," he says. "I'm not sure this building would be here if not for me. Back then, I went out with the laypeople and worked day and night for this place. It took a lot out of me. But I still have relationships with the people who can produce the sums they need."

The final weeks pass in a weepy jump-cut sequence of last times and good-bye events. There's the last Hebrew school Shabbat—one of several Saturday services through the year run by lay groups—for which Jeff and Cindy Blum's daughter, Sammy, gives the farewell speech: "Rabbi Wolpe, you and I go *way* back," she wisecracks.

There's the last Hanukkah, with the Hebrew school's annual family party. (I had to skip that to go home and make latkes—the traditional potato pancakes—with my extended family, using my Pop-pop's recipe: grated potatoes, grated onion and the secret ingredient, knuckle blood from all that grating. We still have all his cruddy old frying pans and aprons, and my Aunt Barb, my brother Dan and I slave over the hot stove until we all smell crisply fried.)

There's the last big society wedding. The synagogue is crawling with Secret Service agents the entire night because Attorney General Janet Reno is attending the marriage of her special counsel, Kinney Zalesne, who grew up at Har Zion.

And there's the last Torah Fund luncheon of the Sisterhood, the women's service organization of the synagogue of which Elaine Wolpe was once queen bee. At the climax of the affair, Elaine surprises the audience by speaking in public for only the second time since her health crisis. She does so with the assistance of a new computerized device that captures snippets of her speech and edits out the pregnant pauses: ". . . thirty years Sisterhood, twenty-seven years Hadassah . . . work hard . . . I love Sisterhood . . . now my reign is through . . . next year, young people, good people . . . my husband, unbelievable . . . kind man, kind heart . . . new rabbi: never, *ever* try to imitate . . . wherever we go, I'm here and the rabbi is here . . . good-bye."

14

GOD, I HOPE I GET IT

THE FIRST RABBI CANDIDATE is highly qualified for the job. He has been on the pulpit for eighteen years, at two strong congregations in New Jersey: first Shomrei Emunah, a tiny gem of a synagogue in the New York suburb of Montclair, and then at larger Temple Beth Ahm in nearby Springfield. He is the head of the rabbinic advisory counsel for his local day school. And he's just published a book that will influence clergy around the world for decades to come: he is coeditor of the new *Rabbi's Manual*. It's the first update in more than thirty years of the little black book—*books*, actually, since it now comes in two handsome, pocket-size leather-bound volumes—used by rabbis to officiate at anything from a bris to an unveiling. It comes with special laminated pullout cards for weddings and funerals.

Yet Rabbi Perry Rank has a problem right away as a candidate, and it's because of the way he wears his kippah. He's nearly bald, which presents a problem for men who wear one all the time: there's no easy place to attach the clip to secure it. So, Perry Rank wears his sidesaddle, sloped down to the right where there's still some hair, instead of centered. It's a completely logical solution to a vexing problem. But it makes him look somewhat goofy.

The search subcommittee gives Rabbi Rank a chance to impress them, and he does: he is personable, smart, committed, experienced. But with the jaunty tip of his kippah, he would have to be the second coming of Rabbi Akiba to convince them to bring him back to meet the full committee.

He starts out with a d'var Torah on the week's parasha, and then takes questions. He grew up in Minneapolis, trained at the Seminary; his wife's a Jewish educator and author, they have three kids. Then he talks a little bit about the *Rabbi's Manual,* the existence of which would normally not be well known outside of the clergy, but his update actually got some lay press. It is the first such manual to contain a grieving ritual to be held after an abortion. And the ritual has an interesting Har Zion tie-in. The prayer itself was written by Rabbi Amy Eilberg, a Philadelphia native who was the first woman to be ordained by the Conservative movement, in the mid-eighties, and who had her first and only pulpit as assistant rabbi at Har Zion. (She left after only one year, eventually becoming a popular teacher and writer.)

Rabbi Rank is doing well enough until he is asked what kinds of source material he uses for his sermons. He begins telling the group about a recent sermon he gave that invoked Bob Dylan and his return to Judaism.

Uh-oh, wrong answer, Cindy Blum thinks to herself. Dylan's freewheeling spiritual search isn't going to fly with this group; they want to hear about rabbinics, scholarly work, religious sources. From the moment the words "Bob Dylan" come out of his mouth, Rank's interview is over, like a first date that has suddenly revealed itself to be the last date. There is nothing left to do but maintain politeness until the interview's conclusion. Fortunately, Lou Fryman knows how to move things along. He begins by subtly cutting off answers to prevent elaboration. And when Rank thanks them for their consideration, everyone in the room knows he will not be the new rabbi.

Over the next weeks, more candidates are shuttled in and out. One whom the committee likes is Rabbi Michael Wasserman, currently at

Temple Beth-El in Birmingham, Alabama. Wasserman is from Boston, went to Harvard and then entered the Seminary in his mid-twenties. His first rabbinic job was as the director of outreach at the 92nd Street Y in Manhattan, where he worked with interfaith couples and young singles; then he had pulpits on Long Island and in Rhode Island before taking the job at Beth-El, a seven-hundred-family synagogue in Birmingham, where he's finishing his second three-year contract.

Wasserman is an interesting prospect because his wife, Elana Kanter, is also an ordained rabbi. Even though they have three growing kids, she serves as his associate rabbi at Beth-El, and as educational director of the synagogue. If Wasserman were selected, Har Zion wouldn't have to worry about a rebbitzin who was too involved in her secular career to play an active role in the congregation. But the rabbi is still just testing the waters. He isn't sure he's ready to leave Birmingham, or whether Har Zion is right for him. Still, he comes right away when the synagogue offers to fly him in for an interview. He gives a strong d'var Torah greeted by a chorus of congratulatory yasher koachs, and before heading back home he visits the nearby Akiba Hebrew Academy, the oldest all-day Jewish high school in the country, which has strong links to Har Zion. The school was located at Har Zion Wynnefield before moving to its own building. One of Wasserman's reasons for considering a new pulpit is that there is no Jewish high school in Birmingham for his kids, the oldest of whom is ten.

In the meantime, the committee attempts to generate more interest in the Har Zion position. Even though it is expressly against the Rabbinical Assembly rules—and Rabbi Herber has given the Two Lews a little lecture on the dangers of getting excommunicated by the RA—the synagogue is reaching out directly to a number of rabbis to see if they would be interested in applying. They have a master wish list that the committee has divvied up.

It includes Bradley Shavit Artson, who recently left a pulpit in Mission Viejo, California, after ten years, in part because he and his wife have an autistic son, and they felt they needed to be in a big city. He applied for the job at Sinai Temple that went to David Wolpe, and now has an academic position at the UJ in Los Angeles. They also want to check into Rabbi Jay Rosenbaum, who has a pulpit at mid-sized Temple Beth Israel in Worcester, Massachusetts, but is nationally known because he let the religion writer from *The New Yorker* tail him for several months while he labored to put together a synagogue trip to Israel. The resulting book, *And They Shall Be My People,* was one that many rabbis around the country, including Rabbi Wolpe, were invited to critique for their local papers.

Rabbi Alan Silverstein, at Agudath Israel in Caldwell, New Jersey, is also on the wish list. Silverstein is a former president of the RA, and has written books on the dilemmas of interfaith dating and marriage; as a nationally known expert on the subject, he addresses both sides of this controversial issue. While he is outspoken in his belief that parents should discourage Jewish children from dating non-Jews, he also believes interfaith couples should be welcomed into synagogue communities with the hope of fostering an environment that might give the non-Jewish spouse an incentive to convert, rather than an ultimatum.

The Har Zion search committee has also reached out to Rabbi Daniel Nevins, the young assistant rabbi at Adat Shalom in the northern Detroit suburb of Farmington Hills. The synagogue is much the same size as Har Zion, and also has a longtime rabbi heading toward retirement age. Ironically, that rabbi is Efry Spectre, who began his career as an assistant rabbi at Har Zion in the 1960s. Danny Nevins has been Spectre's assistant for nearly five years, since graduating from JTS at the age of twenty-eight. He's flattered by the inquiry, but he is happy at Adat Shalom and, besides, he hasn't been a rabbi long enough to apply to Har Zion. With the placement rules, his only chance of becoming a senior rabbi at a large congregation any time soon is if he succeeds Spectre: then he can use the RA's special exception for six years service to one congregation as assistant, and not have to wait until he has been ordained for ten full years. In fact, that's what the congregation has in mind, so Nevins politely demurs.

Of course, Har Zion would love to get Gordon Tucker. A philosophy scholar in his fifties, Tucker is best known to the public because his first wife, Hadassah, is now married to Connecticut senator Joseph Lieberman. (They have a son together, who is a student at the Seminary.) But Tucker has also served as a White House Fellow during the Carter administration. And for a long time he was dean of the Seminary's rabbinical school, until his vocal efforts to liberalize Conservative Judaism—especially when it comes to acceptance of homosexual rights, and then gay marriage—were widely assumed to have jeopardized his position. So, in 1994, he and his second wife and their two children moved to White Plains, New York, where he took a pulpit with an eight-hundred-family synagogue, Temple Israel Center, replacing Rabbi Arnold Turetsky. And he can still get into Manhattan to teach at the Seminary.

Tucker would have the right combination of intelligence and star quality. But he's very taken. He is happy at Temple Israel, and his wife has a job she really loves with the New York Botanical Garden.

The Har Zion search committee has also informally expressed interest in Rabbi Gerald Skolnik, at the Forest Hills Jewish Center, one of the dozens of synagogues in Queens, New York, and Rabbi Stanley Rosenbaum at Tifereth Israel in Lincoln, Nebraska, a town of two hundred thousand people, which has 170 churches and only two synagogues.

And then there's the potential local candidate, David Ackerman, whose name has been thrown into the ring by Danny Wolpe and several others. Ackerman is rabbi at Tiferet Bet Israel, a synagogue half the size of Har Zion, but growing rapidly along with its hometown, the northwestern Philadelphia suburb of Blue Bell. He has taught adult education classes at Har Zion and has done work with Federation, so a number of Har Zion members know him. Some are uncomfortable with the idea of poaching a rabbi from another Philadelphia-area synagogue, but he has been approached informally by several search committee members.

They have yet to hear if Ackerman will apply for the position. But he is clearly mulling it over. So, even though most search committee members have never met the man, and none have seen him run a service, there is a growing feeling that Ackerman could be the guy. He's in his late thirties, a terrific speaker, good-looking. Some say he could be the next David Wolpe.

Rabbi Jacob Herber wipes his hand across his broad forehead and sniffles hard. He looks like a medical student who has just finished a bloody twenty-four-hour shift and knows any chance of sleep is still a long way off. That is, if his eighteen-month-old daughter will allow it.

This is the moment he has been waiting for since his graduation from rabbinical school almost three years ago: the fulfillment of any young rabbi's dream, to be mara d'atra, the "master of the house" who has the last word on all religious debates within the congregation.

At the moment, however, he is so tired and confused that he can barely muster the strength to be miserable. When he agreed to fill in during Wolpe's sabbatical, he was so excited about the unexpected opportunity that he didn't give much thought to the reality. Not only would he be taking on all of the senior rabbi's responsibilities—funerals, bar mitzvahs, weddings, meetings, decisions big and small—but there would be no assistant rabbi, no Jacob Herber, to help him. How was he to run a shul as large as Har Zion without an assistant? Out at Sinai Temple, David Wolpe has two assistant rabbis—although he refers to them as "co-rabbis" in a novel model of shared responsibilities—and the clergy is still overworked.

Ever since Herber and his family returned from a brief vacation before his full responsibilities kicked in, it has been nonstop pressure. A pipe burst in their building while they were away, so the apartment was completely flooded. The moment Herber arrived at the synagogue on his first day as mara d'atra the phones started ringing. He never realized how many calls Rabbi Wolpe fielded in a day, or how much of the follow-up he would be doing himself without a full-time secretary or

administrative assistant. A receptionist in the front office whose job includes answering all the clergy and top executives' phones is his only
support staff. At his first meeting as ranking clergy member he got into
heated discussion with executive director Howard Griffel—the first of
many—about whether men should have to wear kippahs in the sanctuaries during secular events. With the yearlong seventy-fifth anniversary
celebration in full swing, there were going to be a lot of secular programs
held in the sanctuaries. Herber decided that his first act as mara d'atra
would be to make sure that men were requested to cover their heads
during these events.

Griffel claimed that this was contrary to Rabbi Wolpe's way of doing
things. In fact, the synagogue had only followed Wolpe's lead: *he* didn't
always wear a kippah while in the building, unless he was actually praying, or studying, or performing some other specific religious function.
But Herber insisted. He was not going to be able to make wholesale
changes at Har Zion during his six months in charge before the new
rabbi came, but there were a few policies he could initiate. The kippah
laxity had always bugged him. It may have seemed like a small matter,
but it had great symbolic significance. Herber felt it was important for
people to understand that the whole synagogue was sacred space, every
day. And in sacred space, men are supposed to cover their heads.

So, last week, when Har Zion's seventy-fifth anniversary committee
sponsored a speech by former *New York Times* managing editor A. M.
Rosenthal on "Jews, Politics and the Media," there was a prominent request in the printed program notes that men cover their heads in the
sanctuary. It was a modest but meaningful victory for Herber. And the
event itself was a huge success. The sold-out appearance by the legendary journalist was followed by a panel discussion, taped for public
radio, in which he was joined by the editor of the *Philadelphia Inquirer*
and the anchor of the region's top-rated TV newscast—both Jewish. One
highlight was Rosenthal admitting that "A.M. is an idiotic name. In those
days all reporters named Abraham were asked to use initials—it was like
a second circumcision!"

✿   ✿   ✿

When I sit down with him in his study, Rabbi Herber is fighting this cold, his apartment still smells like a wet dog and his patience has been pushed to the breaking point. And he has only been mara d'atra for a few weeks.

But he does his best to paint a cheery picture of his new job. He claims that so far it has been more manageable than he expected. Although he wonders if he has the *sachel,* the wisdom, to handle a congregation this size, he feels that mastery of the task is within his reach. And he has had nice feedback from congregants for the small touches he added to services to make them more his own.

For example, the first week after Wolpe left, Herber posed a question from the bimah during his Shabbat d'var Torah. Not a rhetorical question—an actual question, which he hoped someone seated below him would answer out loud. This technique has become relatively common in synagogues and churches across the country. It is a favorite of younger clergy interested in more participatory services. But it is generally not done in the Har Zion main sanctuary during Saturday morning Shabbat services. Maybe at the more informal Friday night services, or in the small chapel during the summer. But almost never on the big stage.

Many younger rabbis come down off the bimah when they ask these types of questions. Some use wireless lapel microphones and others employ handheld mikes, which is why they are jokingly referred to as "Phil Donahue rabbis." Herber isn't sure Har Zion is quite ready for an off-the-bimah sermon quite yet. It might be too shocking to the older congregants, who love Har Zion precisely because it is High Church. And the older congregants still donate most of the money. Younger people always want change, but they rarely donate anything more than change.

So Herber will continue to ask his questions from the bimah. And he will try to institute other small changes so that his months as mara d'atra might have a lasting impact on this congregation, without impeding the new rabbi from making the place his own.

Yet his time in charge might be brief. He understands that members of the search committee are planning to take a field trip to Birmingham to see Rabbi Wasserman in action.

And more and more people are talking about David Ackerman, even though he still hasn't applied for the job yet, which is why he has asked the committee not to come and check out his services. A crew from the Main Line would be conspicuous, and he prefers that his congregants not know he would consider leaving.

But Ackerman can't stop me from coming. One of the best things about covering rabbis and synagogues is that you always know where your sources, and potential sources, will be on Saturday morning. All I have to do is show up at Ackerman's synagogue, Tiferet Bet Israel, a spanking new temple on a road called Skippack Pike. It was built with the new money from the booming economy around Blue Bell, which is actually a suburb of a suburb: King of Prussia, the superburb built around the buzz of a GE headquarters, a shopping mall that was once the largest in the world and the first Ikea outpost in the United States. The synagogue is a low, beige stucco structure with a drive-through that makes it look like a very long bank. It's on a highway with several growing houses of worship.

The main sanctuary at Tiferet Bet Israel is much smaller than Har Zion's and seems deliberately less dramatic. There is no real separation between the bimah and the seating area, so when Rabbi Ackerman steps away from his pulpit to speak directly to his congregants, which he does easily and often, he is not descending from above.

Ackerman is a Long Islander with the self-assurance of a surgeon. With his winning grin, balding pate and impeccably tailored suit, the man knows how to work a room. As I sit down, he is doing the *misheberach* like a Torah talk-show host.

Misheberach is a special prayer offered for the sick. In more traditional synagogues, congregants alert the rabbi or front office in advance that they want a misheberach said on Shabbat, and provide the Hebrew

name of the person who is ill. A list is printed out for the cantor ahead of
time, and each name is chanted during the prayer. At Tiferet Bet Israel,
like many more informal synagogues, it is the custom for Rabbi Ackerman
to ask if anyone attending services would like to add a name to the
misheberach list. People are requested to stand and, when he points to
them, to recite the name in Hebrew or English. It is then repeated by the
cantor. Anyone can participate, regardless of whether or not they are
synagogue members, or even Jewish. For many, this type of misheberach
can be the most personal, meaningful prayer in the entire service.

Because this is the annual Women's League/Men's Club Sabbath, in
which members of the male and female service organizations run the
service, I don't get to observe Ackerman in action as much as I would
like. But, at first glance, he does seem very presidential, very much the
kind of rabbi who could succeed at Har Zion. After services, I approach
him and introduce myself, asking if he will speak with me. He says that
an interview would be premature, since he's still undecided about applying for the position. He seems sincere in his indecision.

Two days later, I hear that Ackerman has told the RA that he is interested in the Har Zion job and asked them to forward his résumé. An
interview date is announced immediately, because there is no time to
waste. The rabbi search committee has been meeting for well over a year
now, and most members feel they have little to show for it. The candidates have not been what they expected, and they have been expressing
their dismay to the RA for some time—as if the rabbi's union were hiding the really good ones from them. Ackerman is the only rabbi on their
original wish list who has even agreed to be interviewed. And even that
took quite a bit of courting.

The rabbi comes to Har Zion on a Tuesday evening, when the
synagogue is largely empty. Many of the lights in the main rooms have
already been turned off, but they can be reignited by motion detector if
someone enters. The interview is held in the Presidents' room, at a long

conference table. It's the select committee—the Two Lews, Ralph Snyder, Cindy Blum, Carole Karsch, Alan Greenbaum, Dr. Eli Grossman—plus a couple of members of the larger committee filling in for those who can't make it.

The interview begins, as the others did, with a d'var Torah. Ackerman has his written out on three-by-five cards, and when he appears a little nervous, Lou Fryman says, "Relax, you're among friends." And, for the first time in the rabbi search process, a candidate really does seem to be among friends; this is the first person they've seen who they can really imagine as their spiritual leader. Ackerman invokes the week's Torah reading about Moses and the parting of the Red Sea. It is the same parasha that Wolpe expounded on during that disastrous bat mitzvah one year before, but Ackerman's interpretation is completely different. He talks about what Moses and the Israelites had to take with them to make their journey to Israel a positive one, comparing their situation to his own in deciding how to make the journey to the pulpit at Har Zion. He speaks for nearly ten minutes, careful to make eye contact with each committee member. Then the floor is opened to questions.

The first two questions are really statements. Carole Karsch speaks effusively about her experiences with Ackerman at Federation events, which impresses some of the older members of the committee but prompts Cindy Blum to roll her eyes. Ralph Snyder elaborates on the themes of the d'var Torah, as he is wont to do, discussing the need for inspirational leadership until Lou Fryman interrupts him.

"Ralph," he says, "do you have a *question*?"

Eventually, Ackerman is asked about his background, his work at his current synagogue, why he was ambivalent about applying to Har Zion and what he would do with the place. He grew up in Great Neck— which is to New York what Lower Merion is to Philadelphia—and attended public schools. He was active in his synagogue, Temple Israel of Great Neck, where he was inspired by the legendary Rabbi Mordecai Waxman. Now in his eighties and the recipient of many awards from Jewish and Christian groups for his work in interfaith relations—he was the first rabbi to be honored by the pope as a Knight Commander of the Order of Saint Gregory the Great—Waxman is still on the pulpit after more than fifty years.

Ackerman was also very much influenced by one of Waxman's former assistants, Rabbi Harold Kushner, a marvelous sermonizer who began at Temple Israel in Great Neck but later became rabbi at another Temple Israel (there are many more synagogues than there are synagogue names), a smaller, five-hundred-family congregation in the Boston suburb of Natick. It was there that he wrote the 1981 best-seller *When Bad Things Happen to Good People,* inspired in part by the death of his fourteen-year-old son from progeria, a genetic disease that causes premature aging. Kushner was later one of Ackerman's instructors at the Seminary.

But Ackerman also says something very interesting about Waxman and Kushner. He says that twenty-five years ago congregants thought it was a big deal if their rabbi was well known. Today, however, people are looking for a rabbi who *knows them well.*

At Har Zion, of course, they want both.

Ackerman explains that he began as an assistant at Anshe Emet Synagogue in Chicago before being hired by the two congregations that had joined together in Blue Bell to form Tiferet Bet Israel. One of his first major tasks was to help the two groups mend their differences, which he accomplished by holding a series of parlor meetings in people's homes so they could get to know him.

He says he also revamped the High Holiday services at the synagogue to increase participation, which leads to a discussion about the current structure of services at Har Zion. Many older members say they love High Holiday services exactly the way they are. Some of the younger congregants, who aren't willing to pay for the seats closest to the bimah, feel differently, suggesting that perhaps the "fashion show" should be dismantled and the synagogue should run a variety of different services in different rooms. The dialogue prompts Cindy Blum to ask how open he is to entertaining and facilitating change. She likes his answer: he says he believes in change, as long as it has a purpose.

He talks about having a learning session on Shabbat morning before services, and is surprised to hear that Har Zion doesn't offer one. He knows that Beth Am, down the street, has one. For a half hour before services begin, a small group of interested congregants meets informally in the rabbi's study to discuss the week's Torah reading. And those who don't care for formal services spend Shabbat in the library studying.

Ackerman is asked how he would help Har Zion increase the number of young people who come to services. While he offers a few ideas that worked in his current synagogue, he also uses the opportunity to mention that one of his misgivings about coming to Har Zion is the poor youth turnout. The number of Har Zion kids attending Jewish day school, going to Camp Ramah, visiting Israel or just showing up at Saturday morning services and having Shabbat lunch with a few families from the synagogue is certainly not rising. They ask whether he is shomer shabbos, Sabbath observant, but they are only really interested in one aspect of his religious practice: whether he and his family walk to synagogue. He currently drives, only because there is no housing within walking distance of his synagogue. If he changed jobs, he would want to be in a community where his kids knew what it was like to walk home from shul with a group of people and have a meal together. He wonders if that kind of environment can be fostered at Har Zion.

There is a little discussion about money. The Seminary gives candidates a rough idea of the salary range. According to RA estimates, total compensation packages for Conservative rabbis range from $55,000 to $235,000, depending on the location and size of the synagogue. David Wolpe's synagogue in Los Angeles has typically been at the top of the pay scale: he started there, without a day of pulpit experience, at a salary of $200,000 plus a housing allowance and other benefits, and reasonably expects far more if he and the synagogue decide to make a long-term commitment. His father, however, makes far less than that: after thirty years, Rabbi Gerald Wolpe earns only $130,000 a year in salary, plus free use of the home the synagogue owns across the street. His pay is low because he has been there so long and because he is, by his own admission, a really bad financial negotiator. Like many rabbis of his generation, he has always depended on the kindness of parishioners. And they have usually come through. Right now, in fact, a small group of wealthy Har Zionites is quietly putting together a fund so he and Elaine can make a substantial down payment on the condo they want to buy in town.

Younger rabbis can't count on that kind of old-fashioned largesse, and expect high salaries when they first accept major jobs like the senior rabbi position at Har Zion. Jeff Blum has told me Wolpe has been "really underpaid" and that the synagogue expects to spend $180,000, perhaps even $190,000, in starting salary alone for the right candidate.

Ackerman asks if Har Zion has ever had problems negotiating with employees, because he has some experience in that area. Lew Grafman says absolutely not. In fact, he just returned from a convention in Chicago of top officers from the nation's largest Conservative synagogues, and he couldn't believe the horror stories he was hearing about exploded relationships between rabbis and congregations. There has been none of that at Har Zion, he says. After all, the congregation has had only three rabbis in seventy-five years.

Grafman is careful not to share with Ackerman, however, the other insight he had at the convention in Chicago. Almost every congregational leader looking for a new rabbi was complaining about this year's crop of applicants. Most of them said they hadn't seen one rabbi they would consider hiring. While Grafman kvetched along with them, he actually was feeling pretty smug. He knew they had Ackerman in the bag, so if no other good applicants emerged, Har Zion would still end up with a young-star rabbi.

Ackerman's interview goes on for nearly two hours, and while he expresses some frank concerns about the synagogue and the job, it all seems to be going well. He tells the committee a little bit about his scholarly agenda: he is considered among his peers to be a fount of knowledge in many obscure areas of Jewish study. This is welcome news, since not all rabbis are intellectually ambitious enough to even have scholarly agendas.

When they ask for more details about his family, he pulls pictures of his sons out of the folder he brought for his résumé and application. But when the committee asks if they can send a group up to watch him in action, he still balks. Nobody from his shul except a few top leaders know he is here interviewing, and he is still not certain that he will accept the Har Zion job if it is offered. What he would like to do is bring his wife down to synagogue for Shabbat in the very near future. A lot depends on his family's feeling about the place.

15

THE FACE-TO-FACE ROOM

IT'S SUPER SUNDAY, the biggest day of fund-raising on the Jewish calendar, and the grown-ups have taken over the elementary-school wing of the Jewish Community Center in Wynnewood. They have set up a command post in the school auditorium, where large utility tables and chairs have been arranged into five long rows so some three hundred volunteers can work the phones.

Bussed in from various congregations across the Delaware Valley, the volunteers all wear "Super Sunday '99" T-shirts. Next to their phones are piles of cards, each containing the name of one Jew who has given money to Federation at some point in his or her life, and how much. These people are being called to ask if they will give again, preferably more than before. If they're not home, the card goes into one of three large recycling bins: one for $1–$99 givers, another for $100–$249 givers, and a third for $250–$499 givers. After $500, a little more care is taken than just a cold call. And those who give in the thousands each year are invited to come to the Super Sunday site for more personal attention. They get "the face-to-face."

I bump into Ralph Snyder. This is the first time I have ever seen him in a sweater and slacks. In fact, I feel somewhat startled by the casual appearance of so many Har Zionites I am accustomed to seeing dressed in suits. Ralph says he and Lew Grafman are heading to their face-to-face room, and ask if I want to tag along. As we leave, an announcement comes over the PA system that they have just passed the three-hundred-thousand-dollar mark for the day. And it's still only 1:30.

Our destination is a classroom with all the desks pushed into one corner and a sign out front that says "Face-to-Face Room." As we go in, a flock of little girls goes flying by with their oversized Super Sunday T-shirts hanging down to their knees. Among those in the room waiting to assist with the "face-to-facing" are the Goldenbergs, the energetic pair who are this year's Super Sunday cochairs, one of the few positions of significance afforded to younger couples in the world of Jewish society. The Goldenbergs tell me they both grew up at Har Zion and were married there, but now live in Blue Bell and belong to Tiferet Bet Israel, David Ackerman's synagogue.

I look over at Grafman, who is poker-faced. He wouldn't want to let on that Har Zion is in the process of trying to steal their rabbi.

Ralph tells me how the face-to-face soliciting is going. "I got a wife up from $650 to $1000," he says. Her husband, he explains, gives separately, at the over-$15,000 level. That's every year.

Federation fund-raising is a marvel. Over $4 million is raised from this Philadelphia-area Super Sunday alone, and the local Federation raises some $40–55 million annually. Super Sundays in communities all over the country have become a cornerstone of Jewish philanthropy, helping to raise some $700 million each year. The money is used to fund local social service agencies, such as Jewish Family and Children's Services, Jewish day schools, Jewish Community Centers—almost every kind of Jewish institution *except* synagogues (although it does fund some programs that take place at synagogues). Federation, which also funds many non-Jewish social services, advertises itself as the "central address" of the Jewish community, which tends to rankle rabbis who feel that their synagogues should be the central addresses. To some rabbis, Federation has stood for a way for being Jewish without being "too Jewish." The myriad social events connected with Federation fund-raising—the dinner-dances, the golf tournaments, the singles mixers—provide a broad secular Jewish lifestyle that doesn't necessarily involve religious practice.

Federation has also historically raised money along with the United Jewish Appeal (UJA), the major organization through which American Jews send funds to Israel. So Federation/UJA has offered a way of accessing and supporting cultural Israel without getting too involved with religious Israel. Federation, UJA and the synagogues are all on the same side, but they do tend to compete for people's increasingly limited Jewish time and philanthropy.

Until the late 1940s, synagogues like Har Zion were the epicenter of the American Jewish universe. There were Jewish Community Centers (originally called Young Men's Hebrew Associations), as well as those local golf clubs and social clubs that would accept Jewish members, but the synagogues were home to most religious, educational and secular events, and Har Zion was considered a national model of the "synagogue center." In the fifties, sixties and seventies, new, larger Jewish Community Centers were built as Jews moved to the suburbs, and they boomed—as did the Federations and UJA communities, whose offices were sometimes located in the JCCs. These institutions flourished as American Jews gained wealth but were still not invited to fully participate in American culture—or chose not to.

I grew up at a Jewish Community Center—preschool; day camp; iddy, biddy, tween and teen basketball; jukebox dances in the youth lounge; college bowl—and mine was perhaps the last generation of American Jewish kids raised with the assumption that all or most of our time after school and in the summer would be spent exclusively with Jews. In the eighties, much of the interest in all-Jewish institutions—gyms, preschools, summer camps—shifted to more heterogeneous institutions where Jews were finally made to feel comfortable. At the same time, the political situation in Israel made support of the country's actions a little less automatic. While Federation and UJA fund-raising remained strong, JCCs took a hit, and many began accepting non-Jewish members from their neighborhoods. (I'll never forget the astonishment of discovering that the president of my old Jewish Center Youth chapter wasn't Jewish.) By the nineties, national interest in God and spirituality and houses of worship began to increase and the balance of power began swinging away from Federations and Jewish social clubs and back toward the synagogues.

In Philadelphia, one of the most visible signs of this shift is the disintegration of the once-powerful Locust Club. A posh downtown lunch and supper club, it was founded in 1920 by "merchants and professional men"—such as the owners of the Gimbel's and Lit's department stores and the Mastbaum theater chain—because Jews weren't allowed to join the vaunted Union League. Now that the Union League, a Republican stronghold with a history of anti-Semitism dating from the Civil War, is finally accepting Jewish members and welcoming them to come sample their traditional fried oyster and chicken salad lunch platter, the Locust Club is dying. It leased out much of its precious Center City space to a chi-chi restaurant to try and make ends meet, but rumors are spreading it won't last long.

Since these institutions of segregated life are falling by the wayside, it is particularly amazing that Federation and UJA continue to raise so much money. But even they have had to retool for the future. The national Council of Jewish Federations, the umbrella organization for Federation fund-raising efforts, is merging with the UJA. While, together, the two charity groups still raise well over $1 billion a year, they have been stung by accusations of being unresponsive to donors and lacking creativity in giving. The newly consolidated fund-raising effort will be run by Seagram magnate Charles Bronfman, the lesser-known brother of one of the world's most charitable Jewish families. His older brother, Edgar, president of the World Jewish Congress, has been an outspoken critic of secular Jewish fund-raising, claiming it does not invest enough in "Jewish identity."

✿   ✿   ✿

Super Sundays should not be affected by the merger. But clearly, Jewish fund-raising is more challenging than ever. And there is no better indicator than the name on the school we're in. Like nearly every other Jewish elementary school in America it was called, until recently, the Solomon Schechter Day School. The name was in honor of the turn-of-the-twentieth-century rabbi, scholar and president of the Jewish Theological Seminary who founded the movement toward Jewish-American elementary schools that would offer Conservative Jews the same parochial education opportunities as Catholics. It is now referred to as the Perelman School, in honor of Raymond and Ruth Perelman, parents of Revlon magnate Ronald Perelman.

The Perelmans have been trying to give away their vast fortune in large, meaningful blocks—to Jewish charities, as well as secular causes such as the Philadelphia Museum of Art. Normally, a large check from the Perelmans is received with a big hug and an unequivocal thank-you, but the couple's recent educational initiative ran into a very public snag. They offered to give $2 million to the Jewish elementary school and then another $2 million to the high school, on the condition that both institutions be renamed Perelman schools. The Schechter board calmly accepted the deal, and the money, and adopted the cumbersome moniker "Raymond and Ruth Perelman Jewish Day School (a Solomon Schechter affiliate)." But the high school board was unable to keep its concern about the proposed name change quiet while negotiating with the generous Perelmans, and then the students began protesting.

Akiba Hebrew Academy is named for Rabbi Akiba, arguably the most important sage of the Rabbinic Period (first and second centuries A.D.), when the first major work of Torah commentary, the Talmud, was created and codified. Akiba was tortured to death by the Romans, and according to legend his last words were a recitation of the Sh'ma: his dying breath used to utter *adonai echad*, "the Lord is One." The students and faculty at Akiba Academy are known for their feistiness in political causes, which is why they are often called upon to speak out on Jewish issues, especially concerning Israel. But this time, their candor led to philanthropic friendly fire. Some students and faculty were unhappy with the idea of the new name, but instead of handling the friction quietly, the school's leaders let it get out of hand. Eventually the students were holding a public protest against the renaming, daring the Perelmans to give the much-needed money to the school without forcing the name change. The Perelmans, mortified to see their generosity mocked in the pages of the *Philadelphia Inquirer* and on TV news, dug in their heels. With each side in the dispute no doubt believing they had shown the courage of Rabbi Akiba, the high school lost a $2 million gift. They expect to remember their triumph of will each time it rains and the roof leaks.

As the time gets closer to local TV news deadlines, politicians descend to work Super Sunday, soliciting the Jewish vote for the cameras. The upcoming mayoral election is particularly fascinating in the world of Jewish politics, because it will determine the successor to Ed Rendell, whose extraordinarily successful two terms in office, fed by his friendship with President Bill Clinton, earned him the nickname "America's Mayor." Rendell is Jewish, and while his wife and son are not, he has been the most prominent ethnically Jewish public official in modern Philadelphia history and, during the 1990s, one of the most visible in the country, second only to Connecticut senator Joe Lieberman. Rendell never misses a chance to appear at Super Sunday.

Because of Democratic party politics, Rendell has been forced to endorse city council president John Street. But everyone in the Jewish community winkingly knows he has been offering backdoor encouragement to his former finance consultant Sam Katz, who is currently working the Super Sunday main room with his wonky dry humor. Katz, who grew up at Har Zion and whose parents still belong, was a lifelong Democrat. But he switched to the Republican party to avoid local machine politics, just like another well-known local Jewish politician, Arlen

Specter—whose son Shanin, a prominent personal injury attorney, belongs to Har Zion. Specter switched parties in the 1960s to successfully run for DA of Philadelphia, and later for the U.S. Senate.

Sam Katz hopes he has similar success as a Jewish Republican. He is currently the favorite to oppose Street in the general election, which could cause a quandary for many Philadelphia Jews. They would have to consider voting Republican in a local election for the first time in their lives.

Most of the Super Sunday volunteers, however, are too busy to pay much attention to the politicians. There are always more cards, more people to call back. Over the PA system comes news that today's frenzy of phone solicitations has resulted in over four hundred thousand dollars in donations. Also, the bus for Beth Shalom High School students is ready to leave.

16

WAITING FOR ACKERMAN

Hardly anyone comes to shul on time Saturday morning. Services start at 9 A.M., but for much of the first hour, there's nobody here but the clergy, their spouses, a few early-bird daveners and, if there's a bar mitzvah, a sampling of curious non-Jewish guests who were not warned that when the invitation says 9 it is customary to arrive at 10 or 10:30.

Yet, here I am at the synagogue at 9:15. And when I arrive, Lou Fryman, who rarely comes to Shabbat services these days, has already been here for ten minutes. He hasn't gone in, though. He is cooling his heels in one of the outer lobbies, leaning up against one of the preserved memorial plaques that were brought over from the old synagogue in Radnor and staring into the expanse of the parking lot. Fryman probably wouldn't tell me why he's here so early, but I already know.

He is waiting for Ackerman.

It is the worst-kept secret among the Har Zion leadership and clergy—and that's saying something in a synagogue bustling with badly kept secrets. Rabbi David Ackerman and his wife are coming to pay a "surprise" visit to the shul this morning to get a feel for what services are like. I wait with Fryman for a few minutes, then head toward the main sanctuary to check out the morning's kippahs.

It is customary for the bar and bat mitzvah families to order personalized skullcaps, with the name and date of the rite of passage printed on the inside and their choice of color and style on the outside. In the year since I began covering Har Zion, I have amassed an impressive collection, which I pile, like a stack of leather and silk pancakes, on a shelf next to my desk. I've become quite a yarmulkah connoisseur. There are broad ones made of flat satin, for which the classic color is white. Smaller ones are made of plain or etched suede: classic color, black. There's not much you can do to mess up a satin yarmulkah. Even the scariest colors are at least solid, and the only big debate is whether or not to have a button in the middle. With leather yarmulkahs, however, there are a wide variety of options—contrasting trims, computer-generated color—and lots of room for trouble. At one bat mitzvah I got a brown, blue and gray kippah with colors splattered like pieces hacked from a Jackson Pollack painting. My favorite so far has mod swirls etched into the black leather, and the bat mitzvah girl's name printed inside in glowy letters: very Carnaby Street.

The yarmulkahs are placed in a small basket on a table near the entrance to the main sanctuary. If there are two bar or bat mitzvahs that day, each family has its own made, usually in different colors. For today's double bat mitzvah, Jane and Carly, each family has chosen white, so they won't be able to tell whose guests are whose.

Inside, Ralph Snyder is on the bimah, facing the Ark, chanting the early morning service. It's not unusual for him to lead the early morning service—which is run more like a minyan—but today is special. It would be good for Ackerman to see one of the more impressive aspects of Har Zion life, that the leadership knows how to lead services, and do so regularly. But, at 9:35, they are still waiting for Ackerman. So when Ralph finishes, he turns around, scans the small crowd and, a little miffed, comes down off the bimah to warm handshakes and yasher koachs. He takes his regular seat next to Lew Grafman.

At 9:43 the back door opens. I turn to look, and see Ralph and Lew Grafman turn as well. Nope. Just groups of teenage girls, their dresses swooshing, their Kate Spade bags swinging, their perfect long hair sway-ing. At 9:45 Carole Karsch comes in. She quickly scans the crowd, and sits down near her fellow search committee members. Several minutes later, she cranes her long neck to look around again, in case he sneaked in and she didn't notice. In the meantime, the families and friends of the two bat mitzvah girls start filling in the rows closest to the bimah, un-aware of what is going on in the seats behind them. But from the pulpit, Rabbi Herber and Cantor Vogel can watch the whole thing—it's like a lit-tle play, *Waiting for Ackerman*—as search committee members fidget, and Lou Fryman occasionally pokes his head through the back door.

At 10, Lew Grafman leaves his seat and joins Lou Fryman in the lobby. In the meantime, Rabbi Herber is trying to focus some attention on a friend of his, a visiting rabbi from Jerusalem, who is here to give a sermon about the state of Judaism in Israel. At 10:05, Grafman and Carole Karsch can wait no longer: they are due to sit on the bimah, and reluctantly shuffle up to their seats. Finally, at 10:12, Lou Fryman gives up waiting, and comes into the sanctuary to sit down with his wife. He looks upset, embarrassed. The Torah reading has already begun, and no Ackerman.

At 10:20 the back door opens again. Heads turn, but it is Paul and Valerie Wolpe, making one of their first Shabbat appearances since Rabbi and Elaine left for their sabbatical. In the discussions of what life will be like when Rabbi Wolpe has retired, there has been speculation about whether Paul and Val will stay at Har Zion or change synagogues. But as they chat briefly with Fryman before taking their seats, all that seems secondary right now. Where the *hell* is Ackerman? They're here to see him as well.

Finally, at 10:24, the back door opens again. Just as the second aliyah begins, David Ackerman walks in with his wife, Naomi Shapiro. From the looks on their faces, they have no idea of the expectations that have been dashed. Rabbi Herber glances over at Joshua Perlmuter, the sexton, as he reads the Torah and shakes his head in disbelief.

Rabbi Herber taps his fingertips together pensively as he watches the couple take their seats in the last row, behind the Frymans. "Oh, the drama," I scribble on the notepad I keep hidden under my prayer book.

Herber leans toward his rabbinic colleague, who chuckles knowingly when told what is happening. One benefit of Ackerman's visit, no matter how late, is that it assures an audience of heavy hitters for the visiting rabbi's sermon on the precarious state of Conservative Judaism in Israel—and perhaps for his fund-raising session later on. The clergy have also quietly tried to stack the deck to make sure as many young families as possible just happen to be in shul today. They told people, "Just come to synagogue this week. I can't tell you why, but every young kid there will make a difference."

Ackerman is dressed in a well-tailored suit, his dark kippah clipped, dead center, to a tuft of hair in the front. His wife wears a dress and a broad, brightly colored skullcap over her short hair. While Ackerman looks comfortable, his wife appears to regard the congregation with some suspicion. As she scans the room, a cell phone rings—even though it says specifically in the program that congregants are to put "all beepers and cell phones on silent mode." It's *very* Har Zion—but not the Har Zion the committee wants them to see.

The family members of the bat mitzvah girls are called to the bimah for their Torah honors. Before the Torah is read, they must recite a blessing. It is only twenty-four words long and there is another blessing after, which is twenty words. Almost anybody Jewish learned it as a kid, and anybody who forgot it can practice these forty-four words—phonetically if they have to—until they are able to look competent. Yet several family members stumble through the blessings.

Normally, it wouldn't be a big deal. But what will the Ackermans think? Will they feel that Har Zionites are underachievers? Or will they appreciate a certain looseness and imperfection, a casualness not normally associated with the synagogue? At the end of the Torah reading, when the scroll is raised high overhead before rewrapping, the guy with the lifting honor almost drops it. Oh God. Then, at the end of the Torah service, Rabbi Herber forgets that he needs to add the prayer for the new month before Ashrei. The cantor quickly clears his throat, points out the mistake and does the prayer. After which Herber ad-libs, "and now the moment you've all been waiting for . . . *Ashrei!*"

After the Torah service, Herber's rabbinic colleague gives an impassioned sermon about how the religious right in Israel tries to keep Conservative Jews there from practicing their religion as they see fit. It is especially troubling because Orthodox rabbis do not recognize any conversions but their own. In Israel, where the Orthodox make national religious law, that means that the country's constitutional "right of return" for any Jew who seeks the homeland would not apply to Conservative or Reform converts. This policy is being fought strenuously by both denominations—even though, in truth, the Conservative movement doesn't really recognize Reform conversions either. But Judaism, the visiting rabbi says, is supposed to be about placing laws in front of people, not forcing laws upon them. Religion is supposed to be "piety, pleasure, promise and personal commitment."

Throughout the service, search committee members keep turning to look for Ackerman's reaction. At the very end, when all the children come onto the bimah and Rabbi Herber holds his baby daughter while singing the closing prayer, Ackerman smiles broadly. And instead of sneaking out afterward—as he had said he wanted to, in order to keep his visit as "secret" as possible—he and his wife join the congregation at the kiddush. Jacob sees them as he enters the auditorium, and approaches.

"David, what are you doing here?" he asks. "I thought you wanted to be inconspicuous."

Naomi Ackerman answers for him. "He promised me a cookie," she says. She looks happy.

The next week, Ackerman is invited back for a second interview with the full search committee. This time, he comes across as anxious to have the job. He says he and his wife both very much liked the service they attended. The choir and sense of grandeur and elegance reminded her of her youth.

Naomi grew up in a synagogue and, during the summers, at Camp Ramah. Her father, Alexander Shapiro, was a well-known rabbi and a president of the Rabbinical Assembly. He had a brief stint in Philadelphia at the Germantown Jewish Center in Mount Airy, one of the most passionate, intellectually gifted, liberal congregations in the country, and one of the few that did not flee an integrating neighborhood but remained and flourished with it. Most of Shapiro's career, however, was spent on the pulpit at the large, very traditional North Jersey synagogue Oheb Shalom, which resided in a dramatic building in downtown Newark for nearly a century before merging with another congregation and moving to the prosperous suburb of South Orange. Unfortunately, Rabbi Shapiro died of a heart condition at age sixty-three, too soon to enjoy emeritus-hood and the other trappings of a rabbinic job well done.

Ackerman talks about how impressed he is by the prospect of following Har Zion's three great rabbis, and says that he has had a chance to get to know Rabbi Wolpe over the years—and a little better over the past few weeks. He is excited about the job.

It appears that Ackerman has at least the tacit blessing of Wolpe, who is still in Florida. He says he is staying completely uninvolved with the rabbi search, but every once in a while Lou Fryman lets slip that he has asked the rabbi's opinion on something, making some committee members smile and others bristle. There are those who believe that Wolpe has had more quiet input than he lets on when it comes to which candidates Fryman chooses to reject without even an exploratory phone call. If they're thinking about offering Ackerman the pulpit, Wolpe has certainly approved.

One big selling point for Ackerman is that he likes the idea of leading a congregation that has in it so many major leaders in both the Jewish and secular worlds. And he likes the idea of living closer to downtown. Some have compared suburban Blue Bell, where Ackerman currently works, to Penn Valley when Har Zion moved there twenty years ago. But there's one big difference. People who live in Penn Valley are former city-dwellers and, for the most part, they still use the downtown often. They are urban suburbanites. Blue Bell is just far enough away from Center City, geographically and psychologically, that its residents rarely get into town. A transplanted New Yorker, Ackerman says he is surprised how few congregants he and his wife see at, say, the Philadelphia Orchestra.

One search committee member bluntly asks why he had been so ambivalent about applying for the job even after he was approached. He doesn't really answer the question, but makes it clear that he was happy with his growing congregation and not looking for another job, but that this opportunity was just too intriguing. He was initially turned off by the reputation the synagogue has for somewhat impersonal services, but now that he's seen the place in action, he sees great possibilities.

As he begins to talk about starting an adult learning service, Cindy Blum's cell phone rings. It's her kids; they need her to come home. Not long after she arrives at the house, the phone rings. It's Betsy Rentz, a fellow younger mom on the committee, calling from her car to find out what Cindy thought. They pick apart Ackerman's answers, as well as some of the committee's questions, their conversation going on for so long that Betsy has reached home and is sitting talking in her driveway with the car in park. By the time they finish, it seems clear that their year and a half of service on the rabbi search committee is nearly at an end.

Thank God.

All the synagogue's leaders are talking about Ackerman, even though none of them have ever seen him work in his synagogue. I find myself amazed at how consensus can be formed based on so little information, but that is, I suppose, the nature of committees. Still curious to know more, however, I go to another Shabbat service at Ackerman's synagogue. The first thing I notice this time is that in the rabbi's parking space sits a light brown Ford Escort with a baby seat. If he takes the job, he will certainly need a nicer car.

Inside, Ackerman is walking up and down the aisles of the sanctuary;

he has a lapel mike clipped to his tallis, although the place is small enough that his voice would probably carry without it. When he needs a quote from the Torah, he doesn't read it himself. He asks someone from the congregation to read. And when someone raises a hand to respond to a question, he says "talk to me." It is indeed a Donahue d'var Torah.

Ackerman has the appeal of everybody's favorite college teacher. Once he gets the congregation going, he works like an auctioneer of knowledge.

The structure of his service is different than at Har Zion. He gives a sermon on Friday night, not on Saturday. And he isn't the only one to address the bat mitzvah kids after they finish. Another member of the synagogue who knows them well also gives a talk. And then the parents speak.

It's intimate, personal, moving, spiritual. And Ackerman is clearly beloved. What will people think, I wonder, when they find out he's interviewing for a new job on the Main Line?

In the meantime, Rabbi Herber has settled into a level of baseline panic. It shows on his face a little more each day.

"Jacob is a basket case," Jeff Blum tells me, as we sit talking in his den. "He's going nuts."

The previous evening, Blum asked Jacob how the day had gone. Only ten calls, he reported, but three were the kind that hurt the most— complaints that he had failed to make a hospital visit. Also, the car died, on the first day Herber's wife was supposed to take their daughter to day care. And he can't seem to shake the flu.

Blum is the synagogue officer closest to Jacob. So he has been dispatched by the leadership to keep an eye on him, to be Jacob's sounding board and alert them in the event he is going under for the third time.

Blum clearly relishes the role of mentor to the young rabbi. But he also realizes what an odd circumstance this is. Just weeks ago, he had a rabbi with fifty years experience on the pulpit, whose hard-won wisdom he respected completely. Now he has a rabbi with three years experience who is looking to *him* for advice. It's not just the difference in age—Blum is now ten years older than his rabbi—but also a generational difference in education and life experience. When Wolpe was ordained, rabbis were expected to be far more educated than their congregations of immigrant and second-generation entrepreneurs and businessmen. Wolpe was the ultimate example of the Renaissance rabbi: at NYU, he was being prepared for a doctoral program in Renaissance history before he chose the rabbinate. Today's rabbis often have the same, or even less, formal education than their congregants, who have master's degrees, law degrees, medical and dental degrees. The younger clergy especially are often less worldly than their adult congregants.

"In sermons, Wolpe would quote from Browning, and Jacob quotes from *Sports Illustrated*," Blum says, only half joking. "You know I love Jacob, but if he says one more word about the Rangers from the bimah, I'll kill him." However, he must concede that Herber's interest in sports is one of the reasons he is so popular with kids. And, to many young parents, that popularity can be more important than whether the adults' intellectual and spiritual needs are being fulfilled.

Tonight, Blum and Herber are going out to dinner to discuss the most important decisions the young rabbi is expected to make during his tenure: who gets which bar and bat mitzvah dates. Not next year, but three years from now. That's how far in advance these decisions are made. Jeff believes this is one responsibility that Rabbi Wolpe might actually miss, only because the letters they get from parents are often inadvertently hilarious.

Basically, a bar mitzvah is supposed to be held as soon as a child turns thirteen: never before, and preferably not long after. (Bat mitzvahs are a more recent phenomenon and in non-egalitarian synagogues they are still sometimes done when girls are twelve.) While a rite of passage can be held any day the Torah is read, there is, in most synagogues, a "bar mitzvah season," beginning in September and ending in early June. There also tends to be a lull in late December and January because hardly anyone wants a bar mitzvah scheduled in the dead of winter. Snow might keep out-of-town guests away, and family and friends who winter in Florida might consider it too much of a schlepp to come back. But if you're born on January 19 (as I was) it's pretty hard to avoid a dead-of-winter date.

That does not stop parents from trying. One letter this year explains that even though the child's birthday is mid-January, it has been a long-standing "family tradition" that bar mitzvahs be held when the kid is still twelve—so how about a date in September or October?

"Yeah, right," Blum says, shaking his head.

Another letter explains that even though two boys were born only days apart and have grown up to be best friends, they shouldn't share the same bar mitzvah date—because many friends would be unable to participate in their *simcha* (their "happy event," or, in this case, their catered evening affair) because they would have to choose between sim-chas. This letter seems almost OK until the last line, in which the parent expresses hope that this request can be granted and notes they are "pa-trons" of the temple, invoking how much money they give to the syna-gogue each year.

Is "patron" a lot of money? No, Blum says, it's one thousand dollars over normal membership.

Is that a lot of money at Har Zion? Not to the folks Blum refers to as "the six-figure people."

"You would not *believe* the requests we've had," he says. " 'The room at the Ritz is being taken by the mayor, so we need to have another date,' or 'The lanterns we have in our backyard won't be set up in time, so we have to change the date . . . and, by the way, we need to have a solo date.' Are you out of your *mind*?"

With the large number of families who want a Har Zion bar mitzvah, and all the Saturday mornings that are gobbled up by Jewish holidays and festivals, there are hardly any solo dates available. There is even competition for some of the non–Saturday morning dates. Some people prefer Saturday night services, which are generally less demanding on the child, or Sunday or *Rosh Hodesh* dates—celebrations of the new month, often for families who have traditionally observant relatives or clergy members who won't drive to synagogue on Saturday. The few solo dates that do come up are generally undesirable times: in the summer, or right before Christmas. That's how Blum was able to find a solo date for his daughter, Sammy. It's September 7, a date nobody else wanted because it is in that nether zone between the end of beach season and the beginning of the High Holidays. Because he's an officer of the synagogue, he should be able to protect the date "unless, of course, the consul general of Israel moves into the neighborhood, joins the shul and has a daughter born that day."

Once the dates are determined, there's always an outcry. "Oh, my God, the screaming and the fighting," Blum says, chuckling. Then they start trying to trade with each other. That's allowed, as long as the new date isn't so far from the birthday that it begs credulity. Wolpe used to say, "Who told you to have a kid born in January?" Blum recalls. Eventually, the schedule will get finalized, and people can settle down to more important issues, like the bar mitzvah training itself, which takes about two years, and the choosing of caterers, florists, bandleaders and event halls, which can take even longer.

Of course, this is an especially anxious time for Har Zion parents, because they don't know who will be officiating at all these rites of passage. Will the new rabbi be liberal or traditional? Some specifically request in their letters that Wolpe agree to come back and officiate at their children's bar mitzvahs. But the synagogue cannot guarantee that. Who knows what their relationship with Wolpe will be like in three years? And will the new rabbi really want the old rabbi coming in and running services?

In the meantime, the parents this spring must adjust to having Rabbi Herber, rather than Rabbi Wolpe, officiate at their bar mitzvahs. Herber is, of course, a little less sure of himself. Wolpe has mentioned to me that the first time he let the young rabbi handle a Har Zion coming of age, Herber called the bar mitzvah boy by the wrong first name. It's a mistake he says he will never make again. He now knows to always write the names down, and with all the responsibilities suddenly thrust upon him, he may never trust his memory again. Especially since his cold is getting worse and he can barely remember his own name.

When I walk into the Purim Carnival, I am transported back to my youth. In over a year covering this synagogue, nothing has felt more nostalgic than this sight: thirty years later, in celebration of the craziest holiday in the Jewish calendar, kids are still trying to throw Ping-Pong balls into cups and win "valuable" prizes.

Purim, like Hanukkah, is a pretty lightweight festival, making Sukkot seem solemn by comparison. It is built around the public reading of the *Megillah,* a scroll separate from the Torah that is taken from the book of Esther, which tells the soap-operatic tale of the nitwit king of Shushan, Ahasveros. His wife is banished and a new would-be queen, Esther, who just happens to be Jewish, is chosen in a sort of Miss Shushan pageant. The evil courtier Haman (HAY-man) then gets mad because Esther's uncle and protector, Mordecai, won't bow down to him, and seeks revenge by convincing the king to kill all the Jews. Esther uses all her feminine guile to convince the king that this is a bad plan. They all live happily ever after, except for Haman who is, well, hanged.

Haman wore a three-cornered hat, which is why we eat three-cornered stuffed cookies called hamantashen. The highlight of Purim in my family has always been when the mailman arrives with the tin of homemade hamantashen from Greensburg. Grandma, my mother's mother, used to make them, carefully placing them in nests of waxed paper in blue butter-cookie tins, which were then sealed with the thickest, stickiest tape known to man before being wrapped in brown paper. Now the secret recipe, and the responsibility for the mass mailings, has been passed down to my Aunt Phylis, who still dutifully makes them each year.

On the Sunday before the Megillah reading, most synagogues have a carnival for the young kids, who dress up in costumes. The last time I went to a Purim carnival I was probably twelve—preteens are far too cool to get involved with such things, unless they are *working* at the booths. And when I step into the Har Zion carnival, I am pleased to see that the event remains as joyfully rinky-dink as ever, not a hint of the excess normally associated with kids' play these days. They still have a bean-bag toss, a wheel of fortune and a Ping-Pong ball toss. There are a few computer games, but generally, the technology level is lower than what would be found in the toy selection at any grandparent's house. There's a haunted house, miniature golf, an opportunity to shave Haman's head and little kids are running around screaming with glee.

In the evening, adults dress up in costume for the Megillah reading. After all the tension of the past few weeks, it is wonderful to walk into the sanctuary and see on the bimah the entire clergy and leadership of the synagogue dressed like fools and close to tippled. The cantor is outfitted as a king, president Lew Grafman is an Israeli Cat in the Hat and the sexton, Joshua Perlmuter, is reading the Megillah in a clown suit, with full makeup and a red nose. Ralph Snyder is wearing the leather bushman's hat he brought back from his recent trip to Australia. Jeff Blum is in a full Flyers hockey uniform, and next to him is Rabbi Herber in—what else?—a rival New York Rangers jersey and cap. Lurking off the bimah is another congregant dressed as wrestling hero The Masked Marauder.

Every time Haman's name is mentioned in the Megillah, the congregation is supposed to drown it out with noisemakers called *graggers*. But this is, after all, Philadelphia, the booing capital of America, where sports fans are renowned for jeering everyone from hometown heroes to Santa Claus. When Haman's name comes up, the graggers are almost an afterthought compared to the thunderous din of boo-birds. After one particularly loud boo, Herber stops the crowd before the reading continues and says, "How 'bout them Iggles," a taunt to Philadelphia football fans after a particularly bad season. After the next "Haman," a congregant comes up on the bimah, slaps the rabbi on the back and walks back to his seat. It's only when Herber turns his back to the congregants that they see the "Flyers Rule" sign—much worse than "kick me"—that has been taped to his jersey.

As I watch this, it occurs to me that this is probably the first Har Zion Purim in more than a decade that Rabbi Wolpe hasn't attended. And while I realize Purim is zany every year—the whole point of the holiday is to let loose and mock self-seriousness—there is a real sense of generational surge, rejuvenation and liberation. I can't imagine it was ever this wild when Wolpe was on the pulpit. At this moment, Blum and Herber are trading Three Stooges imitations and punching each other.

After the service, I bump into Alan Greenbaum, who I know just returned from the search committee trip to Birmingham to see Rabbi Wasserman in action. I ask him how it went. He says they had an interesting visit to an amazing museum about the Civil Rights Movement and they enjoyed Wasserman's services. When I ask what the next step will be regarding the rabbi candidate, he just waves me off.

"I doubt it will go any further," he says. Which means, I assume, they have decided that Ackerman is their guy.

Cantor Eliot Vogel is the person at Har Zion whose life will probably be changed the most by the coming of the new rabbi. This is why his gut reaction to the entire process is so revealing. At the very beginning of the search, he told Lou Fryman, "The rabbi we want probably doesn't want us." And, when privately discussing the search with Jacob one day early on, he heard the following words come out of his own mouth:

"I can't imagine liking whoever would become the next rabbi of this congregation."

And, like many things he says privately that initially surprise him, he thought about it for a second and realized, yes, he really did mean that.

What is interesting about Vogel—a wiry forty-four-year-old with a calming, public-radio voice and a lot of bite under his mild manner—is that he can have such a seemingly cynical view and still remain powerfully attached to Har Zion and its future. He has had a complex relationship with the synagogue and the community during his eight years here. But, Har Zion is one of the few synagogues left in the country where a cantor can really sing. Musicians will put up with a great deal for the opportunity to *perform*. And they will make what they put up with sound worse than it is, as part of their justification for the compromises they have made in order to be paid to play—especially if part of the pay is the opportunity to raise a family and have a semi-normal life.

The job of the cantor has probably changed more in American Judaism in the past fifty years than the job of the rabbi. In the early twentieth century, Jews clamored for tickets for sold-out concerts by the top cantors, who became the equivalent of opera stars. Even into the 1960s, cantors could still be prima donnas who did little but perform during services, fulfilling their ancient role of cley kodesh, the holy vessel, with the ability to store the prayers of the congregation and directly upload them to God. Yet, by the early seventies, when I was preparing for my bar mitzvah, I do remember thinking how very odd it was that my cantor had a copy of a record he made propped up on his desk. Who in God's name would want that? (It turns out that both my parents and grandparents bought one, although I never heard them played.) Today, cantors have a broad educational role, and share many of the responsibilities that once fell to a rabbi or Hebrew school director. They also do a good bit of pastoral counseling. Ultimately, of course, they are still there to sing, but there are even different kinds of singing. Many congregations are looking for more of a sing-along than the traditional operatic performance, more Mitch Miller than cley kodesh. A sing-along cantor doesn't even need to have a great voice. Through Rabbi Wolpe's era, however, the more operatic style, often with a choir, has lived on at Har Zion. Vogel, who has a powerful voice, still gets to sing.

And, much to his surprise, he may get a new rabbi he actually likes. David Ackerman was high on his personal wish list. They have known each other for years. When Ackerman was a rabbinical student, he came to speak at Vogel's previous synagogue in South Orange for "Seminary

Sabbath," and even then he could see there was something special about him. Later, Vogel was asked to sing at the Ackermans' wedding. Nearly a year ago, Vogel asked Ackerman to drive in and take a walk with him around the Jewish area in Lower Merion, near the Akiba Hebrew Academy and the historic Barnes Foundation, home of the finest and quirkiest early twentieth-century art collection in the world. They talked about whether Ackerman might be a good fit for Har Zion, and what it would be like following Jerry Wolpe. Vogel said he was convinced that while Wolpe had a remarkable career, "he is succeedable. He's most noted for his wonderful oratory, but he wasn't all things to all people— nobody in his position ever is." He thought Ackerman's personality, which was somewhat warmer than Wolpe's, could be successful at Har Zion. He urged him to think about it.

Then, a few months ago, they met again, this time at the Conshohocken Marriott Hotel, a spot that has become popular for suburban businessmen taking power breakfasts and lunches. It was where Vogel had negotiated his last contract, among the high-flying executives from the growing high-tech corridor, spawned by Safeguard Scientific, who always came to "Conshy" to do deals. Ackerman talked frankly about some problems he had encountered with his board in Blue Bell. He was trying to make the jump in his conscience that would allow him to come and interview, but he was afraid of burning his bridges. He was looking for a way, he said, to put his toe in the water. Then, just a few weeks ago, he and Naomi had come over to visit the Vogels and talk about the pros and cons of Har Zion.

Karen Vogel, an affable pediatric social worker specializing in clients with cystic fibrosis, quickly realized the power of Har Zion in her field when she attended her first fund-raiser and was pleasantly surprised to see that many of the big doctors and donors were faces she knew from the shul. When the eldest of their three daughters needed medical attention, they found amazing expertise in the physician-rich community, led by the rabbi who, his former assistants claim, only half-jokingly, "seems to know more world's experts than anybody."

At the same time, the Vogels have been disappointed that Har Zion hasn't changed enough in their eight years here. It is still what is referred to as "the *stadt shul*," the "state shul," the synagogue of record, where somebody who wants to belong to the *right* synagogue belongs. But belonging to the right synagogue doesn't mean you're observant, or spiritual, or learning, or in any way an active member of the Jewish community.

"To be honest with you," Vogel says, lowering his voice, "whenever I hear Rabbi Wolpe addressing someone as a 'fifth-generation Har Zionite,' I just always want to puke. It doesn't mean a lot to me, because I know the Judaism of their home life. So they're fifth generation and I saw them on the High Holidays. Big deal. Why is that to their credit? Are we doing such a great job here?" He's concerned that his kids are growing up in a synagogue where few teens show up after they are bar or bat mitzvahed, a synagogue where nobody completely keeps Shabbat because there is no community of observant families within walking distance. He is pleased that his children will have access to excellent Jewish day schools, but wishes they would see more Har Zion kids there.

While he has a great deal of respect for Rabbi Wolpe and for the synagogue's leadership—both its current leadership, and its amazing history of nurturing strong community leaders—he continues to wonder if Har Zion is the right place for him. And he will probably keep wondering through the next few decades, until his retirement at a ripe old age. In the interim, he takes out some of his frustration doing intensive "platoon training" several days a week with a screaming former marine and, when he can find time, he runs half-marathons.

And he has not given up hope. The synagogue seems to want David Ackerman, a rabbi who shares many of his concerns about observance, increased attendance at Shabbat services, greater enrollment in Jewish day schools and summer camps and generally making Har Zion a warmer, more informal place. So, he and his wife are doing everything they can to encourage the Ackermans to come to Har Zion.

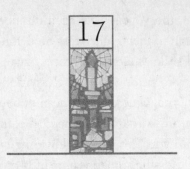

17

THE PLAGUES

R ABBI JACOB HERBER WAKES AT 2 A.M. and greets Shabbat morning with an hour of projectile vomiting. He goes back to sleep and, at 7:30, crawls out of bed to get ready for services. In the shower, he finds himself barely able to lift the bar of soap.

"You're crazy, don't go," his wife says. But what else can he do? There is no other rabbi.

Actually, Rabbi Wolpe has just returned from Florida. But he is supposed to be on sabbatical—he isn't planning to come to Har Zion for Shabbat this week—and Jacob isn't sure he is allowed to call him. Even though, God knows, the Wolpes have certainly called *him* enough times at 8 A.M. on Saturday morning. When he hears Elaine's voice saying, "Jerry is sick," he knows to go throw together a sermon and quickly prepare *something* to say to the bar mitzvah kids. But, truthfully, Jacob doesn't really want to call Wolpe. He only gets to run the shul for six short months before the new rabbi comes, and now that Wolpe is home he will probably be attending more services and synagogue events. Jacob relishes every opportunity he can get to fly solo, without his mentor looking on in what sometimes feels like judgment. If Wolpe is even in the sanctuary, Rabbi Herber feels like he's being scrutinized.

So he walks the mile, mostly uphill, from his apartment building to the synagogue, even though he can barely breathe and his chest radiates pain. The first congregant he meets takes one look at his chalk-white skin and says, "You're going to lie down right now." He goes to sexton Joshua Perlmuter's apartment, in the basement of the synagogue building, and lies on the sofa. Jeff Blum comes down to see him and has four words of advice: "Don't even get up." He agrees to rest for another hour, leaving Blum, Lew Grafman and other officers to run the service.

A little past 10, he lumbers up to the sanctuary to tell the bat mitzvah girl what a good job she did and to give the sermon. It's a new sermon and he doesn't know it that well, all about Shabbat and how one finds time to benefit from the wonder and relaxation of the day. Somehow, he stands and delivers. Then, instead of walking back off the bimah, he decides to stay, assuming the cantor will, for this ragtag service, do the abbreviated version of the Musaf, the additional service. Instead, the cantor does the complete album version, with all the repeats, and Herber is stuck up there, standing and sitting and standing again, for another twenty-five minutes.

Several days later, I ask him if he prayed for strength while on the bimah.

"I was more concerned with sleeping than praying," he says. "God gave me the intelligence to realize what my body needed."

Not only is Rabbi Wolpe back, but he has the whole family with him. Every spring, Har Zion has a symposium called the Levitties Conference, endowed by the family of the late Samuel Levitties (who, along with his wife, also funded the first Center for Pastoral Psychology at the Seminary). The family grant is supposed to be used to "explore issues of contemporary interest on an academic level" by choosing a theme each year and allowing "recognized experts to exchange ideas and provide insights into the complexities of modern society." This year's theme is "Synagogue and Family: Rabbi Wolpe and Sons Reflect." It is a panel discussion, moderated by family friend and longtime Har Zion member Marciarose Shestack—a local celebrity who was the first woman in America to anchor a prime-time news program in a major market.

Some think this year's topic is a marvelous change of pace from the usual menu of Big Questions. Others think accepting the committee's invitation to do this is a rather astonishing example of Wolpe ego. Either way, it promises to be a good show. The house is packed at 1:30 on a snowy Sunday. And the new mara d'atra is pleased to observe that all the men are wearing kippahs.

The five Wolpe men are introduced by Paul's wife, Val, who says she is glad to be able to speak first, because "I rarely get to get a word in edgewise when the Wolpes are in full discourse." Over the years, she has come to understand the Wolpe family ethos, which is: "Be committed, be faithful, be creative, be respectful, be fashionable, be righteous, be loving, be ethical, be knowledgeable, be kind, be generous, be productive, be *r*eproductive, be masterful, be humorful, be observant, be dutiful, be authentic and *behave*." She offers a capsule description of each brother. Steve became a scientist and mice are his primary audience: he likes them because they can't talk back. Paul, her husband, became a social scientist, using the classroom as his theater. He will, she says, "talk on any subject concerning society, whether or not he knows anything about it." David and Danny started out in creative writing and playwriting before deciding "there's no business like shul business." On the pulpit, David can be masterful, Danny authentic.

The moderator asks the boys what it was like growing up at Har Zion. She directs the question first to David.

"Oh, it was wonderful, just wonderful," he says with a grin. "Har Zion was an extremely friendly, warm synagogue where, typically, people took particular interest in the way the rabbi's children conducted themselves. Look, guys, it was almost inevitable that every Shabbat someone would stop me and ask, 'How can you be running in the halls, you're the rabbi's kid?' In the meantime, the lawyers' kids and the doctors' kids were whizzing by. Being a rabbi's kid is a double-edged sword; you gloried in the attention but you didn't want the attention."

Danny, the only one of the four who spent his entire childhood at Har Zion, concurs. "I remember getting into trouble with a friend of mine at Schechter," he says, "and hearing, 'I can understand Robert acting up but you're a *rabbi's son*.' And I replied, 'Do you get angry when Jennifer has a cavity because her dad's a dentist?' "

David jumps back in, "You're constantly reminded of it. A woman comes up to me, 'Are you Rabbi Wolpe's son? You know I used to keep kosher . . .' Lady, *I'm six years old*. I don't *care*. As a result of that, you learn how to hide. You don't come to synagogue and act the way you want to act. Everybody said look how nicely the rabbi's family dressed. That was the hiding part. Even today, if anybody here said anything seriously dissonant about our family, you wouldn't like it. You want to see the family as a perfect family whose foibles can be funny but ought not to be serious . . ."

The moderator interrupts him, and by doing so proves his point. "So you want to be perfect?"

"Yes, *you* want the rabbi's family to be functionally perfect and that encourages us to hide. The truth is, except for a politician, I don't know of anyone whose profession is so dependent on how their family behaves, and that puts an enormous amount of pressure on kids. The only time that hiding broke down, to the extent that it ever did, was when my mother got sick, because then we couldn't pretend we were fine. There was just no way to do it. It was *so* difficult for our family, because it was the first time we couldn't put up a facade of everybody's OK."

"Although we tried . . ." Steve says.

"Yes, and we did a good job," Danny cuts in. "We were in crisis very nicely."

Rabbi Wolpe explains how he tried to keep his sons shielded from the pressures of synagogue life. "We never lived in a city where we had family, so we became very inner-directed, playing off one another," he says. "But I also made a promise, and I paid a penalty for it. I would never discuss anything about the synagogue in front of the family. I knew so many colleagues whose children fled from Judaism because of their father's disillusionment or difficulty with the rabbinate. There are many rabbis' sons who won't walk into a synagogue because they know what their fathers went through. When I *needed* to share something with them, it was very difficult to do because there had been this vow.

"I made a promise to Elaine that I would never attend a dinner meeting. It's still a big joke in our family; whenever the phone rings during dinner they all point at me and go, 'Sit!' And I never took a national office with any organization. When the boys were growing up, anything that wasn't for the synagogue was for them."

Danny says that for the last few years, sons of Conservative rabbis have gotten together annually to have their own RA convention. There's a scholar doing a master's thesis on them.

Some rabbis' children might find the public pressure to be observant a burden. But, David, in retrospect, recognizes in it a crucial element to raising a family that does not become disaffected from religion. "The key to observance in the family," he now sees, "is that it affects everybody equally. My parents had a parent, too. They didn't get to write on Shabbat even though they wanted to. They didn't drop me at shul and give me the message that when you're older you can opt out. For children to be able to see their parents as children, that there is an authority above *them,* is a good thing. So when they grow up they don't think it's natural to throw off all authority."

Rabbi and Elaine were also not didactic when their sons detoured from belief in observance. When David started reading the work of atheist Bertrand Russell, his father bought him a few books he had not read yet and said they should discuss them.

Paul admits that he is the son who went farthest down the path of non-observance, and "my parents almost never got angry at me for acts of rebellion. When I first brought Valerie home and it was serious and she wasn't Jewish, they said nothing to me about it." After a person converts to Judaism, as Val did before she and Paul married, the conversion is not really supposed to be brought up again. There is a fear that being reminded of convert status will make a Jew-by-choice feel less accepted, singled out. It is hard enough for people who have chosen Judaism to hear the vocal disagreement among American Jews about what is required for conversion. But, like everything else about being in a rabbi's family, Val's conversion is still a fairly common topic of discussion at Har Zion, even if it is just to make a backhanded compliment about what a good Jew she became, raising a Jewish family and even becoming a bat mitzvah. Paul has told me privately that Val isn't really aware of this gossip, but he is. He also told me privately that the first time he and Val stopped by his parents' house, it didn't go exactly as he is telling this audience. His father, who was in bed getting over the flu, asked, "Is she nice, do you like her?" And then, of course, he asked if she was Jewish. When Paul said no, he asked, "What is she?" After being told she was raised a Unitarian, he laughed and said, "Well, that's close."

Paul and Val have now been together for over twenty years, and their marriage has been a major source of stability in the Wolpe family; David and Steve haven't been married nearly as long, and Danny is still single. Paul and Val's family is now quite observant; the children go to Jewish day school at Schechter, and Paul takes his spiritual pursuits very seriously. He is a good Shabbat proselytizer.

"You know," he says, "the important thing is not whether or not we'll drive to shul. The important thing is the act of considering whether driving to shul is OK or not. *That* is the Shabbat observance, it is the recognition, the consciousness that it is Shabbat and it means something special and that you take time to evaluate . . ."

"Hey, aren't you supposed to be a *sociologist*?" his older brother Steve interrupts, getting a big laugh.

"Sociologist, my *foot*," Paul says. "I will be applying for the Har Zion position, which I understand is open." The audience bursts into applause.

As the conversation about raising an observant family continues, David interrupts: "I'm going to say something very off the topic. Do you want me to tell you the most illuminating thing you could know about our family? My mother was just telling us to *smile*. OK? Need I say more?"

After the laughter subsides and some of the blush fades from Elaine's face, he continues. "This is actually something important. You heard how much it's a performance-oriented family, a family that was geared to present a certain face to the public. This explains how comfortable we were at home, because no public was watching. But once you set foot outside the door, there's something expected. I mean, this is a lovely afternoon, but it's very unusual to put a family up in front of the public and say, 'Tell us about your family.' And you have to know that our willingness to do it means that we have been trained for a long time to put on a public face. Because otherwise we wouldn't do that—talk about sibling relationships and if you're angry at your parents, and to feel at the end of it, yes, we'll still be lovable. You can only do that if you feel you have a very good handle on the pulse of the public for whom you're performing, and that's what we were trained to do from very early on. Which means that, for all the joys that brings, and the joys are *many* as you can see, the hiddenness I talked about before is real. Because you don't want to see that about our family which is truly potentially ugly, because that would be too discomfiting. So there is about this a genuineness but also a certain artificiality that's inevitable in any public family, a political family, a rabbi's family, that a congregation doesn't want to be aware of. And for good reason."

At that moment, the Wolpes no longer seem like the Kennedys of the Conservative rabbinate, as I sometimes view them. They seem more like the von Trapp family.

There are questions from the audience. If you could turn the clock back thirty years, what changes would you make at Har Zion?

"Well, I think I would have negotiated my salary differently," Rabbi Wolpe says. His kids all break up.

Steve talks about the old Har Zion in Wynnefield, which he liked because it was a social center as well as a shul, a place where he played basketball with friends in the synagogue's gym. Things today are so much more institutionalized that it leads to a bifurcation of Jewish life and non-Jewish life.

Someone asks David how he is adjusting to the pulpit.

He says it's much more emotionally demanding than being a lecturer and scholar, and it requires the same exact skills as being a parent. "Being a parent, at least for me, is the first time in your life when you must be selfless," he says. "It doesn't matter what your needs are when you are urgently needed by a congregant—and that is infuriating, frustrating, hard and terrifically important if you're going to grow as a human being. I switched lives because the other was too easy for me. To be at other people's beck and call is against my grain . . ."

"So," Paul shoots in, "are you saying that you went into the pulpit rabbinate as a form of *therapy*?"

"I know you're only half kidding me. When someone asked Paul why I first went into rabbinical school, he said 'it's a phase.' Someone asked him later, once I was a rabbi, and he said 'to spiritualize himself.' And the truth is I did go into the rabbinate to change from what I was into what I wanted to be. I was too comfortable, it was too easy and too gratifying to just write books and teach and read, which is, even today, what I'd like to be doing but what I ought not be doing all of the time."

On the Wednesday after this Wolpepalooza festival, I rise at 6 A.M. so I can make it out to Har Zion for minyan, which begins at 7, and then *tisch,* the weekly teaching session. I like the concept of tisch—a ten-minute lesson over bagels and coffee—and it is also a convenient place to meet up with the main characters in the rabbi search drama. It's also over by 8:20, so I can often get some time with the rabbi or one of the officers before the day officially begins.

The synagogue I belong to, where I most regularly attend morning minyan, does not have anything like tisch. The minyan is quick, down and dirty, and when it is over people immediately scramble off to work. Still, I like going to minyan in the morning, because it starts the day with something that *matters,* something bigger than work or workout or the morning's e-mail and newspapers. I feel better just being there, being in the synagogue, giving thanks, reading a psalm, thinking about my dad when others say the mourner's Kaddish. I have noticed that the days I go to morning minyan are demonstrably better—more successful, more satisfying—than those when I can't make it.

When I tell my friends this, I get the same look that I got from my parents in 1975 when I told them I was going to start doing Transcendental Meditation. I understand their incredulity. There is something about a morning ritual like minyan that suggests to others that there is *something wrong*. I started going to minyan because something was wrong, but now I'm trying to turn this into a ritual that suggests there's *something right*. That, somehow, religion does not only have to be medicinal or palliative—damage control—but can also be nurturing, broadening, life-affirming. That the "sacred time" Heschel and others spoke about when explaining why to keep Shabbat is not only God's, it's *mine*.

I think about this more during minyan than I used to because, like Rabbi Herber, I just fell into a new job that is sucking the very marrow from my bones and gobbling most of my waking (and too many of my sleeping) hours. The magazine where I have worked as a writer for fifteen years suddenly fired its editor and asked me to take the job. In a moment of piqued curiosity, I accepted—encouraged by my late father, who predicted during his illness that this moment would come one day for me and suggested I try being in charge of something besides myself. It's the first full-time, wear-a-suit, be-at-your-desk-in-the-morning, go-to-meetings job I have ever had. And I often feel as if I am flailing in the quicksand of my new responsibilities.

So, praying feels good. Even sitting in the chapel not praying, listening to others chant familiar phrases in a language I still don't understand, feels good. On Wednesday at Har Zion, with the added bonus of the tisch, it feels even better. After the lesson and the food we *bentsch,* meaning we quickly burn through the recitation of the prayers you're supposed to say after every meal. Judaism isn't big on grace before eating: you just bless the bread and wine, and go for it. It's the after-meal bentsching that takes a little while. I personally haven't sung the *Birchat Hamazon*—the tuneful blessing after eating—other than after Seder since I was at summer camp, where we did it after every meal. I'm not sure I would commit to doing it after every meal (and if I were going to commit to doing anything after every meal, I'm certain my wife would vote for clearing the table and filling the dishwasher instead of bentsching), but I do sometimes think about what prayers I should add to my daily life outside of the synagogue.

I wish I knew how to recommend minyan and tisch to others, to people who are like me before my father died—searching for something, theology, community, but not always looking in the right places. I have a hard time imagining most of my friends getting to the point where they would join me at morning tisch, but I'm pretty sure that most of them would like it.

When I arrive at Har Zion minyan, Ralph Snyder and Lew Grafman are standing outside the chapel doors talking, rather than going inside to pray. Something has happened with Ackerman—that much I can figure out from the snippets of conversation I overhear while putting on my tallis extremely slowly. Snyder mentions something about "making a deal with Landes," which I assume is a reference to Rabbi Aaron Landes, the longtime rabbi at Beth Sholom in Elkins Park. Beth Sholom was the first Conservative congregation in Philadelphia to move to the suburbs, back in the 1950s, and is known nationwide because of its dramatic building, the only synagogue ever designed by Frank Lloyd Wright, and because of its ambitious chorale programs. Landes is also scheduled to retire in the next year, meaning two of Philadelphia's largest Conservative pulpits are open: Beth Sholom is a little smaller than Har Zion, and somewhat less prestigious (largely because of the difference between Elkins Park and the Main Line), but it could be an opportunity for Ackerman as well.

As we get our bagels for tisch, Ralph and Lew are still buzzing, but won't tell me what is happening. I speak to Jacob after the tisch is over. He says he doesn't know what has happened with Ackerman either. The last thing he knew was that the rabbi came in to talk to him about the realities of the job at Har Zion, what it would be like for his wife and his kids. He seemed especially concerned about his wife.

The next day, I find out that Ackerman has withdrawn his application. The leadership is in shock, but also a little relieved because despite his professed enthusiasm for Har Zion, Ackerman remained so ambivalent about the job that they were getting worried about handing it over to him. Ackerman called Cindy Blum, among others, and calmly explained that the decision was made because of family concerns. The word quickly goes around that the sticking point was Ackerman's wife, Naomi. They recalled that she had previously said she liked the services at Har Zion because they reminded her of her father's high-powered synagogue in South Orange. But perhaps Har Zion reminded her of that *too much*. Some who know Naomi and her mother have heard their concerns about whether the pressures of that big job contributed to the early death of Rabbi Shapiro and their complaints about the way they felt they were treated by the synagogue after he died. They've said that the leadership was maybe a little too officious with them, perhaps a little too quick to ask for the house back. Whether the synagogue actually did anything wrong, or the family just forever linked the loss and the shul, didn't really matter—the feelings apparently played a role in the Ackermans' decision.

But those who know Ackerman well are saying the ambivalence, and the decision, were entirely his own. Some suspect that he is hesitant about being on the pulpit at all, and therefore resistant to accepting a bigger job that will call more attention to this ambivalence. They see him as a rabbi torn between pastoral skills and scholarship. It's a predicament that challenges many members of the clergy, the struggle between their abilities as religious politicians and their desire to ignore the rest of the world so they may study intensely. But few come as far as Ackerman without resolving it.

When Ackerman informs Har Zion, he also calls Rabbi Elliot

Schoenberg in New York to let the Rabbinical Assembly know that he will be staying at his synagogue in Blue Bell. He portrays his sudden reversal as a lifestyle decision: being senior rabbi at Har Zion would involve a tremendous draw on his time in ways that his current position does not. He fears the job would have too serious an impact on his family. Like an increasing number of rabbinic placement decisions, it came down to quality and quantity of life, another example of the rabbinate becoming more of a career than a calling.

After he hangs up, Rabbi Schoenberg walks down the hallway to the office of his boss, Rabbi Joel Meyers. He tells him Ackerman has withdrawn from Har Zion.

"Uh-oh," Meyers says.

Only days after Ackerman withdraws, Har Zion suddenly receives a last-minute résumé from a very promising candidate: Rabbi Lee Buckman, from mid-sized Congregation Beth Israel in Milwaukee. I recognize the name immediately. I have relatives who belong to his synagogue, and he officiated at the bat mitzvah of my cousin Marissa, which is how I met him. He is smart and innovative, good with the kids while still challenging to grown-ups. Buckman has been in Milwaukee for almost nine years. Before that, he was a rabbinic intern at the Shelter Rock Jewish Center in Roslyn, New York, the same Long Island synagogue where recently rejected candidate Rabbi Michael Wasserman got his start before moving to Birmingham.

Buckman has been watching the Har Zion pulpit opening—in fact, he has wondered what is wrong with the synagogue, since it has been languishing on the placement list for well over a year. But he didn't apply originally because he and David Ackerman are friends from the Seminary, and it seemed clear to him that Ackerman and Har Zion really wanted each other.

But when he heard that Ackerman pulled out, he quickly applied—although by then he already had four other irons in the fire. His little career gamble had paid off.

Buckman gave notice at his Milwaukee shul in January, even though he didn't have another job lined up. He and his wife have four sons and they became convinced that the local day schools wouldn't serve their needs. Enrollment was shrinking, so their twin boys would likely end up in the same class, which they thought was a bad idea. Even though he loved his job, Buckman was willing to give it up because this was so important.

His wife is a full-time mother and rebbitzin, so they don't have much of a financial safety net if things don't work out. And January is pretty late to start looking. Yet Buckman is unafraid. He knows what the job market is like. Young smart clergy are in demand.

It is, he jokes, "a rabbi's market," and not just for pulpit jobs. Larger synagogues need more rabbis than ever before, as they create teams of second and third seasoned rabbis rather than just relying on a senior rabbi and a revolving door of young assistants. And many off-bimah opportunities are becoming more attractive and lucrative: headmasters of growing day schools, directors of Jewish Community Centers or Hillel centers on college campuses, clergy at large hospitals. Every one of those positions is more family friendly than being a pulpit rabbi. Of the newly ordained rabbis from this year's class at the Jewish Theological Seminary, almost half will choose non-bimah jobs. The same is true for new Orthodox and Reconstructionist rabbis, and in the Reform movement, one-quarter of the new rabbis are choosing positions off the bimah.

Not long after giving notice, Buckman had the usual panoply of offers that greet a Conservative rabbi. He now has a synagogue in the Chicago suburb of Deerfield, B'Nai Tikvah, that wants very much to hire him to replace their retiring rabbi, Reuven Frankel, a former teacher of Buckman's and a good friend. There is a start-up Jewish high school in the Detroit suburb where his wife grew up that wants him to come and be headmaster. There is also a Schechter day school in Chicago with a rabbi-in-residence position. And he has been offered a Jerusalem Fellowship to bring his family to Israel for two years and study. The last two positions would be temporary. He and his wife are looking for something permanent, to provide stability for their kids.

Har Zion sounds like a good fit. It is large and modern, but still fairly traditional—and Buckman is on the conservative side of Conservative. His Milwaukee synagogue is only "Torah egalitarian," meaning that women still don't count for minyan. That's the way he prefers it and since his synagogue is blessed with a robust minyan, there are enough male regulars that his reluctance to count women rarely attracts attention. While Har Zion is entirely egalitarian and would never change back, there are also generally enough men at minyan for Buckman to be able to keep his feelings from causing friction. Also, Philadelphia has excellent Jewish day schools, just what he and his wife are looking for. So, even though he is already interviewing for several jobs, he decides to vigorously pursue the Har Zion pulpit.

The synagogue immediately matches his interest. Besides his strong résumé, Lew Grafman has admired Buckman from afar: he gave a stirring presentation at the Chicago convention of large-synagogue leaders, back when Grafman still believed Ackerman was going to be the one. Buckman had described an exciting adult education program at his Milwaukee temple that was far more aggressive than Har Zion's, as well as some innovative children's programming that made Grafman envious.

While Grafman is still a little baffled as to why Buckman has appeared so late in the process, his application is the first really good rabbi news they have had in a while. They arrange for him to fly to Philadelphia the following Wednesday.

When he arrives at Har Zion, he is informed while sitting in the boardroom in front of the committee that it is "customary" for candidates to begin with a d'var Torah.

"Well, it's great that it's *customary* for you," he thinks, "but it would have been nice to know ahead of time."

With nothing prepared, he nervously collects his thoughts and d'var Torahs away. Luckily, he has done enough impromptu speaking in his career that the committee is impressed. He wins many of them over, and they ask if he would fly back this coming Wednesday to meet with the full committee. This last-minute entry could very well be the answer to their prayers.

✡   ✡   ✡

When Rabbi Herber unlocks his office after minyan, he finds a message that has been slipped under his door. A member of the congregation has died. The message gives only a phone number and a surname that he doesn't immediately recognize, so he assumes the deceased is an elderly family member. He punches in the number, identifies himself, listens for a moment and then the expression on his face shifts abruptly from composure to wide-eyed disbelief.

It's Noreen Cook, his thirty-four-year-old congregant, peer and friend. She's dead. He just officiated at the baby-naming ceremony for her fourth child on Shabbat last week. She had appeared a little shaky in synagogue to Herber, but still radiant, with her other three children gathered around her on the bimah.

After her difficult third pregnancy, Cook, the former assistant DA and wife of the heir to a meat-packaging fortune, was diagnosed with Crohn's disease. While this fourth pregnancy had been somewhat easier than the last one, the doctors were still concerned. This morning she was in bed with the baby when her husband, Robert, went to take a shower and get ready for work. A little while later, one of their daughters came wandering into the bathroom.

"Mommy fell off the bed," she said.

Herber calls Rabbi Wolpe. "I just got the worst telephone call I ever received in my life," he says. "Noreen Cook died."

Wolpe is stunned, but can't immediately help: he agreed to officiate at a funeral this morning, so Jacob has to fly solo. He runs to tell Lew Grafman, who is still lingering in the building after minyan. In minutes, the word spreads through the professional staff, many of whom have just reached their desks. Soon the mothers will start arriving with their kids for day care and preschool. They all know Noreen Cook. She just finished a two-year term as co-president of the Home and School Association, which helps keep parents involved with the teachers in the Hebrew school, kindergarten and all the ambitious preschool programs the mothers rely upon for their sanity: Stay n' Play, Mommy & Me, Kid's Knowledge College, and Bagels, Blocks and Beyond. All the programs for which those moms are now coming in the door to drop off their kids.

The first mother to hear the news wails as her daughter peers up through her bangs, perplexed. Then the next, gasping, crying, shaking her head in disbelief. The women from the front office, old enough to be these mothers' mothers, come out to try to comfort them. But it is not possible.

A woman in a lime-green shirt stands in the stairwell, slumped against a "Torah Talk" poster. "I just saw her yesterday," she says to no one.

As the mothers and children continue to stream in, Herber dashes past them. His car wouldn't start again this morning, so he took his wife's. Now he has to pick her up, so she can drop him off at the hospital on the way to taking their daughter, Mychal, to day care. As they get into the car, he just embraces Cynthia, rendered speechless, thinking about how much of life he takes for granted.

Driving to the hospital, he ponders what he can possibly say to comfort this family. He tries to remember what they taught him at the Seminary in pastoral psychiatry class. Be prepared for their anger, they said, because you are the human representation of the tradition and bear the brunt of their lashing out. The rabbi is God's punching bag.

He thinks he will say, "I wish I had an answer, but I don't have an answer for you. There's nothing wrong with being angry at God. God can take it."

The cantor remains at the synagogue. It is the rabbi's job to pay this hospital visit, so he stays in case anyone at the shul needs to speak to a clergy member. It is going to be a long day and, of course, the rabbi candidate from Milwaukee, Buckman, is coming back this afternoon for a second interview and a meet-and-greet with senior staff.

Cantor Vogel tells me he is having flashbacks to that fateful day in 1991, just after he arrived at Har Zion, when Senator John Heinz's plane collided with a helicopter over the playground of the public school where many of the synagogue's members send their children. Heinz was killed instantly, as were his pilot and the two helicopter pilots. On the ground, two children were killed, and three kids and two adult school employees were injured. The cantor found himself feeling almost grateful because he hardly knew anyone yet, so he maintained some psychological distance from the tragedy. Then he heard that one of the dead children was named Blum, and he immediately thought of Jeff and Cindy, among the only people he knew well because Jeff had been on the cantor search committee. Luckily, none of the victims were from Har Zion.

But this time there is no distance to maintain. He knew Noreen Cook. She represented something incredibly important to him. She was a wealthy Main Line mother who had been drawn into a life of Jewish observance entirely by her experiences at Har Zion, living proof that it could be done. She was also one of the first new Har Zion members who made the commitment to send her children to Jewish day school—even though she had been a product of public schools herself, and her parents had not even belonged to a synagogue.

When Cook and her family first moved to the Main Line in 1993, she decided to put a mezuzah on their front door. The sealed parchment scroll affixed to the entrance of a Jewish home fulfills the biblical commandment to place God's words "on the doorposts of your house and upon your gates." A friend told her there were some prayers you were supposed to say, and since she didn't know them, she called the local synagogue, which just happened to be Har Zion. When the receptionist answered, Cook expected to leave a message and someone would call her back. Instead, she was put on hold for a moment and then Rabbi Wolpe picked up the phone, introduced himself and spelled out the prayers in transliteration for her. She was impressed. She felt instantly welcomed by his kindness and, of course, the voice. Soon after, Cook enrolled her eldest daughter, Danielle, then two and a half, into the synagogue's day camp.

One night, the Cooks sat down for dinner and Danielle started saying *"Baruch atta adonai . . ."*

"What are you doing?" Noreen asked.

"You're supposed to say that before you eat," Danielle replied in toddler language. And she proceeded to teach her mother the *motzi,* the prayer over bread, which, indeed, you are supposed to say before you eat.

When Danielle was old enough, Noreen started her in first grade at the Solomon Schechter day school. Cantor Vogel had found that decision fascinating. He believes that increasing day school enrollment is a key to Har Zion's future. Even though day school students would have no need for Har Zion's after-school Hebrew school, he still feels that more observant congregants in the mix help create a more religiously vibrant shul. And he had always wanted to sit down with Noreen Cook and talk to her about how she came to her decision. He felt that if he could unlock the secret of how she made that leap of faith, it might help him convince others to do it. But they had never made the time to have that talk. And now, instead, he will be chanting at her funeral.

Later that day, Rabbi Buckman arrives in Philadelphia for his second interview. He spends some time with Rabbi Herber and other senior staff. When he meets with the full search committee, everything seems to be going well until they ask if he would go over to the main sanctuary with them and deliver a sermon. He would have been pleased to do so had he been warned ahead of time but, once again, he wasn't asked to prepare anything. Not wishing to disappoint, however, he agrees to deliver the sermon he has almost completed for this coming Shabbat: since it is not written out in the triple-spaced form he would normally work from on the bimah, they enlarge his rough-draft pages on a copy machine.

He does well. Many members are impressed enough to imagine him as the next rabbi of Har Zion. Others would still like to see him in front of a congregation, which means either sending a group to his synagogue in Milwaukee or having him come back to preach at an actual service. These requests are reasonable, but there isn't much time. It is already late March, and he has no job for next year. Unlike other candidates, he can't just keep his current pulpit should his job search fail.

He tells the committee he needs to know quickly if they are serious about him, because the new Jewish Academy of Metropolitan Detroit is really pressuring him to make a decision, and the synagogue in Deerfield is about to make him an offer. The leadership of Har Zion's committee feel that, to some degree, they're suddenly on the other side of the looking glass: three weeks ago their lead candidate wasn't sure he wanted an offer, now their lead candidate wants an offer right away.

Some on the committee wonder: what's wrong with this picture? If Buckman is so right for the job, why did he wait so long in the search process to apply? But nobody asks him. And nobody figures out that his tardiness was actually for a good reason—his loyalty to his colleague, based on the belief that Har Zion and Ackerman really wanted each other.

At the same time, Buckman also wonders what's wrong with this picture? The committee seems indecisive to him, acting as if they have all the time in the world. This is one of the best pulpits in America, yet it has been listed as vacant on the Yellow Sheets from the RA longer than almost any other synagogue. Do they not care about filling the job? Or has it simply been so long since they've hired a rabbi that they don't realize things have changed in the marketplace? It's like buying a home. While people could once sit and deliberate over a house before making an offer, today, if you see something you like, you bid within the hour and pray that nobody outbids you by day's end.

Nonetheless, Buckman does want the job. So, he agrees to wait until they can fly out to Milwaukee and observe him in his natural habitat.

Noreen Cook's funeral is scheduled for Friday morning. In the Jewish religion, burial must take place as quickly as possible after death, usually within twenty-four to forty-eight hours (although never on Shabbat). There is no embalming, no viewing, just a mad rush to arrange everything and to comfort the family who are, of course, in a state of shock.

It is now believed that Noreen's death was caused by long QT syndrome, an abnormality in the electrical system of the heart that is often overlooked on electrocardiograms and, especially in younger patients, isn't picked up until it causes fainting or arrhythmias—so the first symptom can be sudden cardiac arrest. Her husband is struggling with whether her death might have been preventable.

Rabbi Wolpe has, unfortunately, been through this type of deeply resonating tragedy before. This is perhaps the tenth time in his career that somebody so powerfully tied to the life of the synagogue has died so unexpectedly. He recalls too well that day in 1961, early in his career in Harrisburg, when the state troopers called to tell him there had been a car crash and four major leaders of the congregation had been killed. The funeral service was conducted in the main sanctuary because the congregation's memorial chapel could not accommodate four caskets and the crowd. Or the day, also in Harrisburg, in 1966, when the children of two well-known families—a woman in her twenties with advanced cancer and a teenage boy undergoing sugery that was not expected to be life-threatening—died within minutes of each other. Wolpe was at the woman's side, weeping with her family, when the call came that the young man had suffered a heart attack during the procedure. And two days later he had to officiate at both of their funerals, only hours apart.

After those deaths, Wolpe told his wife he had to get out of town. He went to New York the next day, visited the Seminary, walked down Fifth Avenue, wandered around in Saks. He thought about what Einstein said when asked how he survived attending so many banquets and public affairs: "I retire to the back of my mind."

Yet he knows that experience does not make such events any easier. Noreen Cook was very dear to the community, and to him personally. He had just seen her in synagogue the previous Shabbat. It was his first time back at Har Zion since going on sabbatical, and he was actually sitting in the congregation with his family—on the right side, the rabbi side, in the last row. Noreen had approached him, asking if he would please join them on the bimah for the baby naming, but he had demurred.

"Noreen, please," he said, "it's the first chance I've ever had to sit with my grandchildren in shul."

Since Rabbi Wolpe is closest to the Cooks, he steps in and assumes the role of senior rabbi for the funeral—even though, technically, he is supposed to be on sabbatical. At first, Rabbi Herber completely defers to him, as he has for the past three years. They discuss how the Friday morning service will go and, of course, Rabbi Wolpe will give the eulogy, which is what the family is told. But the night before the funeral, Jacob starts feeling that something is wrong with this arrangement. Maybe *he* should be giving the eulogy. He is the rabbi now. And besides, the Cooks are his contemporaries, not Rabbi Wolpe's. Perhaps the younger rabbi should be speaking to the younger congregants who were Noreen Cook's friends. So, the morning of the funeral, he gets up early and begins writing his own eulogy. And when he arrives at the synagogue, he pulls Wolpe aside.

"I wrote something," he says. "I want you to know that I won't give it if you don't want me to. It'll be fine, just tell me. But I felt like I needed to say something."

Wolpe tells Herber to go ahead and give his eulogy first, and then he will adjust the remarks he prepared accordingly. In front of a standing-room-only crowd in the main sanctuary, they both give moving eulogies. Herber makes many of the more salient points about Noreen Cook's death and how much she meant to her family and to the synagogue. Wolpe then explains that when he received the news he had to go somewhere for his own comfort, so he went to *Connections*, the book just published by the synagogue to commemorate its seventy-fifth anniversary, which contains that profile of Noreen. In it, she retold the story of how she had first found Har Zion, and ended by saying of Rabbi Wolpe, "I love that man."

And "that's what strikes all of us," Wolpe says, "that Noreen loved us." She had, he believes, a unique ability to publicly express what she loved.

Afterward, both rabbis are told how touching their remarks were.

Wolpe is not told, however, that some felt his eulogy was a little too much about *himself* and not enough about Noreen Cook. To some younger congregants, the eulogies are a turning point in their feelings about the future of Har Zion. The event clarifies for them that, yes, maybe Rabbi Herber *could* actually be ready to step up and replace his mentor.

Wolpe, on the other hand, is angry about the dueling eulogies. During shiva that evening at the Cooks' home, he approaches his protégé and takes him aside.

"I want to talk to you about something," he says, in a tone that Jacob has never heard before.

A couple of days later, they sit down together in the rabbi's study. Herber is not surprised that Wolpe is upset. In fact, he feels Wolpe's anger is justified and immediately apologizes. He knows he made a mistake.

Although, perhaps he made more than one mistake. Clearly, writing a competing eulogy the morning of a funeral is neither good planning nor smart protégé politics. But, why had he deferred to Wolpe in the first place? This is, after all, supposed to be *his* brief shining moment as mara d'atra of Har Zion. Rabbi Wolpe is gone, but somehow, *he's still here*. It is bizarre for Jacob: he wants to give Rabbi Wolpe the *kavod*, the honor, he deserves. But they can't *both* be rabbi of the congregation.

Neither of them knows exactly how to handle the situation. While Wolpe has developed strong ideas about how to make the transition to retirement—based on watching so many of his colleagues do it badly by staying too involved—everyone has a different definition of "hands-off" and "as far away as possible." While he has kept a respectful distance, he has yet to understand that his very existence makes Jacob feel judged. Handing over the keys to the car isn't the same as relinquishing ownership of the vehicle.

The father-figure issues run rampant in the subtext of their conversation. After all, Jacob currently isn't speaking to his own father. Ever since his parents broke up and he went to live with his mother, he has had a difficult relationship with his dad. But, two years ago, when his daughter was born and Jacob felt "a lack of response" on his father's part, he severed all ties.

Wolpe and Herber talk it through, make some progress. But there's no perfect solution: each is going through a professional metamorphosis, and neither can be sure what will emerge. Yet this is the second heart-to-heart they've had in as many months. The earlier talk had been at Jacob's instigation. He came in to ask about something that had obviously been gnawing at him for some time. When did he get to call Rabbi Wolpe "Jerry" like his other rabbinic colleagues?

Rabbi Wolpe gave this very fair question a moment's thought, and then apologized. He said he probably didn't invite him to do it in the first place because Jacob was in the same rabbinical school class as his son Dan—who calls him Dad and would never call him Jerry. But, yes, it was long overdue for Jacob to start thinking of Rabbi Wolpe as a rabbinic colleague.

"Please," he said diplomatically, "call me Jerry."

18

FIRSTBORN MALE

WITH THE COMING OF PASSOVER five days after the Cook funeral, everything around Har Zion grinds to a halt. Passover, or Pesach, is certainly celebrated in the synagogue—there are morning services on the first and last two days of the eight-day holiday—but otherwise it is the most homebound of the major Jewish holidays. That's because the central observance of Passover is the Seder, the longest family dinner of the year, at which the story of the Exodus from slavery in Egypt is retold.

In preparation for the Seders on the first two nights of the holiday, the home is to be sanitized of all *hametz*—every crumb containing leavening—in keeping with the strict dietary laws of the holiday. As a way of remembering the harsh conditions during slavery, you "keep Passover" by not eating anything leavened, symbolic of the ancient Hebrews hightailing it out of Egypt so quickly that they couldn't wait for dough to rise, so they baked it flat into *matzoh*. Besides purging the home of all that is leavened and filling the shelves with specially pre-pared versions of packaged foods that are labeled "kosher for Passover," many households change dishes and silverware to a special set used ex-clusively for the holiday.

A lot of American Jews "keep Passover" even if, during the rest of the year, they do not follow the more restrictive laws of *kashrut,* keeping kosher. Some of my friends, Jewish and non-Jewish alike, are baffled by this seeming inconsistency of practice. But it has always seemed perfectly logical to me. Keeping kosher every day—by refusing to eat certain foods (pork, shellfish), refusing to mix meat and dairy at the same meal (and keeping separate dishes for each) and eating certain foods, especially meats, only if they are prepared under rabbinic supervision—requires a much broader dedication to traditional Jewish law than keeping the rules of an individual holiday. The decision to keep kosher every day, like the decision to be truly Shabbat-observant every week, is a much bigger commitment, more personal in nature and extremely far-ranging in practical consequences. Rabbis would, of course, prefer it if Jews kept all the dietary and Shabbat laws. But I've never heard a rabbi suggest it is hypocritical to keep Passover if you don't keep kosher. My parents never kept a kosher home. But in my family we have always kept Passover, just as we always fast on Yom Kippur.

I leave Har Zion to its own devices for a few days and go home for Passover, as I always do. The Seder has taken on a new aspect for me in the past few years. Since my father died, I am now the eldest firstborn male of the family, and it has fallen upon me to lead the first Seder. It is a job I sometimes coveted when I was younger, always believing I could do better than my Pop-pop, and later my dad. Now that I have the gig, I wish I didn't, because it so harshly reminds me of who is missing from our Seder table. At the first Seder after my father died, only two months after his funeral, I began with a prayer written for the occasion by my friend Rabbi Michael Monson—a prayer for those no longer at the meal. It was beautiful, but it made everyone so weepy, including me, that I almost didn't include it the second year. This year, the third since his death, I dispense with the prayer, sparing my family the excess emotion. I have learned over the years that while I don't mind making myself cry again over my father's death, not everyone cares for such extreme mourning. The family seems appreciative. There are nearly twenty of us, including my great-aunts and great-uncle who are driven down from New England, and it's nice to start the evening dry-eyed for a change.

The basic Seder narrative is contained in a slim volume called the *Haggadah*. For decades, most postwar American Jews used a Haggadah provided free by Maxwell House coffee as a promotion. But, in recent years, dozens of alternative Haggadahs have been published, and hundreds of new, politically relevant versions of specific prayers have been written; originally printed up and handed out as fliers, they are now more widely circulated on the Internet. Since taking over the Seder, I have become a collector of alternative Haggadahs, an enterprise that is very similar to collecting obscure records and CDs. Each Haggadah has something slightly different; there are Seder rituals for feminists, for Zionists, for kids, for feminist Zionists' kids. But they all tell the same story. And, by threading pieces of them together, I try to make a Seder that is engaging and can be finished in less than three hours, including the meal. Anything longer and the family starts to get cranky.

The retelling of the Passover saga goes well this year. It's a great story with a happy ending, and even though it has been analyzed and parsed for centuries, somebody always comes up with a question that sounds new. At the end, we sing the traditional Passover songs in Hebrew using tunes passed down from my Nana's family. We sing them as quickly as possible—a throwback to our speed-reading classes in Hebrew school—and by the final verses, half the family is complaining that the other half is going too fast. I have only a vague idea what any of these songs are about. I know there's one about a goat, and one that is pretty much just about numbers: my aunt and I are the only ones who sing that one, and we usually crash when we hit the seventh or eighth of the thirteen verses.

It is customary in my family to end the Seder with everyone standing, singing a verse from "America the Beautiful" and then the Israeli national anthem. I have always wondered if those last two should be sung in the opposite order, or if they should be sung at all. Obviously, neither was in the original Haggadah. And I am always suspicious of any attempt to modernize or localize the Seder, because its themes and metaphors are timeless and universal. There is hard-wired into Jewish practice a separation of shul and state. Each Sabbath and festival service, for example, includes a "prayer for our country" to bless the leaders of the nation in which Jews reside. American Jews are sometimes viewed—incorrectly, I think—as struggling with competing national allegiances, de facto dual citizenship. Are we Americans first, or Jews? And even if we're Jews first, is our "country" America or Israel? Prayer books address this by putting the "prayer for our country" first, followed by the "prayer for the state of Israel." The same order as the end of our Seder.

Since I was raised during the first twenty-five years after Israel's founding in 1948, a history capped off by the Yom Kippur War of 1973, there was no doubt then about the need for American Jews to exhibit blind faith toward Israel. Today, that faith is not so blind. At the same time, I now have many more friends who live or vacation in Israel, so the country's safety has a different meaning. But for the purposes of the Seder, we don't debate such things. Our old Haggadah has those two songs at the end, and my Nana and Pop-pop always insisted that we sing them in that order. So we do.

Back in Philadelphia a couple of days after Seder, I drive out to Har Zion on Sunday night for dinner at the synagogue's annual "Passover Restaurant." For thirty dollars, you can get a buffet meal—completely *pesadik,* kosher for Passover—and share the burden of the holiday's dietary laws with your friends and fellow congregants. It's all put on by Betty the Caterer. One of the three kosher catering firms with contracts to serve food at the synagogue, the company is actually run by a guy named Phil. Betty, his mother, has retired.

The spread of food is enormous. In the center there's roast beef being hand-sliced, chicken in some kind of wine sauce with matzoh farfel, perfect round potatoes, kugels of all nations. On one side of the room is a complete deli counter, and on the other is a smorgasbord of sweets, resplendent with fresh coconut macaroons and fruits. While the Passover restaurant is an excellent service for the synagogue to provide, it's also good business for "Betty" to show how the envelope of kosher cooking can be pushed. The synagogue recently mailed out the next round of bar and bat mitzvah dates, and many in the congregation are planning weddings and other life-cycle events for the coming year.

I bump into Cindy Blum, and we laugh about the absurdity of our appetites on Passover. When we can't eat certain things, like bread, we suddenly *must have them,* so there is a tendency to gorge ourselves on the Pesach version of foods we might never eat otherwise. I admit that I downed the whole roll of pesadik kishka—a kind of bready stuffing that looks like sausage—even though I never eat regular kishka. I also ate every macaroon in sight, even though I would not touch a macaroon the rest of the year.

During dinner, Jeff Blum pulls me aside to tell me about a startling development. The leadership has suddenly decided that Jacob Herber should be the next rabbi of Har Zion. "The guy from Milwaukee," Rabbi Buckman, is still in active consideration, and a group is supposed to go visit his synagogue this weekend. But the passage of time has increased their caution about his candidacy. They feel he is intellectually gifted and experienced, but he doesn't seem as warm and engaging as Jacob. And, of course, Buckman is rushing them.

"If they're ambivalent about him," Jeff says, "then why not just have Jacob, who everyone loves?"

He says he is taking Rabbi Herber to the Flyers game on Tuesday, and will discuss this turn of events with him there. Perhaps he also hopes that having a rabbi at the First Union Center will change the Flyers' sputtering fortunes. The team's star, Eric Lindros, has gone down with a collapsed lung, which caused Jeff's son to turn to him and exclaim, "So where is your God *now?*"

I call Jeff after the hockey game to see how it went. He says in their conversation he compared the situation to the movie *The Natural,* which is appropriate because Herber, like Robert Redford's character in the movie, started his career late: he is almost ten years older than most "young" rabbis. It is also appropriate because Herber is a real sucker for schmaltzy sports films, quoting from them in sermons almost as often as he quotes from scripture.

"You know that scene where Redford is smacking balls over the fence," Blum told Herber, "and one coach is marveling over this and the other points out, 'it's only practice'? Well, that's what you've been doing, practicing. But now you're in the game."

Jacob also heard from Lou Fryman, who told him to sit down with his wife and discuss whether they were interested in his becoming a candidate for the Har Zion position. When Jacob reminded him that it was against the rules for such an inexperienced rabbi to be considered, Fryman apparently told Jacob not to worry about that. The powerful lawyer had been serving on committees for more than twenty-five years and had successfully challenged rules far more rigorous than those of the Rabbinical Assembly.

"Apparently," Blum tells me, "Cynthia Herber said yes in a heartbeat, much to everyone's surprise, and Jacob came back to Lou with a yes."

I, too, am surprised by these events, as well as by Blum's excitement about them. Only weeks ago he was telling me he feared Jacob might not survive his six months as fill-in rabbi of Har Zion. He says that the people who actually come to synagogue have watched Herber over these few months and feel he is growing into the job. Even Ralph Snyder, Wolpe's close confidant, is now supporting a Herber candidacy. Yet some of Snyder's older colleagues on the committee are still against moving in this direction. They adore Jacob, but he is too young, too green, to guide so large an institution at such a pivotal moment. He doesn't bring enough to the table other than what he has learned under Rabbi Wolpe. And the synagogue needs truly fresh blood after thirty years with the same rabbi. Har Zion needs someone who thinks outside the box. But Jacob's entire rabbinic career has been spent inside the box Wolpe built. It's all he knows.

And the old-timers know from experience that whenever a synagogue has an old rabbi and a younger rabbi, a cult tends to grow around the younger rabbi, simply because he is younger, more enthusiastic, different. It is the basic group psychology of all houses of worship, which is why Har Zion has always had a rule about never keeping assistants longer than two or three years. After that, a certain number of younger congregants and older contrarians will almost always start asking why the young, good-cop rabbi can't take over.

But the opinions of the Jacob naysayers may not have the same weight as they did before. After all, many of them are the same people who had been backing David Ackerman as the savior of Har Zion, and now that his candidacy has crashed and burned, they have lost some clout. And there are signs that Ralph Snyder is having some success in his attempts to soften their opinions. Bernie Fishman, who led the committee that chose Rabbi Wolpe and is still, in his advancing years, the softest touch in the synagogue—he and his son Mark are the first ones Har Zion asks to pay for almost *anything*—just came back from Florida last week. He looked tan although somewhat frail: he is in his seventies, and his daughter is dying of cancer, which has taken its toll. After services, he made a very public beeline to Rabbi Herber and told him how much he had enjoyed the sermon. It was considered a sign that the rest of the old guard might come on board.

While all this is happening, in Milwaukee, Rabbi Buckman is beginning to sense that Har Zion is not really serious about his candidacy, and the committee is coming out to visit him as a formality. Since he and his wife have decided against the Deerfield pulpit—it's either Har Zion or the school—he withdraws his name from consideration at the other shul. His call reaches the Deerfield president just as their committee has voted to offer him a contract, so their search is now back to square one. He then calls Lou Fryman, to let him know the committee members should cancel their trip to Milwaukee. He is going to take the position at the Jewish high school in suburban Detroit after all. When nobody at Har Zion begs him to reconsider, his suspicions are confirmed. They have obviously decided they want to elevate their assistant rabbi.

If they have that much confidence in Jacob's ability, he thinks, that's wonderful. But Buckman actually feels sorry for him. He can only imagine the demands that will be placed on his inexperienced colleague. He wonders if Jacob has fully imagined them yet.

Jeff Blum tells me that he is sure Jacob will grow into the job, although he does point out that this entire process has been proof that anything can happen. At the hockey game, he told Herber that he would be pleased to have him as his rabbi and to have him officiate at the bat mitzvah of his daughter. By his estimate, 85 percent of the committee is convinced he is the guy.

Rabbi Wolpe, Blum thinks, will be very pleased.

Well, no. Actually, Rabbi Wolpe isn't very pleased at all. But since he has vowed to stay out of the rabbi search process, he can't really tell that to anyone but his wife—and me. As we sit in his almost completely dismantled office, the once-jammed shelves now denuded of books, he expresses deep concern. The synagogue leadership is panicking, he says. And he is very worried for Jacob. In no way is he surprised that the leaders are trying to draft the young rabbi into service; in fact, he would have been more surprised if this *hadn't* happened. But Jacob is not yet eligible for the job, and perhaps he shouldn't be.

"He is *most* advanced for a young man. He's exceptional," Wolpe says. "But I'm afraid his inexperience will catch up with him." Wolpe has been warning Herber for months about the dangers of being seduced by a congregation like Har Zion. What happens when the seduction is over, and the year or two honeymoon period that all new rabbis get comes to an end?

"That's when you begin to deal with reality," he says. "You tick off somebody important and soon 90 percent of the congregation still likes you but enough people don't that you start hearing things you *never* heard during the honeymoon. I'm sure I made gaffes at my first pulpit in Charleston, and they were willing to overlook them because I was new. By the time I made it to Har Zion, they didn't expect to have to tolerate what the people in Charleston would. I don't want him to get caught in a mature situation at the beginning of his career."

He can't really share these feelings with the leaders at Har Zion: he must even be circumspect in talking with his old pal Ralph Snyder. When Ralph first asked whether Wolpe thought Herber was ready to run Har Zion, he had answered honestly, "I hope so." He didn't mean to sound critical of Jacob—in fact, he was being critical of Ralph and the others for thinking that a rabbi with so little experience could handle the congregation's incessant demands. But, he could see by the look on his friend's face that all Ralph wanted to hear was unqualified support for the plan. So Wolpe decided then and there to excuse himself from any conversations about Jacob's candidacy, because he knew anything he said would be wrong.

We begin talking about other perils of rabbinic placement. He tells me that, besides the situation at Har Zion, his son Danny has resigned his position in Boca Raton and is also looking for a new job. That's an amazing coincidence, I say, because my mother just told me that the new rabbi at my old synagogue in Harrisburg, Eric Lankin, has suddenly announced that at the end of his contract he will leave to take a non-pulpit job in New Jersey. My mom is especially annoyed because she lobbied for Lankin on the search committee—in part because I told her how strongly my friend Rabbi Michael Monson recommended him.

While she doesn't come out and say so, something Jewish-motherly in her voice suggests that she believes the synagogue's troubles are now partially my fault.

I ask Rabbi Wolpe if his son Danny would consider applying for the job at his father's old shul. It would be fitting and, more important, it would mean my old synagogue might actually have a rabbi next year. He says he didn't know about the opening, and he'll discuss it with him right away.

Apparently Har Zion is not the only synagogue, and Judaism not the only religion, having problems filling pulpits at this, the late-April height of clergy employment season. In my e-mail several mornings later is this unsigned parody memo, which Rabbi Monson received anonymously and forwarded to almost every rabbi I have ever heard of.

The following is a confidential report on several candidates being considered for a pulpit.

- Adam: Good man but problems with his wife. Also one reference told of how his wife and he enjoy walking nude in the woods.
- Noah: Former pulpit of 120 years with not even one convert. Prone to unrealistic building projects.
- Abraham: Though the references reported wife-swapping, the facts seem to show he never slept with another man's wife, but did offer to share his own wife with another man.
- Joseph: A big thinker, but a braggart, believes in dream-interpreting and has a prison record.
- Moses: A modest and meek man, but poor communicator, even stuttering at times. Sometimes blows his stack and acts rashly. Some say he left an earlier church over a murder charge.
- David: The most promising leader of all until we discovered the affair he had with his neighbor's wife.
- Solomon: Great preacher but our parsonage would never hold all those wives.
- Elijah: Prone to depression. Collapses under pressure.
- Elisha: Reported to have lived with a single widow while at his former church.
- Hosea: A tender and loving pastor but our people could never handle his wife's occupation.
- Deborah: Strong leader and seems to be anointed, but she is female.
- Jeremiah: Emotionally unstable, alarmist, negative, always lamenting things, reported to have taken a long trip to bury his underwear on the bank of a foreign river.
- Isaiah: On the fringe? Claims to have seen angels in church. Has trouble with his language.

- Jonah: Refused God's call into ministry until he was forced to obey by getting swallowed up by a great fish. He told us the fish later spit him out on the shore near here. We hung up.
- Amos: Too backward and unpolished. With some Seminary training he might have promise, but has a hang-up against wealthy people—might fit in better in a poor congregation.
- John: Says he is a Baptist, but definitely doesn't dress like one. Has slept in the outdoors for months on end, has a weird diet and provokes denominational leaders.
- Peter: Too blue-collar. Has a bad temper—even has been known to curse. Had a big run-in with Paul in Antioch. Aggressive, but a loose cannon.
- Paul: Powerful CEO-type leader and fascinating preacher. However, short on tact, unforgiving with younger ministers, harsh and has been known to preach all night.
- James and John: Package-deal preacher & associate seemed good at first, but found out they have an ego problem regarding other fellow workers and seating positions. Threatened an entire town after an insult. Also known to try to discourage workers who didn't follow along with them.
- Timothy: Too young!
- Methuselah: Too old . . . WAY too old!
- Jesus: Has had popular times, but once his church grew to five thousand he managed to offend them all, and then this church dwindled down to twelve people. Seldom stays in one place very long. And, of course, he's single.
- Judas: His references are solid. A steady plodder. Conservative. Good connections. Knows how to handle money. We're inviting him to preach this Sunday. Possibilities here.

THE GHOST OF HAR ZION PAST

I MMERSED IN ALL THIS placement Kremlinology, it has been easy to forget exactly what is at stake here—just what this synagogue has meant, and why it matters so much who its fourth rabbi will be. So the seventy-fifth anniversary event honoring the historic relationship between Har Zion and Conservative Judaism could not come at a better time. On a Sunday afternoon, we sit in the small chapel waiting to be regaled by the leading lights of Conservative Jewry: the chancellor of the Jewish Theological Seminary, Ismar Schorsch, is scheduled to speak, along with Rabbi Dov Elkins, who began his career at Har Zion Radnor in the mid-1960s, and is now a nationally known lecturer, author and teacher with a pulpit in Princeton; and Rabbi Alan Kensky, an associate dean at the Seminary and well-known Midrash scholar who was a scholar-in-residence at Har Zion during the late 1980s.

But the highlight for me is that Chaim Potok is on the program. He is very much the ghost of Har Zion past. It should be an excellent opportunity for me to bone up on what the synagogue has meant to American Judaism.

Wolpe arrives with the news that the chancellor can't make it, and his last-minute replacement, historian Jack Wertheimer, the provost of the Seminary, is caught in bad weather. His plane hasn't arrived at Philadelphia International Airport yet. So Wolpe has to stall. He is, no surprise, a crackerjack staller. And he begins telling stories from the good old days.

He talks about the year the first Camp Ramah was started in Wisconsin, and many Seminary students went out to be counselors. He traveled out there with a young Norman Podhoretz, who had yet to make his place in the world of literary criticism and punditry as the neo-conservative editor of *Commentary*. Podhoretz was, Wolpe recalls, "the village *shagetz* then"—using the Yiddish term for a non-Jew or a Jew who flouts Jewish law—"and he hasn't changed. He told us about all the outrageous things he did. We got on a train to Eagle River, Wisconsin, and stopped at a non-kosher restaurant for lunch. Norman turns to us and says, 'We are in Eagle River, Wisconsin . . . have a meat sandwich, who will know?' And in walks Dr. Louis Finkelstein, the head of the Seminary. Norman was never the same."

As he tells these stories, something finally clicks for me. For the past several months, I have been attending these seventy-fifth anniversary events without fully understanding what everyone is talking about. Basically, these well-funded symposia preach to the converted, offering old-timers and their kids and grandkids a chance to waltz down memory lane. Nobody bothers to explain much to the uninitiated, which is, of course, one way that tight-knit communities tighten the knit: at a family reunion, nobody has time to bring the new son-in-law up to speed, they are too busy kissing (or dissing) cousins.

Even though Wolpe has done his best during our private discussions to explain bits of back story, there are still times when I am baffled. I will recognize from the look in his eyes that he is probably being reve-latory, but only someone who has done a Ph.D. on, say, Har Zion presi-dential politics during the Vietnam War would really appreciate what he is revealing. In fact, Wolpe recently gave me what amounts to his dissertation on just that subject, the rocky period when he first came to Har Zion. It's a private, unpublished memoir—thirty-four pages, single-spaced—giving his detailed perspective on how he came to be hired by the synagogue, the state it was in when he arrived and how the leadership eventually came to move Har Zion to the suburbs. It is dated September 1992, and in the text he claims it was written in response to then-recent books on the Jewish history of Philadelphia and Boston. Since those books were published in 1986 and 1991 respectively, a more likely explanation for the enterprise is that he had open-heart surgery in the spring of 1992, and realized the risk of leaving his legacy in the hands of other writers.

This document would probably shock and enthrall any of the veteran Har Zionites who were around back in the late sixties and early seventies, and would fascinate Wolpe's children, from whom he kept all hints of the psychodramas within the synagogue. His son Paul has told me he still does not know many of these stories, and believes a big reason two of his brothers chose the rabbinate is because their father never really let on how difficult it is to maintain a pulpit and one's sanity. Yet, even after several readings, I still wasn't sure I understood the story he was trying to relate.

Listening to Wolpe and Potok, however, I'm starting to make connections, the major dramas of the Har Zion saga becoming clearer. Perhaps I have at last just heard the stories enough times. Or maybe it's the way the two are needling each other. Potok refers to Wolpe as "Jerry" in front of his congregants—which is, of course, never done. When he apologizes for the gaffe, Wolpe shoots back, "No problem, you're lucky I didn't call you 'Herman,' " which is, I assume, what Potok went by before deciding to use only his Hebrew name, Chaim. I can suddenly see them as young men, characters from Potok's fiction. And the story they lived through takes on strong narrative lines and swelling background music.

In 1922, the members of a minyan in the growing West Philadelphia neighborhood of Wynnefield decided to start their own synagogue. They raised money by employing the European custom of "rimpling," going from house to house after services and making a Kiddush and a sales pitch at each one. Then they held a fund-raising dinner, and between twenty-seven men they raised thirty thousand dollars. In less than two years, they built a temple for $175,000 and began with a membership of one hundred families. They named a president and hired a young rabbi by telegram the day he graduated from the Seminary. Both proved to be excellent choices, ambitious and committed: president Harry Cohen and Rabbi Simon Greenberg remained in their respective positions at Har Zion for more than two decades, as did the original Hebrew school principal and the sexton.

The synagogue grew to 250 families by the end of its first year, and quickly made a reputation in a city that was home to many of the oldest Jewish institutions in America—including a congregation, dating from 1740, that included Benjamin Franklin among its early donors and spawned the country's first Hebrew school. Philadelphia was where the Conservative movement was conceived in America—by immigrants who believed both main forms of European Jewry, Orthodox and Reform, were too extreme, and so founded short-lived Maimonides College, the precursor to the Jewish Theological Seminary, as well as the Rabbinical Assembly. Philadelphia was where the first sermon in English was preached and the first English-language Jewish newspaper was published. And Har Zion grew to become the city's largest and most powerful synagogue, the stadt shul. The neighborhood around it, Wynnefield, became increasingly Jewish, to the point where it was derisively referred to as "Kike's Peak."

Simon Greenberg, whose family moved to America from Russia when he was four, was one of the first English-speaking rabbis in the United States. He was a charismatic Zionist who was coaxed away from a teaching track at the Seminary to take Har Zion's pulpit. And his multiple allegiances to the synagogue, the Seminary and Israel became the cornerstones of Har Zion's international reputation. Nor did it hurt that after the Depression many of the synagogue's members amassed great wealth as entrepreneurs and were extremely generous to Jewish causes. But Har Zion members had more than deep pockets; they became known for proudly investing in meaningful innovation and unique pro- gramming, along with buildings to which plaques could be affixed. In 1946, Rabbi Greenberg left Har Zion—although in many ways he never really left—to work full-time under Louis Finkelstein as provost of the Seminary. Because he had more American pulpit experience than anyone else at the Seminary, an institution then run primarily by European- trained scholars, Greenberg became a role model for an entire generation of American rabbis—as well as clergy in other faiths.

And his experiences at Har Zion were filtered into the Seminary's lessons. Solomon Schechter may have been the first major commentator on the peculiar experience of being a rabbi in twentieth-century America. (His observation that "you have to be able to talk baseball to be a success as an American rabbi" is often quoted.) But it was Greenberg who brought the practical wisdom of twenty years on an American pulpit to the religious and intellectual training of Conservative rabbis, helping trainees understand all the places where God is in the details. He was joined in this role by another longtime pulpit rabbi from Pennsylvania whom Finkelstein hired to teach practical rabbinics and fund-raising: Max Arzt, who was a father figure and mentor to young Jerry Wolpe, and whose son, David Arzt, was Wolpe's rabbinical school roommate and later served as best man at his wedding. Since the Seminary and the Conservative rabbinate were the driving force in American Judaism through much of the twentieth century, Greenberg and Arzt made an in- delible impact on the practical world of the modern clergy.

Greenberg's successor at Har Zion, David Goldstein, was one of the first American-born pulpit rabbis. Born and raised in Minnesota, Goldstein came to Har Zion from a synagogue in Omaha, Nebraska, and he brought a Midwestern straightforwardness and quiet Machiavellianism to a congregation that had grown accustomed to a little more charisma. (One former assistant describes his sermonizing style as "very natural, never bombastic, like the way Robert Frost spoke at John Kennedy's inauguration.") So he never quite escaped Simon Greenberg's long shadow, yet it was under Goldstein's leadership that Har Zion membership grew to some eighteen hundred families in the postwar period, with fourteen hundred children in the Hebrew school. And unlike Greenberg, who was an active Zionist caught up in national and international issues, Goldstein was a master fund-raiser and a builder of local Jewish communities. Unfortunately, he was quickly afforded an opportunity to build when, in the winter of 1947, a fire broke out in the synagogue that destroyed the pulpit, the Ark, all the Torahs and most of the stained-glass windows. Har Zion did more than rebuild that synagogue; it re-created the idea of the "synagogue center" for postwar American Jews. Goldstein raised the money to add an auditorium, which also became the city's first large space available for kosher catering. The synagogue built a gym and a community center, making Har Zion the true center of a Jewish universe in West Philadelphia—a place that children and teenagers would walk by in the afternoon to see if their friends were there.

Part of Goldstein's talent was his ability to recognize the good ideas of others and raise money from his machers—up on the bimah after services, or out on the golf course—to make these innovative dreams reality. One example of his investing in intellectual development was the innovative scholar-in-residence program he initiated in the early 1950s to expand the synagogue's intellectual reach. The first scholar-in-residence was Nahum Sarna, a young British student of Bible and Semitic languages who went on to become one of the most important biblical scholars of the twentieth century, beginning with his authoritative work *Understanding Genesis.* He was followed by Dr. Fritz Rothschild, who went on to teach at the Seminary and became a protégé of Heschel, editing some of the great rabbi's work after his death. And then came Chaim Potok, long before he became known as a popular novelist. He was recommended to Goldstein by both Heschel and Greenberg.

Potok had been ordained at the Seminary in 1954, served as a chaplain for sixteen months on the front lines in Korea, returned to live in New York and then moved to California, where he was director of the

Camp Ramah in Ojai and taught at the University of Judaism. In 1959, he became scholar-in-residence at Har Zion in Wynnefield and also ran the first services at blossoming Har Zion Radnor, imbuing the place with his creative spirit. On the side, he was working on his first novel (which was never published but allowed him to learn how to write a novel) and was completing course work for a Ph.D. at Penn in philosophy. When he finished his term as scholar-in-residence, he was offered three excellent pulpits, but he was ambivalent about continuing in the rabbinate. His wife, Adena, a psychiatric social worker, asked him what he most wanted to do with his life; he said he wanted to write. So he turned down the jobs, and they decided to move to Israel—a move that was made possible only after Rabbi Goldstein quietly gave them what was then the very large sum of two thousand dollars from his discretionary fund. It was typical of Goldstein's intellectual largesse.

During their year in Israel, Potok wrote *The Chosen,* along with a somewhat less commercial work: his dissertation on the epistemology of Solomon Maimon. The Potoks then returned to America, living in their native New York until Potok sold the book to Simon & Schuster, and then moving back to Philadelphia, where Potok was offered the excellent day job of editor-in-chief at the Jewish Publication Society (JPS). The couple also rejoined Har Zion. The synagogue still had a great, galvanic davening minyan, in which he remained active. Potok was the best-known member of Har Zion's *chevra,* a group of rabbis and educators, many associated with the nearby University of Pennsylvania, which functioned as a minyan within the congregation and also had other benefits: there was an investment club, headed by a banker in the congregation, to help the clergy make the best of their small salaries.

It was in this warm, supportive environment that Potok wrote his next two novels—*The Promise* and *My Name Is Asher Lev*—while working at JPS. But the Potoks privately had to admit that Har Zion was no longer the same synagogue they had enjoyed in the early sixties. Behind the bimah, it was an increasingly unhappy place. While it still had its national reputation as a utopian congregation, Har Zion was under attack from without and from within.

The rise of the counterculture in the late sixties hit hardest at the most traditional houses of worship, like Har Zion, where women were still not allowed on the bimah and younger members had trouble moving into leadership positions. Besides the generational and gender tension, there were growing problems of geography. The shift of population from the city to the suburbs was increasing, eroding the walk-in community in Wynnefield and forcing younger suburban members to drive their children back into the city for Hebrew school at the main synagogue. Many of Har Zion's younger, more energetic members worshipped at the Radnor campus and came to the main synagogue primarily for High Holiday services. And when they came back, they could see how much the neighborhood was changing. Although it had always been ethnically integrated, Wynnefield was now becoming poorer, less white and, to some, appreciably more dangerous.

These national trends, which were facing major urban houses of worship all around the country, combined with a situation very specific to Har Zion: the relationship between Rabbi Goldstein and the leadership had gone sour. Some of the problem was simply the bad timing of a rabbi nearing retirement age just as America and American Jewry were changing drastically with the times. But Goldstein didn't help the situation. He was reluctant to retire, and distrustful that the new, younger leaders of the synagogue would do the right thing for him after he stepped down. He harbored an unrealistic dream that his son, a rabbi in Atlantic City, might succeed him. And it also became clear later on that he had pressures at home, as he quietly struggled with the failing health of his wife, who was slowly slipping into premature senility.

Potok had always admired Goldstein as "an enormous person with a blunt face to him. He had vision beyond any twenty rabbis. All of the great ideas of the synagogue came from him. He did all the hard work, but didn't get the credit. And then he was bludgeoned by spiteful men." Among the leaders of those men was philanthropist Abner Schreiber, which was ironic since Schreiber had helped fund some of Goldstein's initiatives over the years and was very much part of the embattled generation the rabbi represented. But when Schreiber became president

of the synagogue in 1965, he sided with some of the younger reformers—
the synagogue's executive director, and the next generation of leaders,
who were business executives and professionals rather than self-made
entrepreneurs. And he quickly became Goldstein's nemesis. Under attack, Goldstein grew increasingly mercurial.

"It was the most vicious, mean-spirited thing I've ever seen," recalls
Schreiber's grandson, Marshall Herskovitz. "And it made me aware of
the tendency in successful men when they reach a certain age to get involved in turf wars just to fight over turf. It was as if they were fighting
for control of a company. The ugliness of the struggle astonished me
as a young boy. I couldn't tell you the particulars. I know he thought
Goldstein was arrogant and mean. But that could also describe my
grandfather."

The leadership leaned on Rabbi Goldstein to create a succession plan,
and they began discussing whether or not to build a new Har Zion in
the suburbs—a move Goldstein opposed. The rabbi's longtime assistant
rabbi, Efry Spectre, was interviewed for the job, but he was viewed as
too closely aligned with Goldstein, his mentor, to be an agent of change.
Spectre then abruptly left Har Zion and became senior rabbi at nearby
Beth Am Israel—which at the time was still in the city and was also
struggling with whether to relocate to the suburbs. But Spectre realized
that his predecessor at Beth Am "hadn't fully retired, he didn't want to let
go," so he quickly moved on to become founding rabbi of a congregation created by fleeing members of Har Zion and Beth Am.

The battles continued over who should be the next rabbi and
whether or not Har Zion should move. There were theological battles,
which were not surprising because Har Zion had become an extremely
diverse synagogue. Not only did it have two campuses, each with its
own services, but on the High Holidays there were seven different
services within the main building, reflecting a wide variety of beliefs
and levels of observance. There were also generational battles, eventually leading the two silver-haired presidents after Schreiber to resign
prematurely—the second, in 1968, followed by all his officers. The

Jewish Theological Seminary stepped in to try and stanch the bleeding, convincing a young leader from the Radnor congregation—Bernard Fishman, who ran his family's large boys-apparel manufacturing business—to assume the embattled presidency. What he took over was a synagogue tearing itself apart.

The struggles were then exacerbated by a decision typical of Har Zion's largesse and intellectual high-mindedness, and one that backfired in a most public way. While trying to decide if younger Jews would continue to flee Wynnefield for the suburbs, the leadership decided to do a study. They selected prominent Penn sociologist Dr. Samuel Klausner, who was a member of Har Zion's observant chevra and owned a home near the synagogue, for the seventeen-thousand-dollar commission. Klausner's university-based Center for Research on the Acts of Man had a larger social agenda, consistent with its rather lofty name and the political climate of the late 1960s. The passionate sociologist was interested in bigger Big Questions than whether or not Har Zion should move. Besides his fears for Wynnefield, he was concerned about how a largely urban religion could survive in the auto-driven world of the suburbs, where he saw Jews becoming more assimilated and secularized.

During the year of Klausner's study, the synagogue solved its clergy problems by inviting Rabbi Wolpe to take over Goldstein's pulpit. While negotiating with Har Zion, Wolpe began to realize that the synagogue was much more deeply divided than he had been led to believe, and that the situation with Rabbi Goldstein had been more painful than anyone had let on. Wolpe also discovered that Goldstein was against the idea of the young rabbi from Harrisburg succeeding him. This was especially painful because Goldstein had been the main speaker at Wolpe's installation in Harrisburg, and he was under the impression they had an excellent relationship. Wolpe appealed to Simon Greenberg at the Seminary for assistance, but the vice-chancellor could not get directly involved. He had already been doing damage control behind the scenes for some time, as Goldstein became more embittered and unpredictable. Eventually, however, a compromise was worked out, Goldstein stepped aside and Wolpe was hired.

In mid-1970, Sam Klausner delivered the results of his study to the thirty-man planning committee of Har Zion. His research found that the racial and social changes in the neighborhood weren't nearly as drastic as the synagogue's leadership believed; his conclusion was that the only real danger to the racial balance of Wynnefield would be if Har Zion left. This analysis did not dissuade them from their plan—which Wolpe clearly had been hired to help execute—to move Har Zion away from the socially and racially changing neighborhood. When Klausner realized that his recommendations were being ignored, he stunned the synagogue's leadership by releasing his study to the media, insisting that Penn's research regulations required such a public dissemination of information. The newspaper stories completely accepted Klausner's socially optimistic analysis. The stories also captured some of the more incendiary findings of the study, including assessments of the percentage of Jews who were "more enthusiastic about the advantages of an integrated neighborhood" and those who were "more prepared to integrate with higher-status white Gentiles."

In response to the stories, synagogue president Bernie Fishman was forced to issue a public statement clarifying the congregation's position: Har Zion *was* going to move to the suburbs. Of the congregation's seventeen hundred member families, only 350 still lived in Wynnefield, and few of them had children. Even though the move would take some time, he said, the board of directors had authorized the committee to find and purchase a piece of property in the suburbs.

The battle continued in the press. In a follow-up article, another prominent member of Har Zion joined Klausner in publicly criticizing the idea of a move: Harry Sylk, the drugstore entrepreneur whose name was on the grand auditorium in the synagogue that would be left behind, a room that had cost him and his three brothers a one-hundred-thousand-dollar donation back in the 1950s.

A year later, the holy war of Har Zion was still raging, and even worsened after a *Newsweek* cover story entitled "The Battle of the Suburbs" featured a full-page sidebar on the synagogue's situation in Wynnefield. The author of the sidebar so completely accepted Klausner's findings that it was entitled "The Suburb That Struck a Truce" and reported that Wynnefield was one of the few places in America where "white flight" had actually been stopped. Klausner was quoted roundly criticizing "the oligarchy of the synagogue" for rejecting a study commissioned merely to "cover its tracks."

Behind the scenes, the congregational leadership was in turmoil over the divisiveness and the public attacks. The Jewish community was not accustomed to such critical coverage in the lay press. And while the leadership still wanted to move Har Zion to the suburbs, there was no plan and no money. Wolpe was starting to reinvigorate Shabbat services with his sermons—which were more dynamic than Rabbi Goldstein's had been, and touched on more socially relevant topics—but membership was slipping further. Then Har Zion's influential executive director resigned, in part, Wolpe felt, because the administrator was concerned that the synagogue might never get past the planning phase of the move.

Soon, Wolpe himself started talking to his wife about the possibility of quitting Har Zion. He had been brought in to help a divided congregation unite and rise to its former greatness—in a new synagogue he could help build from scratch. Instead, it looked as if Har Zion was crumbling under its own weight. It could actually implode or at best remain a small, moderately significant congregation in Wynnefield. The frustrated rabbi made a trip to New York to speak to the head of the Rabbinical Assembly about which other pulpits might be available if he left.

In the midst of his desperation, Wolpe called a meeting at his home of the synagogue leadership and several key congregants, to tell them just how close he was to giving up. Instead, he was pleasantly surprised when Al Grosser, a gruff developer known for saying what was on his mind, blasted the group for their complacency, which he claimed would

destroy Har Zion. He insisted they commit to raising the money needed
for the move, and he volunteered to be a leader and constant irritant.
Sadly, he didn't live to see the result of his infectious enthusiasm: two
weeks later, he had a heart attack and Wolpe officiated at his funeral. But
Wolpe would always believe Grosser was the key catalyst responsible for
getting everyone motivated.

Finding a site for the new synagogue became the next nightmare, especially after it was determined that the Radnor campus was unsuitable.
It had extreme topography—the new building would have to sit on top
of a steep hill with all the parking at the bottom or vice versa, either way
not a great idea for older members—and the site was considered too far
from the city. Eventually a tract of land was found that was an equal
distance from Wynnefield and Radnor, and had the added advantage of
being less than a mile from an exit of the Delaware Valley's main thor-
oughfare, the Schuylkill Expressway. It was a huge old estate and the insurance company administering its sale would not break it up. So the
congregation arranged to buy all eighty-four acres, picked twenty-five
choice acres of plateau land for the new complex and made plans to re-
sell the rest of the parcel for residential development at a price that
would make their own plot cost-free.

Word of the tentative purchase was leaked to the press by Sam
Klausner. Har Zion officials publicly denied they had bought the land, or
even that they were definitely leaving, because the decision still had to
be put to a congregational vote. And on January 7, 1973, it was. Before
the meeting, Wolpe and the synagogue's leaders rehearsed and rehearsed
their answers to the questions they knew would be coming from the anti-
move forces. They truly had no idea how the vast majority of members
would feel about the move when given the opportunity to actually cast
ballots. The meeting was high drama: more than a thousand Har Zion
members attended, and the main auditorium was standing-room-only.
The meeting was chaired by Jerry Shestack, the outgoing president and,
more important, a brilliant attorney capable of maintaining some control
over so charged a situation.

The anti-move forces did not have much ammunition other than their own abilities of persuasion and their heartfelt commitment to the future of their neighborhood. But in the three years since their fight began in earnest, conditions in Wynnefield had not really improved; there had been murders and break-ins where swastikas had been painted on the walls of the synagogue. Daniel Elazar, a chevra member and renowned scholar—a world expert on political culture and the international Jewish community—stepped up to the microphone to attack the kind of synagogue Har Zion was likely to become in the suburbs, protesting that the new building would become nothing more than a catering hall with a chapel attached, and lower educational standards. Wolpe had prepared long and hard for this issue, marshaling all kinds of proprietary statistics to show how catering income was the only way to maintain standards in the synagogue's schools—and pointing out that part of the current crisis was that neighborhood safety issues were causing congregants to hold their rites of passage elsewhere, hurting the congregation's bottom line.

In the end, the vote wasn't even close. The membership overwhelmingly supported the move.

Not long after the vote, Wolpe was in town and ran into Rabbi David Wice, the leader of Philadelphia's largest and oldest Reform synagogue, Rodeph Shalom, which had a magnificent old building near city hall and a newer one in the suburbs.

"I hear you are building a new Har Zion," he said. "Well, I built one synagogue building. If I had to do it over again, I would retire from the rabbinate." Wolpe soon understood what he meant.

They initially hired renowned architect Percival Goodman for the project. That didn't work out, and they ultimately had to pay him thirty thousand dollars before starting over with another design concept from a local firm.

The fund-raising was also difficult. A meeting was held at the Locust

Club, where the initial major gifts were made. Bernie Fishman, of course, made the key donation, along with his cousin Sylvan Tobin, which led to the main auditorium being named Fishman-Tobin in honor of their parents. In the middle of fund-raising, however, the Yom Kippur War broke out. This not only diverted even more Jewish philanthropy than usual back to Israel, but led to the oil embargo that wreaked havoc on America's economy and its psyche. Interest rates skyrocketed, and the financing arrangements for the new synagogue were suddenly in jeopardy. While the leadership had hoped to keep the thirty-two-acre Radnor campus as a summer camp and retreat, the change in rates forced them to arrange to sell it to Sun Oil to raise cash.

Membership continued to drop. In fact, the new building was designed for a lower head count, adjusted to what Wolpe and the leadership hoped they could maintain: one thousand families, which during the burgeoning 1950s and into the 1960s would have been considered a disaster, but now seemed like a hopeful round number.

Other corners had to be cut to save money, leading to auditoriums so faceless that they needed redecoration almost immediately. Even the most esthetic achievement of the new synagogue, the modern stained-glass windows inspired by Ben Shahn's Hebrew calligraphy, caused controversy. They were stunning in design and execution, using a revolutionary technique employing much larger chunks and shards of prestained glass than usual to let in a maximum amount of shimmering colored light. But those Har Zionites who had grown up enchanted with the more traditional stained-glass windows of the Wynnefield sanctuary—as well as those families who had donated the money for those windows—were shocked to find out that they would not be incorporated into the new building. Not only that, they weren't even going to be put into a museum or in storage. Apparently they had been created using a process that didn't allow them to be taken apart: if the lead holding them together was melted, the heat would also melt the paint that had been applied to the glass. Some of the furious members who had donated the windows asked to take theirs, until they found out how expensive it would be and how little chance there was of keeping them intact. When the Wynnefield synagogue building was finally sold to Pinn Memorial Baptist Church, all the old windows remained in place.

On September 12, 1976, just after the nation's bicentennial had been celebrated in Philadelphia, Rabbi Wolpe stood in the central entrance of the new building and blew a shofar, a hollowed-out ram's horn used as a call to prayer. At the other entrance, the synagogue's sexton echoed with his own shofar, and the full house rose as the Torah scrolls from Wynnefield and Radnor were carried in a processional into the new sanctuary.

Har Zion was reborn in the house that Wolpe built. And those who had opposed him were gone, but neither forgotten nor forgetful. Nearly thirty years after the war for Wynnefield was lost, there are still plenty of older people in Philadelphia who refer to Wolpe as "the new rabbi" at Har Zion, the one who "ruined the place."

Chaim Potok would never be so impolitic as to say such a thing in an address at the new Har Zion. And, in fact, he never blamed Wolpe personally for what happened—nor did Klausner, with whom Wolpe later studied sociology at Penn. But as the sagacious bearded writer and rabbi speaks here today in the Har Zion chapel, it is clear that time has not dissipated all his displeasure. His comments are directed more toward American Judaism as a whole. He believes that Conservative Judaism is floundering (an opinion shared by many inside and outside the movement, evoking untold gigabytes of debate). But, long after he and his wife quit the synagogue, he still believes that Har Zion, on the eve of its seventy-fifth anniversary, is a special congregation devoted to its original ideals.

"Why is there only one Har Zion like this in the United States?" he asks. "That's not a celebration, it's a disaster!" He dismisses the "big questions" about the Seminary listed on the afternoon's agenda—"Why are you asking *these* dumb questions"—and says he has some bigger ones.

"Will we be split over homosexuals as we were over women?" he asks. "And why haven't we *gotten rid of the bar mitzvah*? Can't they have a rite of passage without throwing money at them?"

Now he's on a roll. "Some say that to American Jews, religion is a hobby. But is it? Not to the Orthodox. But how about the Conservative?" He looks down at the crowd. "Is Judaism something serious? Or is it . . . *golf*?"

He lets the question linger for a moment. "Because, if it's golf, I'd rather be home writing a sentence."

Later in the program, Potok laments the number of Jews who are losing their religion. "For every one hundred Jews who leave, we get only sixty converts," he rails. And then, with a twinkle in his eye, he notes, "By the way, Sam Klausner gave me those statistics."

THE RABBIS' CONVENTION
TOTE BAG

"I LOVE THE PEOPLE here at Har Zion," Rabbi Herber tells me, "but I'm not really a part of the family. My family is other rabbis. That's my chevra. And I'm really looking forward to having a chance to see my friends and classmates, and just clear my head." He's headed off to Baltimore for the annual convention of the Rabbinical Assembly. I let him know that I'll see him there.

Two days later I'm coming up the escalator at the Sheraton Inner Harbor Hotel, and as I reach the top nearly the entire cast of characters of the Har Zion rabbi search is milling about the registration area. To my right, Perry Rank is telling a colleague about the pulpit he just accepted in Syosset, Long Island. To my left, Michael Monson spies me from a distance and approaches: he is now the rabbi at the tiny congregation in Montclair, New Jersey, that used to be Perry Rank's synagogue.

And right in front of me, like actors cued in a play, David Ackerman and Jacob Herber, both dressed casually in khakis and shirtsleeves, walk toward each other and give a firm soul-brother handshake. I almost expect them to turn to me and give a thumbs-up sign, like the beginning of *Starsky and Hutch*.

The clock strikes, and everyone begins shuffling toward the Chesapeake Ballroom for the day's main plenary session. It is entitled "The Renewed Yearning and Search for God: A New Jewish Spirituality?" but I can tell from some of the grumbling comments of the older rabbis that the subtitle probably should be "A New Jewish Spirituality or Just a Bunch of Crap?" The moderator for the morning session is Rabbi Neil Gillman, the brilliant and bombastic Seminary philosophy professor whose High Holiday moonlighting job is running the upstairs services at Beth Zion Beth Israel, the synagogue my wife and I now belong to and attend when I'm not at Har Zion. As a speaker, Gillman rarely disappoints, and this morning he's in fine form.

He discusses a paradigm shift that is "allegedly going on" in America, with Judaism as its nexus. There is now more interest in the Jewish person than the Jewish people. The "peoplehood" agenda of the early and mid-twentieth century is giving way to a new centrality of religion and belief. When he was a student at the Seminary, the peoplehood concept in American Judaism was very strong, and "there was precious little attention paid to religion, prayer, sin, all the stuff that now comes under the umbrella term *spirituality*." But this New Spiritualism, he says, is now everywhere, with renewed interest in the body, *feelings*, meditation that borders on Hasidic practice and a general shift toward speaking to the heart rather than the mind.

The Chesapeake Ballroom is a big gray rectangle with the kind of modern-garish hotel chandelier that I can't imagine anyone actually commissioning, but I've seen too many to believe they *all* could have been found at yard sales. The room is overflowing with clergy, so many that every chair is taken and rabbis are seated on every available inch of floor along the walls. It is heartwarming to see them, young and old, returned to their original roles as teachers and students—which is what rabbis are *supposed* to remain, though along the way too many of them get turned into CEOs and therapists and lonely, angry men and women of faith.

In front of me are rows and rows of kippahs from around the world, like the uniforms from a clergy all-star game. There is a lot of hair, but it is unevenly distributed: in general, the less on the head, the more on the face. While Gillman talks, I see some of the younger rabbis whispering to their colleagues, slapping their foreheads, as if to say, "Why can't these older rabbis just *give it up already*?" Finally, they are rather harshly shushed by an older rabbi dressed in a shirt and sweater vest and a swirling colorful yarmulkah. It turns out to be Rabbi Wolpe, looking every bit his seventy-one years in civilian clothes, unwittingly recast as a cranky grandpa of the Rabbinical Assembly.

I also notice, sitting on the floor some distance from the shushees, Rabbi Jeffrey Wohlberg, who replaced Wolpe at my synagogue in Harrisburg and officiated at my bar mitzvah. His well-trimmed beard has gone from red-blond to white, but he still looks youthful, like the "young rabbi" he was when we first got to know each other in 1969, during a "rock service" he organized to try to rekindle the interest of "the young people." While I haven't seen Wohlberg in years, we have been in contact sporadically. He left my old synagogue in the mid-eighties for Washington, D.C., where he took over one the city's oldest and largest synagogues, Adas Israel. He will call or drop a note when he sees something I've written for *The Washington Post Magazine*. And I will never forget his kindness for calling our home when we were sitting shiva for my father.

Except for the fact that he is an excellent sermonizer, Wohlberg is nothing like Wolpe. Given to informality, he always seemed more comfortable provoking the mind of a teenager than swaying the mind of an adult. But the two rabbis seem forever destined to be linked: both vaulted from Beth El in Harrisburg to huge Conservative pulpits in major Eastern cities. Both have sons who became rabbis. And since both of their last names begin with "Wo," they are often listed back-to-back in programs and print ads for social and political causes. I catch Wohlberg's eye and he waves an inquisitive "what are *you* doing here" hello.

Gillman introduces the speakers. (Conspicuously absent is David Wolpe, who didn't have the time to fly east for the convention.) First up is James Fowler, a Methodist minister, prominent academic and the author of many books on the psychology of religion, including the classic *Stages of Faith: The Psychology of Human Development and the Quest for Meaning*. Fowler talks about the changing perceptions of God, from "God the void," to "God the enemy," to "God the companion," and makes comparisons between post-Holocaust Jews and the children of abusive parents. He says we all hunger for a "renewed and compassionate relationship with God," which puts him firmly in the pro-spirituality camp. He ends with a nice image, invoking a biblical verse and calling upon the rabbis to "breathe life upon the dry bones of our secularity."

Then comes Elliot Abrams, a top Republican political appointee turned ethicist after being convicted of lying to Congress about the Iran-Contra affair and then being pardoned by President George Bush in 1991. Abrams, who has a lot of time on his hands while the Democrats control the White House, has been out speaking to synagogue groups about politics and the future of the Jewish people, supporting his book *Faith or Fear: How Jews Can Survive in Christian America*. He is, predictably, conservative. "All this talk about the need for spirituality is *wrong!*" he exclaims. "It's a product of all the worst trends in American culture. People won't attend synagogue no matter how many reforms the *kavanah* [spiritual meaning] committee recommends. We must avoid marketplace religion, which is not saying, 'Here I stand,' but asking, 'What do they want?' Does spirituality mean a more informal, less structured service, or privatized religion that stresses self-realization? I say, 'Just Say No to spirituality!' "

And when he does, a young female rabbi sitting on the floor nearby turns to her colleague and says, "God, I hate this stuff."

"It's come down to ritual and order versus spirituality," Abrams continues. "I'm not *against* spirituality. To me the most important spiritual moment is at home when we bless our teenagers [before Shabbat]. But I am impatient with Jews who are non-practicing screaming for changes in Jewish practice. In the end, they will abandon us anyway . . . Spirituality is the *wrong answer* to the *wrong question!*" And with that, much of the crowd bursts into applause, with those seated on the floor literally pounding on the walls.

The young rabbi just rolls her eyes.

As does the next speaker, Rodger Kamenetz, poet and author of *The Jew in the Lotus,* which created a dialogue between Judaism and Buddhism, and *Stalking Elijah: Adventures with Today's Mystical Masters.* He just walks up to the microphone and says, "*What* am I doing here? I suppose I am the simple son." It gets a chuckle, and then he discusses his own distrust of the term *spirituality*. He finds the notion of "adding spirituality," as if it weren't already part of the religion, downright offensive.

The last speaker is Rabbi Martin Cohen from Beth Tikvah in far-off Richmond, British Columbia. Before Cohen begins to speak, his momentary pause is broken by the plaintive moan of a distant shofar—which someone is obviously testing out in a vendor's booth down the hall. Everyone laughs and, after listening to Cohen for a few minutes, everyone thinks. He develops an astute analogy, comparing our relationship to God to teenagers who yearn for love without really knowing much about love. It is the truest thing anyone has said all morning, and the only aspect of this high-powered debate on spirituality that will stay with me.

Which makes it all the more amazing when I find out that Cohen applied for the job at Har Zion and didn't even get an interview. He was rejected by form letter and is about to assume a pulpit in Mission Viejo.

After the session, I finish scribbling some notes and then walk down to the registration area, where my entire life as a Jew passes before my eyes. Rabbi Wolpe and Elaine are standing near the escalator talking to Rabbi Wohlberg and his wife, Judy, who has the face of a Jewish Diane Sawyer and never seems to age. Walking up behind them is Rabbi Ira Stone, my current rabbi, looking especially high-spirited. It strikes me as amusing to see these revered rabbis as any group of ordinary conventioneers, milling around with RA tote bags stuffed with Jewish Theological Seminary pens and United Synagogue refrigerator magnets. They talk shop, ask about each other's kids, normal convention stuff.

Conversation is cut short by the next round of seminars. I attend one on "Practical Rabbinics," in this case the "Legal Issues Impacting the Rabbinate," being led by Robert Jossen, the RA's lawyer. It is fascinating and horrifying. He begins by noting that in the past two years, two rabbis have been held legally liable for breaching congregant confidentiality, and *The Wall Street Journal* reported that pastors are doing less counseling than ever before for fear of legal claims. He explains that while the courts still uphold the idea of rabbi-congregant privilege, the question is who *controls* the privilege. The test is whether the communication was in confidence. "If they come up to you during Kiddush with others around you, there's less confidentiality than if they take you aside and say 'it's confidential' and then you tell everyone else." He notes that this can be a problem even if the person has *already told* everyone else, "because you may be the only person they've told the truth to."

The talk turns to counseling teenagers, and how much you can tell their parents afterward. This is especially tricky with suicidal kids. For psychologists and psychiatrists, there is such a thing as malpractice in counseling. The courts, he explains, have so far rejected the idea of malpractice for clergy counseling, but "the further you get from spiritual counseling and move more toward therapy, the courts say there can be liability . . . also, the further you get away from your office, there's a suggestion that you aren't doing religious counseling." He recommends never counseling outside of the rabbi's office, and saying out loud during any session, "I am not a psychotherapist."

There is also a danger of being accused of sexual harassment or inappropriate touching. A rabbi's embrace, or even a firm holding of the hand, can be misconstrued. When counseling a person of the opposite sex, the lawyer recommends that rabbis take care to position themselves in the room so there is "no perception of you wanting to be physically close. If anything happens that can be misinterpreted, act immediately by calling in a third person, such as a secretary, to help defuse the situation. But if you *avoid physical touching completely,* you won't be misinterpreted." Some rabbis, he says, have a personal rule of not seeing a congregant alone in the office more than once. Others arrange to have their secretaries buzz them after five minutes so sessions don't get too complex and personal.

After his prepared remarks, he takes questions. What about making anonymous references to counseling experiences in sermons? Well, the issue hasn't been tested in the courts yet, but he worries about a case like that. What he's suggesting is that the legal climate has become so tense that rabbis can no longer invoke their *own* experiences risk-free, even if names and situations are properly disguised.

What about a social kiss, one rabbi asks, or a comforting embrace? Surely you're not saying those are wrong?

"Remind yourself," the lawyer says sternly. "No physical contact. On a shiva call, maybe an embrace can't be misinterpreted. But it's different in the study by yourself."

After the seminar on legal issues and the rabbinate, I wait around to introduce myself to Joel Meyers, the executive vice president of the Rabbinical Assembly. He's an affable, gangly, clean-shaven rabbi, who bears a vague resemblance to actor Martin Landau, and he remains cordial even after I explain that I'm the writer who has been following the Har Zion rabbi search. This search has been a topic of much discussion in the offices of the RA and not only because of Har Zion's importance to the movement. Jacob Herber has been a special young rabbi to them ever since he worked for the RA while a rabbinical student, so it is especially ironic and troubling that he finds himself in such a sticky situation. Meyers says he will be happy to speak with me after the convention.

Later in the convention week, Meyers sits Jacob down and, in the most gentle and fatherly way possible, lays down the law. Over coffee, he lets the young rabbi know that he is concerned about what is happening at Har Zion, and does not want Jacob to get hurt in this process—either from within the congregation or by his colleagues. He understands that the situation developed naturally and nobody is to blame. But it would be wise for Jacob to signal to everybody that he is not in the running for this position because he *cannot be*. There is absolutely no way the Rabbinical Assembly will allow him to be a candidate for the job at Har Zion. It is expressly against the rules of the RA, and it is a bad idea for the synagogue and for Herber as well.

Meyers believes the main reason the Har Zion committee members have circled their wagons around Jacob is because they are still in shock that Ackerman turned them down. And since they did not love any of the other candidates who applied, they have come to believe that they will never find anybody good enough to replace Wolpe—even though Meyers believes they have already ignored several fine prospects. So they might as well just hold on to Jacob. It's not "let's take Rabbi Herber," he thinks, so much as "he's a part of us."

Jacob says he understands. But he also knows that the search committee has requested a meeting with Meyers. They plan to make him an offer he can't refuse.

Back at Har Zion the Friday night after the convention, I get a taste of this "new spiritualism" everyone is so upset about. The synagogue hosts a traveling version of what has come to be called "Friday Night Alive," a tuneful, high-energy, participatory service with lots of singing and dancing. It is a spin-off of the service so successfully pioneered in New York at the liberal Upper West Side synagogue B'nai Jeshurun—which now gets a phenomenal turnout every Shabbat, including hundreds of singles. It is looked at with skepticism by some Conservative rabbis, who when they describe the movement spawned by B'nai Jeshurun as "BJ Judaism" are not necessarily referring to the synagogue's initials.

B'nai Jeshurun was a dying old synagogue in the 1980s when it hired Rabbi Marshall Meyer, a student of Heschel's who had left the United

States after his ordination in 1958 to take a pulpit in Buenos Aires, where he later set up a Seminary branch to train Conservative rabbis for South America. He became a hero to human rights activists when he challenged the military junta in Argentina, which was turning its enemies into "the disappeared." And his efforts became internationally known in 1981 after the publication of *Prisoner Without a Name, Cell Without a Number,* the prison memoir of one of his congregants, editor Jacobo Timerman, who was arrested because of his newspaper's antigovernment stance. Rabbi Meyer returned to New York in the mid-1980s, but his politics were considered too liberal for a Seminary post, so he accepted the pulpit at BJ and remade it in his own image of what Judaism was supposed to be. It was a combination of Heschel's teachings on God and spirituality with some of the hippie song-and-dance Judaism that was popularized in the late sixties. Meyer was one of the first Conservative rabbis in the country to adopt a gender-neutral liturgy and to welcome gay and lesbian members, and he ultimately disaffiliated BJ from the Conservative movement. He was also a founding member of the editorial board of the upstart Jewish journal *Tikkun,* so when its editor Michael Lerner became well-known—especially after his phrase "the politics of meaning" was picked up by the Clinton White House—the BJ story got even more publicity.

Even though Rabbi Meyer died in 1993, B'nai Jeshurun's influence continues to grow. The synagogue is about to be used as a location for the filming of the religious comedy *Keeping the Faith,* starring Ben Stiller and Edward Norton as best friends who become a rabbi and a priest struggling to update the roles of the clergy (and who vie for the same woman's affections). One of the film's highlights is a scene in which the young rabbi, in an attempt to jump-start his congregation, leads a black choir into BJ and turns *Ein Keloheinu,* an upbeat song near the end of the Shabbat service, into a gospel romp.

Even synagogues that are too traditional to accept the entire liberal BJ model have begun trying out the basic concept of a Friday night service geared toward singles and younger couples. When David Wolpe took over at Sinai Temple in Los Angeles, for example, he instituted a version of the service with musician Craig Taubman and attendance has been huge. Har Zion has nothing like it.

The Friday night service at B'nai Jeshurun employs electrified musical instruments. Like many more traditional synagogues, Har Zion doesn't allow the playing of musical instruments during Shabbat; playing them has been interpreted as *work*. So, this traveling version of Friday Night Alive is a capella. Or, as they are introduced: "Shabbat unplugged with Rabbi Margo Stein." Four people, three women and a man, stand on the bimah in front of microphones and begin snapping their fingers, do-wopping into a ditty called "Moving Into Shabbos." When the song is over, all are asked to shake hands with the persons sitting nearest them and wish them a *shabbat shalom*. The service is an interesting combination of praying and cheerleading and Rabbi Wolpe watches it all from the rear of the sanctuary, where, instead of sitting, he leans against the back wall with Lew Grafman.

We are encouraged to review the week that was, and then let it go, so we can be connected with God. "We connect with the kabbalists of old who went out and danced in the field," says one of the rabbis, and the clapping eventually leads to a conga line around the sanctuary. As at any good bar mitzvah party, those who dance are accusing those who won't of being sticks-in-the-mud. Cantor Vogel and Rabbi Herber are in the conga line, as is Ralph Snyder, along with many families who have brought their young children. But Wolpe and Grafman abstain, just leaning and watching.

I stay out of the conga line as well. While I greatly admire the basic concept of loosening up services and bringing some outright joy and exuberance to synagogue worship, I'm not sure about the execution. I am having trouble connecting with this; it seems a little too forced for me. It also seems somewhat anachronistic. This kind of service was popularized in America during the Vietnam War by a liberal folksinger named Rabbi Shlomo Carlebach, who traveled from town to town whipping Jews into a frenzy. I can vividly recall when he came to Harrisburg in the early seventies; the demand for tickets was so large that they held the event not in the synagogue but at the larger Scottish Rites auditorium. Carlebach, who was dark and hairy, like Francis Ford Coppola during his *Apocalypse Now* days, spirited the normally stodgy members of our community into frantic dancing and swinging around the auditorium. It was the first time I ever saw Jews sweat in prayer.

Yet even Carlebach's infectiousness—in his heyday, he was like the Jim Morrison of Judaism—carried me only so far. Mostly because of the music he had to work with. I have affection for the Jewish songs and tunes I learned in my youth, and am happy to hear them again in synagogue (which is why, like many other Jews, I tend to resist the new tunes that cantors are always trying to foist on us just because *they* crave, understandably, a little variety). I find myself especially moved by the song at the end of the Torah service, *Etz Chaim He,* in which we say good-bye to the scrolls as the Ark is closed, because it has drama, and most congregations sing it together with great choral fervor. But, in general, the music of Judaism, even the Friday Night Alive stuff, strikes me as a little thin: some decent, recognizable melodies, but as a songbook short on depth and counterpoint, and almost completely lacking in rhythm or backbeat. The first time I ever heard a gospel choir, at an interfaith assembly at public school put together by Baptist and Jewish groups, I realized immediately that there was a better way to inspire musically than what I was hearing in shul. And I have always wondered why American Jews don't embrace the musical lessons of gospel, a completely American art form, and make more joyful noise. It is my dream to one day take the greatest gospel songs and edit the bejesus out of them, so that they are only about God and can be enjoyed by people of all faiths.

Herber comes back to the bimah and invites all the kids up to join them in a Kiddush. As he does, one of the Shabbat Unplugged rabbis says, "Your inner child is invited, too."

While Herber seems to be enjoying himself, later, when I ask him what he thought of the service, he just laughs. It obviously was not to his taste and as he smiles I realize for the first time what an old young guy he can be. He tells me about a letter he got from a congregant who had walked out of the service, which she described as "toxic noise," expressing her concern that he was lowering the standards of the congregation and worrying about Har Zion's future. He kindly reassured her that the service was a one-shot thing, not part of a plan to introduce change, but was careful not to throw Rabbi Wolpe under the bus. After all, he tells me, it was Wolpe who originally agreed to host Friday Night Alive.

It's showdown time. Late Monday afternoon, Rabbi Joel Meyers arrives at Har Zion for the long-awaited confrontation between the RA and the search committee over the fate of Jacob Herber.

Meyers enters the auditorium and immediately does not like what he sees: the room is set up with a podium and rows of chairs, too formal, too theatrical. As the committee members are shuffling in, he asks Fryman if they can get rid of the podium and put the chairs in a circle. When Fryman looks a little startled, Meyers starts moving the chairs himself and other committee members follow his lead.

Fryman begins the meeting by welcoming everybody and, in a very lawyerly fashion, reviews the facts that have led them to this moment. He makes it clear that, as far as the search committee members are concerned, they have faithfully executed their responsibilities and have selected the best possible candidate to be their next rabbi.

It is, Meyers thinks, a wonderful example of a prosecution as well as a summation. But he's not buying it.

When Fryman finishes, Meyers throws him another curve: instead of responding, he suggests they first go around the room, introduce themselves and tell a little bit about who they are and how long they have been at Har Zion. Some members are very cordial, and talk about how much Rabbi Wolpe means to them. Others, especially Ralph Snyder, offer Meyers little lectures. Har Zion has this prestigious history, the rabbis of Har Zion have been tremendous figures in the movement, and how dare you tell us what we can and cannot do? Or, what choice do we have but to hire Rabbi Herber after all the lousy candidates you sent us? But each time, Meyers just says thank you and moves on to the next person.

Finally, he tells them some of his own feelings. He finds them an unusually bright and diverse committee, and they have obviously worked very hard. He believes that the pool of candidates was better than they had realized, suggesting that if they had not summarily discarded so many résumés, they might know that. He talks about just how hard it is to replace a rabbi who has been loved for so many decades, but also notes that their situation is not really unique: it happens all the time. The only thing unusual here is that Wolpe took a sabbatical so Herber has been running the congregation by himself for a few months during the search. He explains how much he admires Rabbi Herber, and says he understands how difficult it is to hear that they cannot consider him for the job and have to go back and look for rabbis for another year. But the rules are the rules. They are there to protect the rabbis as well as the congregations.

Ralph Snyder is the first to respond, and he explodes. "We know you're a *union boss* . . ." he spits out.

Meyers tries to deflect him with his stock response to that common accusation. "If we were really a union," he says, "I'd join with the United Mineworkers and bring a few big guys to come with me to the meeting . . ."

Snyder is neither amused nor deterred. He stares directly into Meyers's eyes, battle of the alpha males, and raises his voice well above the line of decorum—even for a heated discussion among Jews—saying he has called the chancellor *personally* about this matter. He says he knows that Har Zion gives an enormous amount of money to the Seminary and the RA—although he stops short of actually threatening to cut off that support. He is livid. Cindy Blum, sitting next to him, has never seen him so angry.

The conversation remains heated until it is clear that Meyers is not going to change his mind. Herber is not eligible to be a candidate at this time and he expects them to go back next year and do a fair and proper search. They want him to guarantee they will get excellent candidates this time around and he says that of course they will, but he can't guarantee anything. He runs an employment agency, not a popedom, and he can't control which rabbis will be looking for jobs next year. He urges them to be very careful about what they're doing, reminding them they have a responsibility to the legacy of the synagogue. But they also have a responsibility to Rabbi Herber: it would be wrong if he were harmed by the process.

The committee leaders want a guarantee that if they look for another year and do not find anyone better than Herber, then the RA will let them bend the rules and hire him. He can't guarantee that either. In a year, Herber will still only have been an ordained rabbi for four years. He needs to be at Har Zion for six years before he can be a candidate for the job.

In summation: keep the search going, protect Rabbi Herber, follow the rules. Now, let's break for dinner.

And so they eat. No argument is so intense that it should keep anyone from dinner—although before his first bite Meyers jokes, "Do you think I should have somebody else try my food?"

At the table, the conversation continues but it is less heated. It's clear that not everyone on the committee is necessarily ready to anoint Rabbi Herber, but they like him and they don't want to lose him as well as Wolpe. They are concerned that he will seek another pulpit, leaving them at square one again.

The dinner ends cordially, and the RA has spoken. Har Zion must start looking for another rabbi again next fall. The committee members are in shock but resigned to their fate. In the meantime, the leadership suddenly has a lot of decisions to make. Rabbi Herber's contract is going to expire soon. And if he is going to continue running the synagogue for the next year, they had better get him some help.

21

OFFICE POLITICS

THERE'S A TUNE I can't get out of my head as I'm driving out to Har Zion for services, but I also can't quite identify it. And then I realize it's that silly "Moving Into Shabbos" song from the Friday Night Alive service. I think it's with me not because of the melody, such as it is, but the sentiment: going to Har Zion for Shabbat has now become a regular part of my life, something I look forward to every week. It is, in some way, still my job, but it is also my relief, my respite from my office job. When I first started this project, most of my time was spent in Rabbi Wolpe's office interviewing him. Now he's on sabbatical—in town occasionally, but busy giving talks on bioethics. And I am still with his people.

They no longer regard me with such suspicious looks. Perhaps they were waiting to see if I would keep coming around once Wolpe left. Or perhaps they were just keeping their distance during a one-year trial period. But I am slowly starting to understand what it feels like to be a member, albeit honorary, of a community that prays together and knows one another's business.

In many ways, I feel that way more at Har Zion than at my own synagogue, BZBI. This is not surprising, because in this odd religious experience I've created for myself, I spend more quality Jewish time out here.

But there are times when I feel the call of community—as opposed to just the quick comfort of minyan—at my own shul. Last week I played hooky from Har Zion and Diane and I went to Sabbath services at BZBI, because our rabbi, Ira Stone, and his wife invited us to their home for Shabbat lunch to meet the new editor of the *Jewish Exponent,* Philadelphia's thriving weekly Jewish newspaper. During the service, Rabbi Stone made a point of congratulating me from the bimah on my new job, proud that a member of the synagogue was now editor of *Philadelphia* magazine. When he said that, I actually blushed, and felt a strange rush that I was actually part of a welcoming community.

As an adult, I have never really had a community that wasn't some- how either work-related or associated with the hometown community of my family. And I doubt many of my friends, even the ones who have joined synagogues and churches for their kids, are involved enough to have some good news in their lives noted from the pulpit. I feel like part of a generation that does not expect true community and usually settles for camaraderie. The most we can reasonably hope for is to maintain our own nuclear families.

How do you know when you're in a community? Well, for me, one sign is that when I skip Saturday morning services at Har Zion, I feel guilty. And when I return the next week, people say, "We *missed* you last week," or ask, "Where have you been?" Although, is that community or just peer pressure? Is there any difference?

During the service today I feel especially engaged, not by what's hap- pening on the bimah but by what's happening in the prayer book. Shabbat is becoming more alive to me, more of an entity, more of an an- tidote to the burdens of the working week. When I was mourning, I usually took the most expedient route and went to minyan Saturday eve- ning rather than the whole drawn-out Saturday morning service. So I've never invested this kind of time in community ritual before. It makes me feel involved with religion in a whole new way. It also makes the stakes in the rabbi search seem that much higher.

✡   ✡   ✡

Jacob seems particularly stiff and lackluster today. For his sermon, he begins by telling the time-weathered parable about the two brothers and the sheaves of hay they secretly share with each other. I think I first heard this one early on in Hebrew school, probably by *gimel,* the third letter in the Hebrew alphabet, corresponding to third grade.

He's not thirty seconds into his sermon before the people behind me start talking. What he's delivering sounds like some old student sermon or something he downloaded off the RAVNET at the last minute. I can't feel any conviction. It seems as if he is just *reading* it.

"Our connection with Jerusalem transcends space and time," he says, and, behind him, sitting on the bimah, Jeff Blum appears to be staring off into space.

What is interesting to me is that part of the reason the sermon isn't working is that it is somehow *too religious.* I am accustomed to Rabbi Wolpe's sermons, which use Jewish material in a more provocatively secular way. This is just straight-up Torah and Israel stuff, preaching to those who don't need to be converted.

"A wonderful example of this is the story of Alfred Dreyfus," he reads on, and at that, the guy behind me makes a snoring noise to his wife. Many older men in the congregation have fallen asleep. Others are reading the week's program or leafing through the welcome pamphlet that explains how the service runs and what each of the stained-glass windows means. A few people actually get up and walk out.

Jeff Blum leans forward and makes eye contact with Cantor Vogel. I wonder what they're saying to each other with that look. Is it a good-natured, "Well, Jacob will learn"? Or a more cynical, "Boy, we're in trouble"?

Several days later, I find out that it was probably neither. It was likely a look of empathy. Because in any normal situation, Jacob wouldn't even have been on the bimah giving that sermon. He would have been by his wife's side in Mexico City, where his father-in-law has just been diagnosed with a brain tumor. Jacob is extremely close to his father-in-law, a developer in his mid-fifties who is a cultivated lover of Yiddish literature. While he and his wife have known each other only for four years,

Jacob already has a much more loving relationship with his father-in-law than he ever had with his own estranged father.

I feel like a schmuck for being so critical of his sermon—even if it was just to myself—and wonder how many times over the years I have condemned an oration without knowing if the rabbi had a good reason for distraction. Although, I suppose, the show must go on.

The next time we meet, Jacob tells me his father-in-law had been experiencing some headaches and impaired vision. Then, the week after Jacob returned from the RA convention in Baltimore, the diagnosis was made. The tumor is malignant and inoperable, but there is hope that it might respond to radiation. Since they got the news, life has been . . . well, he wants to say *crazy*, but that seems insufficient. It was crazy *before* this happened. Now it is trying. It is difficult. With his wife and daughter away, it is lonely. There has been an outpouring of love and support from the synagogue, however. People are asking him to dinner, or just dropping by unannounced with food. People call just to see how he is. It makes him realize just how many close and wonderful relationships he and his wife have made.

He changes the subject, and we begin talking about the place of the rabbi in the congregation. He notes that with the ancient rabbis, there were people whose job it was to commit to memory what the rabbis said during worship and then to write it down after Shabbat. I wonder where he is going with this, until he looks at me with great disappointment.

"I know you've been taking notes in shul during Shabbat," he says. "You know you shouldn't be doing that, and I would like you to stop it."

Busted. How did I get caught? The only possible explanation is my seat change. When I first started covering services, I sat all the way on the left side of the synagogue, near the front: as far away from where Wolpe stood preaching as possible, but with a perfect vantage point to watch him when he was seated or standing. I was also on the far aisle, so I always got to look at the stained-glass window dedicated to Passover, with colorful abstract figures, arms outstretched in yearning, from seat level to ceiling. It is the last area that fills up, because some of the seats are held for kids who come up to the main sanctuary when the children's service ends. Over there, my hands were well hidden from the clergy. While at first I would leave and take notes in the bathroom after the sermon, I soon became bolder and started jotting down notes under my prayer book, either on a reporter's notepad or the week's program. I assumed nobody noticed.

At services, the regulars almost always sit in the same seat every week; when they move, everyone notices. When Herber took over, I decided to change my seat to the same position on the other side of the sanctuary, so I could observe him better and, frankly, because I now knew more people and wanted to sit close enough to watch them, too. I am now next to the High Holiday psychedelia of the Rosh Hashanah window, with its primordial stew of deep reds and blues becoming a yellow double-helix leading to a white-hot sun and blue shofar. I have tried to be more discreet with my note-taking because I am closer to the rabbi and congregants who know me. But apparently this hasn't worked. Either Herber has seen me himself, or somebody else ratted me out.

I apologize profusely and tell him it won't happen again. I'll have to go back to scribbling notes in the bathroom.

Jacob could certainly leave and go to Mexico. The synagogue's leaders could cover for him and run a Shabbat service or two. But he feels the need to stay and do his job. He remains in touch with his wife and family in Mexico by phone and e-mail, and discreetly seeks Rabbi Wolpe's advice on matters professional and personal. It is a busy time in the synagogue. May and early June are the last burst of the Jewish High Season, with the end of bar mitzvah season and the last major holiday of the year.

Shavuot, the Feast of Weeks, which commemorates the giving of the Torah at Mount Sinai and the covenant between God and the Jewish people, is coming. It is usually greeted with a celebration of the study of Torah: it was, after all, Jewish mystics who invented the "all-nighter" when they created the Shavuot tradition of staying up all night to study on the holiday. Many American synagogues also mark Shavuot with a more recent custom: the service is run by the confirmation class, a group of young men and women who have continued their formal Jewish studies several years beyond the age of bar or bat mitzvah. The idea of confirmation was first borrowed from modern Christianity by the Reform movement in Germany, which felt that thirteen might be too young to come of age and tried to institute the confirmation as a later substitute— the religious equivalent of raising the minimum age for driving or drinking. But the bar mitzvah of course survived, and now both rites of passage are marked in most Reform and Conservative synagogues—even though the percentage of bar mitzvahed kids who complete confirmation classes has fallen dramatically in recent years. Har Zion typically bar or bat mitzvahs seventy to eighty young people a year. This year's confirmation class has only twenty-three members.

In addition to Shavuot and the bar mitzvahs, the season is especially packed with events because of the convergence of the seventy-fifth anniversary and Wolpe's formal retirement. The week of Shavuot, for example, is a perfect time for the synagogue to dedicate one of the parting gifts it has been preparing for Rabbi and Elaine; the congregation has been restoring one of its treasured Torahs in their honor, with a fundraising drive that allows members to "purchase" anything from an individual name in the scroll, for eighteen dollars, all the way up to an entire book of the Torah for $360. The next week is the annual congregational meeting, which includes the election of new board members, the annual "state of the congregation" message and budget presentation and, to lighten things up, a repeat performance of the Har Zion Follies, "a gleeful romp through Wynnefield, Radnor and Penn Valley" featuring "Eat a Little, Pray a Little." Three weeks later comes the synagogue's annual black-tie dinner dance, which will be a seventy-fifth anniversary ball this year honoring Rabbi and Elaine. The committee chairs for the ball are Janet and Ralph Snyder, Annabelle and Bernie Fishman and Carole and Sam Karsch, the heart of Rabbi Wolpe's inner circle.

And Rabbi Herber needs to be present for all these events. Rabbi Wolpe can't very well be expected to fete himself.

Even though the good-bye is starting to feel a bit long to everyone, including the Wolpes, the events are nonetheless touching, especially in the interaction between Wolpe and Herber. At the conclusion of the Torah dedication service, Jacob says from the bimah, "It has been an honor and a privilege to be your assistant and be part of your family."

At the black-tie affair for five hundred, Rabbi Wolpe—OK, Jerry—returns the compliment. He says, to a crowd that includes his own children, that he considers Jacob Herber to be "another son."

This comment comes during a scene that is very Har Zion. After cocktails and butlered hors d'oeuvres in the lobby, all five hundred tuxedoed and bejeweled guests are ushered into the main sanctuary to daven *Mincha*. The crowd is more mixed than usual: the old guard is here, as well as young socially active couples who are rarely in evidence on Shabbat. The evening service concludes, as it always does, with the mourner's Kaddish. And then the microphones are brought out—"test, test, one-two, one-two"—so that friend after Wolpe friend can come up to the bimah and laud him with words of praise, thanks, hope, sadness, but no regret.

Wolpe's old pulpit colleague, Cantor Isaac Wall, gets a huge round of applause when he takes the bimah, and his full voice returns them immediately to the Har Zion of their youth. Ralph Snyder gets up, calls Rabbi Wolpe a "living example of rare dignity" and Elaine a "source of inspiration for all of us." Bernie Fishman bursts into tears when he recalls the scene at Lankenau Hospital the night they were told Elaine would die. Wolpe looks relieved, Elaine sort of sad.

Carole Karsch recites from the Emily Dickinson poem she always remembered hanging on the wall behind Rabbi Wolpe's desk:

> *If I can stop one heart from breaking,*
> *I shall not live in vain;*
> *If I can ease one life the aching,*

Or cool one pain,
Or help one fainting robin
Unto his nest again,
I shall not live in vain.

Elaine Wolpe speaks to the congregation, again with the help of the computer program that allows her to create a recorded message without pauses and unexpressed thoughts. "Passages," she begins, ". . . thirty years ago I was vibrant and young, size ten . . . passages . . . always president, like my mother, Ruth . . . passages . . . new rabbi, but never, *ever* try to imitate rabbi . . . I'm a lucky girl."

But the most attention must be paid when Rabbi Wolpe himself takes the bimah, his voice breaking with emotion. He thanks and honors his old friends and his young colleague. And then he speaks of one of his favorite books, *The Lonely Man of Faith*. It was written in the 1960s by Joseph Soloveitchik, the Renaissance rabbi from Berlin who studied the sacred texts of Judaism and then physics, mathematics and philosophy, before joining the Orthodox rabbinate and coming to Boston in 1932 to be the city's chief rabbi and, later, the leading theologian of Modern Orthodoxy. The slim volume is one that most rabbis know well, its opening paragraph a sprawling statement that crystallizes the sentiment of a modern clergy immersed in scripture, but also awash in the ideas of a psychotherapeutic era.

The nature of the dilemma can be stated in a three-word sentence. I am lonely. Let me emphasize, however, that by stating, "I am lonely," I do not intend to convey to you the impression that I am alone. I, thank God, do enjoy the love and friendship of many. I meet people, talk, preach, argue, reason; I am surrounded by colleagues and acquaintances. And yet, companionship and friendship do not alleviate the passional experience of loneliness which trails me constantly. I am lonely because at times I feel rejected and thrust away from everybody, not excluding my most intimate friends, and the words of the Psalmist, "My father and my mother have forsaken me," ring quite often in my ears like the plaintive cooing of the turtledove. It is a strange, alas, absurd experience engendering sharp, enervating pain as well as a stimulating, cathartic feeling. I despair because I am lonely and, hence, feel frustrated. On the other hand, I also feel invigorated because this very experience of loneliness pressed everything in me into the service of God. In my "desolate, howling solitude" I experience a growing awareness that, to paraphrase Plotinus's apothegm about prayer, the service to which I, a lonely and solitary individual, am committed is wanted and gracefully accepted by God in His transcendental loneliness and numinous solitude.

Later on in the book, Soloveitchik disparages the idea that the congregation is able to help assuage this loneliness. "In the majestic community," he writes, "in which surface-personalities meet and commitment never exceeds the bounds of the utilitarian, we may find collegiality, neighborliness, civility, or courtesy—but not friendship." Other rabbinic scholars have noted that Conservative rabbis might be the loneliest rabbis of all, since, unlike Orthodox and Reform clergy, they often don't even share a level of religious practice with their congregants. Most Conservative rabbis are far more observant than those to whom they preach.

Yet here, at Har Zion, at this moment, it appears that Wolpe can indeed claim friendships within his congregation, friendships that have sustained him and Elaine during a nearly equal number of best times and worst times, since her stroke is now remembered as the midway point of his tenure. Life since then has been "brutal, enervating and lonely," he says, "and one of the most inspiring experiences one could imagine."

He turns to Elaine. "I am married to the most miraculous woman God ever created," he says. "As Byron wrote, 'She walks in beauty, like the night.' "

And then he talks of his father. "Wherever I have gone," he says, "it has been with the presence of my father. When he died in 1938, I vowed he would never leave me. And I have made this the theme of my life. I pray that he and my mother are watching together and they are smiling."

The sound of weeping can be heard throughout the room, tears not so much of loss but of awe for something almost as powerful as loss: profound change without tragedy. The "new rabbi" is now old, the "new Har Zion" is now middle-aged, and the twentieth century, the century when Judaism became American because of what happened to most of Europe's Jews, is almost over. The tears are tears of heart-wrenching joy, of happiness that they have all survived to see one brilliant rabbi's career end the way he wanted it to. After fifty years, his public struggle with God can be called a draw.

Summertime and the davening is easy. After bar mitzvah season ends, Shabbat services move to the small chapel where daily minyan is held. Even though the room holds two hundred people, the service is still quite intimate. Regular shul-goers refer to the feeling in these summer services as "the real Har Zion."

When I walk into services, my friend Ruth, whose father Wolpe eulogized with the great menorah metaphor, is up on the bimah halfway through the chanting of the Haftarah. She asked me to come, because of a conversation we had that inspired her to do this. When her dad died, we had talked a lot about the mourning process and I had shared some of my experiences—including my study project in memory of my father. She had decided to memorialize her father by relearning the Haftarah from her own bat mitzvah and chanting it in her new synagogue. One of the great freedoms of summer services is that they allow this sort of participation from the adult members: during bar mitzvah season, there is rarely an opening on the schedule for a non-thirteen-year-old who wants to do the Haftarah.

I've been thinking about doing mine over. The reading for my bar mitzvah week is called *Vayera,* a fairly resonant parasha to be associated with for the rest of your life. The Torah portion itself is from Exodus 6, and includes one of the most debated passages in the liturgy, in which God's many names are revealed to Moses: "I am the LORD. I appeared to Abraham, Isaac and Jacob as *El Shaddai,* but I did not make myself known to them by My name, *Adonai.*" Vayera also includes the confrontation with Pharaoh in which the rods are turned into serpents, as well as the first seven of the ten plagues against the land of Egypt. (I missed out on locusts, darkness and killing of the firstborn, which is just fine with me.) The Haftarah is from Ezekiel 28, which includes a prophecy against Egypt that involves a lot of fishing imagery—"I will put hooks in your jaws . . . with all the fish of your channels clinging to your scales . . . I will fling you into the desert"—which seems appropriate since fishing is the primary hobby I inherited from my father. It would be great to chant my Haftarah again, either at my own shul or . . . wouldn't it be interesting to ask to do it at Har Zion? Now *that* would be pushing the envelope of investigative reporting. But since Vayera comes in late January, I would probably have to get myself on the schedule several years in advance.

After services, I try to get a little kiddush face-time with Jacob, whom I haven't been able to reach on the phone. He looks harried. I assume it is because of the pressures of his father-in-law's illness and the toll it is taking on Cynthia. But there's also something else. He is moving, he tells me. In fact, he is in the midst of trying to make two moves at the same time. Both moves, however, are being held up because the present occupants have been slower than expected in packing up.

He is moving into Rabbi Wolpe's office at Har Zion.

He is also moving his family into Rabbi and Elaine's house.

I can't decide which move is more telling. The house is more surprising, only because Lew Grafman had led me to believe that the synagogue planned to rent it out for a year until a new rabbi could be chosen. But according to Jacob, the synagogue leadership came to him and "generously offered" the office and the parsonage, saying it would be a waste for them to sit empty.

Since a line of people are waiting to talk to Jacob, we agree to speak next week. There is a groundbreaking scheduled for the new addition to the building to expand the Har Zion Hebrew school. The fund-raising for the addition has gone more slowly than expected but the kids need the space, so they are going ahead with the construction anyway. We will meet afterward.

The groundbreaking ceremony takes place in a grassy area near the front entrance: even with the schematic drawings right there, it is hard to imagine where a new wing for the school is going to fit. But they all have faith. And, much to my amusement, they all have yellow plastic hard hats over their kippahs, even Rabbi Wolpe.

The whole event has come together at the last minute, because someone realized that if it isn't held during this particular week in July, they will have to wait for nearly a month. There is a traditional period of Jewish mourning in the summer, the Three Weeks, which corresponds with several catastrophes that befell the Jewish people during the period that ends with the ninth day of the Jewish month of Av—*Tisha Ba'av*, a fast day commemorating the destruction of both temples in Jerusalem, the first by the Babylonians in 586 B.C., and the second by the Romans in 70 A.D. Because the Three Weeks usually begins in late July, when most American Jews are on vacation from everything, including Judaism, this is probably the least-observed holiday in the Jewish year. But it does have rules that rabbis and synagogues keep, and a joyous event such as a groundbreaking would not be appropriate during the Three Weeks.

After the groundbreaking, I talk to Jacob. We sit in his office, which he is anxious to vacate, but Rabbi Wolpe still hasn't quite finished packing up his stuff. Rabbi and Elaine have also been unable to get their things moved out of the parsonage to their new apartment in town, in a high-rise building not far from the Liberty Bell and Philadelphia's historic district. This means Jacob and Cynthia will not be able to get contractors into the house—which needs to be painted, among other things—before they leave for their summer vacation, the long-overdue trip to Mexico City to visit with Cynthia's family. When they return, the High Holidays will be upon them, so they probably won't be able to get the place ready until after Sukkot.

This messes up their master plan at a time when everything is suddenly moving very quickly for them. Jacob is unhappy about how the housing logistics have worked out, but says he does not blame it on Rabbi Wolpe personally. He realizes it is hard to leave your office and home of twenty-five years, and no matter where you go, there are contractors to make you crazy.

He tells me a little more about what has been happening with the synagogue leadership. Not only did they give him the office and the house, but they have negotiated a new employment contract for him, which he has just signed. They offered him considerably more money than he has been making. And the contract is for three years. The deal has all kinds of outs for either side once they see how the rabbi selection process goes this year. They are, he says, committed to doing another full search just as the RA ordered. But a three-year contract is a pretty big hedge on the bet that they won't find anyone they like better than Jacob. And, considering what they have just gone through with Rabbi Meyers and the RA, it's a rather aggressive move for the leadership to make.

In the meantime, the RA has arranged to get Herber some help. They found an "interim" for the synagogue, a seasoned rabbi who is not on the tenure track and will agree to serve for just one year, to help get the shul through a transitional period. In most cases, an interim replaces a departing senior rabbi. (Actually, in some Christian denominations, there is a mandatory interim period after the departure of a long-term senior clergyman, to give the congregation a breather before it begins searching for a new spiritual leader.) It is extremely rare for an interim rabbi to work under a young former assistant with such limited pulpit experience. It sounds a little bit like the baseball movie *Bull Durham*.

I ask Jacob how his father-in-law is doing. Better, actually: the radiation seems to have shrunk the tumor somewhat, and he finds the side effects tolerable enough. We talk a bit about what it is like to be a rabbi in a situation like this. He explains that while he seeks solace in the same prayers he has always recommended to congregants, he has to admit that the prayers speak to him differently now. He no longer says them by rote, but consciously stops and recites the words about what God will do.

"It's not that I'm asking God to intervene directly and cause my father-in-law's body to physiologically change," he explains. "I pray asking to *enable* the people to whom God has given wisdom. I believe there are laws of nature and that those laws of nature run their course. Whatever happens in nature has already been set into motion, and God does that. God doesn't come and change the laws of nature after the fact. If God is the source of all creation, then the things in life that aren't so great have their source in God, too. But I don't have any special access or specific powers. I have no greater ability than you do to serve as a direct conduit to God."

I am interested in his sentiment but also the way he expresses it—carefully, with no gender pronouns. This is one of the results of full egalitarianism in much of the Conservative movement. It is no longer appropriate to refer to God as only "he." It is also not appropriate, except in feminist synagogues, to refer to God only as "she." I have seen rabbis clumsily attempt to make some compromise—using "he" in the first half of a responsive reading in English, and then "she" in the second half, or alternating line by line. But many do what Jacob does, repeat the name God over and over, sometimes two or three times in a sentence.

Jacob tells me he is getting ready for that trip to Mexico City. But he is also acutely aware that relationships are shifting all around him. His wife, Cynthia, for the first time, has to start thinking seriously about her role as rebbitzin—even if she doesn't *want* a role as rebbitzin in this new world of clergy from two-career households. I note that she attended the groundbreaking ceremony today, which she might not have done six months ago.

Cynthia generally comes to Shabbat services, but I rarely see her work the crowd. Even though she's an international lawyer and certainly knows how to shmooze, she often seems reluctant to do it; in part, I've heard, because she still feels somewhat like a foreigner in American sub- urbia, but also, I'm guessing, because she just doesn't want to play the game. She didn't really sign up for all this. Four years ago, she was a sin- gle lawyer in Mexico City working on high-level trade negotiations. By last year, she was a married mom in the suburbs of Philadelphia, raising an infant daughter, doing a little substitute teaching in Spanish at the Shipley School (she isn't yet licensed to practice law in the United States) and waiting to find out where her husband's next job was going to force them to move. Now, all of a sudden, her husband is all but running for office at a very demanding synagogue where she had grown accustomed to not really being very involved. She is cordial, and graciously accepts dinner invitations from congregants, trying her best to reciprocate. But she is not planning to become Elaine Wolpe, who was in her heyday the Martha Stewart of rebbitzin, always having congregants over to the house, where everything—the food, her clothes—had to be perfect. And some congregants have noted Cynthia's lack of enthusiasm for hand- shaking and baby-kissing. "Y'know, she could say *hello* once in a while," I've heard people grouse.

Jacob is also watching his relationship with Rabbi Wolpe change, and he has become a little more open with me about when there is friction between the two of them. It is not easy to renegotiate the terms of a mentorship. It is as hard as recasting the relationship between a father and son. While a strong sense of loyalty exists between the two of them, there is also a weariness with the roles they have played in each other's lives, and a question of whether, in their new roles, they will be col- leagues or friends or, who knows, maybe nothing, maybe just former work-friends at a company where they both toiled for a while.

Rabbi Wolpe said that he would always be there to help out, but the first time Jacob asked him to fill in on a Shabbat so he could go on vacation, Wolpe wasn't available. "He said, 'Jacob you can always call me, I'm ten minutes away; if you need advice, help, I will always be here for you,'" Herber recounts. "And I will continue to seek out his advice and counsel. But I'm not his assistant. There is a difference in our relationship. I revere him and respect him. But, I don't have to answer to him any longer—technically. Now, if he tells me, 'You're making a mistake,' that doesn't mean I won't listen to what he says. He's one of smartest men I know, he knows this place better than anybody else. And he's a rabbi's rabbi. It would be foolish and stupid not to seek out his help or to shut it off when it's offered. But he said to me he does not want to be an issue here anymore. He wants his replacement to have the opportunity to grow here. He doesn't want to cast a great shadow over everything. He wanted to go out on his own terms, and he has.

"I believe it is my responsibility to create a collegial and warm relationship with him as emeritus, and give him the respect he deserves."

Jacob is starting to think about his High Holiday sermons. Clearly, he's scared to death. He has never spoken in front of the High Holiday crowd in Har Zion's main sanctuary. Wolpe never allowed his assistants to preach in the main room on the High Holidays. They always ran the more informal services in the small chapel.

"I never asked him if I could," he admits. "I never had the guts to bring it up. I took it as a given. In most other congregations of this size, it's common for rabbis to rotate, with the assistant preaching the second day. But I've never set foot in there on the High Holidays. I just hope that the things I do are well received. And I'm not going to be shocked if some of them aren't."

I ask what he plans to talk about. "Well, this is not my installation, and I'm not presuming that I'm going to be the rabbi here," he says. "In a way, it's sort of an audition. I'm thinking about giving this sermon, as a rabbi and as a Jew, about how the congregation should think about this synagogue. A sermon that will lay out my theology on what synagogue life is about. I don't want to be the rabbi of a congregation where I don't think my viewpoint is something people share. If it's not a good match, I would be miserable."

It sounds like he's planning a real Jerry Maguire moment.

"You know, *Jerry Maguire* is one of my favorite movies. In theory he was right and in reality it almost led to his destruction. That's not going to be my approach. But, at the same time, I'd like people to get an idea of how I think as a rabbi."

22

"BUT WE *NEED* THAT MONEY"

T HE WEEK BEFORE THE HIGH HOLIDAYS, I call Barbara Schwartz to see how the seating chart is going. She tells me they've had a net loss of sixty families in the annual flurry of membership resignations. This is a substantial number, nearly 5 percent of the congregation, but it is not surprising, and the resignations have been fairly predictable. Most of the members were older couples who no longer lived in Penn Valley or even had family there, but came back every year on the High Holidays just to hear Wolpe's sermons. She doesn't see the resignations as being any comment on Rabbi Herber.

One of the more notable resignations is that of Paul and Val Wolpe. They decided that, for this year at least, it would be too strange to worship at Har Zion without Rabbi Wolpe on the pulpit. They joined the Germantown Jewish Center, where the more casual, participatory style is closer to what Paul would have chosen for himself all along had his father not been the rabbi of another synagogue in town. Paul explained to Jacob that their decision had nothing to do with him: "It's not you, it's us." He also told him that they intended to maintain memberships at both shuls, but through "benign neglect" neither he nor executive director Howard Griffel made sure that happened. Rabbi and Elaine plan to attend services with Paul and Val at Germantown for Rosh Hashanah. But for Yom Kippur and the rest of the year, they have joined my synagogue, BZBI, where Wolpe has always admired Rabbi Stone.

I call Cindy Blum to wish her *l'shana tova,* a happy and healthy new year, and find out if there has been any search committee activity. She says it's been quiet for several months. She tells me she has been impressed with how Rabbi Herber has grown in that short time, but then she was taken aback when the interim rabbi, Moshe Tutnauer, arrived a few weeks ago from Israel. His style, his ease and his depth of knowledge and teaching ability reminded her just how unpolished a diamond Jacob really is.

When I speak to synagogue president Lew Grafman, he asks if I read the recent article in the local *Jewish Exponent,* "Where Have All the Rabbis Gone?" about the nationwide shortage of good rabbinic talent. I tell him I saw it. He says he is unclear about how the next year will go, and is not sure what the RA will do if they decide to renominate Herber.

Lou Fryman is, predictably, the most lawyerly about the upcoming season. He is now heading into his third year as head of the Har Zion rabbi search committee, the longest he has ever spent on any committee in his decades of high-level volunteer work. He makes it clear to me that Rabbi Herber has his proponents on the committee and in the shul but that there are also many who feel he is not ready, and the synagogue should be making a decision for the next twenty years, not the next year or two.

He is cryptic when I ask about the RA's position on how things are going. I later find out why. Apparently Rabbi Meyers went ballistic when he found out that Jacob was occupying the senior rabbi's office and moving into The House. He had confrontational phone conversations with Fryman and Herber. Fryman asked, "What did you expect us to do, leave the office and house empty?" Meyers said yes, while he didn't care as much about the house, the office certainly should have been kept empty. This all felt a little too much like Al Haig moving into the Oval Office and taking charge prematurely. Herber told him that the synagogue's leaders insisted he move into the office. "What was I going to do, tell them no?" Exactly, Meyers said. If he wanted to abide by the RA's rules, he should have insisted on staying in *his* office. He knew the line between kosher and *traif.*

But it was already done, and there was no undoing it. Herber had already put his books on Wolpe's shelves. He had hung his family photos and New York Rangers banner on Wolpe's walls. All Fryman and Herber could do was say they were shocked, shocked, by Rabbi Meyers's reaction to these minor housekeeping decisions, and perhaps do a little extra atonement during the High Holidays.

Rabbi Wolpe is in the living room of his half-unpacked apartment, perched on a kitchen chair in the middle of a sea of new white shag carpeting. Dressed in his civilian clothes—a blue T-shirt, jeans with a sharply ironed crease and light-colored shoes—he has the unmistakable look of a man playing hooky. Tomorrow will be the first Rosh Hashanah in fifty-four years that he is not preaching. For the first time since he was eighteen, he will be prohibited from work just like every other Jew, sitting with his family and praying in another synagogue, not his own.

Yet while he is fascinated by the possibilities of his new surroundings and freedom, there is also a weary sadness about him. He starts talking about the way in which he retired, all the decisions he made so that nobody could accuse him of hanging on. He stayed away from the rabbi search, he didn't insist, as some of his retiring colleagues have, to be given an office at Har Zion from which to second-guess his successor. Yet something has obviously gone wrong, although he will not say the word *wrong* because that would sound too judgmental, and he does not want to be one of those judgmental old rabbis.

He will say only that he finds the situation "strange," a word that he delivers as ominously as Vincent Price.

As I can see, the apartment is overflowing with housewarming plants and flowers and fruit baskets. He and Elaine have received dozens of phone calls from holiday well-wishers at Har Zion. Yet he is surprised by the phone calls he has *not* received. Perhaps the signals he has sent that he would prefer not to be involved anymore have been *too* convincing.

Actually, he tells me, he is *amazed* by the calls he hasn't received. Although it is clear he is only talking about one call.

It's Jacob. Jacob hasn't called to wish him l'shana tova.

In fact, Wolpe laments that his protégé hasn't called him much at all since the retirement. Maybe he just needed to make some distance, to find his own way. But not to call him before Rosh Hashanah? He just finds that so . . . strange.

I tell Rabbi Wolpe he sounds like my mother.

"Well, if you don't call your mother, this is how she'll feel," he says. "As it turns out, I had to send him something, so I wrote and wished him well. But I still haven't heard from him. Maybe he'll call later today . . ."

The next morning, I go to services at Har Zion. Just as Rabbi Wolpe did so graciously, Jacob has arranged complimentary tickets for me. But they are much better tickets. As I keep walking forward, farther forward, looking for my seat, I suddenly realize he has placed me in the second row, just beneath his lectern. Amazing seat, the kind that usually comes with a backstage pass.

I have arrived fairly late, showing up during the long, rustling pause before the sermon begins. As I take my seat, Herber ducks his head away from the microphone and mouths a message to me with a smirk. Three thousand people are probably wondering what he said. It was: "I thought I'd wait until you got here."

I can't decide if he is trying to impress me with the great seat or just make sure that I don't take notes on Rosh Hashanah. But he doesn't realize that even I wouldn't take notes during a High Holiday service. Instead, I have smuggled in my portable tape recorder, which fits perfectly in my tallis bag, so I can have full audio of his first sermon.

Much to my surprise, he does not attempt to make global

pronouncements about the state of the synagogue or the themes of his rabbinate. Instead, he plays to his strength, goes with what he knows, what he feels most passionate about: kids. His goal is to make the parents of Har Zion think again about the quality and quantity of time they spend with their children. While he begins nervously, he eventually gets on a roll. He does not pull punches, does not make excuses. And as the sermon builds to a crescendo, he makes a statement that literally elicits gasps from the congregation. He tells them they should, this year, work 5 percent less, even if that means *earning* 5 percent less, and spend that time with their children.

While many people are nodding in agreement, in the middle section, a well-appointed Main Line mom is heard whispering too loudly, "But we *need* that money."

When the sermon is over, Herber looks relieved and proud of himself. While there will be plenty of congregants who spend their family luncheon complaining that he's "no Rabbi Wolpe," he has, at the very least, gotten their attention. If this turns out to be his first and last Rosh Hashanah in the main sanctuary at Har Zion, nobody will ever accuse him of playing it too safe.

The announcement of the 5 percent rule, a kind of child-rearing tithe, is one of several dramas that play out over the High Holiday services. During Kol Nidre, Lew Grafman gives the annual state-of-the-synagogue address. But this time he has surprising news. The Cook family, in memory of Noreen Cook, has made the largest single gift in the history of the synagogue—a high-six-figure donation to endow programs in the new school building. To recognize this largesse, the leadership is breaking its long-standing policy of never offering what are called "naming opportunities" on the exterior of the synagogue. The new structure will now be called the Noreen Cook Center for Early Childhood Education of Har Zion Temple, and the name will be visible on the outside of the building.

Kol Nidre goes well, but on Yom Kippur day there is a snafu in the services. In an effort to give the new rabbi-in-residence some main sanctuary pulpit time, Herber has decided that after Yizkor, the memorial prayer, he will go to the small chapel and Tutnauer will get the main stage for the afternoon. Unfortunately, it is impossible to keep the two services in sync, so when Herber is about to start Yizkor, he receives word from the chapel that Rabbi Tutnauer is already finished and waiting to switch sanctuaries. After conferring briefly with Grafman and other leaders, Herber makes an executive decision. To save time, they will eliminate the seemingly endless responsive reading in English that Har Zion has always done during Yizkor. But, instead of explaining the problem and solution to the congregation, he just skips the prayer and moves on.

The problem is that this is more than just a regular responsive reading. It is a prayer with presold adjacencies. Like almost all American synagogues, Har Zion raises money by publishing an annual Book of Remembrance, in which congregants pay to have the names of their loved ones listed. This long responsive reading is literally printed across the tops of some ninety memorial pages in the small, paperbound book. Since the reading is made up of snippets from various verses in the Torah, the prayer can be expanded or contracted based on the number of pages sold each year. Congregants are accustomed to reciting the prayer and lingering for a moment on the page listing their lost relatives.

Some welcome the last-minute edit: they always thought the prayer went on for too damn long anyway. But others are crushed. Without that prayer, their ritual is ruined, their remembrance tarnished.

In the hours and days after the service, many people replay the Yizkor mistake. When Rabbi Wolpe gets home from services at BZBI, his answering machine has several messages on it from congregants calling to tattle on his would-be heir apparent. One young woman comes into Herber's new office and just bawls her eyes out, asking why he did it.

Jeff Blum tells me he is amazed by how the story is being embellished. "In two years," he says, "it will be told that everybody walked out of the congregation." He does concede that there were members who said that if they knew he wasn't going to read the prayer, they wouldn't have paid to put the names in the Book of Remembrance. But, "Hey, he's a young rabbi and he made a decision. People will recover, and he has to be thick-skinned, too. If he's gonna be senior rabbi here, he'd better get used to people taking shots."

But Rabbi Wolpe is worried about how many shots Jacob can take. "You know, there's an old joke," he says. "How do you teach a pretty girl how to swim? Well, you take her in the pool, put your arms around her and hold her close to you. And what if it's your sister? You push her in the pool. I would love to see Jacob held close, with someone making sure he isn't hurt. But he's being pushed in."

This year's Simhat Torah is wilder and crazier than ever. The kids and grandkids have completely taken over, and the grandparents, like Ralph Snyder and Bernie Fishman, just stand there on the bimah watching the spectacle, laughing and marveling at the energy exploding all around them.

There are several special aliyahs in the Simhat Torah service: the two most important are *hatan Torah,* "groom of the Torah," the last verse on the final scroll of Deuteronomy, and *hatan Bereshit,* "groom of Genesis," the first verse of the Torah, the first seven days of creation. At Har Zion, these crucial aliyahs have always been reserved for the rabbi and cantor. But, this year, Rabbi Herber is trying something different: these two aliyahs, and another special aliyah just before them, are given to active congregants. It's an interesting symbolic gesture, a way of signaling a new relationship between clergy and worshippers.

After the reading of the Torah and Haftarah, Herber walks solemnly up to the lectern, lowers his voice and says, "Today, I'd like to speak to you about . . ." before bursting into laughter and scooting back to his seat. When the cantor sees it's a fake-out sermon, he yelps, "Oh, thank goodness," and everyone breaks up. As the service is winding down, the clergy and leaders down shots poured from a bottle of whiskey on the bimah, and the cantor tries to rush through the concluding prayers by chanting them to the tunes of secular songs—which must be something cantors do for fun at their conventions. He does the reader's Kaddish to "God Bless America," among other things, and finishes with a breakneck *adon olam* sung perfectly to the "William Tell Overture."

As the service ends and we stream to the exit, Jeff Blum pulls me aside. He is tipsy and out of breath, unbuttoning the top button of his collarless shirt.

"That was unbelievable!" he says. "This place is being reborn! It's youthful, exuberant, everything it's supposed to be!" And then he sees his daughter Sammy and dashes off after her.

Rabbi Wolpe is settling into his new life as a retired rabbi and active bioethicist. He has two part-time jobs. He is still chairman of the advisory committee for the University of Pennsylvania's Center for Bioethics. And he has been named director of the Louis Finkelstein Institute at the Seminary, which has been through several permutations since being founded by the esteemed Talmud scholar and Seminary chancellor in 1938. It began as an Institute for Religious and Social Studies, and was used for the interfaith colloquies that Finkelstein so successfully employed to increase the profile of the Seminary in the Jewish and non-Jewish world. In 1939, the institute held a Conference on Science, Philosophy and Religion that widened its reach to interdisciplinary dialogues as well. Every Tuesday during the school year, Finkelstein would present classes and lectures by renowned theologians, scientists, politicians and authors.

After Finkelstein retired in 1972, his institute was turned over to Rabbi Burton Vizotzky, who began holding regular sessions on interdisciplinary Bible study. The classes became known as "the best conversation in town" and attracted a glittering cross-section of New Yorkers, including financier Ivan Boesky and, eventually, public television intellectual guru Bill Moyers. He was inspired by the rabbi's unorthodox classes and books to produce the groundbreaking 1996 public television series *Genesis: A Living Conversation,* which prominently featured Vizotzky.

The chancellor gave Wolpe the Finkelstein Institute in the hope that

it can become a premier voice in the exploding world of Jewish
bioethics. What he will do with it remains to be seen. He is setting up
some conferences, but it is unlikely that the institute will become a regular weekly or monthly forum for him in Manhattan anytime soon. He
has already been booked for too many lectures, study weekends and
meetings with everyone from religious groups to the Human Genome
Project. DuPont, based in nearby Wilmington, has asked him to be their
company ethicist. He was the only Jew to write an invited paper for an
interfaith symposium sponsored by the Aspen Institute on the challenging topic of "the limits of dialogue," using abortion as a paradigm.

It's a heady time, the life he had imagined for himself years ago when
he planned to leave Har Zion before Elaine's stroke. He is energized and
fortified by the work and the intellectual challenges. He tells me repeat-
edly that he is having the time of his life.

There is, however, one thing still gnawing at him. His relationship
with Har Zion is still *strange*. He expected to be involved with fund-
raising, but they never really called to ask him to do anything. And the
rewarding relationship he expected to have with Rabbi Herber hasn't
come to pass either. Herber, he tells me, never did call that day to wish
him a happy new year. Indeed, Wolpe was so vexed by the breakdown
in communications that he actually wrote Herber a letter as part of the
cleansing and atonement process of Yom Kippur. He asked in the letter if
he had done anything to offend Herber, and hoped that the gesture
would jump-start a more active dialogue between them. But, in his view,
it didn't work. They met for lunch at Penn, talked about some things,
and while it was clear Herber felt badly about his mentor's disappointment, nothing really changed. Wolpe can't help flashing back on the
conversation they had last winter, when Jacob complained about not being able to call him "Jerry." He keeps wondering if that is a key to their
seeming inability to grow closer as rabbinic colleagues.

"I still believe he's making a terrible mistake," Wolpe tells me. "I
think I could be of help to him. It's very, very strange. I have had a
tremendous, unbelievable amount of contact with individuals from the
synagogue, but almost no contact with the leaders of Har Zion. Lew

Grafman calls me about retirement issues. But that's about it. I suppose
it's a strange combination of people not wanting to disturb me and life
going on and . . ."

He shakes his head. "Elaine gets upset with me, because when something disturbs me, I try to internalize it. Elaine is much better at just getting it out. Me, I probably have it buried in a deep part of my brain. It
comes out through stomach disorders and headaches."

Of course, when I talk to people at shul, they tell just the opposite
story. They are baffled at how distant Wolpe has been. "It has been the
biggest disappointment," Jeff Blum tells me. "Wolpe promised he would
be involved, especially with fund-raising for the endowment." In addition to the new construction project, Har Zion is trying to build a nest-
egg endowment fund. "And he hasn't been seen or heard from in *months*.
And the longer he stays away, the less likely it is he can come back. Jacob
says he doesn't know if there's been a falling out or what. But why can't
the guy just show up at shul sometime? I guess it's possible he's doing it
to give Jacob space. But I doubt it. And the endowment drive is hurting."

The next time I speak with Rabbi Herber, I try, as carefully as possible, to bring up his relationship with Wolpe.

"I sense there's a different chemistry between us," he says, "but it
hasn't affected our working relationship. To Rabbi Wolpe, I'll always be
his kid. He's told me he considers me like a son."

He says Wolpe sent him a nice note before the holidays, and says he
really hasn't called much to seek his counsel because "nothing has been
earth-shattering." He does admit, though, that during the High Holidays
he thought about Wolpe's close friends—who sit right down front, so he
sees their faces—and wondered what they would report back to him. He
mentions Carole and Sam Karsch in particular. This is interesting because not only are they close to the Wolpes, it is well known among insiders that while Carole Karsch adores Jacob personally, she is probably
his biggest adversary on the rabbi search committee.

According to Jeff Blum, the committee isn't really getting any new résumés of note. "Unless the Messiah applies," he says, "it's Jacob's job." But there has been some discussion among synagogue leaders about creating a new rabbinic model if Jacob is ever allowed to become a candidate and is selected. They wouldn't have a senior rabbi so much as their own little "rabbinate," a number of clergy members with varied experience hired to fulfill different responsibilities, led in a collegial way by Jacob.

"I think it could work," he concludes.

KING TUT

MOSHE TUTNAUER IS ONE of the great characters of the American rabbinate, and he'll be the first person to tell you so. He is an unapologetic egotist, a relentless communicator and, by the standards of American religious life, a complete and utter misfit. Yet this pudgy, ambling grandfather with the look of a veteran character actor and a New York accent something between delicate and delicatessen has a sort of pulpit brilliance.

Few understand American synagogue life better than Tutnauer— "Tut" to his friends, which one can become almost instantly—because few have run as many shuls. Long ago, he once had a regular pulpit at Beth El Congregation in Phoenix. After ten years of that, he and his wife, Margie, moved to Israel in 1972. He had a "normal life" there for another ten years, mostly teaching, went on a sabbatical to Argentina and then began a new career as an "itinerant rabbi," taking interim jobs all over America and then returning to Israel when each was completed. Tut is a close friend of Rabbi Joel Meyers at the RA, and as such has become the RA's "fixer," a sort of rabbinic James Bond whom the Conservative movement sends to help ailing or imploding synagogues and report back from the hot spots.

Tut and his wife have been airlifted into quite a few rabbinic war zones. His first interim job was Sinai Temple in Los Angeles in 1984, not long after Hillel Silverman left the synagogue and his wife to marry a congregant. Although interim rabbis generally stay only for a year—so neither the congregation nor the rabbi gets the wrong idea about long-term relationships—Tut remained at Sinai for two years because the RA knew he would leave quietly, gladly, and return to Israel. During that time, he helped stabilize the congregation and also invited young rabbinical student David Wolpe to give his first talk at the synagogue he would one day lead.

After working in Israel and Russia for the next ten years on behalf of the Conservative movement and the Seminary, Tut began taking interim gigs again. In 1996 he went to Shaarey Zedek, a mega-congregation in suburban Detroit, the next year to Temple Beth El in Rochester, then to Ahavath Shalom in Fort Worth, Texas. Each synagogue had a specific problem Tut could help them through: at one, the rabbi was developing a chronic illness, at another, the rabbi was accusing the congregation of age discrimination.

Every year, at the end of May, his phone starts ringing. There are calls from all over the country. But last year, he got a call earlier in the month, before he was even packed to leave Texas.

It was Rabbi Meyers. He didn't sound happy.

"Don't speak to anybody until you speak to me," he said. "I'm not yet at liberty to discuss it, but there's something important we may need you to do."

Tut says he has never walked into a situation as complex as Har Zion. And it is made all the more difficult by the circumstances of his job. Here he is, a man in his mid-sixties with thirty years experience in the rabbinate, and he's been hired to work with Herber, who is in his mid-thirties and has been ordained for only three years. And the synagogue isn't really using Tut the way he expected.

While Jacob has impressed everyone with his growth—seeming much more presidential than his naysayers had ever expected—the leadership has also tried to impress upon him that he really needs "seasoning" regardless of his natural talent. They suggested he take as many weekends and even weeks away from the synagogue as possible to visit other congregations, ostensibly those run by the kind of rabbi Har Zion had hoped to attract. There he could gather a variety of perspectives by seeing how other rabbis do things—funerals, weddings, bar mitzvahs, introducing prayers—and perhaps get a cram course in what other rabbis learn during their first and second pulpits. He could leave Tut in charge, knowing that the services would run relatively smoothly and Tut would say something wise or provocative at the appropriate moments to keep the congregation interested.

Unfortunately, it is now late winter 2000, and Jacob hasn't been away even once. He seems afraid to leave, convinced, perhaps, that the only way to really run for the job of senior rabbi at Har Zion is to be there and available to congregants every minute. And while the leadership laments that he isn't out gathering pointers, they are simultaneously very demanding of his time and energy.

Tut understands this dynamic all too well. "Rabbis get bored with the day-to-day business of congregational life—especially the talented ones," he says. "They seek to go out into the community and become personalities, and then the congregation basks in their rabbi's glory. While the congregation is basking, the rabbi isn't paying sufficient attention to the nuts-and-bolts issues of the congregation. How many Sisterhood installations can he get himself up for? How can he stay fresh talking to all these bar mitzvah kids?"

Rabbi Herber is doing everything he can to show he can take care of the nuts and bolts. "This very often happens with divorce and second marriage, right? Either you try to marry the same person or you marry the opposite person. Neither of them works very well," he says, with a nasal laugh.

The young rabbi also knows that the search committee has begun bringing in candidates again—and this year's crop is considered better than last year's. Some rabbis already sense that the job is Herber's, and the word is out that Har Zion might be putting on another search just to keep the Rabbinical Assembly at bay. But there are still mid-career rabbis who would like a shot at the job and the RA is heartily encouraging them to apply. Rabbi Meyers would like nothing better than for Har Zion to fall in love with an eligible candidate for its pulpit, because he doesn't really want to have the same conversation with them about Jacob this May.

In fact, my own rabbi at BZBI recently confided to me that the RA has encouraged him to apply. He's not really looking to leave BZBI, but both he and the cantor are up for long-term contract renewal this year. So to make sure he is covered for all possible employment scenarios, he did put his name on the placement list for open jobs. But he wouldn't apply to Har Zion.

"Would I suggest to one of my protégés to come here because this is a great job?" Tutnauer asks, and then answers himself, "No, because whoever would come here to replace Rabbi Herber would have a lot of shit to deal with, and it doesn't make sense to do that. You'd split the congregation down the middle."

Tutnauer is in a rare position to view Har Zion from inside and outside. I ask him what he thinks about Wolpe's role in the synagogue since retirement. "He has been the ultimate gentleman," he says. "He has maintained a cordial relationship but noninterfering. It's an act of statesmanship: you gotta get out of your kid's life. And you probably can never get too far out of the way. There is a theological concept that God, in order to create the universe, had to shrink God's self. If not, he would fill the universe and wouldn't have room for anybody. You only get too far away if you never show up, or you demonstrate hostility and hurt. He has not done that. He has been a real gentleman."

While Tut feels that the synagogue is not making full use of his own skills, there is no question that he has made quick impact on its culture. He did so the first time he stepped down off the bimah on Shabbat to deliver a teaching session—rather than a sermon—at ground level. He paced the area in front of the first row without a microphone. And in one extended teaching riff, he changed everyone's idea of what a Har Zion rabbi could be. It helps, of course, that his casualness, even his occasional self-effacement, during services is countered by nuggets of provocative, hard-won insight.

I've heard several congregants talk about the way Tut speaks to bar and bat mitzvah kids, comparing his and Herber's styles. Jacob appears to want to speak to the kids completely at their own level, often about sports. He swaddles them with personal history gleaned from talking to them or their family members, asking for acknowledgment after each one: "You have been a ranked tennis player since you were ten, right? But you have always been as concerned with *fairness* as with winning, right?" Herber's approach seems to be a direct reaction to the way Wolpe spoke to the kids, usually with more adult language and on more adult themes, with comments more likely to be remembered by their parents.

Herber also tries very hard to draw parallels between the boys or girls paired up for each week's rite of passage, even if the two have absolutely nothing in common except the proximity of their birthdays. It's a noble effort, but it can get clumsy when one kid appears far more accomplished than the other and there is no way to hide that. The comparisons sometimes seem to translate into: "You, Billy, are a straight-A student and captain of the soccer team and you, Bobby, really try hard in school and sports."

Tut, too, is obsessed with sports, and almost any conversation with him will veer into the imagery of basketball, his game of choice, or football. In fact, at sixty-six, he still plays basketball, and since he knows I'm in a regular Sunday game, he tries to recruit me for some post-Shabbat hoops on the court behind the shul when the weather warms up. But he uses sports metaphorically, and he talks about the gods of sport, rather than trying to elevate little league to big league status. On the bimah, he is more likely to stick to theology and big ideas.

"I remember Tut speaking to a bar mitzvah boy, very movingly, about the difference between what you do on special days, which are just for show and pretend, and the things you do *every day*, which represent who you are," Jeff Blum tells me. "This touched me deeply, and pointed out to me the power of having a rabbi for whom a little offhand comment can be an opportunity to touch deeply. I don't think Jacob has *ever* made a comment that touched me deeply.

"Look, he's no Wolpe and he's never going to be a Wolpe, but it's the right thing for us now. It's a new era of rabbis who do constituent service. And Jacob is a mensch."

Interestingly, the rabbi whose epic ambivalence is partly responsible for Har Zion's clergy dilemma is making news again during this placement season. In early February, Rabbi David Ackerman's name shows up on the short list for a plum university job, as Jewish chaplain and Hillel director at Brandeis University in Massachusetts. The day after his name is published as a finalist, Ackerman withdraws from consideration, reportedly because he has accepted and signed a new long-term contract with his synagogue in the Philadelphia suburbs.

Ackerman is replaced as a finalist for the Brandeis position by Rabbi John Schechter, the great-grandson of Solomon Schechter. Apparently, Schechter had not originally applied because he was one of Ackerman's references and didn't wish to compete with his colleague. The job later goes to another rabbi.

It begins as a normal late-February double bar mitzvah. The parking lot isn't as full as usual—the snowbirds, including the Wolpes, have yet to migrate back from Florida—and drifts cover the expanding frame of the new Noreen Cook Center addition to the building.

Both bar mitzvah boys make strong impressions on the bimah. The first, a basketball player, jokes during his speech about reading in *Sports Illustrated* that "bar mitzvah age is when a young Jewish boy realizes he is more likely to own a team than to play on one." The second is more serious-minded, giving the "honored rabbi" talk about his Torah portion and his responsibilities as a man. Herber smiles broadly as he speaks to each of them, but it is a political smile, a work-smile, and clearly something is wrong. He is really distracted: while talking to the boys together at the lectern, he actually uses the phrase "screwing up" and there's an audible gasp from the congregation. A few minutes later he announces the wrong page for Ashrei. Before delivering his sermon, he apologizes, saying this has been a really terrible week for him personally and he begs forgiveness.

"I am here in body," he admits, "but not really in spirit."

Then in the first line of the sermon, he tries to explain something he was taught at the Seminary, but the word comes out "cemetery." Another gasp.

Oh, God, I think. And he had told me only recently that his father-in-law was responding well to treatment.

During the kiddush after services, I work the room quickly to find out what has happened. The cantor tells me Rabbi Herber's father-in-law has not died, as I feared, but his health has taken a dramatic turn for the worse.

Because people are lined up to speak to Jacob, I make the rounds. Executive director Howard Griffel and I talk about the latest Philadelphia-area synagogue scandal. According to the *Exponent,* Griffel's counterpart at another local congregation has been accused of stealing some seven hundred thousand dollars from the congregation over the past few years, hiding the money in a "breakfast club fund," and then siphoning it off to capitalize a business venture with the synagogue accountant. I track down Lew Grafman, who fills me in on the rabbi search. He says they are still interviewing candidates, but the big issue is still what will happen in their upcoming shoot-out with the RA. He worries that it could get ugly.

Noticing an opening at last in the line to Jacob, I shake his outstretched hand and give his forearm a reassuring squeeze. I ask how he is.

He says that his father-in-law was doing pretty well, actually. And then suddenly the dread call came and they were told to fly down immediately, there wasn't much time.

"Now he is in a hospice," he says. "It's done."

He fixes his eye on me, which takes me by surprise.

"Well, *you* know," he says, "you've been through this yourself."

And with these words he connects with me in such a powerful way that I can hardly speak. I extend my hand, mustering the wherewithal to tell him how sorry I am for him and his family. We give each other's shoulders a grip, which turns into a hug.

To me, in this moment, Jacob Herber has become the new rabbi. Because he has done what rabbis are supposed to do: in receiving my empathy, he remembered that I needed some as well. Especially since the third anniversary of my father's death has just passed. And I miss him more than ever.

I remember the way he would squeeze my hand a couple of times. Every so often, I would feel the quick one-two pulse of paternal reassurance, a private message hidden in a public display of affection. In my worst childhood fears, I could not imagine that one day I would hold my father's hand and a faint double-squeeze would be all that was left of him.

Growing up, I was the kid with the dad you could really talk to. Friends would come to visit me and, invariably, end up talking to him. He was easy, with a real talent for friendly engagement. He would blanch at the formality of his given name, Gerald, and roll his eyes when referred to as Mr. Fried. My father was such a Jerry.

I suspect that his popularity, and maybe even his youthful appearance, had a lot to do with the fact that he never really left home or grew apart from the daily influence of his own parents. Except for his college days at Penn State, just a couple of hours upstate, he remained a hometown Harrisburg boy. He had dreams of being a chemist until a bottle whose contents he had been analyzing all semester fell and broke just as he was about to identify the last layer of gunk. According to his retelling of the story, he walked out of the lab and never came back, promptly changing his major to journalism/advertising and facing up to who he really was: the son of a traveling salesman and an angel. His goal was to marry a woman prettier than he deserved, which was my mom, and to prove he could be successful in business without also being a scoundrel like my charming street-taught Pop-pop. My dad wanted to be a Boy Scout in the gritty world of retail.

He started out as a toy buyer, and fondly recalled putting in his order for the first Barbie dolls, the year they debuted at the New York Toy Fair. He spawned an unplanned kid (me) and then my two brothers, and had a heart attack at the age of twenty-nine. And after a miraculous recovery he grudgingly decided it would be best if he went to work with his father after all in the furniture store Pop-pop had opened after coming off the road. My father built up the business with his clever radio ads, featuring a kindly old salesman character, Mr. Martin, who was forever fighting with his son, the "whippersnapper," for trying to gouge the customers. It was a telling inversion of real life: a shrink would have had a field day with that one.

When my dad bought a store of his own, hoping to escape his father's gravitational pull, Pop-pop surprised everyone by closing his own place at the last minute and asking my father to make room for him as a salesman. While the balance of power in their relationship shifted with ownership, my father still had to contend with his father every day of his life. Even after the store closed, and my father opened a small advertising agency that successfully marketed his city smarts and small-town heart to family furniture stores around the world, Pop-pop was given an office down the hall and some small ongoing task to manage.

I was oblivious to their friction. Unconditional love sometimes skips a generation. To us grandkids, Pop-pop was a loving and generous man. To my father, he was something of a bully. Consequently, my father's act of defiance was to refrain from telling his kids what to do. He had the courage to hold his tongue. He taught me that the key to being a great parent—or spouse, or friend—is often in what you *don't* say.

My father was not a religious man. He was fascinated by Judaism and enjoyed reading and learning about it, but he never expressed much spiritual affinity. He didn't have to be dragged to synagogue like my Pop-pop—who was a president of our Jewish Community Center, but came to shul only when Nana forced him—but I suspect he was more moved by being there together with his family than by praying. He understood the concepts of mitzvot, good deeds, tzedakah, charity, and *gemilut khasadim,* acts of loving-kindness, better than anyone I have ever met, and gave generously of his time and money. Mostly, he believed in the spiritual power of earthly relationships. To him, God was the force that assures that what goes around comes around. His form of worship was to be there for family and friends even before they knew they needed him.

In the summer of 1996, my father called from the shore house to tell me he had just been to the doctor. Six months later, he was dead at sixty-two from colon cancer. The illness leached him from the inside until there was virtually nothing left but bones and eyebrows: for some reason, while all the rest of his hair fell away, his brows grew more lush. But as his voice grew weak his hands still talked, in the emotional Morse code of the double-squeeze, reassurance that something familiar remained.

I took the better part of those six months off work to be with him. Although we discussed almost everything, the subject of religion came up only once. It was when the rabbi paid a sick call, asking my father, who by that time was pretty much bedridden, if he wanted to discuss Jewish ideas about life after death. But Dad waved him off, saying: "I was always taught that Jews don't believe in an afterlife."

Later, we talked about whether that was really true. I told him that I was certain he had been taught that, but at a time when American Jews were going through a somewhat assimilated period of being told what they "believe" and "don't believe." That kind of teaching, however, had gone out of style, because it is actually contrary to traditional Jewish thought. There are commandments one is supposed to follow, mitzvot to perform. But the only thing all Jews believe is that "the Lord is One." Everything else is up for informed debate. There are, in fact, many fascinating Jewish mystical texts about life after death.

My father didn't want to hear this. "I lived my whole life based on the idea that there was nothing after death," he said. "It's *way* too late to start thinking about it now."

But, of course, I've been thinking about it ever since.

24

MARCH MADNESS

CINDY BLUM SITS IN her crowded office at Elwyn, an agency that provides early intervention for public school kids with learning problems. The black metal furniture crammed into the small room is humanized by the pictures of her kids over her desk and a bookcase full of teddy bears and other toys. She is telling me about her painfully mixed emotions over what has happened to the rabbi search and what will happen to Har Zion.

Cindy is starting to change her mind about Jacob. Six months ago, she was feeling pretty positive about a Herber candidacy. Now she's not so sure. She likes the idea of her and Jeff being part of the new rabbi's inner circle, just as Ralph and Bernie were with Wolpe thirty years ago. And she loves the fact that her kids actually have a close relationship with the rabbi. What a great experience it would be for Sammy, her youngest, to be bat mitzvahed by Rabbi Herber—with whom she has spent so much time because he is often at the house picking Jeff's brain. But, still, she says, "Maybe there's a reason why somebody should have more experience. Maybe there's a reason for the rules. I adore Jacob as a person, and I think he has some really great qualities. But I think it's apparent there are certain areas of his professional development he needs to work on. And what concerns me is I haven't seen any great proactive approach on his part to work on them." She wonders why he's not visiting other synagogues to learn from other, more experienced rabbis. She wants to know how he is going to expand his horizons, so he can help her to expand her own.

"I'm looking for a spirituality that I don't see coming through Jacob in services," she says. "There's a mechanical formality to him. I know Wolpe is a hard act to follow. But, remember, when the search committee first did that huge survey, being able to deliver an inspiring sermon was the number-one priority. At the time I thought, 'Why? It's such a small part of what a rabbi does.' But now that I've been to shul on a regular basis, I see the difference between someone able to get up there and be inspiring and work at an intellectual level that will keep people coming to shul, give them something to go away with. And it's not something I feel from Jacob."

The rabbi search committee is supposed to get together this coming Wednesday. The inner circle is going to interview a new candidate at 4 P.M.—this is only the third candidate they have invited in this season, and the other two have already been rejected—and then the entire group is meeting at 7. Cindy has decided that she is going to raise these issues at the general meeting. She really is having second thoughts about Jacob being handed the pulpit at Har Zion just because he's there, just because he's already in the house and in the office. She wants more out of services than this and she has heard other congregants, even other search committee members, privately say the same thing. It is time for the conversation to take place among the whole search committee. Before it's too late.

When I call Cindy the next week to find out what happened at the big meeting, she sheepishly admits that she didn't go. She missed it because her father was in the hospital with third-degree burns on his foot. He was supposed to soak it in Epsom salts, but he has so little feeling left in the foot that he didn't realize the water was burning him.

She tells me that she didn't feel so bad about missing the meeting, however, because Jacob has been so great to her dad in the hospital. He visits every day. He even offered to drive Cindy's mother, who lives near him, to the hospital. And he has generally been a caring, loving rabbi and friend. Maybe, she says, he doesn't need to be superintelligent from the pulpit if he can connect like this as a person. They haven't had this kind of feeling at Har Zion in a long time.

She uses almost the same words to describe Jacob's ability to connect as I did while sitting in the car after services scribbling down my description of his searing gaze and his galvanizing recollection of my father's death. The similarity is eerie, and also a little troubling, because it now occurs to me that I heard these same words long ago. Isn't this the way people used to describe the appeal of Ronald Reagan as president?

Cindy tells me she heard that this new rabbi candidate who came in from Toronto, Philip Scheim, was pretty impressive. She heard it from Carole Karsch, who sidled up to her at kiddush and said, "Where was he a year ago?"

Lew Grafman tells me the same thing when I see him at kiddush. He says they are finally seeing some good candidates. "But where were they a year ago?" he asks. And then, while everyone is reaching for the little spinach puffs on the steam table, he looks at me solemnly and says, "We started too early." And now it's too late.

I go to Tut and ask for his assessment of the situation. "Look," he says, "I think Jacob should be the rabbi of this congregation. I do have a problem with him being the rabbi of this congregation *tomorrow*. But that is what it's going to be. If I'm Joel Meyers, I don't have a choice. The RA can't continue going through the charade of bringing people here who everybody knows are going to be rejected: that's ugly. And the rumor is that there are some excellent people who, in unfairness to them, haven't been invited to interview because *it's too late*. And nobody in the room wants Jacob to go to Milwaukee. They like him, respect him. He's earned it. I think the RA is up against a wall now."

But at this very moment Tut has a more pressing concern.

"Are you gonna play ball with us today or what?" he asks.

✡   ✡   ✡

By late March, Philadelphia's hotels are teeming with rabbis and college basketball fans. The NCAA men's semifinals and the women's finals are both being held here, as is the one-hundredth annual convention of the Rabbinical Assembly. "March Madness," as the NCAA describes its tournament, is everywhere. Har Zion is no exception.

All the top brass from the RA are in town just as the synagogue is ready to announce that although they have searched high and low, they can't find anybody better than Jacob, so they want an unprecedented dispensation.

But the synagogue has another, even more urgent problem. Last week, a bomb threat was left on its voice mail system. The building had to be immediately evacuated, Rabbi Herber had to run an emergency meeting the next evening to calm down parents and kids, and new security measures were rapidly put into place. Actually, Lew Grafman and the leadership had been discussing for some time whether security needed to be tightened up. During the week, the doors in front of the office have always been left unlocked and largely unmonitored, and on Shabbat, all the synagogue's doors are left open and accessible. They had been reluctant to restrict any access to the shul or incur the possible costs of increasing security. But the decision has now been made for them, and the most extreme and expensive measures have been taken. There are armed guards at the entrances for the moment, but a new, sophisticated security system will be put into place so that everyone must be buzzed in by the main office. Only on Shabbat and holidays will some doors be left open.

All this hangs over Rabbi Herber's head as he struggles with his personal pressures. His father-in-law is still languishing in the hospice, somehow holding on to a thread of life. Jacob still has no way of knowing what will happen with his position at Har Zion. He can't sleep at night, playing out the scenarios in his mind. If the RA rules against the synagogue, he'll be looking for a new job next year and they will be moving. But if the RA ultimately agrees to let him be a candidate, there is another problem: the ruling may come too late for the synagogue to hire an assistant for him. And Tut will be heading back to Israel soon. So, Jacob could be working even harder next year than he is now. And all this is complicated by a development that nobody else knows about yet: Cynthia is pregnant with their second child.

On its surface, the Rabbinical Assembly convention at the Wyndham Franklin Plaza Hotel looks pretty tame. For the hundredth anniversary of the RA, which was started in Philadelphia, the leaders wanted a cele-bratory, non-controversial meeting, leaving political battles for another year. They even called it the "Centennial Celebration Convention" and packed the agenda with relatively feel-good, optimistic sessions.

But behind the scenes the drama is playing out. Word spreads that Har Zion is asking the RA for an exemption from the placement rules. It is one of the most elaborate and public games of chicken any synagogue has ever played with the RA, especially ironic because it concerns Jacob Herber, who many rabbis know from his years as that personable young man at the RA.

Some of Rabbi Wolpe's colleagues at the Seminary have heard that Jacob isn't getting along so well with him, or with Rabbi Tutnauer for that matter. Some who attend the gala dinner for the RA leadership at Har Zion note that when Rabbi Herber rises to give the opening greetings—in front of everyone who matters in the Seminary, from the chancellor on down—he neglects to make any special mention that Wolpe and Tutnauer are in attendance. Nobody thinks Jacob really did this on purpose to hurt them. It is simply evidence that he has yet to fully understand the political nuances of mentorship.

The afternoon after the dinner, I go to the big keynote speech by Rabbi Harold Schulweis, whom I've always wanted to hear lecture. He is one of the most widely quoted of the pulpit rabbis of Wolpe's generation, an excellent, thoughtful writer whose sermons read as profoundly as they sound, and whose pulpit work has been smartly, tastefully preserved and promoted for decades. On the website for Congregation Valley Beth

Shalom in Encino, California, a seventeen-hundred-family synagogue where Schulweis has been spiritual leader since 1970, there are audiotapes available of his sermons all the way back to the beginning of his tenure, and full-text versions from the past decade that any clergy member can download and appropriate, as long as the rabbi gets proper attribution. Schulweis has been closely involved with the California Conservative world of the University of Judaism since not long after its inception—he came west in 1952, taking a pulpit in Oakland after being ordained and briefly teaching at City College of New York. And this easy access to his fine body of work has made him a homiletic guru for rabbis young and old. His popular books are less well known to the public than those of his colleague Harold Kushner, but Schulweis is probably more influential among working clergy, because his work is more focused on core theological issues.

I am interested in Schulweis's lecture, which is predictably provocative and full of quotable lines, such as: "Belief in God is not delivered on a silver platter, it requires courage," anything less "reduces Judaism to pots and pantheism." But I am also interested in Schulweis as a role model, since it is clear that in many ways David Wolpe has followed the venerable rabbi's lead. Schulweis is the nationally prominent Conservative rabbi David's father might have been. Why he isn't is an interesting question. If it gnaws at Rabbi Gerald Wolpe, he has never mentioned it to me, but I know it is something his children have thought about. Paul Wolpe once told me something very interesting about his brother: he said he felt that David, especially earlier in his career, attributed their father's lack of national stature to a "failure of courage." His father has told me that it was because he always turned down national posts to spend every extra minute with his family. The truth is probably somewhere in between, and complicated.

Clearly, Elaine's illness forced Wolpe to retreat professionally at a moment when he might have blossomed into more of a national multimedia force. But his fascination with bioethics, which predates Elaine's stroke, also moved him away from concentrating his intellectual energies on core religious issues. This goes as far back as college majors: Wolpe is, at heart, fascinated with history. Schulweis studied and taught philosophy, and is more focused on theology.

Wolpe is also, I think, an interesting example of the kind of Jew who early on recognized his abilities in public speaking and intellectual thought, and chose the rabbinate not only because of the Holocaust, but, on a more subtle level, because other professions might have been closed to him because he was Jewish. When congregations lament today, "Where are the great rabbinic sermonizers of yesteryear? Why are so many young rabbis mensches at the hospital visit but low-wattage from the pulpit?" the answer might be in the experiences of Renaissance rabbis like Gerald Wolpe and Harold Schulweis. Intellectually gifted public speakers don't have to be rabbis anymore. They can be university professors, pundits, senators from Connecticut.

The intellectual role of the American rabbi has also changed since the days when Wolpe and Schulweis were coming up. The rabbi used to know more about *everything* than his congregants. Now he (or she) is likely to know more only about Judaism.

"I don't give sermons anymore," Moshe Tutnauer tells me, "because I don't know more than those people. So I teach Torah. In the day of Simon Greenberg, when much of this congregation was smart but not educated, you developed a rabbi who interpreted *The New York Times* for the congregation. Now the people who write *The New York Times* are sitting in your congregation, along with two professors of psychology and three doctors of philosophy. What are you gonna tell *them*? Don't be a jerk!

"There's also a basic democratic thrust in this country. Even your doctor doesn't tell you what to do anymore—you go until you get the opinion you want to hear. So I'm not playing the role of his highness looking down from the pulpit. I don't want to pretend to be an authority except for the area in which I am an authority. And even though I've studied more about Judaism than them, I'm not gonna say, 'This is what Judaism says.' That doesn't sell anymore."

✡   ✡   ✡

While the rabbis' convention is in town, a quiet meeting is held be-tween several members of Har Zion's search committee, including the Two Lews, and some of the top RA brass. The Har Zion group goes expecting to do some business, make a deal. They assume that Rabbi Meyers has already gone to the RA's placement commission—an inde-pendent panel that rules on placement issues for Conservative Judaism—and received a tentative ruling on the Har Zion situation. They also assume that a deal can be made, because their recollection of the diffi-cult meeting last year is that Meyers all but promised they could hire Jacob if they searched for another season.

But of course, he never said that, didn't mean that and has been watching with great concern as this freight train of Jacob's candidacy keeps barreling toward him. He is worried for the synagogue, worried for Jacob. And he's also frustrated because other Conservative syna-gogues with open pulpits seem to be doing just fine in their searches. In fact, the committee at another of Philadelphia's big Conservative congre-gations, Beth Sholom, the Frank Lloyd Wright–designed synagogue in the northern suburbs, has already seen several candidates they like, in-cluding one Har Zion interviewed and rejected, and another who ap-plied to Har Zion and didn't even get a cursory pre-interview on the phone, just a polite form rejection letter from Lou Fryman.

Meyers tells the synagogue's delegation that the RA is not prepared to make a decision, and is not very happy with what Har Zion has done. While the synagogue's leaders keep saying they don't want to endanger Rabbi Herber's career, they have, in his opinion, clearly put the young rabbi in harm's way.

The meeting ends in a draw. The Har Zion group says they will keep looking, although they probably won't. The RA group says they will take the matter under advisement, but they don't want to. It is three weeks un-til Passover, when rabbi search season begins to wind down. Two weeks after that, Tutnauer's phone will start ringing and he'll be off, either to an-other synagogue that needs help or back to Israel. This could get ugly.

✡   ✡   ✡

All the while, most people in the congregation have no idea what is happening. At the bar mitzvahs over the next two weekends, life in the main sanctuary appears normal. There have been no major announcements in the temple bulletin about the search, and most members don't know to ask.

I'm reminded of a point Rabbi Schulweis made in his lecture at the convention. He offered an interesting interpretation of the Fourth Son in the Seder, the son who is usually described as too uneducated to know how to ask. "The Fourth Child is not *dumb*," he said. "He doesn't ask because he *doesn't believe we have the answers.*"

During one Shabbat service, an older couple, members who don't attend often, are sitting behind me discussing the rabbis.

"I don't like Tutnauer," the husband says. "He's too . . . well, *something* . . ."

"I like Rabbi Herber," the wife says. "He's nice, friendly."

"I don't like Herber either," the husband says. "He's *too* friendly. I don't want a rabbi who's friendly."

One of the bar mitzvah boys gives a truly original speech, talking about his mother's work as a physician treating cancer. He wows the congregation with his unusual plan for tzedakah: he's donating part of his bar mitzvah money to one of his mother's patients. She needs a second opinion on her breast cancer from Sloan Kettering and her HMO won't pay for it.

At the kiddush, Tut and Cantor Vogel tell me that the formal request has gone into the RA for Jacob to be considered a candidate. Tut is engaged, fascinated, watching the whole thing like a sports fan who has access to both teams' locker rooms. But he is also a fan who can leave when the game is over. Vogel, who has to stay and live with the decision, seems more resigned than enthralled. However the RA rules, it means more pulpit friction for him.

Tut says that he has suggested a compromise to Rabbi Meyers. Let Jacob be rabbi-elect—or some such made-up position—for the next two years, and then he can be made rabbi when he reaches the six years of experience required by the Rabbinical Assembly bylaws. It's a compromise that a Philadelphia lawyer could love, bending the rules into a soft pretzel without breaking them. Tut has also shared this scenario with Jacob, who he says is getting his head around the idea that this might be all they offer him. Then he would have to decide whether to take it or to put himself into placement at the last minute, which would leave Har Zion completely in the lurch.

"Jacob is totally torn up about this," Tut tells us.

A week later, there's a call from Mexico City: it's almost over, come and say your good-byes. Jacob and Cynthia rush to book flights. When they arrive, Cynthia's father can no longer speak; he communicates only by the look in his eyes. His breathing is labored, he is obviously in pain. All they want for him is that the suffering ends. We're all here with you, they tell him, you don't have to keep fighting, let go.

Jacob struggles to figure out who he is in this wrenching scene: is he the son-in-law or the rabbi, the husband or the rabbi? He thinks about his own father, who stopped being part of his life not long after Cynthia's father became part of it, just after Mychal was born. Soon he will have lost them both.

While they are in Mexico City, word comes that the issue of his candidacy is finally going to be addressed by the RA. Lew Grafman and his recently named successor as president, Alan Greenbaum, are invited to meet with Rabbi Meyers and Rabbi Schoenberg. It is time to make a deal, or at least a proposal that can be put in front of the placement commission, which will make the final decision.

The meeting is much friendlier than the others. They have already gone fourteen rounds and there is little punch left. Several scenarios have been discussed. One is that Herber would be named rabbi of Har Zion and Rabbi Wolpe would be spirited back to temporarily serve as "mentor-rabbi." When that was run by him, Wolpe immediately shot it down as "bizarre." His career had exploded since leaving the synagogue, he didn't want to go back and he knew Jacob would be aghast if anyone suggested he return.

Another option, the most expedient for Har Zion, would be to allow Jacob to become a candidate for senior rabbi right now. There could be several ways of justifying that, going back to the intention of the rule—which was to keep young assistant rabbis from pushing out their older, more established senior rabbis. Since Wolpe had retired, obviously the synagogue was not trying to bend the rule to force him out. At least two other synagogues had been allowed to elevate assistants with fewer than six years experience. Both cases were emergency situations after the senior rabbi had taken ill or died, but still the precedent had been set. Also, Jacob is several years older than the typical rabbi only four years out of Seminary. The rule was meant to keep twenty-seven-year-olds off the largest pulpits, not thirty-seven-year-olds.

But Rabbi Meyers and Rabbi Schoenberg are emphatic: the rule says Jacob cannot be made senior rabbi of Har Zion until he has been ordained for six years. So Jacob would have to technically remain in his current position—the title of which is simply "rabbi"—for almost two more years. If he and the synagogue agree to do this, then perhaps a deal can be struck in which the RA would allow Har Zion to interview him for the senior rabbi job right away, but not technically install him in the job until after the two years passes. They would also be allowed to hire an assistant rabbi or another rabbi-in-residence immediately.

Grafman and Greenbaum agree that this could work for Har Zion. Meyers and Schoenberg agree to present the proposal deal to the placement commission. There will still be a wait for the commission's official stamp of approval. But it does appear that after nearly three years, the search to replace Rabbi Wolpe is finally over.

Jacob gets the call in Mexico City. He shares the good news with Cynthia and then, overwhelmed by the extremes of emotion he is feeling, he talks to his father-in-law, who has been so worried for so long about the uncertainty of their lives in Philadelphia. The dying man squeezes Jacob's hand to let him know he is pleased, relieved. It is such a bittersweet moment: their *nachas,* their good news, appears to be helping him locate his peace, bringing him closer to rest.

Three days later, he is dead. And if Jacob Herber was ever really a young man, he isn't anymore.

The placement commission goes on to approve the deal between Har Zion and the RA, and Jacob is finally allowed to formally interview for the job with the rabbi search committee. As he prepares for the interview, Cynthia and Mychal arrive back from Mexico City, where they sat shiva. There is an outpouring of emotion and support for them in their time of grief. And they are going to need it.

The morning of Jacob's interview, the couple goes to the hospital so Cynthia can have a special ultrasound to verify what they already suspected. She is having a miscarriage, losing the baby she told her father about on his deathbed.

Jacob tries to pull himself together for his interview. He feels he should be home with Cynthia, but he also knows that this meeting can't easily be postponed. The committee has to vote on his candidacy and make a recommendation for the annual board meeting next week. If he tells them Cynthia had a miscarriage, they will certainly understand and reschedule, but the Herbers don't want everyone to know their business right now. And Jacob doesn't want sympathy to play a part in their perception of his readiness for the job. So he sucks it up and goes in.

He can't tell how he is doing, because his mind is really elsewhere. Then, halfway through the meeting, Ralph Snyder scribbles a note, hands it to another member and leaves. Cindy Blum also gets up, and heads out with Ralph.

Jacob is sure he has blown it. In fact, he is sure that what Ralph wrote was "He's blowing it." He finishes his presentation, answers all questions, and Lou Fryman, sitting next to him, thanks him for his time. He walks down the long quiet hallway with nothing but the hum of the fluorescent lights to comfort him. Out the door, down the concrete steps to the parking lot, where his car sits in the space marked "Reserved for Rabbi Herber."

And just as he gets to the car, the members of the search committee come streaming out the glass door toward him, smiles on their faces, congratulating him, shaking his hand, telling him he is the one. Ralph's note, it turns out, said, "You know what? He did terrific."

Jacob is approved by the board, and Har Zion's torturous three-year rabbi search is finally at an end. And as the rabbi placement season finishes, I get news of all the other working rabbis and synagogues I've been following. My synagogue in town, BZBI, gives Ira Stone—my rabbi and Rabbi Wolpe's rabbi—a new long-term contract. My cantor, however, tells me after minyan one day that he has received an unacceptable offer and is leaving for another congregation. My hometown synagogue, Beth El, hires a rabbi from Winnipeg, Allan Meyerowitz. He was interviewed once at Har Zion and was not brought back to meet the full committee, but was brought back twice to the other big Philadelphia Conservative shul looking for a rabbi, Beth Sholom, before they decided on someone else: Gershon Schwartz, from Congregation Shaarei Shalom in Baldwin, New York. Rabbi Daniel Wolpe never did apply for the job in Harrisburg, choosing instead to remain in Florida. He has just been hired for his first solo pulpit by a small shul, Temple Ohalei Rivka—The Southwest Orlando Jewish Congregation, which prides itself on being "the closest synagogue to the Walt Disney World Resort."

As for Moshe Tutnauer, he announces he is leaving in early June, and we try to get in as many Shabbat basketball games as possible before he goes, whenever the weather permits. The games are one of many ways that Tut has helped loosen up Har Zion, trying to return it to its historic roots as a community center, not just a sanctuary and catering hall. I feel a guilty glee as I change out of my sport coat and slacks into wrinkled gym shorts, a sleeveless basketball shirt and Nike high-tops in the men's bathroom just off the sanctuary. Sometimes we even return to the kiddush dressed like that, trying to talk one more guy into playing. Tut's knees are shot, but his mid-range set shot is still pretty accurate. And there is something extremely wonderful about throwing a behind-the-back pass to the sixty-six-year-old who just finished explaining the Torah portion, and watch him touch-pass to a man open underneath, or just pop the fifteen-footer.

On his last Shabbat, when I walk into the sanctuary, Tut is sitting on the bimah, just next to where Rabbi Wolpe used to sit. He catches my eye, and makes a pronounced dribbling motion, which is his way of asking if I can play today. It is something I never expected to see from the bimah at Har Zion Temple. But then, that is true of a lot of things I've seen over the past three years.

I later discover that the synagogue has made Tut an offer he can't refuse, and he will be joining Har Zion for a second year. So the games will continue.

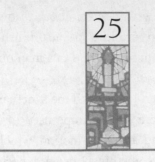

25

PULPIT FRICTION

IT BREAKS MY HEART to watch what is happening between Rabbi Wolpe and Rabbi Herber. As one of the few people who speaks to both of them often, it is amazing to see how each yearns for the other's attention, affection, support, respect, yet they seem incapable of connecting. It is so difficult to make the transition from where they were two years ago to where they are now, especially for two men whose wives aren't particularly close, so they can't function as a backdoor source of communication.

Tut once told me that success as a rabbi "depends on how smart you are and how ready your wife is to tell you, 'Stop being a schmuck.' "

Their problems touch a chord for me right now because my last mentor is dying. Ed McFall, the former UPI Philadelphia bureau chief who gave me my first job out of college, is in the final stages of cancer. Ed has been the perfect mentor: supportive, kind, fatherly when it's appropriate, collegial when it's necessary. His impending loss makes watching these two rabbis float near each other, like astronauts trying again and again to dock on a space station, that much more painful.

For some time now, Ralph Snyder has been trying to instigate a rapprochement between the two rabbis, suggesting they go out for lunch, hash it out. Wolpe feels they have already done that a couple of times to no end, because after the lunches he doesn't hear from Jacob for months. At the same time, Herber feels disconnected both from Wolpe and from his colleagues in New York, his mentors at the Rabbinical Assembly, whom he refers to collectively as "my rabbis." He understands they are upset with him over what has happened during the Har Zion rabbi search. But between the synagogue and his dying father-in-law and the loss of the baby, he is under an enormous amount of pressure. It would be nice just to get a call from someone concerned about how he is holding up.

Ralph arranges for Wolpe and Herber to have another lunch to try and settle their differences. It quickly becomes emotional. Jacob tries to apologize, but Wolpe says he does not trust the apology. He still doesn't understand what the problem is between them. Jacob has already apologized several times before, yet their relationship never improves.

Jacob is taken aback, teary. He says he has already lost two fathers, and doesn't want to lose a third.

Wolpe now thinks he made a mistake and should have gotten involved in the rabbi search, especially when it bogged down after Ackerman withdrew. He knows he stayed out of it for all the right reasons, and he has had dozens of notes and phone calls from other rabbis congratulating him for doing what so few of them would have been able to. But now he worries that doing the right thing might have been the wrong thing.

And he is not the only one thinking this. I speak to several rabbis who privately express their incredulity that Wolpe could allow the search for his successor to get so out of hand. One pulpit rabbi, who likes Jacob very much personally but fears for his future, calls his hiring at Har Zion "the first major casualty in the country to a new trend in the rabbinate—a move away from the huge congregation."

Wolpe doesn't quite agree with that analysis. He concedes that the candidate pool for Har Zion may have been affected by the trend of talented rabbis preferring to remain at small and mid-sized congregations instead of going after such a huge pulpit. He knows there is a growing belief in the rabbinate that while the huge synagogues often pay better and have more prestige, nothing can compensate for the increase in pressure. But he doesn't believe that was the main reason Har Zion's search got into trouble. And while large American synagogues are clearly at a critical juncture, he has no fear that they are in real danger.

"There has been a return to the small, intimate, non-cathedral synagogue," he says, "but there will always be a place for Har Zion, I'm convinced of it. You need a synagogue that big to handle the diversity that can't be handled in a smaller group—where it's easier for people to feel out of sync with the defined position of the congregation. There will always be the special-interest synagogue and the larger synagogue, which is like an umbrella covering people who want to go to shul and not be involved in an ideological crunch."

He believes this is more about America than Judaism. "In America there is such a desperate need for self-definition in an amorphous society where people don't have the opportunity to understand what they want to be. So there's a grasp for anything that speaks of defined ideology. That's why right-wing religions are expanding. People *want* to be put into slots. Sociologically, Americans are always teenagers. And the one thing you discover about your teen years is how quickly they go by as you're trying to define yourself. We are the most desperate seekers of self-definition of any nation in history. And whatever helps you in self-definition, be it a cult or a religion, survives."

Wolpe tells me he thinks he would make an excellent cult leader. "I could be very dangerous," he says. "If I had the energy—it takes great energy—and if I weren't as eclectic as I am, I'd be a great cult leader. I know all the secrets. I just don't want to put in the time."

I have now been talking to Wolpe several times a month for over two years, and have come to believe I know him fairly well, at least professionally. So I am truly shocked, just like everyone else who knows him, when he announces that he is coming out of retirement.

He has agreed to spend one year as interim rabbi at Temple Emanu-El in Palm Beach, Florida. The congregation is particularly important to organized Judaism, because it is the winter synagogue of so many major donors to Israel, to American Jewish causes and to the Conservative movement. Among its better known congregants are Seagram's co-owner Charles Bronfman, the head of the combined Federation/UJA, Slim-Fast magnate S. Daniel Abraham, assorted Lauders and Resnicks, and other less conspicuous but nearly as wealthy givers. The synagogue also hosts many of the snowbird season's biggest Jewish fund-raisers and political speeches: last winter, both presidential candidate Al Gore and V.P. candidate Joseph Lieberman reached out to South Florida's Jewish voters from its pulpit.

So a lot of prominent people were upset when news spread that the rabbi of Temple Emanu-El, Leonid Feldman, had punched the president of the synagogue in the face.

With one blow, Rabbi Feldman knocked the president to the living-room floor of his $9 million Palm Beach mansion, blackening his right eye and setting into motion an ugly internal struggle that threatens to blacken the eye of Conservative Judaism. And Rabbi Wolpe has been asked by the Seminary to bring the Solomonic wisdom necessary to save the synagogue before the *wintermachers* migrate south for fund-raising season.

Leonid Feldman was a rabbi other rabbis gossiped about even before he decked his synagogue president. A tall, striking émigré often referred to as a "rock star rabbi," he was the first Soviet Jew to be ordained by the Conservative movement. He worked the national lecture circuit during the eighties, and then accepted the pulpit at Emanu-El, a sleepy little congregation in a section of Florida not always hospitable to Jews. He reportedly told the synagogue's board during negotiations, "I want to be a role model for your sons and daughters, granddaughters and grandsons. Therefore, I'm going to drive a nice car; I'm going to wear nice clothes; I'm going to ask for a very nice salary. When some of your brilliant children and grandchildren are sitting in the sanctuary looking up at me, I want them to think, 'I could be a doctor, I could be a broker, I could be a lawyer, but I want to be a rabbi, just like Rabbi Feldman.' "

He was not afraid of being bombastic and confrontational. He told *The Palm Beach Post* that "if you don't give 10 percent of your earnings to charity, you're a bastard." Many of his rabbinic colleagues regarded him with suspicion, believing some of his best *refusenik* sagas to be possibly apocryphal. But while some chided him for providing nothing more than what one congregant called "religious entertainment," they had to admit that he could fill seats and raise money.

Under Feldman's leadership, Emanu-El grew from three hundred families to over eight hundred, expanding along with the Jewish population of Palm Beach, adding more and more younger families to the core of senior citizens. He also put down roots in the community, marrying the daughter of the synagogue's treasurer. But as the synagogue grew, along with Feldman's cult of personality, splits emerged. There were generational and cultural gaps between the old guard and the new younger families. Feldman claimed that old-fashioned Palm Beach Jews did not always appreciate public displays of affection to God, like dancing in the street with the Torah scrolls on Simhat Torah. Others complained that Feldman had too many outside interests that took him away from his primary obligations to the synagogue: lectures, TV appearances. His supporters, including his father-in-law, blamed the problem on the fact that the growing congregation wouldn't hire Feldman a full-time assistant rabbi.

Then Stephen Levin was elected president. A successful fast-food and beverage-bottling entrepreneur, Levin had been a close supporter of Rabbi Feldman, chairing the campaign that had raised $8 million to rebuild the synagogue and update the Hebrew school. But when he assumed the presidency of the synagogue in 1998, there was an immediate clash. Levin said the rabbi wasn't focusing enough of his time and attention on daily synagogue business.

Last November, just before snowbird season began, Levin called a meeting of the ten-member executive committee of Emanu-El with the rabbi. It was held in his massive, fifteen-thousand-square-foot home, which is appointed with Chagalls, Miros and other twentieth-century art and sculpture. The meeting went on for an hour, with members openly criticizing Feldman's commitment to the synagogue and the time he spent away from the congregation. Then Levin demanded a detailed schedule of where Feldman planned to be. When Feldman noted he had already provided them a schedule of his upcoming travel, a copy of which was sitting on the glass coffee table, Levin looked at it, crumpled it into a ball and threw it toward the rabbi.

Whereupon Feldman stood up and clocked Levin, who was sitting on an ottoman next to the table. Levin crumpled onto the unforgiving granite floor.

The rabbi apologized, and everyone at the meeting agreed to keep the incident a secret. In March Feldman announced plans to resign, even though he still had three years left on his contract. And all the turmoil might have been forgotten had it not been for the timing of the resignation—which came too late for the congregation to search in a timely way for a permanent replacement. So Feldman's supporters, who believed he had been forced out unfairly by Levin, were trying to lure him back.

The synagogue needed a strong interim rabbi, and soon Wolpe was being love-bombed by national leaders urging him to consider the Palm Beach pulpit. The flurry of complimentary and beseeching phone calls was very gratifying; he had never realized before how many people nationally were aware of the success of his pulpit at Har Zion. They were saying he was a legend, the only one who could save Emanu-El. It was nice to hear, an ego trip as satisfying as any he's ever had. And they threw big numbers his way, David Wolpe numbers, nearly twice what he was making annually after thirty years at Har Zion. It was flattering, tempting, especially since his relationship with his old synagogue had turned so strange. His kids begged him not to do it. But he was seduced and Elaine supported his decision.

Why does he need this aggravation? Perhaps there is something he still needs to prove. Before he goes off to be a bioethics lecturer for the rest of his life, he wants one last chance to show some of the most powerful Jews in the country that all those nice things they are saying about him are true: that his voice from the pulpit is the stuff of legend. I also suspect there is something about the disaster of this synagogue that feels familiar to him. I recognize the language he uses to describe it: he is employing a lot of the same phrases I've heard him use to describe what Har Zion was like when he arrived. Nobody remembers anymore what he did to save Har Zion thirty years ago. It's ancient history. Maybe this is his chance to do it again, to be a Solomon for a new century. And, in so doing, seal his place in the history of the rabbinate.

By the time Wolpe's deal is finalized in mid-summer, the situation down in Palm Beach is worsening. Armed guards are called to one board meeting to separate angry synagogue members. Levin, the president, becomes as much of an issue as Rabbi Feldman. Levin is publicly criticized for his "dictatorial" actions, but is also whispered about for conduct supposedly unbecoming a synagogue president: his new wife, Petra, a former Miss Germany, is not Jewish, and some feel he doesn't come to synagogue enough. A petition is circulated to force Levin out, but he refuses to call a congregational meeting at which it can be presented. So, congregants go to circuit court, seeking to strip him of his power and stop him from releasing a sixteen-page internal report detailing the problems the synagogue had with Feldman—including the punching incident, which has been kept from the general public thus far.

Three weeks later, the whole sordid story is on the front page of *The Palm Beach Post,* the Sunday edition, no less. It is not only a "*shanda* for the *goyim*"—a disgrace that reinforces to non-Jews all the cultural stereotypes of Jews—but may well qualify as Palm Beach's first shanda.

In the meantime, Feldman takes another job: at a temple in Miami, which is also called Emanu-El. It's a famous old Conservative synagogue that once had more than fifteen hundred families, but has now grown so moribund that at its current size of 250 families, it cannot, at the moment, afford to affiliate with the United Synagogue of Conservative Judaism. For taking a job outside of the RA's placement system, Feldman is officially sanctioned by the Rabbinical Assembly. He is suspended from the RA for three years, during which time he is not allowed to do any rabbinic work within twenty-five miles of the synagogue that he left.

As the Wolpes arrive in Palm Beach for the High Holidays, the synagogue's civil war continues. The very morning of erev Rosh Hashanah, a three-hour meeting is held to try and get what are now two complete rival boards to stop suing each other over who should be able to vote in the next synagogue election. They decide to drop their lawsuits for the time being, and agree to continue negotiations after Yom Kippur.

On the High Holiday bimah, Wolpe does not leave anything to chance. He delivers an old, time-tested sermon right out of the handsome red leather-bound volume Har Zion had made for his retirement. He adds only one comment about the acrimony at Emanu-El.

It is the story of a yeshiva director who decides he wants to start a rowing team. He gets eleven yeshiva buchers into a shell, and they lose every race. Baffled, he tells his assistant to find the best rowing team in the country and then figure out how *they* do it. He comes back and says he has discovered their secret.

At Harvard, he says, ten men row and only *one* yells.

"It is time," Wolpe tells his Rosh Hashanah audience, "for more rowing and less yelling."

For the first time since I began covering Har Zion, I decide not to attend High Holiday services there. My mentor, Ed, just died and I need to be with my family in Harrisburg. At my synagogue at home, I am able to sit next to my wife during shul, following along with her in Hebrew and interacting at all the moments we've come to share in the service. She knows that during the *Kedushah,* when the congregation chants *kadosh, kadosh, kadosh,* holy, holy, holy is the Lord, and we're supposed to stand on tippy-toes, I will put my arm around her waist and lift her just off the ground. I can sit with my mother, my brothers, my aunt and uncle, my cousins, in the same row where I've sat since childhood, with the same people in front of us for as long as I can remember: the ever-expanding Isaacman clan; the Cohens, our old neighbors, one of whom, Sandy, married one of my first girlfriends, Marcia, who always turns to gab with me or my mom, with whom she is friendly through the synagogue. There is a big difference between praying at home and at Har Zion. At home, I talk to everyone and miss half the service; at Har Zion, where I usually sit alone, I concentrate on the prayers.

A pall hangs over my hometown synagogue. The longtime cantor, Paula Victor, who has courageously carried the Harrisburg congregation on her own shoulders as rabbis go in and out the revolving door, has ovarian cancer. She was treated successfully, but there has now been a recurrence. The synagogue has hired a backup cantor to be at her side on the bimah in case she is unable to continue, and they place a chair directly behind her lectern so she won't have to expend the energy to walk back and be seated. During the Musaf service, she loses her strength halfway through one of the major prayers and can't continue singing. Holding on to both sides of the lectern, she insists on speaking the prayer in Hebrew rather than letting the substitute cantor finish. Later, during one of the big call-and-response prayers, *cain y'hee rotzon,* she urges the congregation to sing louder, louder, louder to fill in for her own waning voice. It occurs to me that while prayers on Rosh Hashanah and Yom Kippur are always supposed to be approached as if it is your last chance, this may very well be the last time Cantor Victor ever leads us in urging God to inscribe us in the book of life.

The new rabbi, Allan Meyerowitz, does his best to get his new congregation through the emotional experience of Cantor Victor's illness, and to pep-talk everyone into believing that the synagogue's darkest days are in the past. He is the fourth rabbi in five years running the High Holiday services, at a synagogue that had grown accustomed to the stability of only three rabbis over the previous forty. He is unabashedly optimistic and enthusiastic during all his remarks between prayers, but makes a mistake in his first Rosh Hashanah sermon. Like many rabbis, he is excited that Senator Joseph Lieberman, a Jew, is running for vice president in the upcoming election. He tries to use this as an opportunity to speak about anti-Semitism, but eventually his sermon becomes political, and then too political, basically calling for Jews to vote for Lieberman because he is Jewish. This is dangerous territory for any rabbi, but especially risky in Harrisburg, the state capital, a company town where the company is government and the current governor is a Republican who almost got the vice presidential nod himself. Several people actually get up and walk out during the sermon, which I have never seen before. It will be interesting to see if he makes it.

When I get back to Philadelphia, I catch up with Har Zion's services, which a friend of mine generously offered to audiotape—using my technique of hiding the handheld recorder in the tallis bag. Interestingly, Rabbi Herber does not speak about politics, national or international, at all, but instead responds to something else in the air. He has spoken to me over the past months about the fact that since his father-in-law died, it seems as if everywhere he goes people are getting cancer, treating cancer, fighting cancer, succumbing to cancer. He finds himself asked to make sense of death by cancer a couple of times a week. So he gives a very basic, simple sermon about the synagogue community as a place of comfort, about the synagogue as a place where one explores why life is still worth living in the face of so much darkness.

He says he hears the voice of Hagar, the slave of Abraham who bore him a son and was banished by Sarah, when he listens to all the lonely unhappy people who want to know, "How can you gather at your synagogue and pray for life? Life isn't a bargain. Life is pain. Life is rejection.

You know what life is? The longer you live, the more life becomes a story of something being *taken* from you. Why look forward to another year if it's just going to be more of the same?" He offers what sounds like a rather elementary solution to this existential problem: "Find someone else to help," he says. But it is the way he invokes the darkness itself that is intriguing, the way he speaks to the miserable, and in so doing catches the ear of those brought down by their misery.

He tells of an elderly aunt whom he called to relate the exciting news that he had been accepted into rabbinical school. "Did you hear?" he said, "I'm going to be a rabbi! Isn't that great?"

"How could I hear?" she asked. "Nobody ever calls me."

"And I think I know why," Herber jokes. It isn't a famous story from a famous rabbinic scholar. But it is true at a level I don't often hear in synagogue. Even when he is expectantly asking people to "go out and find somebody else to rescue," he says this technique "works not only for the elderly, the divorced, the widowed, but also for the middle-aged middle manager who realizes he's gone as far as he will go in his company, and instead of resenting people who got promoted over him, instead of allowing his soul to become corrupted, chooses to become a mentor to younger coworkers. It works really well for young people who are disillusioned."

He finishes by explaining that one of the biggest problems for these disenfranchised people is that nobody hears them, nobody takes them seriously.

"We promise you," he announces, "that we will take you seriously. This is a place where people leave their pain, their anguish, their fear God has abandoned them, and walk out knowing that somebody truly cares about them. There are so many institutions in our lives that don't take us seriously, that exploit our innocence, answer our mail with a form letter and our calls with a recording. We desperately need this one place that exists for the purpose of caring about us."

Har Zion reborn as a place that feels your pain? There's an ambitious goal for the new year.

26

THE GRINCH WHO
STOLE PASSOVER

Now that he is several months into his second term, Tut is giving me a personal "state-of-the-congregation" address. There is, he believes, a new spirit of casual camaraderie at the synagogue, which he finds really wonderful and inspiring. It is counterbalanced, however, by the Har Zion bar mitzvah culture. "Har Zion has become, if you'll excuse the language, an easy lay," he says. "They let too many kids go through the bar mitzvah process, regardless of knowledge, because the synagogue needs to be known as a great place to have a bar mitzvah."

He continues to be concerned about Rabbi Herber, who he feels has been put into an impossible situation, a "quarterback with no offensive line." Since last year's rabbi search, there have been several staffing cutbacks. The full-time program director resigned, and he was not replaced. Not only was that a position that Rabbi Wolpe had worked very hard to create and get funded, but the program director had functioned as an extra clergy member, taking on many jobs, including helping with some bar mitzvahs, which will now revert to the rabbis and cantor. Also the scholar-in-residence program has been suspended. Even though the scholar-in-residence mostly taught, he or she was also usually available for some clergy duties. While Rabbi Wolpe hasn't been around a lot since his retirement, he has at least officiated at the funerals and weddings of families he was close to in the congregation. But now that he is in Palm Beach full time, he can't help out.

"Without an offensive line, even the best quarterback stinks," Tut says. "And the management has to be ready to spend money; especially when you have an unseasoned quarterback. You need to learn how to read the defenses. They're out to get you all the time, like cornerbacks always ready to intercept you. Congregations always want to save money. But if I was running this place I would have as much backup as I could find for Rabbi Herber. They are stretching him *very* thin."

In fact, crunch time is fast approaching. Tutnauer's deal is that he spends half the year at Har Zion and half the year home in Israel. November is here, and he is about to fly back—just after this week's bat mitzvah, which everyone has been dreading since it was first put on the calendar.

It is the return of the nightmare bat mitzvah family, the Landises, whose controversial rite of passage was my first experience in the Har Zion main sanctuary nearly three years ago. They have had another bat mitzvah since then, although they decided to hold it away from Har Zion. And their thermonuclear divorce, which was covered in the media, has been finalized. While Michelle, the ex-wife, has quit the congregation—remaining active in Jewish causes and education without a formal synagogue affiliation—Martin and the kids still belong to Har Zion. So, they've decided to give it another try.

Gingerly, the cantor and Rabbi Tutnauer have been doing everything they can to make sure there's no repeat of last time. Rabbi Herber hasn't been as involved, because he is not planning to be in shul that day. While the leadership begged him for a year and a half to take some weekends away and visit other synagogues, he never got around to scheduling one until faced with the prospect of officiating at the Landis bat mitzvah.

"The hand of coincidence is amazing, isn't it?" Tut laughs.

I ask Tut how he plans to make sure there isn't a repeat of the last performance.

"I've laid the groundwork by trying to build a strong personal relationship with the major player, the father, on the assumption that he will not want to embarrass *me* if I make him feel comfortable," he explains. "I also think the dynamic is different. The child is a different child. The wound is either deepened or healed or time has taken care of the tensions, but I don't anticipate a problem. I met with the father and mother separately. You're dealing with a brilliant guy whose thought processes are hard to anticipate. I have no illusions. Who knows what it's gonna be?

"I might take a Valium, and just say, 'Moshe, you're going home on Monday, just handle it.' And that's pretty much what I told his ex-wife. Anticipate bad things that might happen and just figure out how to handle it. But I am probably overly optimistic."

The morning of the bat mitzvah, the synagogue is packed. Politically and socially connected, the Landises attract a broad and interesting crowd. The only one not here is the father. He arrives a half hour later than requested, along with his son and the special lavender kippahs for his guests, which he forgets to put in the basket at the entrance, so he has to go back out and misses the Torah being taken out of the Ark. The cantor and rabbi simply roll their eyes to each other, "Here we go," and get on with the service.

Tut is right about the bat mitzvah girl: Lori Landis* is different from her polished older sister. A little zaftig, round-faced, wearing a long blue dress, she looks like a happy, hippie bridesmaid from the sixties in her first dressy outfit.

Tut makes a point of putting the bat mitzvah into a community context. He announces before the Torah reading all the simchas that are being celebrated by those receiving aliyahs. There are two congregants in their eighties who are celebrating birthdays, with children or grandchildren reading portions in their honor. There are two marriages in the congregation being celebrated. Two bat mitzvahs—and, of course, Tut is returning to Israel.

The Landis parents, Martin and Michelle, have separate aliyahs, which is depressing but probably prudent. Michelle goes up on the bimah to wait for her aliyah to be called. She sits alone on one of the benches on the side, looking over her shoulder out into the congregation like Wyeth's Christina, so sad and isolated among the family that she brought onto this earth. The Torah reading is Genesis 22, the story of God testing Abraham by asking him to sacrifice Isaac. Given this family, there could be a great sermon in that material if anyone dared to broach it.

Lori and her bat mitzvah partner do well with the Torah reading and the Haftarah. Lori stumbles a bit at one point, but recovers. In some ways, I think that's better. It is the kids who do everything perfectly that worry me. When the Torah is read, it is customary for there to be a person on either side of the reader following along in the book form of the Torah, so when a mistake is made, it can be immediately corrected. There is nothing wrong with making a mistake as long as it is corrected, which is one lesson the Torah teaches even before you read it. And, to me, there is something comforting when the reading breaks down momentarily, when it becomes a group effort rather than an individual performance.

Then Lori gets up to give her speech, which sounds awfully well written to have been penned exclusively by a thirteen-year-old. She speaks about the good work of the charter school her family started and how it changes the lives of underprivileged children. She says the school can combat the harmful effects of bad parenting. While it all sounds more like a fund-raising appeal for the school than a bat mitzvah speech, it is obviously a worthy cause for her to support with her bat mitzvah money. And, in what might be seen as a gift to the congregation in general and her mother specifically, she finishes her talk without thanking anyone at all.

When the rabbi speaks to Lori and her bat mitzvah partner at the lectern, he does not pretend they are on equal footing. The other girl is the daughter of a couple who are very active in the synagogue; she is the most popular girl he has ever seen at Har Zion, arriving at every bat mitzvah class with an entourage. Lori, on the other hand, he only got to know recently when she followed him out to the basketball court one day and shot around with him. Tut tries to charm Lori, but she appears a little bored, even yawning once while he is speaking to her.

After the bat mitzvah girls return to sit with their families and the Torah scrolls are returned to the Ark, Tut comes down off the bimah to teach. Since today is his last day at Har Zion for a while, his topic is "The End of My Prayer." And as he hands out the orange sheets he'll be teaching from, I see he has chosen a prayer that has fascinated me since the first day I came to shul after my father's death. In fact, I'm not alone, because the rabbi says that many people tend to pay special attention to this prayer during services. It is the final prayer of the silent portion of the Amidah, *elohay n'tzor l'shoni mayra:*

> *My God, keep my tongue from evil, my lips from lies. Help me ignore those who would slander me. Let me be humble before all. Open my heart to Your Torah, that I may pursue Your mitzvot. Frustrate the designs of those who plot evil against me; make nothing of their schemes. Act for the sake of Your compassion, Your power, Your holiness, and Your Torah. Answer my prayer for the deliverance of Your people.*
>
> *May the words of my mouth and the meditations of my heart be acceptable to You, my Rock and my Redeemer. May the One who brings peace to His universe bring peace to us and to all the people Israel, Amen.*

The orange sheet compares different translations of the prayer, which is in every Jewish prayer book, and details the biblical sources of the various lines, which were culled from Psalms 19 and 33, and Deuteronomy 16.

Tut talks about the first lines of the prayer, discussing the pain we inflict with words rather than rocks or guns. He is standing right in front of the Landis family as he says this, but they don't appear to be listening intently: at one point Martin whispers to his daughter Lori and they share a giggle. Tut talks about asking God to cleanse not only our actions but our feelings, because only then can our hearts be open to Torah. With spiraling intensity, he hammers away about the importance of not harming with words.

He appears to change the subject when he starts talking about Israel, where his seventeen-year-old grandson is not going to Stanley Kaplan to boost his SAT scores, but rather is in physical training to join the army. The peace process has fallen apart and the terrorist attacks are the worst they have been in years; he notes that the plane back to Israel will be empty and it will be terribly easy to get through customs. He chants the lyrics from a song currently popular in Israel, about "the children born in 1973," and as we hear these chilling lines a cell phone starts ringing just behind the Landises. Tut goes on to describe the first time he ever had to put a gun together, and realized the single most important thing on a gun is the safety catch.

"Have you ever seen a machine gun go off by itself, how it sprays bullets and spins around?" he asks. It is a gorgeous and painful analogy for what happens when anything potentially harmful—a mouth, a brain, a person, a people—spins out of control. He says we all need a safety catch.

During the Musaf service, I lose my concentration on the prayers as well as the Landises, and find myself turned away from the congregation, staring instead at the massive stained-glass window to my right. I see these windows every week as I walk into services, but I have never really looked at them closely from this perspective: in my aisle seat, I'm only three or four feet from the bottom of the window, which rises some thirty feet above my head. Light floods through the richly colored glass, yet from this vantage point I can't really make out the images that are so apparent from afar. Instead I look closely at the windows themselves. They are constructed from hunks of glass of various colors, sizes and textures that are splintered and shattered in fascinating ways, joined with a black epoxy that is an inch thick in some places and razor thin in others. While the windows, one for each major holiday, appear perfect in their glistening modernity from far away, up close you can see just how massive each piece is and just how distressed. None of the glass seems to have been cut into shape, but rather smashed, broken with a hammer, ripped off, bitten off. Yet the pieces are held together by a nearly hidden force that somehow keeps them from crumbling under their own imperfections.

It occurs to me that these windows are a mirror of this community: big, unwieldy, colorful, opaque, dazzling uncut jewels that don't exactly match up but are held together anyway by something powerful and amorphous that fills in both the cracks in the pieces and the cracks between the pieces. Each piece changes in color and intensity depending on the quality of light shining through it and the perspective of the viewer. In this stained-glass community, every piece has great value, no matter how distressed or distressing, because it holds something else in place. I look to my left at the congregation, and then turn back right to the window, and they are both bathed in the same light.

Afterward, at the kiddush, I bump into a lawyer who represents the magazine I have been editing—a job I mercifully just left—in a lawsuit. It turns out she is a close friend of Michelle Landis and is here to lend her moral support. Just then, Michelle approaches. She seems relieved. When she is told I am writing a book about the synagogue and the rabbi search, the first thing she says is that Herber should not be replacing Wolpe, he's not a heavy-duty enough rabbi. She says Tutnauer was the savior of this bat mitzvah, the only voice of reason in her family's relationship to Har Zion. She is happy about today. Her daughter did well, and everybody behaved.

Tut is happy, too: happy there was peace in the sanctuary, happy to be heading home. He will be missed, but he'll be back in the spring, when the temperature rises and the snow melts away from the basketball court.

While tranquillity reigns at Har Zion, a dark cloud still hangs over Rabbi Wolpe's new synagogue in Palm Beach. Snowbird season is fast approaching but so are the elections for the new synagogue leaders and another lawsuit has been filed by rival factions over who gets to vote. When I speak to Rabbi Wolpe, he tells me the situation is the most disgraceful thing he has ever seen in a synagogue. More than one hundred families have already quit. He believes Rabbi Feldman is attempting to orchestrate events from behind the scenes, but it is clear there is plenty of blame to go around in this circus of Jews behaving badly. Wolpe recently called both sides together for a meeting he hoped might help clear the air. Instead, the next thing he knew, someone put out a press release on Temple Emanu-El stationery describing the previously secret details of Rabbi Feldman's suspension by the RA three months ago.

"It's just *horrendous*," Wolpe says, "a phantasmagoria of absolute horror."

He now feels he may have made a mistake by accepting the pulpit. The Wolpes have made some new friends in the congregation, but there are many days when he regrets being seduced by the money and the attention and all those national figures calling to say he is a legend. This feeling has been reinforced by some setbacks in Elaine's health and their fear that medical care in Florida isn't as good as at home in Philadelphia. The standing joke he has heard is: "Do you know where you go when you get ill in Florida? To the airport."

Recently, Elaine woke up in the middle of the night and her legs wouldn't move. She was put in the hospital for tests, which all came back negative, and some movement in her legs returned. One theory is that it was either a passing problem—such as an adverse drug reaction—or the long-term effect of the way she has to walk and stand to compensate for her partial paralysis. The fear, however, is that she is having ministrokes. And, clearly, she can no longer walk or stand as confidently as before. She is now using a cane.

Rabbi and Elaine come back up north for a short time before the snowbird season begins. He uses the opportunity to meet with the chancellor of the Seminary, Ismar Schorsch, in New York. Wolpe has kept the Seminary top brass informed about the situation in Florida, but he is not certain they understand just how bad things are. He implores Schorsch to consider the unusual step of flying down to Florida and meeting with the rival factions himself.

Reluctantly, Schorsch comes to Florida several days before the planned election. In the early evening, he addresses the congregation about the impact of their actions on the synagogue, the community and the Jewish people. A synagogue, he says, has to set and abide by some moral standards of behavior.

After he leaves, Wolpe herds the battling eight-member groups into different rooms and does shuttle diplomacy, trying to build a compromise slate of officers and trustees for the coming year. The process breaks down several times. Once, they are close to a final slate until one would-be vice president announces that he wants his name above all the others, even though the names are being listed alphabetically and his does not come first. By midnight, a tentative agreement is reached. The next afternoon, lawyers for both sides go back into circuit court to present the judge with the settlement order. Shabbat comes and goes, and on Sunday more than four hundred people arrive to vote.

The vote appears to be unanimous, but still, when the recording secretary asks, "Those opposed?" everyone looks around the room nervously. Afterward, the new president-elect shakes hands and accepts the collective mazel tov as a writer from the *Post* looks on, preparing to report the first good news about the synagogue in quite some time.

Wolpe is thrilled. People are coming up to him and kissing his hand, thanking him for saving the congregation, saying he performed a miracle. It's a heady feeling. But he knows it is only the beginning. "I led them to the shoals of talking to one another," he tells me on the phone several days after the election. "Now the tough stuff begins. But that's for the new rabbi coming in to do. I'm just here to keep things going."

In fact, he says, he would prefer not to be there at all. But he made a commitment. He and Elaine will stick it out. It certainly does help that now, at this synagogue, he is a hero.

✡   ✡   ✡

The job, however, has taken its toll. It is visible as Rabbi and Elaine come north again in April for a visit, and we get a chance to catch up. Not long after the election, Elaine took a bad fall, tripping over a traffic cone as they were heading into a concert. Unable to brace herself, she fell right onto her face.

It is all catching up with her, he fears, the years of battling every challenge. Her ability to speak has been diminished even from the impaired level she had come to accept. Her walking is getting worse. The congregants at Emanu-El have been wonderful to her, and she has also seen old friends from Har Zion and from Harrisburg who have migrated south: they could have lunch and dinner dates every night, and they will now forever have a broadened social world in Florida. But it has been a difficult time, too hard to be worth what was gained.

He fills me in on his rabbinic sons' careers, which, to some degree, he is beginning to live through vicariously. David, he says, is doing exceedingly well but is working terribly hard. He has become the major figure in the rabbinate in Los Angeles, called *everywhere* to speak. But he would like to get back to writing another book, and he just can't do it. He is overtaxed and the synagogue has a deserved reputation for being difficult. But it will be at least another six years before he will have an opportunity to make any changes that might free up time, because he just signed what his father calls a "most gratifying" new contract.

David's salary is a source of much speculation among rabbis, several of whom have told me he is the highest-paid pulpit rabbi in America. But he isn't. When negotiating his new contract, David was told by an official in the Reform movement that its recent compensation survey showed at least ten rabbis reporting annual salaries around three hundred thousand dollars, which is what Sinai Temple is now paying him. According to a recent national survey of all organized religions, the highest pulpit clergy salary reported in the country is four hundred thousand dollars, paid to a nondenominational senior pastor at a church in the south-central section of America with weekly attendance of over fifteen hundred congregants.

Wolpe's youngest son, Danny, is also doing well at his first solo pulpit in Orlando. "Danny is just remarkable," he says. "He's the kind of person who leaps into the congregation. They adore him there and he's having a wonderful time. He'd like to get married, and we would like him to, and then he will really be the most happy fellow." Danny is less interested in being a star than being a pastor; he is a good speaker, but his real skill is getting involved in his congregants' lives. He called the other day, excited that a woman in a mixed marriage had decided to become Jewish, and thanked him for inspiring her to do it.

Since Danny is single and working in Florida, the Wolpes see him quite frequently. They don't see David and Elli and the baby nearly as often, and when they do, it is usually because they go to L.A. to visit. Yet David and his father communicate often by e-mail and phone. And David is such a public presence in the media and on the Internet that his exploits can be easily followed through his writings and clippings.

In fact, he is about to trigger an international incident.

On the first day of Passover, David delivers a sermon about the historical validity of the Exodus story. He discusses how new discoveries in biblical archaeology are confirming what some have been suggesting for decades: there is mounting evidence that the Exodus never happened, or didn't happen the way it is told in the Bible. He wants his congregants to think about how we as Jews are to maintain our faith in the face of scholarship that calls into question the historical accuracy of the Torah.

This would not normally be *that* provocative a sermon, even if delivered by a provocative speaker like David on the one day of the Jewish calendar when the subject matter would be most likely to provoke. But several factors combine to make it more resonant. At Sinai Temple, the first day of Passover draws nearly as many congregants as Rosh Hashanah, because there is a large Iranian-Jewish population in the synagogue who also celebrate the Persian New Year, NoRuz, on that day. So there are more than two thousand people at a service for which most rabbis would be pleasantly surprised by two hundred. In addition, David has invited the religion reporter from the *Los Angeles Times,* Teresa Watanabe, to cover the sermon, following up on a recent call she had made to him about some of these new archaeological findings.

He assumes she will write something small for her well-buried Saturday religion column, in which he is sometimes quoted. Instead, she writes a long, provocative story that runs on the front page of the paper's well-read Friday edition (during the week that Good Friday and Friday the thirteenth coincide). There's a photo with the caption: "Rabbi David Wolpe of Sinai Temple in Westwood called his sermon a search for truth: 'I think faith ought not rest on splitting seas.'"

The *L.A. Times* article is e-mailed furiously around the globe. I get the first of many copies forwarded to me from a writer at ABC News in New York. I barely know her, but when my book project came up in a recent conversation, she explained that she grew up at Har Zion and still follows the exploits of the family Wolpe. When I go to temple on Shabbat, Tut tells me he is hustling to get a copy of the sermon to find out what the fuss is about.

The local media reports that Sinai Temple had to put in an extra phone line to take all the calls, which only increase when L.A.-based radio host Dr. Laura Schlessinger rips the *Times* article on her nationally syndicated show. David is then publicly condemned by the Orthodox rabbinate in Los Angeles, which takes out an ad in the *Times* to blast him. Soon the chief Sephardic rabbi in Israel comes after him. He is actually accused of undermining the entire Middle East peace process, by popularizing theories that might help those who question Israel's historic right to its homeland. In the process, he gets tagged with a new nickname in the *Jerusalem Post.*

David Wolpe now looms as "the Grinch who stole Passover."

The controversy is particularly fascinating because of the window it opens on the relationships between the Jewish denominations, especially the friction between Conservative and Orthodox Judaism. One of the better-known rabbis who writes denouncing David's sermon is Avi Shafran, the director of public affairs for the Orthodox group Agudath

Israel of America. Shafran is the midst of his own controversy for an article he recently wrote for the Jewish national magazine *Moment,* which
was entitled "The Conservative Lie." The article called Conservative
Judaism "not only dishonest but superfluous," and was especially critical
of Conservative Jews for claiming to observe *halachah,* the body of
Jewish laws, but not really practicing what their rabbis preach. He accused the movement of becoming what sociologists have called a "marketplace religion," in which rules are changed or bent because of pressure
from congregants. While Conservative rabbis are clearly not happy
about the low level of Sabbath and ritual observance in their congregations, they do not share Shafran's bold sentiment that "sincere and dedicated Conservative Jews need to face an uncomfortable fact: Their
movement is a failure." The article came on the heels of journalist
Samuel G. Freedman's well-received book *Jew vs. Jew,* which explores
what he calls "the struggle for the soul of American Jewry . . . Who decides what is authentic and legitimate Judaism?"

By questioning the historical facts of the Exodus, David has stepped
directly into these controversies. The Orthodox rabbis take his sermon
as a deliberate attack on their true—or *truer*—Jewish ideology, especially
irksome coming from Conservative Judaism's rising golden boy.

Within his own synagogue, the controversy brings packed houses
and spirited debate. A question-and-answer session about the sermon
draws more than three hundred people, and a lunchtime Bible study
class about the Exodus attracts more than a thousand. While many of
the more traditional members of the synagogue are upset, there is only
one resignation out of sixteen hundred families. And one of David's most
high-profile congregants comes forward to defend him: actor Kirk
Douglas, who has been studying with the rabbi weekly for the past two
years as part of his return to religion after a near-fatal helicopter crash
and then a stroke. David also officiated at Douglas's second bar mitzvah
back in 1999, a star-studded event held on a Thursday morning in Sinai
Temple's small chapel, with guests including Lew Wasserman, Karl
Malden, Don Rickles, Larry King, Catherine Zeta-Jones, Angie Dickinson

and Steven Spielberg's mother, Leah Adler. Douglas writes a supportive letter to the *Jewish Journal of Greater Los Angeles* detailing the impact that studying with Rabbi David Wolpe has made on his life.

I call David to discuss the Exodus sermon. He is dazed and confused by its impact, but is also clearly loving it. This is one of the advantages of the built-in drama of the pulpit, something you don't get as an author or traveling lecturer. The religion writer from *The New York Times,* Gustav Niebuhr, would go on to marvel at the Exodus phenomenon more as evidence of the enduring power of the well-delivered sermon than anything having to do with biblical archaeology or theology.

"Part of what a rabbi is supposed to do is expose him or herself, theologically, religiously, spiritually, even emotionally to the congregation— because we're supposed to grow together," David says. "Being a rabbi can be a cloak and a veil: exposing oneself as a person and saying things you know will disturb is difficult for a rabbi, who is supposed to be after all a dispenser of comfort, a soother of wounds.

"The generation previous to mine felt the collective danger to the Jewish people to be so great that anything you said that could be taken amiss was a great communal transgression. And you see that, for example, in discussion of Israel. There was a time that any open criticism of Israel was considered harmful, virtually heretical. It's less so now, and in part that's because people feel more secure than they did then. There is also a therapeutic ethic that is very powerful now that people should be honest, and social relations that are based on mutually comfortable dishonesties are less admirable than people used to believe."

Isn't this kind of honesty easier said than done? "Yes, it's impossible to do completely. When Mrs. Schwartz says to you, 'Wasn't my daughter wonderful at her bat mitzvah?' it's a poor rabbi who would say, 'No, actually, she was terrible.' "

27

THE END OF MY PRAYER

THE TERRORISM IN ISRAEL is escalating and the Middle East peace process seems dead. The economy is sputtering locally and nationally. It would be a great time to be peddling a book called *The Diminished Expectations Diet Plan*. Yet, here at Har Zion, we are all caught up in a kind of communal euphoria. The same is true for the entire Philadelphia region. Our pro basketball team, the 76ers, is marching triumphantly toward the NBA finals. Our star players, Iverson, Mutombo and McKie, have made a clean sweep of the league's top awards, and our Jewish head coach, Larry Brown, has been named coach of the year.

Nobody can talk about anything but the 76ers. Avid listeners of all-news radio KYW have switched to sports-talk on WIP. Bernie Fishman and his son Mark, who has become one of the synagogue's most active young philanthropists, are suddenly even more popular than usual, because their family has a box at the First Union Center. Rabbi Tutnauer now understands why God wanted him to come back to Har Zion for a second year: to help Rabbi Herber, yes, yes, of course, but, a box for the NBA playoffs? Let us give thanks. This is even better than the year he worked in Detroit, at the congregation of Bill Davidson, the billionaire owner of the Detroit Pistons.

Inspired by the spirit of 76, the basketball games after Shabbat services become more popular. People who barely know the rules, like Cantor Vogel, come out to play anyway because it's in the air. Tut's weekly basketball e-mails—long, rhyming verses that combine Shabbat imagery with predictions for the next 76er playoff series—get funnier and sillier as the Sixers advance and everyone is loopy with excitement. But there is a method to the madness of "Old King Tut, the merry old nut," and his plot is succeeding. Unable to truly mentor Rabbi Herber the way he expected to, he is instead trying to loosen up the congregation for him. And, as a result, Har Zion has never felt less like a country club and more like an old-fashioned Jewish Community Center.

Tut tells me he is still concerned about the lack of sufficient backup for Rabbi Herber—although, with the change of sports season, he has switched metaphors from a weak offensive line to weak power forwards and perimeter shooting. But he is pleased to report genuine progress in other areas that matter: two dozen new Har Zion families sending kids to Jewish day schools, more adult education classes, a new study group for young couples, all good first steps.

And there are big changes coming in the Hebrew school. Sara Cohen, who has been running the award-winning school for more than twenty years, is being nudged into retirement. The school has been her life, since her husband, Irv, a well-known music teacher, died over a decade ago. She has labored for years to make sure the synagogue can maintain high educational standards, but she is very old-school and she has held the hard line about shortening the Hebrew school week to two days. She was being protected by Rabbi Wolpe, who told her straight out when he retired that her position wouldn't last forever. Har Zion has the gentlemanliness and wherewithal to be more patient and benevolent than most synagogues, giving someone like Sara a year or two to get used to the idea of retiring, rather than, say, a month. But nobody is surprised by the announcement. Somewhat more surprising is the announcement that the leader of all the children's services has also resigned. She is taking a job at David Ackerman's synagogue.

There are changes in store for Rabbi Herber's family as well. His wife is pregnant.

Tut's last week finally arrives, and it is a very emotional moment for Har Zion. Not the same as when Wolpe left but, in some ways, more poignant. Wolpe's departure was the end of an era. The new era, for the past two years, hasn't been just Rabbi Herber, but Herber with Tutnauer. Even though Tut is technically the rabbi-in-residence, the hired help, he has in some ways better served certain rabbinic functions at the synagogue than Herber. He is more learned in Jewish law and custom. He is better at extemporaneous speaking. And he is extremely young for a man his age. He is, of course, a bit of a flake, and will never be a full-time rabbi anywhere again. But that is a built-in problem of the rabbinate. The people you wish would be your rabbi often don't want full-time pulpits. I recently spoke about this with Chaim Potok. When he was a young rabbi at Har Zion's Radnor campus, he was brilliant and fascinating and everyone wanted him to take a pulpit. "But who wants to be on call forty-eight hours a day?" he recalled thinking. "Besides, what I wanted to do most in life was write. And you can't write and be the rabbi of a major pulpit."

When Tutnauer leaves, Herber will be, for the first time, truly on his own. And, after all the talk about a "new model" for the Har Zion rabbinate, the synagogue did what it has always done. It went to the Seminary, identified one of the top rabbis in the class—a smart, confident female rabbi, Jill Borodin, who grew up in Toronto, where the Conservative congregations are all so huge that this congregation doesn't seem so big—and wooed her to Har Zion. She may not be called assistant rabbi as Jacob was: they want to call her "rabbi *shaynee*," rabbi number two. But she is still another student right out of the Seminary just like Jacob and every assistant rabbi before him. They've just gotten their licenses, and they're driving in the Indy 500.

Still, this is a day for a joyful good-bye. Tut talks during sermon time, parsing the priestly blessing at the end of the service. He talks about all that has been accomplished at Har Zion during his two years here. And then he segues into what is weighing upon him, the situation in Israel, where suicide bombers just killed dozens in a Tel Aviv disco. His children and grandchildren could have been in that disco.

He ends by reciting the priestly blessing: "May the Lord bless you and protect you. May the Lord deal kindly and graciously with you. May the Lord bestow his favor upon you and grant you peace."

Amen.

As he returns to the bimah, Jacob is waiting for him with tears in his eyes. And, when the service ends, he calls Tut back to the lectern for more. He wraps Tut in a full bear hug, and then delivers his prepared remarks, which sound a little too well prepared. He seems at first emotionless, too worried about getting the words right. But he finally breaks down when he says that in Tut, he has finally found his "Rav," his rabbi, his mentor. If memory serves, it is actually a stronger statement than the one he made about Wolpe two years earlier. He is now choking out the words but fighting to keep talking. And he is making everyone else weepy, too. Wolpe could make people cry, but not by crying himself. Jacob shares emotion rather than invoking it. At the end of his tribute to Tut, the congregation rises in applause, like the farewell to a brilliant headmaster of a school. For many of them, this is the last good-bye. There will be a dinner dance tomorrow night honoring Tut and his wife, but he knows attendance will be light. Even though he predicted in his last e-mail that the Sixers would eliminate the Milwaukee Bucks in six, the Eastern Conference finals are now heading to a decisive game seven at the Sixers' home arena. Like many people, I tell Tut I'd love to be there for his dance. But it's game seven. He understands.

The Sixers win, the city busts loose in one big all-night street parade, and our miracle team goes into the NBA finals. And then they shock the world by winning the first game in Los Angeles against the Lakers, who are led by hometown hero-turned-nemesis Kobe Bryant, who went to Lower Merion High School, where many Har Zion kids go. The day after

David whups Goliath in an overtime win, I get an e-mail from Tut. He's turning around and flying back from Israel to be here for the home games of the NBA finals. He doesn't say how this happened, but it isn't hard to figure out.

The Fishmans have arranged for Tut to be able to fly back to the States. He can watch the games from the family box. And then he can also be there over the weekend for the bar mitzvah of Eddie Fishman, Mark Fishman's son, Bernie's grandson. Tut can, to some degree, take the place of Rabbi Wolpe, who is unable to return for the Fishman bar mitzvah because of his responsibilities in Palm Beach. Tut's presence will increase the nachas, the joy brought by the next generation.

And the Fishmans need all the nachas they can get. They have had an utterly heartbreaking year. Bernie and Annabelle's forty-something daughter, Jane, recently died after a protracted battle with breast cancer. Janie was truly beloved at Har Zion; when Danny Wolpe was a kid, he always said he wanted to grow up and marry her. Since her death, Bernie has been a wraith. The last time I spoke to Rabbi Wolpe about Bernie, who he considers his closest living friend, he just shook his head, the way rabbis do when they know too much. "He's not doing well," he said. "I'm afraid he won't recover. She was the most marvelous girl, a lovely, sweet, complete human being who made everybody feel as if they were her best friend. She and her mother spoke on the phone every single night. They miss her so."

The bar mitzvah takes place the morning after the 76ers are eliminated. The team far exceeded anyone's expectations, and its few stars played through what normally would have been season-ending injuries. So, even though the season is over, the communal buzz continues, carrying over into this important rite of passage.

Eddie is, after all, the next generation of the family that has been Har Zion's most important benefactor. Jacob looks nervous. Eddie himself looks a little nervous. Tall, with his mother's blond hair, he starts the blessing before the Haftarah and messes up the first line. And with just the right amount of chutzpah, he stops, says, "No, no, I gotta start again," and then laughs, allowing everyone else to laugh with him. Then he does it perfectly. And the Fishmans get all their well-deserved nachas.

After the service, the kiddush is abuzz. Some are *kvelling* about the Herbers' new baby; it was a boy, Adin Avraham (the middle name after Cynthia's father), and they just had the bris. Some are kvetching about Jacob's remarks during the bar mitzvah, which they feel went on a little too long and too thick; although I recall Bernie once telling me he never forgot what the rabbi said at Mark's bar mitzvah—"You'll be known by three names, one is the name you're given at birth, the second is your nickname and the third is the name that people really know you by." Others are still talking Sixers basketball, replaying the last week of games. If they had only left Mutumbo in during game two after Shaq fouled out, everything might have been different.

As I speak to Lew Grafman, Tut grabs me by the shoulder. "Come," he says, "the basketball players must drink." He drags me over to where the other guys from our Shabbat game are gathered around a table: Jeff Blum, who is destined to be the next president of the synagogue; Cantor Vogel; Steve Chopnick, a lawyer who never failed to put some hurt on me after I scored on him; several others. Someone is pouring shots of whiskey.

We raise our glasses to inspired basketball players, pro and extremely amateur, to Tut's safe flight back to Israel, the second in two weeks, to the end of several eras and the beginning of a new one, Har Zion, the next generation. And then we drink.

It is September 11, and the country has never needed great rabbinic voices more. But this time, Rabbi Gerald Wolpe really is closed for business. And in his retirement he is relieved. Sitting in the crowded study of his Philadelphia apartment, he gets to share in the country's pain and anger for once, instead of stepping outside himself to ponder what he will say to memorialize the pain and anger of others. He has done too many of these: the assassinations of Kennedy and Martin Luther King and then another Kennedy, the Six-Day War, the Yom Kippur War, the massacre at the Munich Olympics, so many moments from which the world would never recover, moments that would "change life forever" but were ultimately remarkable for how they showed what stays the same. His job now is to process what is happening by himself for himself, to be there for Elaine and to offer sage advice when David and Danny call, exasperated over what they are going to say to their congregations this coming Shabbat and on Rosh Hashanah, less than a week away.

I ask the rabbi what advice he gave his sons, what scripture he suggested they quote. He says the one thing he keeps thinking about is a line from a book he read long ago.

"Are you familiar with the work of Albert Payson Terhune?" he asks.

No. After spending much of the last three years tracking down the literary and Judaic references he tosses off in casual conversation, I can only imagine who the owner of this lofty name must be, no doubt some obscure but important existentialist philosopher.

"Terhune wrote *Lad, a Dog,* and all the other dog books that became *Lassie,*" he explains. "I loved those books as a child, read them over and over, and read them to my kids as well. And there was a line in one of those Lad stories that I've always remembered. The story is about a little boy who is walking with Lassie—Lad—and he falls over the side of a cliff. And he grabs a tree branch. Lassie, of course, takes off for help. And as the boy is dangling there, he remembers a phrase his grandfather taught him:

"A hero is someone who holds on one minute longer."

He has never forgotten that line. And, he thinks it might prove useful for one of his sons' sermons. If not, they should go with their own instincts. He's just glad he isn't the one up on that pulpit.

As we talk, Elaine comes into the room in a housedress, gesturing broadly. She wants us to come with her, immediately. "Cathedral," she says, "Service. Now . . . Service. Cathedral. *Now.*" We're both momentarily baffled, and then Rabbi Wolpe figures it out. The memorial service from the National Cathedral is on TV. We should come watch with her.

We go into the den and sink into the soft sofa. An opera singer is belting out a bravura performance of "God Bless America," accompanied by a classical guitarist. Then come the clergy. Rev. Nathan Baxter, dean of the National Cathedral, begins his remarks with a biblical quote. As he speaks the first line, Wolpe begins reciting along with him:

> *A cry is heard in Ramah—*
> *Wailing, bitter weeping—*
> *Rachel weeping for her children.*
> *She refuses to be comforted*
> *For her children who are gone.*
> *Thus said the Lord:*
> *Restrain your voice from weeping,*
> *Your eyes from shedding tears;*
> *For there is a reward for your labor*
> *They shall return from the enemy's land.*
> *And there is hope for your future*
> *Your children shall return to their country.*

"That's from Jeremiah," Wolpe says. "Excellent choice. You know, I think that's my favorite book of the Bible."

We sit and critique the clergy. The dean, a female bishop and the Muslim cleric do very well. The rabbi is a bit of a disappointment. Any one of the rabbis Wolpe could have touched us more.

When the rabbi finishes on TV, we rise to go back to our interview. Elaine says we can only speak for a couple of minutes longer. She has an appointment, to which he must accompany her. She is going to finish getting dressed, and then they have to leave.

You are retired now, her eyes seem to be saying. You are finally all mine.

Two days later Rabbi Wolpe calls to tell me that I left my tape recorder at his apartment. But I suspect that isn't really why he called, because he normally would let me know something like that by e-mail. No, what he really wants to tell me is that he and Elaine spontaneously went to Shabbat services at Har Zion, for the first time in months. And Jacob gave a sermon that was "marvelous, really impressive," about the attack on the World Trade Center, repeating the idea that "now we are *all* Israel." Wolpe was very pleasantly surprised. Jacob was mobbed with well-wishers after the service, and Elaine was not really prepared to handle the crowd, so Wolpe sent his compliments via Herber's wife, Cynthia, before they hustled out.

After Shabbat, Jacob called to thank him and they had a terrific conversation, very warm. It made Rabbi Wolpe feel better about the situation for the first time in a long time. He wants me to know that. He also wants me to know that David was just on CNN for an hour, on the *Talk Back Live* program. So he is feeling very good about not being on the pulpit.

"On both coasts," he says, "there are strong young men carrying on."

Yet, several days later, I hear that Jacob has stumbled professionally. Since the "we are all Israel" sermon went over so well, he decided to give it again—on the first day of Rosh Hashanah. This may have gone over well with the thousands of congregants who only come for the High Holidays. But to the people who truly matter to Jacob's future at Har Zion, the synagogue's leaders and regular attendees, it was a gaffe. And the reaction to it reminds me of how synagogues and their rabbis often act like lovers: after ending a long-term relationship, there can be a torrid affair that either blossoms into marriage or is ultimately revealed as the "transitional romance" needed before the next major commitment.

On the morning of Yom Kippur, I go to synagogue, my synagogue, BZBI, alone because my wife, Diane, has the flu. I arrive at 9:30, before the crowd. The regular cantor isn't on stage yet: he and the choir don't come on until 10:30. From 8:30 until 10:30, it's the opening-act cantor, and the room feels more like a minyan, with a wizened guy chanting quickly without flourishes and a small crowd following along. When I survey the room, looking for a seat that will be comfortable for the next six hours, I spy Rabbi Wolpe in the pews, immediately identifiable by his blood-red tallis. He's not sitting in the back row as is his custom. He's in the middle of the sanctuary, one seat from the aisle. When I wish him *gut yontiff,* good holiday, he tells me Elaine is ill. Her impairments are worsening. She sat through Kol Nidre last night, but she couldn't follow, unable to read since the last series of mini-strokes. He sighs, clearly crestfallen by her condition. He will have to say her Yizkor for her.

Since I am also praying stag, he offers me a seat.

As I sit down and ask what page we're on, I realize in all the time I have been with him over these three years, I have never simply sat with him and prayed. We have talked endlessly about the life of the synagogue, but we never have been together in the synagogue. There is something fascinating about observing him in prayer—not in performance, just praying, for himself, for his wife. I notice that when our rabbi, Rabbi Stone, does a responsive reading in English—there is, for example, in the Yom Kippur liturgy, the repetition of the *al hait,* a long listing of "for the sin which we have committed before thee by . . ." —Wolpe does not participate. Instead, he chants all the al haits rapidly in Hebrew. It is as if he had to perform this prayer the way an American congregation wanted it, responsive reading in English, for fifty years and now he can finally pray in the way he is comfortable.

I am delighted to find that he is just like a "regular" congregant. He has brought along some non-prayer books to read during the long Day of Atonement. And he turns out to be quite a chatty shul companion. He recalls something I asked him about the other day and elaborates on a point. We had exchanged e-mails recently about his favorite passages from the Torah. Besides several from Jeremiah, and the one everyone likes from Ecclesiastes, he cited something from the daily prayer book, "God re-creates the world every day." Now, he says, he wants to show me another one he forgot, and he riffles through the pages to find it. It's in

Hinini, one of the central prayers from last week's Rosh Hashanah service. *"V'lo y'hee shum mikhshol bitfelati,"* he reads aloud, and then looks at the English. "But I don't like this translation. What it means is 'let there be no obstacles to my prayer.' "

One of the lay books he brought is by the British science fiction writer Olaf Stapledon, whose classic *Last and First Men* I was forced to read (and almost understand) in college. This particular Stapledon book is a collection of his philosophical writings on religion and mysticism, and Wolpe starts reading it during the chanting of the Haftarah. At one point, he leans over to me and taps his finger on a provocative sentence in the introduction, which he wants me to read. He is amazed that the sentence was written in the 1930s, when it seems to him so relevant today. And his excitement about the sentence touches me, his continued hunger for knowledge, even in the few moments he can steal between prayers.

As he talks, it occurs to me that Rabbi Stone might soon send a harsh look our way. He would send it to me, of course, because it wouldn't do to be shushing Rabbi Wolpe.

As we talk and pray, I am reminded of a story Rabbi Wolpe once told me. Actually, he has told it to me more than once, probably half a dozen times over these past years, and I've also heard him tell it in sermons, too. But he always recounts it well, as if it were the first and last time, which I recognize as one of the reasons my father loved him so as a rabbi. He is a great salesman. A sales rep for God.

One day a man asked his father, "If you don't believe in God, why do you go to shul?"

His father replied, "People go to shul for different reasons. My Orthodox friend, Garfinkle, goes to shul to talk to God. And I go to shul to talk to Garfinkle."

For three years, Rabbi Wolpe has been my Garfinkle. Even when he hasn't been there, he has been there: because he was my father's rabbi, because he was my rabbi, because he was Har Zion's rabbi. And now he is just a friendly gentleman sitting next to me at synagogue, just like the gentleman who took him in when he was eleven and his world changed forever.

The time comes for Yizkor, the memorial prayer. As the rabbi announces it, half the congregation gets up and leaves. But Wolpe does not seem to notice. It's not his congregation walking out. He's not trying to save the world anymore. He is just trying to say his own prayers. This might be the first time in his life that he has said Yizkor by himself, without an audience and without his family.

The service begins with that verse from Ecclesiastes, the one he told me was among his all-time favorites.

> There is a time for everything, for all things under the sun
> a time to be born and a time to die,
> a time to laugh and a time to cry,
> a time to dance and a time to mourn,
> a time to seek and a time to lose,
> a time to forget and a time to remember.
> This day in sacred convocation we remember those who gave us life . . .

We continue with a personal meditation, each of us asking God to "give me the gift of remembering," so my memories can be "tender and true, undiminished by time, not falsified by sentimentality." We ask also for the gift of tears, the gift of prayer and, finally, the gift of hope, that we may "always believe in the beauty of life, the power of goodness, the right to joy."

And then Rabbi Wolpe and I pray, alone and together and in the loudest of silences, for the souls of our fathers.

Amen.

AFTERWORD

It is time for me to stop praying at Har Zion. Not because I feel in any way uncomfortable there, but maybe because I feel too comfortable. And being comfortable where you work can be risky. Just as a rabbi gets to enjoy the familiarity and warmth of a community only as long as the employment contract stipulates, my job at Har Zion is coming to an end. After nearly four years, I know more people there than I do at my own synagogue in town, and it is time to change that. So I make a Jewish New Year's resolution to start doing my praying closer to home, in the congregation where I belong.

But I remain a member of the Har Zion diaspora, and Judaism is still a small town. So I hear stuff.

In mid-October, as the Jewish holidays end—and Americans are emerging from their mental air-raid shelters after 9/11, returning to what passes for normal life—I get an ominous e-mail from Rabbi Wolpe.

"I do not know what the last chapter will be in your book," he writes, "but there is activity going on at HZ that may require an epilogue."

I e-mail back asking if he can give me a hint.

"There is unrest in the ranks. There is unrest in the administration. There is unrest in the working corps."

Some unrest, of course, is to be expected. Even if a well-seasoned rabbi had taken over, this would be a rough transition. And I suspect that Rabbi Wolpe, who still doesn't feel comfortable returning to Har Zion very often because his relationship with Rabbi Herber has never moved much beyond a wary optimism, is likely to be hearing from the congregants who miss their old rabbi the most. So I ask whether he is sure the situation is really in jeopardy.

"It is more serious than I realized," he writes back. "It is a story that is unfolding and I am very very uncomfortable and sad about it. . . . I gave thirty years of my life to Har Zion; I do not want anything detrimental to happen to it."

Over the next months, I have little contact with the ongoing life of Har Zion. Since my book is already done and edited and fact-checked, I am catching up with all the other work I've been putting off for the year I spent writing.

I am so busy that, for the first time, my father's yartzeit seems almost routine, just as going to minyan once or twice a week, or going to say the Yiskor prayer four times a year, has become. I say Kaddish at the evening service, I light the twenty-four-hour yartzeit candle, I say Kaddish at the morning service, I go to work, and then at 5:30 return to say my third Kaddish at the afternoon service. The yartzeit does not feel shallow, just more efficient than before. Perhaps I am slowly learning how to mark the anniversary of my father's death without completely reliving it.

Synagogue news travels more slowly in winter; when key links in the gossip food chain migrate to Florida, word doesn't get out quite as efficiently. So weeks pass before I hear the news: Har Zion has quietly postponed the installation ceremony of Rabbi Herber, which had been tentatively scheduled for the spring.

When I make inquiries about the postponement, even insiders seem vague on what is happening and what it means. They insist this is not what it might appear to be—the beginning of the end for Rabbi Herber at Har Zion—but rather part of a positive action in support of his rabbinate to ensure that he and the congregation have a long and productive life together. If they know more, they are reluctant to share it. So I finally drive out to Har Zion one Saturday morning for Shabbat services to see what is going on.

I haven't been there in over seven months. The last time I was in the sanctuary was for Sammy Blum's bat mitzvah, on the Shabbat before September 11. I walk in, take my old seat and observe the congregation. Among the congregants and guests here for today's bar mitzvah, everything seems normal. But on the bimah, I discern a certain brusqueness, an excessive formality between the rabbi and the cantor. This is not normal. They're interacting like a married couple staying together for the children.

After services, as I make my way to the Oneg Shabbat, I am approached by a thirty-something man who turns out to be the grownup version of the little kid who lived next door to my Nana and Pop-pop, one of the boys we used to run around with outside after Friday night dinner. I haven't seen him since I stopped running around outside after dinner, and we are friendly and nostalgic. Then he begins telling me how happy he is to have recently joined Har Zion, in large part because he likes Jacob and his casual and comfortable style. As I nod and listen, I wonder how he could have missed the bimah family dysfunction during the service. And then I remind myself that most people don't pay attention to such things—they're in synagogue to share a familiar ritual, be part of a happy event, hear the rabbi say nice things about the bar mitzvah boy, maybe even pray.

At the Oneg Shabbat, I make the rounds, greeting my sources in the synagogue who are, in general, quite cordial toward me. When I ask for updates, however, I get an assortment of demurrals. The cantor makes it clear with a roll of his eyes that things haven't been easy, but avoids going into detail. Lew Grafman is friendly, but when asked specific questions notes instead how quickly a past president can fall out of the loop.

Then I see Jeff Blum, who is full of nervous energy, like a kid who just poked a guy, ran away, and now sees him giving chase. He assures me that Jacob's installation has been postponed, not canceled, and that the action was taken in the hope of preserving and sustaining the rabbi's career at Har Zion, not undermining it. Too many members of the clergy and senior staff have been complaining about aspects of Jacob's managerial style, he says. If the leadership had installed the young rabbi before there was major improvement in these internal relationships, the congregation would run the risk of insulting, and perhaps even losing, some of the most important people who are providing continuity at Har Zion during the rabbi change: the cantor, the executive director, the ritual director, among others. The decision to postpone, made by president Alan Greenbaum with strong support from Jeff and other synagogue vice presidents, was clearly a risk. But they have brought in a management consultant—an executive psychologist Jacob requested some time ago—and remain hopeful that these actions will have the desired effect.

Jeff Blum still believes in his friend Jacob Herber's rabbinate at Har Zion. At the moment, however, he has to concede that relations with the new rabbi are pretty icy. Jacob clearly does not appreciate getting this professional time-out.

I wander around, refilling my coffee, nibbling at what's left of the food, killing time until the line of people waiting to see the rabbi has shortened. I am hoping to get a moment of Jacob's time, because he has not responded to any of my calls or e-mails over the past several weeks. They weren't urgent, and this has happened before when he was especially busy, so I haven't been too concerned. But I'm still hoping to speak with him again. And, on a more personal level, I am worried for him because I sympathize with his situation.

I have watched this community take a process they hoped would be a bold reconsideration of their direction for the future—a chance to reclaim the passions of the synagogue's founders and to choose a new leader based on broadly shared beliefs and lofty goals for the new century—and allow it to devolve into a debate about one man. This happens all the time in houses of worship, just as it does on sports teams, which Jacob knows well from following hockey. I'm not sure whether a rabbi is more like a coach or a star player. But I do know firsthand that when all the problems of a large group become focused on the performance of a single person, it is a reductionist nightmare to be that person. Many rabbis have been there before Jacob, but that doesn't make it any easier.

I wait in line, and finally it is my turn. I make eye contact with Jacob, and extend my hand to wish him a good Shabbat. He looks down at my hand, but does not take it. At first I think he is joking, so I keep it extended, waiting for him to grasp it. And then I realize he really is refusing to shake my hand.

He looks me in the eye. "If this is about the book," he says, coldly, "talk to my lawyer."

I try to explain to him that the book is finished and I have no need to talk to his lawyer. I primarily wanted to address a couple of questions he had asked my researcher about facts he had confirmed for the book. But clearly, this postmortem isn't going to happen. He stares at me, his eyes wide open but completely closed.

"Jacob," I stammer, "if you don't want to talk to me for the book anymore, that's fine; you've been more than generous with your time. But is this really the way you want to leave it—that you won't even shake my hand on Shabbat?"

"Talk to my lawyer," he says again. And with these words he disconnects so harshly that I can feel myself shaking as I walk away.

I leave the auditorium, amble through the wide corridor where parents chat while their cookie-infused kids whiz by or wrestle on the floor, toss my yarmulkah in the bin, grab my coat, and leave the synagogue building for what will probably be the last time. I should have stuck to my Jewish New Year's resolution. It is time for me to stop praying at Har Zion. Perhaps it is time for me to start praying *for* Har Zion.

Over the next few months, my only communication with the synagogue is a group e-mail I send to the cast of *The New Rabbi* for Passover, wishing them a wonderful holiday and moist macaroons.

In mid-May, however, I suddenly start getting cryptic confidential e-mails from various people that something is happening at Har Zion with Rabbi Herber. Apparently his working relationships with Cantor Vogel, Rabbi Borodin, Executive Director Howard Griffel, Ritual Director Joshua Perlmuter and other key staff have become so fractured that synagogue leaders doubt they will heal properly. Even the expensive executive psychologist, hired with a donation from a Herber supporter on the board, says Har Zion has the most dysfunctional senior staff he has ever seen. While the entire professional staff has contributed to the problem, and the lay leadership hasn't done much to stop it, an overwhelming majority of synagogue officers and consulting past presidents now believe that Jacob's inexperience is to blame.

Although the rabbi is usually calm and warm in emotional situations with congregants, with his colleagues and staff he sometimes responds to pressure by being temperamental, uncommunicative, even imperious. On several occasions, Jill Borodin has left his office in tears, after Jacob abruptly ended a discussion with a pronouncement that he is the rabbi, the mara d'atra, and has final say. As a manager, Rabbi Herber can be so inconsistent that the cantor has admitted to him, "Half the time I want to wring your neck, and the other half I want to hug you." As a result, little problems have been looming large.

The final incident that leads synagogue officers to dramatically reconsider their support for the rabbi begins as nothing more than a disagreement over a family's request concerning who would officiate at their small evening bar mitzvah in early May. Rabbi Borodin has been working closely with the young man, and his family wants her to officiate. Rabbi Herber is refusing their request, saying he does not approve of "clergy shopping." The argument is still going on early in the week the bar mitzvah is to take place. Synagogue president Alan Greenbaum and Jeff Blum urge Jacob to accept a compromise in which Jill officiates but he still participates. On Tuesday, he finally relents. The next morning, however, Blum and Greenbaum receive an e-mail from Jacob, a missive they view as a disturbing manifesto, insisting that as mara d'atra he wants a new policy statement regarding the roles of the rabbis. The tone of the e-mail, more than its content, is troubling. To Greenbaum, the problem isn't that Jacob is demanding some new authority they don't want to give him. The problem is, he already *has* the authority and he still doesn't seem to understand that or feel secure with it. It is as if everyone knows who the rabbi is—*except the rabbi.*

The day after the e-mail, the cantor, who has negotiated a precautionary out-clause in every year of his new employment agreement, tells Jeff Blum he is thinking about leaving. And Blum is forced to confront his mounting fear that Jacob Herber is not the right rabbi for Har Zion, and that this issue should be addressed now, before he becomes president. Greenbaum, it turns out, has been thinking the same thing.

An informal meeting is called at Greenbaum's home for current synagogue officers and past presidents. The vast majority of the twenty-three people assembled there agree that it is time to tell Rabbi Herber that his contract is very unlikely to be renewed next year, and perhaps to offer to buy him out now. Everyone agrees that the substance of their discussion, including the fact that they are having the meeting at all, should remain confidential until Greenbaum and Blum can speak to Herber privately. But, of course, the meeting remains secret only until it is adjourned.

"They all leave sworn to secrecy," laments one insider, "and this is kept for as long as it takes them to get their cell phones out of their pockets."

Nothing splits a community faster than rumors of a major decision made at a clandestine meeting. So the behind-the-bimah approach backfires miserably. Various factions within the board of directors—which usually just rubber-stamps the decisions of the synagogue's president and officers—are now gearing up for a legal battle, claiming that if Herber is forced out without a board vote, it is a by-law violation. One of the most vocal supporters of this position is board member Len Lundy, the attorney Jacob told me to speak to, who turns out not to be his personal lawyer after all, but a close synagogue friend and consigliere: his Ralph Snyder. Lundy, who is also godfather to Jacob's one-year-old son, brings his background in confrontational real-estate and business-transaction law to the conflict.

As a result, many of the difficulties that the synagogue's leaders and clergy have been trying to keep quiet—for Jacob's sake as well as their own—are now spreading like a computer virus through the community. As everyone interprets the tidbits of fact and rumor they've heard, filling in the blanks as they go along, the synagogue appears to be descending into a kind of midrashic chaos.

Some of Jacob's supporters are, like Lundy, younger members of the congregation, more familiar with its schools and the bar mitzvah training of their kids than the harsher realities of grown-up synagogue politics. And maybe some of his older supporters have forgotten how truly ugly congregational disputes can get, having been lulled by decades of suburban peace under Wolpe's relatively stable reign. They don't seem to understand the accepted wisdom that when there is a power struggle in a house of worship, nobody wins.

On the other hand, the "experienced leaders" Jacob's supporters are challenging are the very ones who told the RA it was wrong about the risks of giving a rabbi three years out of seminary one of the largest, most challenging pulpits in the world. So who is more guilty of ignoring accepted wisdom?

It occurs to me that everyone involved could probably benefit from the sage and calming words of a trusted rabbi. But Rabbi Wolpe is sitting at home trying not to interfere. And Rabbi Herber is keeping his mouth shut—on advice of his newly hired counsel.

Every few days, I get an e-mail from Wolpe, each one concluding with a similar sentiment. "I weep for the institution to which I gave thirty years of my life, " says one. "It is like watching a sick child," says another. And then finally, "I suffer with the tragedy of Har Zion. I am in pain beyond description."

In early June, another synagogue insider sends me an e-mail with the subject line: "Synagogue Implodes."

"Morale has sunk to an all-time low," it says. "The pro-Herber forces are apparently doing a little investigative work of their own and are planning an assault on Jeff Blum. . . . If this weren't so ugly it would be ridiculous. I never thought that I would live to see the day when I'd be living as a character in a soap opera. . . . God Save the Queen and Har Zion Temple!"

In response to a petition, a special board of directors meeting is called to discuss the situation. While board meetings are always open to the public, they usually attract few spectators: since the board includes all twenty current officers of the executive board, many past officers and all the past presidents, most of those normally interested in the day-to-day life of the synagogue are already among the governing body's eighty-seven members. This board meeting, however, is held in the main auditorium, with a court reporter brought in to make a record of the proceedings and some extra security guards in case things get out of hand. More than six hundred people attend.

The meeting is loud and angry and painful. There are attacks on Jeff Blum, who has been president for only a week. And there are attacks on Alan Greenbaum, who actually made most of the decisions that led to the meeting. Neither of them wants to fight with the congregation, or get baited into a public discussion about why they want to buy out Jacob's contract. So they basically sit there and take it.

After the meeting, Jeff Blum announces the appointment of a special blue-ribbon board advisory committee—including none of the main combatants on either side—to undertake an independent fact-finding mission about what actually led to the crisis at the synagogue, and to make a recommendation to the board of directors about Rabbi Herber's future at Har Zion. Its work will be strictly confidential, and until the committee makes its recommendation to the board, all issues concerning Rabbi Herber and the future of Har Zion are officially tabled.

In the meantime, synagogue life is expected to proceed as usual. And for a little while, it actually does. Then, in mid-August, *The New Rabbi* is published. First an excerpt appears in *Philadelphia* magazine, under the title "Synagogue Confidential," and then the book starts showing up in stores and being reviewed. There is passionate debate about it among Har Zion members (and later among rabbis nationally), but the most obvious immediate response is that a few young families become afraid that the media attention could make the synagogue more of a security risk—a potential target—and withdraw their children from the Noreen Cook Center for Early Childhood Education. Also, those people who became incensed at Jeff Blum three months ago when he first changed his mind about Jacob's rabbinate are even further inflamed by some of his quotes in the book. His openness becomes part of the critique of his personal style as president, which is certainly bolder and more in-your-face than that of his two predecessors.

But nobody from Har Zion comments publicly about the book, and when I am interviewed, I steer clear of discussing the current situation at the synagogue. The only semi-public comment comes from Tut, who reaches out to the Har Zion community by way of e-mail.

His High Holiday message is titled "War Zones," and begins by describing two places near his family's Jerusalem home, the French Hill junction and the Mount Scopus campus of the Hebrew University, which have been the sites of recent deadly terrorist attacks. "Both are so close that we regularly hear the ominous sound of ambulance sirens rushing victims to the Hadassah Hospital on Mount Scopus," he writes.

So, no matter how complex and no matter how bitter synagogue wars get, they are relatively trivial compared to what we face on a daily basis.

I do not mean that the synagogue wars should be taken lightly by us. People have strong feelings about their synagogues. They expect their synagogues to be above petty power plays. They are profoundly disappointed to discover that "clergy" cannot resolve interpersonal relationships and professional problems with love and grace.

Clergy, on the other hand, often find themselves victims of unrealistic expectations by congregants and poor management by synagogue leaders. They are thrust into situations beyond their ability to handle. The result is often anger and frustration that impacts on the entire rabbinic family. Because rabbinic work is of a public nature, rabbis often find their spouses and children drawn into conflicts they have not created. Rabbinic war zones, though usually not life-threatening, are often areas of emotional hell for congregants, rabbis, synagogue staff, and their families.

. . . I pray that the coming year will bring peace and reconciliation not only to French Hill junction, but to all areas of conflict. I pray for peace and understanding for all the synagogues of the world, for their members and their leaders and for all the souls of individual human beings whose hearts long for love and peace.

To which I e-mail back, "Amen."

✿   ✿   ✿

It is unclear what Rabbi Herber thinks of all this. Nobody is sure whether he rallied his supporters to fight for him, or whether people just decided to fight on his behalf, and either he couldn't stop them or he didn't *want* to stop them, hoping they would win and save his job. And, of course, he has to know that some of the people aren't fighting *for* him at all—they're just fighting as people do in any community when they perceive some tyranny of the "in-crowd."

I am told that much of the time Jacob keeps his own counsel and won't discuss the situation, not even with close friends. He says he doesn't want people to make a big issue out of his personal employment matter. Privately, he expresses concern that the congregation could become fractured beyond repair if he stays, but if he leaves, those members who rely on him the most will feel abandoned. If he can, he would really like to keep the pulpit.

Most of those I hear from are no longer in contact with Jacob, except superficially or professionally. He has, it appears, stopped shaking hands with many of the people who were so much a part of synagogue life when I was covering Har Zion. This includes Jeff Blum, who finally approaches Herber on the pulpit during Kol Nidre services and does what Jews do on Yom Kippur: he says how sorry he is for what has happened to Jacob and his family and asks for the rabbi's forgiveness. The gesture is met with a blank stare, all that remains of a friendship cultivated over six emotional years.

Otherwise, the high holidays pass without incident. Much to the surprise of many insiders, Jacob conducts services and gives fine sermons almost as if nothing has happened.

My wife and I go to Harrisburg for Rosh Hashanah, where my old congregation has moved its services back to the synagogue building after decades of renting a larger hall. They've also added a new "alternative" service. This is a dramatic change, with much to recommend it, and it might help attract members lost to the Reform temple down the street. But I hear grumblings among childhood friends of mine, who are now grown-up machers, about what will happen when the rabbi's contract comes up for renewal later in the fall.

For Yom Kippur, we are back in Philadelphia at our synagogue, BZBI, where the new cantor pushes the musical envelope by replacing the traditional choir with soaring duets performed with an amazing female singer—who turns out to be a member of the congregation—and Rabbi Stone is as fascinating and thoughtful as ever.

I look around on Kol Nidre evening, and don't see Rabbi Wolpe anywhere. The next day, I scan the place periodically to see if he has arrived. But he never makes it. Concerned, I call him after the fast. He says it was the first time he ever missed high holiday services in his life, but he was too sick to attend: his stomach was really bothering him. I am reminded that he is now nearly seventy-five, and he has been mentioning his health quite a bit in the past six months. I recall one cryptic comment he made in an e-mail, "I am now totally involved in Elaine's needs and my own campaign to remain healthy for both our sakes. I am reevaluating my schedule and what I hope to do in whatever productive days/years may still be ahead. It is an interesting and challenging process." Not long after the holidays, I see him in synagogue and he tells me that he has decided to stop taking speaking engagements that require him to travel much farther than New York or Washington.

In the Har Zion community, everyone awaits the report of the blue-ribbon board advisory committee, which will decide the fate of Rabbi Herber just as the rabbi search committee did not so long ago. Since beginning its work in early August, the committee has been calling in past and present members of the clergy and senior staff, as well as current and former lay leaders of the synagogue. It may be the stealthiest committee in the history of Har Zion Temple, or any temple. Not a word about its proceedings seems to leak out to anybody.

Diane and I leave town for a Northwest trip that is part work—I'm now speaking at a lot of synagogues—and part fifteenth anniversary getaway. When we return ten days later, I hear from my rabbi at morning minyan that word is circulating in Jewish Philadelphia: the big meeting at which Jacob's fate will be announced is taking place tonight. Rabbi Wolpe e-mails to confirm that the special committee will deliver its report this evening.

As the meeting is called to order in the Fishman-Tobin auditorium, Jeff Blum walks to the lectern. He looks gaunt. Instead of his usual banter, he reads from a prepared statement.

"During these volatile times," he says, "Har Zion needs a leader who is strong, practical and will not fall prey to the presence of a small, vocal minority of vindictive malcontents who permeate our meetings and our e-mails, and seek to ruin reputations."

He challenges the audience: "Let me ask you something . . . is there anyone gathered here this evening who has made an error in judgment . . . paid a price for that mistake . . . and then strived to rededicate his life to good works? I know I have."

While many in the auditorium look confused, synagogue insiders know that Blum is referring to a savage effort to force him to resign—by bringing up and throwing in his face a closed legal matter from sixteen years ago, when he was first out of graduate school. It is, ironically, a matter he had been careful to disclose and have vetted by Har Zion leaders before he was first put on the board of directors back in the eighties, precisely to prevent anything like this from ever happening to him or the synagogue. But apparently some of Herber's supporters had dug up the paperwork from that legal matter in June. They let newly elected president Blum know they were willing to use the material against him if he didn't reverse his position on buying out the young rabbi's contract. This hadn't happened, and the issue of the legal matter didn't come up again for months. But then, just after Simhat Torah ended in late September, two board members—a married couple who were less pro-Herber than anti-Blum—circulated its details in two vicious letters that were spread via mail and e-mail. Many synagogue leaders, appalled by the couple's actions, are quietly moving to force them to step down from their leadership positions. But it's too late for Jeff.

When he says "I am resigning as your president," many gasp. A few of his detractors actually clap before being stared down by the vast majority of congregants who can see this is a man who has just publicly shared the most difficult decision of his Jewish life.

As he finishes, Jeff steps away from the lectern and hugs his wife, Cindy, who has already started crying. He takes her hand, and then the two of them walk down the aisle, as stunned congregants rise to their feet in appreciative applause. They are leaving the synagogue they have been part of since they were kids. Nobody knows if they're ever coming back.

As the buzz in the sanctuary from Blum's dramatic exit dies down, the board advisory committee presents its report. It is marked "confidential" but is read aloud to the assembled congregants, each member of the committee reciting a couple of its eighteen pages. The report is extraordinary in its openness, its evenhandedness and its ability to address intense interpersonal issues without throwing anyone in particular under the bus. It is very Har Zion in the best possible sense, a communal self-evaluation that could have much to offer any organization facing internal problems. The report frankly discusses mistakes and miscues large and small, even noting, for example, how the failure to consult the cantor, executive director and other senior staff before deciding to elevate Rabbi Herber may have made the decision even riskier. The committee members wrestle with issues of mentor management, and how Herber and the synagogue's leaders could have made better use of the RA, and Rabbis Tutnauer and Wolpe. They explore the many difficulties of replacing Wolpe—exacerbated by the senior rabbi's reservations about elevating Herber—and how synagogue leaders didn't fully anticipate or prepare for the challenges they faced. The committee even makes an attempt to plumb the psychodynamics of Rabbi Herber. While acknowledging the pressures of his "frantic personal and professional pace," the report also states that "many of the tensions in the rabbi's relationships . . . can be traced to . . . his perception that he was not given enough respect." But the committee then observes that the word "respect" hardly ever came up in their interviews with the clergy and senior staff. The term they usually heard was "support." They came to understand that, to Herber, respect and support were the same thing. But they also learned that the rabbi and the leadership disagreed on what "support" meant. Herber thought it meant "sending a clear message" that they were unflinchingly committed to him for the long term. Leaders thought it meant "identifying specific issues he needed to address."

Most of the people assembled in the main sanctuary this evening, however, are waiting to hear only one thing amid the report's various findings, recommendations and interpretations. Can the fight for Rabbi Herber's job still be won, or will this report signal the true beginning of the end?

What they finally learn is that the battle over the new rabbi has been over for quite some time. The generals just never told the soldiers to stop fighting. In September, Rabbi Herber privately informed the committee that he no longer felt comfortable at Har Zion; he wanted to leave, and he had asked his lawyer to negotiate a separation package.

But before recommending that the board agree to the negotiated settlement, the committee wants a few things to be said out loud in this synagogue where so much has been whispered.

The committee member reads: "Rabbi Herber clearly has the potential to be a special rabbi. . . . But the lack of experience that rendered him ineligible to accept the position in the first place proved to be an overwhelming burden.

Rabbi Herber made mistakes during his tenure . . . but his biggest mistake was agreeing to accept a position he simply was not ready for. The leadership also made mistakes with respect to Rabbi Herber, starting with the decision to elevate him." And then the committee quotes from an article by the Rabbinical Assembly about leadership transition: "Nothing undermines a change in leadership more than the failure to be aware of and think through transition issues. Often, both rabbis and congregations under-invest time and planning in the transition process. However, transition time used wisely can become an *Eitz Ratzon*, a time of learning, progress and productive growth."

Rabbi Herber appears at synagogue one more time for Shabbat, and then withdraws from the public life of the congregation, although he and his family continue living in the rabbi's house across the street. Two weeks later, his farewell letter is mailed out. It calls for *shalom bayit,* "peace and harmony," and explains that he is discussing a mutual termination of his rabbinic contract "to heal the fissures within our congregation and to provide my family with *sipuk nefesh,* with peace of mind."

Herber shares a story of a colleague who found a boy waiting for him in the synagogue parking lot one day, a boy who had just learned that his father had cancer. The rabbi wasn't sure how to respond. "Was the boy looking for some explanation," he wondered, "some justification, some philosophical insight, some spiritual epigram that would lessen the hurt?" No, the boy said, "all I want is a hug from my rabbi." The lesson is that "we influence by *who* we are, not by what we say. A rabbi has only one sermon: his or her life. During my tenure, I have tried to extend my hug to you." He ends with a popular poem by an anonymous author—the one that begins "count your garden by the flowers, never by the leaves that fall"—and then, simply, "thank you, shalom, goodbye."

Steps are taken to try to begin the healing of Har Zion as quickly as possible. Some are public. A new synagogue president is selected from among the remaining vice presidents. Instead of lawyer Steve Chopnick, Jeff's choice, the board picks someone who was close to Jacob, Harry Sauer, an affable entrepreneur with a wolfish beard and extra time on his hands since semiretiring young after selling his executive recruiting firm.

Other steps at healing are quieter. The couple whose letters triggered Jeff Blum's resignation are pushed into resigning their leadership positions, and instead decide to quit the synagogue. The board reaches out for help to the RA, as well as to the Alban Institute, a highly regarded non-profit in Bethesda that specializes in consulting services for at-risk houses of worship.

A committee is formed to update and clarify the bylaws. A veteran clergyman, Rabbi Matthew Simon, is hired as interim senior rabbi. And a new search committee is appointed. Since Jacob Herber was never actually installed as senior rabbi, the committee will be finishing the work begun by Lou Fryman's committee in 1997. They will be choosing the successor to Rabbi Wolpe.

And they will be doing so with more input from their retired rabbi than the leadership has had for some time, because Wolpe suddenly feels welcome again in his old synagogue. Now that the situation that kept him away has been resolved, people feel freer to seek his counsel and he is more comfortable giving it. He meets privately with the new president, pledging support and discretion. Sauer asks if Wolpe would come and speak at his installation, a request that carries special significance. The rabbi has not spoken from the pulpit at Har Zion since his retirement. For a while, he felt unwanted. Most recently, he demurred when Jacob invited him because he didn't want to fuel the absurd rumor that the young rabbi was being pushed out so Wolpe could have his old job back.

Wolpe agrees to run the service on the Shabbat after Thanksgiving. He asks Jeff Blum to attend, along with the other past presidents. Jeff is reluctant. He hasn't set foot in the main sanctuary since the night he resigned. Still, Wolpe is his rabbi. And he knows that the couple who had come to make his life at Har Zion so unbearable will no longer haunt Shabbat services for him. So he and Cindy decide to go.

Back at his old lectern on Saturday morning, Wolpe is euphoric. It's a feeling he hadn't quite expected, and wasn't sure he would ever have again at Har Zion. During his sermon he speaks about leadership, and how very often a leader has to sacrifice himself for the greater good: to walk away so that what he has built can continue to provide shelter. He could be talking about himself or Jeff Blum. And while Wolpe would never interpret it that way, some would say that he is also talking about Jacob Herber.

The new president is summoned to be installed. He speaks only briefly, thanking his family and offering prayers for the congregation to heal. Wolpe thanks him for his words, and, returning the Torah to the Ark, makes a point of welcoming all the past presidents in attendance. "I particularly want to welcome Jeff Blum," he says, "who knows the affection I have for him." Jeff and Cindy burst into tears. And at least for that Shabbat, Har Zion feels like their synagogue again.

As I complete my reporting and pack up to leave the world of Har Zion for good, it is that time of year again. This is not a milestone yartzeit—it has been six years since my father's death. But it feels like one.

I have become Jewish in a more rewarding way than I ever could have imagined, and the deeper my spiritual and intellectual search goes, the more I realize I've just begun. I am also part of my own local Jewish community, which is there when I need it, and I do my best to return the favor. And I now understand how and why to pray. I still can't translate Hebrew, and there are many prayers and tunes I don't know. But I am invariably moved and intrigued when I come to worship, because I have learned various ways to find meaning in a main sanctuary or chapel.

Yet while many Jewish observances come naturally now, others still feel like a diet I'll never be able to stick to. I have yet to commit to coming to services every Shabbat or holiday. But even though my fellow minyanaires sometimes greet me with "welcome back" instead of "hello," I believe they understand that observance is not a community competition but a deeply private journey best taken in public.

On the evening of my father's yartzeit, I go to my synagogue and am pleasantly surprised to find more than enough people to pray. But when I walk into the chapel the next morning, I am disappointed to see that we are nowhere near minyan. If we don't get four more people, I won't be able to say Kaddish for my father for the first time in six years. I take a seat next to the chapel's glass door and stare at the synagogue's entranceway attempting to conjure more congregants.

Whenever getting a minyan appears precarious, I find myself wondering how this reflects on the spiritual health of the congregation. I look at my rabbi's face as he silently scans the room to see if he somehow counted to six incorrectly—and I wonder if he views daily attendance figures as a referendum on the state of his rabbinate, or the future of American Judaism. I know he is especially concerned about rabbi/congregation relations. While our synagogue is stable, many are still searching for their futures. Most of the congregations I've been following are hiring *new* new rabbis. Jacob Herber is about to accept a pulpit in Milwaukee—close enough to Chicago for him to be able to see the Rangers occasionally. And Har Zion is interested in Rabbi Jay Stein, the thirty-seven-year-old leader of a small congregation in central New Jersey. Stein has experience as an assistant at a large suburban Chicago synagogue and as a rabbi's kid in Bridgeport, Connecticut.

The only good thing about not having a minyan is that when much of the service can't be recited aloud there is more time for personal reflection. Nestled between the first two Kaddishes we can't say is David's "Song of Dedication," which I pay attention to for the first time. It is a prayer that tiptoes along the line between life and death: "I called to You, O Lord; You healed me; You brought up my soul from the grave . . . What profit is there if I am silenced? What benefit if I go to my grave? Can the dust give thanks? . . . You turned my mourning into dancing. You changed my sackcloth for robes of joy."

The abridged service continues, but the more prayers we have to cut out, the less chance we have to wait for enough people. As we head into the home stretch—the Ashrei on page 91, "Happy are they who dwell in Your house"—the synagogue entrance opens and a man walks in. The door is about to shut behind him, when someone catches it and another man walks in. We're still two short, but as the prayer ends, the door opens again. It's a couple. We have ten.

I nod to the rabbi so he can stall until they get to the chapel. And when the mourner's Kaddish arrives, I rise.

While reciting the prayer, I'm still thinking about King David's bereavement being transformed into revelry. And I remember something my father said not long before his death. He was lying in bed one morning having what I can only describe as an attack of poetry. He riffed about getting "an extinguisher to put out the fire of all nations," and free-associated about the port in his chest and the tubes that were feeding him.

"How do you get out of this?" he asked, tugging on the tubes. "How do you get out of these bells and whistles?"

I asked him why he wanted to get out of it.

He said he needed to be freed so he could go "harvesting rainbows."

And as I pray I wonder: in all the wisdom of the rabbis, will I ever find words more comforting?

ACKNOWLEDGMENTS

This book began in the quiet moments between prayers at minyan—mornings and evenings at Temple Beth Zion Beth Israel, and the unconventional lunchtime minyan in the crowded library of attorney Allen Rothenberg's firm, both in Center City, Philadelphia. So I must first thank my fellow minyanaires past and present, especially Rabbi Michael Monson, Rabbi Ira Stone, Rabbi Abraham Powers, Cantor Marc Kushner and Cantor George Mordechai.

But the book never could have happened, of course, without the cooperation of Rabbi Gerald Wolpe, who has given me an enormous amount of time, as well as intellectual and emotional energy, over the nearly four years we've been talking.

Rabbi Wolpe opened the doors for me at Har Zion, where I must thank Rabbi Jacob Herber, Cantor Eliot Vogel, Rabbi Moshe Tutnauer, Joshua Perlmuter, Howard Griffel, Barbara Schwartz, Sara Cohen and all the lay leaders and congregants who were interviewed on tape or over the buffet tables, especially Jeff and Cindy Blum, Lewis Grafman, Louis Fryman, Ralph Snyder, Bernie Fishman and Alan Greenbaum. Rabbi Wolpe's family was also very generous with their time and patience. Thanks to Elaine Wolpe, Rabbi David Wolpe, Dr. Paul Root Wolpe, Valerie Root Wolpe and Rabbi Daniel Wolpe. At the Rabbinical Assembly, thanks to Rabbi Joel Meyers and

Rabbi Elliot Schoenberg. Thanks to the rabbis who were involved in the search and agreed to tell me their side of the story, especially Rabbi Lee Buckman and Rabbi Danny Nevins. A special thanks to Chaim Potok, who graciously made time to see me even though he wasn't feeling well.

While this book is based in Philadelphia, New York, Los Angeles and Palm Beach, my Jewish sensibilities were formed in the rich, supportive Jewish community in Harrisburg, Pennsylvania, and in Jewish summer camp. My thanks to the clergy and staff at Beth El Temple and the Jewish Community Center of Greater Harrisburg, where I became a man; at Pinemere Camp, where I became myself; and at the Jewish Home of Greater Harrisburg, where most of the people I've loved and lost spent their last days. And thanks to the teachers who mattered most in my Jewish education: Ernest Weiss (and his endless supply of cherry cough drops), Rabbi Jeffrey Wohlberg and Rabbi Arthur Green.

The research for this book was begun by Ben Brody, who was my Guy Friday, assistant and protector during most of the years I worked on it; he also offered valuable input on the finished manuscript. I also received important encouragement and feedback from Carolyn Starman Hessel of the Jewish Book Council, Nina Zucker and a rabbinic source known only as "Deep Voice." Erin Alden and, later, April White did a nice job with the fact-checking. And interns Sharon Male, Michael Sonsino and Jo Piazza helped greatly with the research.

Many thanks to the colleagues who made my eighteen-month foray into magazine editing a joyful challenge, and my return to full-time writing a pleasure: Sabrina Rubin Erdely, Tim Baldwin, Tim Haas, Jim Graham and Lawrence Goodman. And thanks to those who were there for me during the transition, especially my brother, Dan, and my best friend and consigliere, Joel Perilstein.

While almost all the reporting in the book is original, for the section about Palm Beach and Temple Emanu-El, I did rely on the excellent reporting in *The Palm Beach Post,* especially the work of then-religion writer Doug Belkin. I also relied on clips from the *Philadelphia Bulletin* archive at Temple University Library for the retelling of Har Zion's move from Wynnefield.

This is my second book with my brilliant and relentless editor, Ann Harris, the high priestess of insight and Post-its, and the entire Bantam family—publisher Irwyn Applebaum, publicity queen Barb Burg, sharp-shooting publicist Chris Artis and in-house counsel Matthew Martin. It is a rare treat in publishing to work with the same people at a house for five years (or five months, for that matter) and they have been especially supportive with this project.

This is my third book with agent extraordinaire Loretta Fidel. Every writer should be so lucky to have such a nurturing, patient and exuberant agent (although if they did, then Loretta might not have as much time for me so, um, never mind).

This book was inspired by some of the most glorious times in my life, but was researched and written during some of the most difficult. I want to thank those who helped me through the death of my father, and the years of searching that came after: my family, the clans Fried, Ayres, Schultz and Caplan; my friends Kim and Moon, Lisa and Joel, Ronnie and Noel, Daph and Frank, Sally and Rob, Reenie, Doug and Jill, Jeff and Beth, Diane and Steve, Geoff and Meg, Barry and Julie, Edie and her kids, and Kay and Richard.

My sanity was maintained during the last year of writing by the Philadelphia 76ers, as well as the bruising brothers in my regular halfcourt basketball game at the Sporting Club.

And God bless Ed McFall, who didn't get to see this book finished but whose influence on journalists and good men will live on forever.

My wife, Diane Ayres, took care of me and this book for four years—even, at times, when she had no idea what either was about. I can never thank her enough for her love, her friendship, her constant inspiration, her astonishing editing skills and her giggle. But I do plan to keep trying.

SELECTED BIBLIOGRAPHY

Diamant, Anita. *Saying Kaddish*. New York: Schocken, 1998.

Eliade, Mircea. *The Sacred & the Profane: The Nature of Religion*. New York: Harcourt Brace Jovanovich, 1959.

Finkelstein, Louis. *Akiba: Scholar, Saint and Martyr*. New York: Atheneum, 1964.

Frankl, Victor E. *Man's Search for Meaning* (Revised and Updated). New York: Washington Square Press, 1984.

Freedman, Samuel G. *Jew vs. Jew: The Struggle for the Soul of American Jewry*. New York: Simon & Schuster, 2000.

Friedman, Murray, ed. *Jewish Life in Philadelphia 1830–1940*. Philadelphia: Institute for the Study of Human Issues, 1983.

———. *Philadelphia Jewish Life 1940–1985*. Philadelphia: Seth Press, 1986.

Geffen, Rela M., ed. *Celebration & Renewal: Rites of Passage in Judaism*. Philadelphia: Jewish Publication Society, 1993.

Gillman, Neil. *Conservative Judaism: The New Century*. Springfield, NJ: Behrman House, 1993.

Gordis, Rabbi Daniel. *Becoming a Jewish Parent*. New York: Three Rivers Press, 1999.

Gordon, Noah. *The Rabbi*. New York: McGraw-Hill, 1965.

Green, Rabbi Arthur. *Seek My Face, Speak My Name: A Contemporary Jewish Theology*. Northvale, NJ: Jason Aronson, Inc. 1992.

Heschel, Abraham Joshua. *God in Search of Man: A Philosophy of Judaism*. New York: Farrar, Straus and Giroux, 1957.

————. *The Prophets: An Introduction.* New York: Harper Torchbooks, 1969.

————. *The Sabbath: Its Meaning for Modern Man.* New York: Farrar, Straus and Giroux, 1951.

Jewish Publication Society. *Tanakh.* Philadelphia: Jewish Publication Society, 1985.

Rank, Rabbi Perry Raphael, and Rabbi Gideon M. Freeman, eds. *The Rabbinical Assembly Rabbi's Manual.* New York: Rabbinical Assembly, 1998.

Robinson, George. *Essential Judaism.* New York: Pocket Books, 2000.

Siegel, Richard, Michael Strassfeld, and Sharon Strassfeld. *The First Jewish Catalog.* Philadelphia: Jewish Publication Society, 1973.

Singer, David, ed. *American Jewish Year Book,* Vols. 96–100. New York: American Jewish Committee, 1997–2000.

Soloveticheck, Joseph. *The Lonely Man of Faith.* Northvale, NJ: Jason Aronson, Inc., 1996.

Strassfeld, Michael. *The Jewish Holidays: A Guide & Commentary.* New York: Harper & Row, 1985.

Wieselteier, Leon. *Kaddish.* New York: Alfred A. Knopf, Inc., 1998.

Wilkes, Paul. *And They Shall Be My People: An American Rabbi and His Congregation.* New York: Atlantic Monthly Press, 1994.

Wolpe, Rabbi David J. *The Healer of Shattered Hearts.* New York: Henry Holt, 1990.

————. *In Speech and in Silence.* New York: Henry Holt, 1992.

————. *Teaching Your Children About God.* New York: Henry Holt, 1993.

————. *Making Loss Matter.* New York: Riverhead, 1999.

Zucker, David. J. *American Rabbis: Facts and Fiction.* Jerusalem; Northvale, NJ: Jason Aronson, Inc., 1998.

PRIVATE PUBLICATIONS:

Abel, Anne, ed. *Connections: Har Zion Temple Celebrating 75 Years 1924–1999.* Har Zion Temple, 1998.

Wolpe, Rabbi Gerald I. *Collected High Holiday Sermons 1974–1998.* Har Zion Temple, 1999.

————. "From Wynnefield-Radnor to Penn Valley: A Personal Memoir of the Move of Har Zion." Unpublished, 1992.

INDEX

© MICHAEL AHEARN

ABOUT THE AUTHOR

Stephen Fried is an award-winning investigative journalist and essayist. He is the author of the widely praised books *Thing of Beauty: The Tragedy of Supermodel Gia* (which inspired the Emmy-winning HBO film *Gia*) and *Bitter Pills: Inside the Hazardous World of Legal Drugs* (which triggered an FDA investigation into antibiotic safety). A two-time winner of the National Magazine Award, the highest honor in magazine journalism, Fried has written frequently for *Vanity Fair, The Washington Post Magazine, Glamour, GQ, Rolling Stone* and *Philadelphia* magazine. He teaches journalism at Columbia University, and lives in Philadelphia with his wife, author Diane Ayres.

www.stephenfried.com

Chapter notes for *The New Rabbi* are available at *www.thenewrabbi.com*